Praise for the First Edition

From the first edition of *Node.js in Action* by Mike Cantelon,
Marc Harter, T.J. Holowaychuk, and Nathan Rajlich.

"The content ramps up nicely from basic to advanced."
> From the Foreword by Isaac Z. Schlueter, Node.js Project Lead

"The definitive guide to Node and the Node.js ecosystem."
> Kevin Baister, 1KB Software Solutions

"Superbly written with practical (and even funny) real-world examples."
> Àlex Madurell, Polymedia SpA

"Thoroughly enjoyable...will get you up and running very quickly."
> Gary Ewan Park, Honeywell

"An excellent resource written by the people behind the code."
> Brian Falk, NodeLingo, GoChime

Node.js in Action

SECOND EDITION

ALEX YOUNG
BRADLEY MECK
MIKE CANTELON

WITH
TIM OXLEY
MARC HARTER
T.J. HOLOWAYCHUK
NATHAN RAJLICH

MANNING
SHELTER ISLAND

For online information and ordering of this and other Manning books, please visit
www.manning.com. The publisher offers discounts on this book when ordered in quantity.
For more information, please contact

Special Sales Department
Manning Publications Co.
20 Baldwin Road
PO Box 761
Shelter Island, NY 11964
Email: orders@manning.com

Manning Publications Co.
20 Baldwin Road
PO Box 761
Shelter Island, NY 11964

Development editor:	Cynthia Kane
Review editor:	Aleksandar Dragosavljević
Technical development editor:	Stan Bice
Project editors:	Kevin Sullivan, David Novak
Copyeditor:	Sharon Wilkey
Proofreader:	Melody Dolab
Technical proofreader:	Doug Warren
Typesetter and cover design:	Marija Tudor

ISBN 9781617292576
Printed in the United States of America
2 3 4 5 6 7 8 9 10 – EBM – 22 21 20 19 18

brief contents

contents

preface

Since the first edition of *Node.js in Action*, Node has merged with io.js and has dramatically changed its governance model. Node's package manager has been spun off into a successful new company, npm, and technologies such as Babel and Electron have transformed the development landscape.

And yet, not much has changed in Node's core libraries. JavaScript itself has changed: most developers now use features from ES2015, so all of the original listings have been rewritten to take advantage of arrow functions, constants, and destructuring. Node's libraries and built-in tools still look broadly similar to Node pre 4.*x*, though, so we've looked to the community for updates to this edition.

To reflect the realities a Node developer now faces, we've restructured the book. There is less focus on Express and Connect, and more focus on a broader range of technologies. Everything you need to be a full-stack developer is here, including front-end build systems, choosing a web framework, working with databases in Node, writing tests, and deploying web apps.

In addition to web development, we've included chapters on writing command-line applications and Electron desktop apps. This lets you take full advantage of your Node and JavaScript skills.

Understanding Node and its ecosystem isn't the only thing this book is about. Where possible, I've tried to add background details on what has influenced Node. Ideas such as Unix philosophy and using databases correctly and safely are covered alongside the usual Node and JavaScript topics. Hopefully, this gives you a broad enough picture of Node and JavaScript to seek out your own solutions to unique problems.

—ALEX YOUNG

acknowledgments

This book was built on the work of the previous authors and owes a great debt to their efforts: Mike Cantelon, Marc Harter, T.J. Holowaychuk, and Nathan Rajlich. This edition wouldn't have been possible without the encouragement of the team at Manning. Cynthia Kane, my development editor, kept me focused during the long process of updating the original content. Without Doug Warren's detailed technical proofread, this book and the sample code wouldn't be half as good as it is. Finally, thanks to the many reviewers who provided feedback during the writing and development process: Austin King, Carl Hope, Chris Salch, Christopher Reed, Dale Francis, Hafiz Waheed ud din, Harinath Mallepally, Jeff Smith, Marc-Philippe Huget, Matthew Bertoni, Philippe Charrière, Randy Kamradt, Sander Rossel, Scott Dierbeck, and William Wheeler.

—ALEX YOUNG

about this book

The first edition of *Node.js in Action* was about web development with a particular focus on the Connect and Express web frameworks. *Node.js in Action, Second Edition* has been updated to suit the changing requirements of Node development. You'll learn about front-end build systems, popular Node web frameworks, and how to build a web application with Express from scratch. You'll also learn how to create automated tests and deploy Node web applications.

Node is being increasingly used for command-line developer tools and desktop applications with Electron, so you'll find chapters dedicated to both of these areas.

This book assumes you're familiar with basic programming concepts. The first chapter provides an overview of JavaScript and ES2015 for those of you who haven't yet discovered the joys of modern JavaScript.

Roadmap

This book is organized into three parts.

Part 1 provides an introduction to Node.js, teaching the fundamental techniques needed to develop with it. Chapter 1 explains the characteristics of JavaScript and Node and steps through example code. Chapter 2 guides you through fundamental Node.js programming concepts. Chapter 3 is a full tutorial on how to build a web application from scratch.

Part 2, the largest section of the book, focuses on web application development. Chapter 4 dispels some of the mystery around front-end build systems: if you've ever had to use webpack or Gulp in a project but didn't really understand it, this is the chapter for you. Chapter 5 reviews some of the most popular server-side frameworks available for Node, and chapter 6 goes into Connect and Express in more depth.

Chapter 7 is dedicated to templating languages, which can improve your productivity when writing server-side code. Most web applications need a database, so chapter 8 covers the many types of databases that you can use with Node, from relational to NoSQL. Chapters 9 and 10 deal with testing and deployment, and this includes cloud deployment.

Part 3 goes beyond web application development. Chapter 11 is about building command-line applications with Node so you can create developer-friendly text interfaces. If you're excited about the prospect of building desktop apps such as Atom with Node, then take a look at chapter 12, which is all about Electron.

We've also included three detailed appendixes. Appendix A has instructions on how to install Node for macOS and Windows. Appendix B is a detailed tutorial on web scraping, and appendix C reviews each of the officially supported middleware components for the Connect web framework.

Code conventions and downloads

The code in this book follows common JavaScript conventions. Spaces, rather than tabs, are used for indentation. Lines longer than 80 characters are avoided. In many listings, the code is annotated to point out key concepts.

A single statement per line is used and semicolons are added at the end of simple statements. For blocks of code, where one or more statements are enclosed in curly braces, the left curly brace is placed at the end of the opening line of the block. The right curly brace is indented so it's vertically aligned with the opening line of the block.

Source code for the examples in this book is available for download from the publisher's website at www.manning.com/books/node-js-in-action-second-edition.

Book Forum

Purchase of *Node.js in Action, Second Edition* includes free access to a private web forum run by Manning Publications where you can make comments about the book, ask technical questions, and receive help from the author and from other users. To access the forum, go to https://forums.manning.com/forums/node-js-in-action-second-edition. You can also learn more about Manning's forums and the rules of conduct at https://forums.manning.com/forums/about.

Manning's commitment to our readers is to provide a venue where a meaningful dialogue between individual readers and between readers and the author can take place. It is not a commitment to any specific amount of participation on the part of the author, whose contribution to the forum remains voluntary (and unpaid). We suggest you try asking the author some challenging questions lest his interest stray! The forum and the archives of previous discussions will be accessible from the publisher's website as long as the book is in print.

about the author

ALEX YOUNG

Alex is a web developer based in London, England, and is the author of *Node.js in Practice* (Manning, 2014). Alex created the popular JavaScript blog DailyJS, and is currently employed by Sky as a senior developer for NOW TV. You can find him on GitHub (https://github.com/alexyoung) and Twitter as @alex_young.

BRADLEY MECK

Bradley is a member of TC39 and part of the Node.js Foundation. When not working his time is spent working on tooling solutions for Javascript, gardening, and mentoring students. His work at GoDaddy comes after a long resume of using Node.js for other companies like NodeSource and Nodejitsu. While always eager to teach and explain, he tries to keep people motivated because learning is hard for him as well as for many others.

about the cover illustration

The figure on the cover of *Node.js in Action, Second Edition* is captioned "Man about Town." The illustration is taken from a 19th-century edition of Sylvain Maréchal's four-volume compendium of regional dress customs published in France. Each illustration is finely drawn and colored by hand. The rich variety of Maréchal's collection reminds us vividly of how culturally apart the world's towns and regions were just 200 years ago. Isolated from each other, people spoke different dialects and languages. Whether on city streets, in small towns, or in the countryside, it was easy to identify where they lived and what their trade or station in life was just by their dress.

Dress codes have changed since then, and the diversity by region and class, so rich at the time, has faded away. It is now hard to tell apart the inhabitants of different continents, let alone different towns or regions. Perhaps we have traded cultural diversity for a more varied personal life—certainly for a more varied and fast-paced technological life.

At a time when it is hard to tell one computer book from another, Manning celebrates the inventiveness and initiative of the computer business with book covers based on the rich diversity of regional life of two centuries ago, brought back to life by Maréchal's pictures.

Part 1

Welcome to Node

Node is now a mature web development platform. In chapters 1 to 3, you'll learn about Node's main features, including how to use the core modules and npm. You'll also see how Node uses modern JavaScript, and how to build a web application from scratch. After reading these chapters, you'll have a solid understanding of what Node can do and of how to create your own projects.

Welcome to Node.js

1

This chapter covers

- What is Node.js?
- Defining Node applications
- The advantages of using Node
- Asynchronous and nonblocking I/O

Node.js is an asynchronous, event-driven JavaScript runtime that offers a powerful but concise standard library. It's managed and supported by the Node.js Foundation, an industry consortium with an open governance model. Two actively supported versions of Node are available: Long-Term Support (LTS) and Current. If you want to learn more about how Node is managed, the official website has plenty of documentation (https://nodejs.org/).

Since Node.js appeared in 2009, JavaScript has gone from a barely tolerated browser-centric language to one of the most important languages for all kinds of software development. This is partly due to the arrival of ECMAScript 2015, which solved several critical problems in previous versions of the language. Node uses Google's V8 JavaScript engine that's based on the sixth edition of the ECMAScript standard, which is sometimes called ES6 and abbreviated as ES2015. It's also due to innovative technologies such as Node, React, and Electron, which allow Java-Script to be used everywhere: from the server to the browser, and in native mobile applications. Even big companies such as Microsoft are embracing JavaScript, and Microsoft has even contributed to the success of Node.

In this chapter, you'll learn more about Node, its event-driven nonblocking model, and some of the reasons that JavaScript has become a great general-purpose programming language. First, let's look at a typical Node web application.

1.1 A typical Node web application

One of the strengths of Node and JavaScript in general is their single-threaded programming model. Threads are a common source of bugs, and although some recent programming languages, including Go and Rust, have attempted to offer safer concurrency tools, Node retains the model used in the browser. In browser-based code, we write sequences of instructions that execute one at a time; code doesn't execute in parallel. This doesn't make sense for user interfaces, however: users don't want to wait around for slow operations such as network or file access to finish. To get around this, browsers use events: when you click a button, an event fires, and a function runs that has previously been defined but not yet executed. This avoids some of the issues found in threaded programming, including resource deadlocks and race conditions.

1.1.1 Nonblocking I/O

What does this mean in the context of server-side programming? The situation is similar: I/O requests such as disk and network access are also comparatively slow, so we don't want the runtime to block business logic from executing while reading files or sending messages over the network. To solve this, Node uses three techniques: events, asynchronous APIs, and nonblocking I/O. *Nonblocking I/O* is a low-level term from a Node programmer's perspective. It means your program can make a request for a network resource while doing something else, and then, when the network operation has finished, a callback will run that handles the result.

Figure 1.1 shows a typical Node web application that uses the web application library Express to handle the order flow for a shop. Browsers make requests to buy a product, and then the application checks the current stock inventory, creates an account for the user, emails the receipt, and sends back a JSON HTTP response. Concurrently, other things happen as well: an email receipt is sent, and a database is updated with the user's details and order. The code itself is straightforward, imperative JavaScript, but the runtime behaves concurrently because it uses nonblocking I/O.

In figure 1.1 the database is accessed over the network. In Node, that network access is nonblocking, because Node uses a library called libuv (http://libuv.org/) to provide access to the operating system's nonblocking network calls. This is implemented differently in Linux, macOS, and Windows, but all you have to worry about is your friendly JavaScript database library. While you're writing code such as `db.insert(query, err => {})`, Node is doing highly optimized, nonblocking networking underneath.

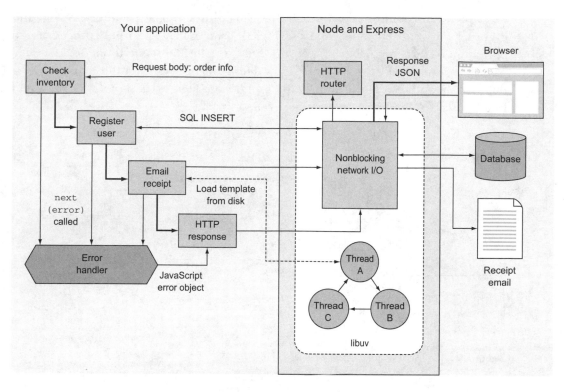

Figure 1.1   Asynchronous and nonblocking components in a Node application

Disk access is similar, but intriguingly not the same. When the email receipt is generated and the email template is read from the disk, libuv uses a thread pool to provide the illusion that a nonblocking call is being used. Managing a thread pool is no fun at all, but writing `email.send('template.ejs', (err, html) => {})` is definitely much easier to understand.

The real benefit to using asynchronous APIs with nonblocking I/O is that Node can do other things while these comparatively slow processes happen. Even though you have only a single-threaded, single-process Node web app running, it can handle more than one connection from potentially thousands of website visitors at any one time. To understand this, you need to look at the event loop.

1.1.2   The event loop

Now let's zoom into a specific aspect of figure 1.1: responding to browser requests. In this application, Node's built-in HTTP server library, which is a core module called http.Server, handles the request by using a combination of streams, events, and Node's HTTP request parser, which is native code. This triggers a callback in your application to run, which has been added using the Express (https://expressjs.com/)

web application library. The callback that runs causes a database query to run, and eventually the application responds with JSON using HTTP. This whole process uses a minimum of three nonblocking network calls: one for the request, one for the database, and another for the response. How does Node schedule all these nonblocking network operations? The answer is the event loop. Figure 1.2 shows how the event loop is used for these three network operations.

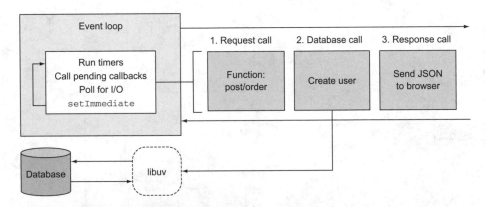

Figure 1.2   The event loop

The event loop runs one way (it's a first-in, first-out queue) and goes through several phases. Figure 1.2 shows a simplified set of the important phases that run on each iteration of the loop. First, the timers execute, which are the timers scheduled with the JavaScript functions `setTimeout` and `setInterval`. Next, I/O callbacks run, so if any I/O has returned from one of the nonblocking network calls, this is where your callback is triggered. The poll phase is where new I/O events are retrieved, and then callbacks scheduled with `setImmediate` run at the end. This is a special case because it allows you to schedule a callback to run immediately after the current I/O callbacks already in the queue. This might sound abstract at this stage, but what you should take away is the idea that although Node is single-threaded, it does give you tools to write efficient and scalable code.

Over the last few pages, you might have noticed that the examples have been written using ES2015 arrow functions. Node supports many new JavaScript features, so before moving on, let's look at what new language features you can use to write better code.

1.2   *ES2015, Node, and V8*

If you've ever used JavaScript and been disheartened by the lack of classes and strange scoping rules, you're in luck: Node has fixed most of these problems! You can now make classes, and using `const` and `let` (instead of `var`) fixes scoping issues. As of Node 6, you can use default function parameters, rest parameters, the `spread` operator, for...of loops, template strings, destructuring, generators, and more. A great summary of Node's ES2015 support can be found at http://node.green.

First, let's look at classes. ES5 and earlier versions required the use of prototype objects to create class-like constructs:

```
function User() {
  // constructor
}

User.prototype.method = function() {
  // Method
};
```

With Node 6 and ES2015, you can now write the same code by using classes:

```
class User {
  constructor() {}
  method() {}
}
```

This uses less code and is a little easier to read. But there's more: Node also supports subclassing, super, and static methods. For those versed in other languages, the adoption of class syntax makes Node more accessible than when we were stuck with ES5.

Another important feature in Node 4 and above is the addition of const and let. In ES5, all variables were created with var. The problem with var is it defines variables in function or global scope, so you couldn't define a block-level variable in an if statement, for loop, or other block.

> **Should I use const or let?**
>
> When deciding whether to use const or let, you almost always want const. Because most of your code will use instances of your own classes, object literals, or values that don't change, you can use const most of the time. Even instances of objects that have properties that change can be declared with const, because const means only that the reference is read-only, not that the value is immutable.

Node also has native promises and generators. *Promises* are supported by lots of libraries, allowing you to write asynchronous code with a fluent interface style. You're probably familiar with fluent interfaces already: if you've ever used an API such as jQuery or even JavaScript arrays, you'll have seen it. The following short example shows you how to chain calls to manipulate an array in JavaScript:

```
[1, 2, 3]
  .map(n => n * 2)
  .filter(n => n > 3);
```

Generators are used to give a synchronous programming style to asynchronous I/O. If you want to see a practical example of generators in Node, take a look at the Koa web application library (http://koajs.com/). If you use promises or other generators with Koa, you can yield on values rather than nesting callbacks.

One other useful ES2015 feature in Node is *template strings*. In ES5, string literals didn't support interpolation or multiple lines. Now by using the backtick symbol (`` ` ``), you can insert values and span strings over several lines. This is useful when stubbing quick bits of HTML for web apps:

```
this.body = `
  <div>
    <h1>Hello from Node</h1>
    <p>Welcome, ${user.name}!</p>
  </div>
`;
```

In ES5, the previous example would have to be written like this:

```
this.body = '\n';
this.body += '<div>\n';
this.body += '  <h1>Hello from Node</h1>\n';
this.body += '  <p>Welcome, ' + user.name + '</p>\n';
this.body += '<div>\n';
```

The older style not only used more code but also made introducing bugs easy. The final big feature, which is of particular importance to Node programmers, is arrow functions. *Arrow functions* let you streamline syntax. For example, if you're writing a callback that has a single argument and returns a value, you can write it with hardly any syntax at all:

```
[1, 2, 3].map(v => v * 2);
```

In Node we typically need two arguments, because the first argument to a callback is often an error object. In that case, you need to use parentheses around the arguments:

```
const fs = require('fs');
fs.readFile('package.json',
  (err, text) => console.log('Length:', text.length)
);
```

If you need to use more than one line in the function body, you need to use curly brackets. The value of arrow functions isn't just in the streamlined syntax; it has to do with JavaScript scopes. In ES5 and before, defining functions inside other functions makes the this reference become the global object. Here's an ES5-style class that suffers from a bug due to this issue:

```
function User(id) {
// constructor
  this.id = id;
}

User.prototype.load = function() {
  var self = this;
  var query = 'SELECT * FROM users WHERE id = ?';
```

```
    sql.query(query, this.id, function(err, users) {
    self.name = users[0].name;
    });
};
```

The line that assigns `self.name` can't be written as `this.name`, because the function's `this` will be the global object. A workaround used to be to assign a variable to `this` at the entry point to the parent function or method. But arrow functions are bound correctly. In ES2015, the previous example can be rewritten to be much more intuitive:

```
class User {
  constructor(id) {
    this.id = id;
  }

  load() {
    const query = 'SELECT * FROM users WHERE id = ?';
    sql.query(query, this.id, (err, users) => {
    this.name = users[0].name;
    });
}
}
```

Not only can you use `const` to better model the database query, but there's also no need for the clumsy `self` variable. ES2015 has many other great features that make Node code more readable, but let's look at what powers this in Node and how it relates to the nonblocking I/O features that you've already looked at.

1.2.1   Node and V8

Node is powered by the V8 JavaScript engine, which is developed by the Chromium project for Google Chrome. The notable feature of V8 is that it compiles directly to machine code, and it includes code-optimization features that help keep Node fast. In section 1.1.1, we talked about the other main native part of Node, libuv. That part handles I/O; V8 handles interpreting and running your JavaScript code. To use libuv with V8, you use a C++ binding layer. Figure 1.3 shows all of the separate software components that make up Node.

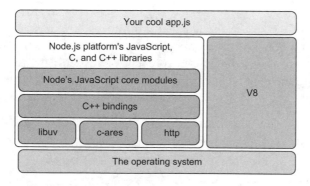

Figure 1.3   Node's software stack

The specific JavaScript features that are available to Node therefore come down to what V8 supports. This support is managed through feature groups.

1.2.2   *Working with feature groups*

Node includes ES2015 features based on what V8 provides. Features are grouped under *shipping*, *staged*, and *in progress*. The shipping features are turned on by default, but staged and in progress can be enabled using command-line flags. If you want to use staged features, which are almost complete but not considered complete by the V8 team, then you can run Node with the `--harmony` flag. In-progress features, however, are less stable and are enabled with specific feature flags. Node's documentation recommends querying the currently available in-progress features by grepping for `in progress`:

```
node --v8-options | grep "in progress"
```

The list will vary between Node releases. Node itself also has a versioning schedule that defines which APIs are available.

1.2.3   *Understanding Node's release schedule*

Node releases are grouped into Long-Term Support (LTS), Current, and Nightly. LTS releases get 18 months of support and then 12 months of maintenance support. Releases are made according to semantic versioning (SemVer). SemVer gives releases a major, minor, and patch version number. For example, 6.9.1 has a major version of 6, minor of 9, and patch of 1. Whenever you see a major version change for Node, it means some of the APIs may be incompatible with your projects, and you'll need to retest them against this version of Node. Also, in Node release terminology, a major version increment means a new Current release has been cut. Nightly builds are automatically generated every 24 hours with the latest changes, but are typically used only for testing Node's latest features.

Which version you use depends on your project and organization. Some may prefer LTS because updates are less frequent: this might work well in larger enterprises that find it harder to manage frequent updates. But if you want the latest performance and feature improvements, Current is a better choice.

1.3   *Installing Node*

The easiest way to install Node is to use the installer from https://nodejs.org. Install the latest Current version (version 6.5 at the time of this writing) by using the Mac or Windows installer. You can download the source yourself, or install it by using your operating system's package manager. Debian, Ubuntu, Arch, Fedora, FreeBSD, Gentoo, and SUSE all have packages. There are also packages for Homebrew and SmartOS. If your operating system doesn't have a package, you can build from source.

NOTE   Appendix A provides more details on installing Node.

The full list of packages is on Node's website (https://nodejs.org/en/download/package-manager/), and the source is on GitHub (https://github.com/nodejs/node). Bookmarking the GitHub source is worthwhile in case you want to poke around in the source without downloading it.

Once you've installed Node, you can try it out straight away by typing `node -v` in the terminal. This should print out the version of Node that you just downloaded and installed. Next, create a file called hello.js that looks like this:

```
console.log("hello from Node");
```

Save the file and run it by typing `node hello.js`. Congratulations—you're now ready to start writing applications with Node!

> ### Getting started quickly in Windows, Linux, and macOS
>
> If you're fairly new to programming in general and you don't yet have a preferred text editor, then a solid choice for Node is Visual Studio Code (https://code.visualstudio.com/). It's made by Microsoft, but it's open source and a free download, and supports Windows, Linux, and macOS.
>
> Some of the beginner-friendly features in Visual Studio Code include JavaScript syntax highlighting and Node core module completion, so your JavaScript will look clearer and you'll be able to see lists of supported methods and objects as you type. You can also open a command-line interface where Node can be invoked just by typing Node. This is useful for running Node and npm commands. Windows users might prefer this to using cmd.exe. We tested the listings with Windows and Visual Studio Code, so you shouldn't need anything special to run the examples.
>
> To get started, you can follow a Visual Studio Code Node.js tutorial (https://code.visualstudio.com/docs/runtimes/nodejs).

When you install Node, you also get some built-in tools. Node isn't just the interpreter: it's a whole suite of tools that form the Node platform. Let's look in more detail at the tools that are bundled with Node.

1.4 Node's built-in tools

Node comes with a built-in package manager, the core JavaScript modules that support everything from file and network I/O to zlib compression, and a debugger. The npm package manager is a critical piece of this infrastructure, so let's look at it in more detail.

If you want to verify that Node has been installed correctly, you can run `node -v` and `npm -v` on the command-line. These commands show the version of Node and npm that you have installed.

1.4.1 *npm*

The npm command-line tool can be invoked by typing npm. You can use it to install packages from the central npm registry, but you can also use it to find and share your own open and closed source projects. Every npm package in the registry has a website that shows the readme file, author, and statistics about downloads.

That doesn't cover everything, though. npm is also npm, Inc.—the company that runs the npm service and that provides services used by commercial enterprises. This includes hosting private npm packages: you can pay a monthly fee to host your company's source code so your JavaScript developers can easily install it with npm.

When installing packages with the npm install command, you have to decide whether you're adding them to your current project or installing them globally. Globally installed packages are usually used for tools, typically programs you run on the command line. A good example of this is the gulp-cli package.

To use npm, create a package.json file in a directory that will contain your Node project. The easiest way to create a package.json file is to use npm to do it for you. Type the following on the command line:

```
mkdir example-project
cd example-project
npm init -y
```

If you open package.json, you'll see a simple JSON file that describes your project. If you now install a module from www.npmjs.com and use the --save option, npm will automatically update your package.json file. Try it out by typing npm install, or npm i for short:

```
npm i --save express
```

If you open your package.json file, you should see express added under the dependencies property. Also, if you look inside the node_modules folder, you'll see an express directory. This contains the version of Express that you just installed. You can also install modules globally by using the --global option. You should use local modules as much as possible, but global modules can be useful for command-line tools that you want to use outside Node JavaScript code. An example of a command-line tool that's installable with npm is ESLint (http://eslint.org/).

When you're starting out with Node, you'll often use packages from npm. Node comes with lots of useful built-in libraries, which are known as the *core modules*. Let's look at these in more detail.

1.4.2 *The core modules*

Node's core modules are similar to other languages' standard libraries; these are the tools you need to write server-side JavaScript. The JavaScript standards themselves don't include anything for working with the network, or even file I/O as most server-side developers know it. Node has to add features for files and TCP/IP networking at a minimum to be a viable server-side language.

FILESYSTEM

Node ships with a filesystem library (fs, path), TCP clients and servers (net), HTTP (http and https), and domain name resolution (dns). There's a useful assertion library that's used mostly to write tests (assert), and an operating system library for querying information about the platform (os).

Node also has libraries that are unique to Node. The events module is a small library for working with events, and it's used as a basis for much of Node's APIs. For example, the stream module uses the events module to provide abstract interfaces for working with streams of data. Because all data streams in Node use the same APIs, you can easily compose software components; if you have a file-stream reader, you can pipe it through a zlib transform that compresses the data, and then pipe it through a file-stream writer to write the data out to a file.

The following listing shows how to use Node's fs module to create read- and write-streams that can be piped through another stream (gzip) to transform the data—in this case, by compressing it.

> **Listing 1.1 Using core modules and streams**

```
const fs = require('fs');
const zlib = require('zlib');
const gzip = zlib.createGzip();
const outStream = fs.createWriteStream('output.js.gz');

fs.createReadStream('./node-stream.js')
  .pipe(gzip)
  .pipe(outStream);
```

NETWORKING

For a while, we used to say that creating a simple HTTP server was Node's true Hello World example. To build a server in Node, you just need to load the http module and give it a function. The function accepts two arguments: the incoming request and the outgoing response. The next listing shows an example you can run in your terminal.

> **Listing 1.2 Hello World with Node's http module**

```
const http = require('http');
const port = 8080;

const server = http.createServer((req, res) => {
  res.end('Hello, world.');
});

server.listen(port, () => {
  console.log('Server listening on: http://localhost:%s', port);
});
```

Save listing 1.2 as `hello.js` and run it with `node hello.js`. If you visit http://localhost:8080, you should see the message from line 4.

Node's core modules are minimal but also powerful. You can often achieve a lot just by using these modules, without even installing anything from npm. For more on the core modules, refer to https://nodejs.org/api/.

The final built-in tool is the debugger. The next section introduces Node's debugger with an example.

1.4.3 *The debugger*

Node includes a debugger that supports single-stepping and a REPL (read-eval-print loop). The debugger works by talking to your program with a network protocol. To run your program with a debugger, use the `debug` argument at the command line. Let's say you're debugging listing 1.2:

```
node debug hello.js
```

Then you should see the following output:

```
< Debugger listening on [::]:5858
connecting to 127.0.0.1:5858 ... ok
break in node-http.js:1
> 1 const http = require('http');
  2 const port = 8080;
  3
```

Node has invoked your program and is debugging it by connecting on port 5858. At this point, you can type `help` to see the list of available commands, and then `c` to continue program execution. Node always starts the program in a *break* state, so you always need to continue execution before you can do anything else.

You can make the debugger break by adding a `debugger` statement anywhere in your code. When the `debugger` statement is encountered, the debugger will halt, allowing you to issue commands. Imagine you've written a REST API that creates accounts for new users, and your user creation code doesn't seem to be persisting the new user's password hash to the database. You could add `debugger` to the `save` method in the `User` class, and then step over each instruction to see what happens.

Interactive debugging

Node supports the Chrome Debugging Protocol. To debug a script using Chrome's Developer Tools, use the `--inspect` flag when running a program:

```
node --inspect --debug-brk
```

This will make Node launch the debugger and break on the first line. It'll print a URL to the console that you can open in Chrome so you can use Chrome's built-in debugger. Chrome's debugger lets you step through code line by line, and it shows the value in each variable and object. It's a much better alternative to typing `console.log`.

Debugging is covered in more detail in chapter 9. If you want to try it right now, the best place to start is the Node manual page on the debugger (https://nodejs.org/api/debugger.html).

So far in this chapter, we've talked about how Node works and what it provides to developers. You're probably also itching to hear about the kinds of things that people are using Node for in production. The next section looks at the types of programs you can make with Node.

1.5 The three main types of Node program

Node programs can be divided into three typical types: web applications, command-line tools and daemons, and desktop applications. Web applications include simple apps that serve up single-page applications, REST microservices, and full-stack web apps. You may have already used command-line tools written with Node—for example, npm, Gulp, and webpack. Daemons are background services. A good example is the PM2 (www.npmjs.com/package/pm2) process manager. Desktop applications tend to be software written with the Electron framework (http://electron.atom.io/), which uses Node as the back end for web-based desktop apps. Examples include the Atom (https://atom.io/) and Visual Studio Code (https://code.visualstudio.com/) text editors.

1.5.1 Web applications

Node is server-side JavaScript, so it makes sense as a platform for building web applications. By running JavaScript on both the client and server, opportunities exist for code reuse between each environment. Node web apps tend to be written with frameworks such as Express (http://expressjs.com/). Chapter 6 reviews the major server-side frameworks available for Node. Chapter 7 is specifically about Express and Connect, and chapter 8 is about web application templating.

You can create a quick Express web application by creating a new directory and then installing the Express module:

```
mkdir hello_express
cd hello_express
npm init -y
npm i express --save
```

Next, add the following JavaScript code to a file called server.js.

Listing 1.3 A Node web application

```
const express = require('express');
const app = express();

app.get('/', (req, res) => {
  res.send('Hello World!');
});
```

```
app.listen(3000, () => {
  console.log('Express web app on localhost:3000');
});
```

Now type `npm start` and you'll have a Node web server running on port 3000. If you open http://localhost:3000 in a browser you'll be able to see the text from the `res.send` line.

Node is also a big part of the front-end development world, because it's the main tool used when transpiling other languages such as TypeScript to JavaScript. Transpilers compile languages from one high-level language to another; this contrasts with traditional compilers, which compile from high-level to low-level languages. Chapter 4 is dedicated to front-end build systems, where we look at using npm scripts, Gulp, and webpack.

Not all web development involves building web apps. Sometimes you need to do things such as extract data from a legacy website to use when rebuilding it. We've included appendix B, which is all about web scraping, as a way of showing how Node's JavaScript runtime can be used to work with the Document Object Model (DOM), as well as showing how to use Node outside the comfort zone of typical Express web apps. If you just want to quickly make a basic web app, chapter 3 provides a self-contained tutorial on building Node web applications.

1.5.2 *Command-line tools and daemons*

Node is used to write command-line tools such as process managers and JavaScript transpilers that are used by JavaScript developers. But it's also used as a convenient way to write handy command-line tools that do other things, including image conversion, and scripts for controlling media playback.

Here's a quick command-line example that you can try. Create a new file called cli.js and add the following lines:

```
const [nodePath, scriptPath, name] = process.argv;
console.log('Hello', name);
```

Run the script with `node cli.js yourName` and you'll see `Hello yourName`. This works by using ES2015 destructuring to pull out the third argument from `process.argv`. The `process` object is available to every Node program and forms the basis for accepting arguments when users run your programs.

You can do a few other things with Node command-line programs. If you add a line to the start of the program that starts with `#!`, and grant it execute permissions (`chmod +x cli.js`), then you can make the shell use Node when it invokes the program. Now you can run your Node programs just like any other shell script. Just use a line like this for Unix-like systems:

```
#!/usr/bin/env node
```

By using Node this way, you can replace your shell scripts with Node. This means Node can be used with any other command-line tools, including background programs. Node programs can be invoked by cron, or run in the background as daemons.

If all of this is new to you, don't worry: chapter 11 introduces writing command-line utilities, and shows how this type of program plays into Node's strengths. For example, command-line tools make heavy use of streams as a universal API, and streams are one of Node's most powerful features.

1.5.3 Desktop applications

If you've been using the Atom or Visual Studio Code text editors, then you've been using Node all along. The Electron framework uses Node as the back end, so whenever I/O such as disk or network access is required, Electron uses Node. Electron also uses Node for managing dependencies, which means you can add packages from npm to Electron projects.

If you want to quickly try Electron now, you can clone the Electron repository and start up an application:

```
git clone https://github.com/electron/electron-quick-start
cd electron-quick-start
npm install && npm start
curl localhost:8081
```

To learn how to write an app with Electron, flip ahead to chapter 12.

1.5.4 Applications suited to Node

We've walked through some of the types of applications you can build with Node, but there are certain types of applications that Node excels at. Node is commonly used to create real-time web applications, which can mean anything from user-facing applications such as chat servers to back ends for collecting analytics. Because functions are first-class objects in JavaScript, and Node has a built-in event model, writing asynchronous real-time programs feels more natural than other scripting languages.

If you're building traditional Model-View-Controller (MVC) web applications, Node can do this well. Popular blogging engines are built with Node, such as Ghost (https://ghost.org/); Node is now a proven platform for building these types of web applications. The style of development is different from WordPress, which is built with PHP, but Ghost supports similar features, including templates and a multiuser administration area.

Node can also do things that are much harder in other languages. It's based on JavaScript, and it's possible to run browser JavaScript in Node. Complex client-side applications can be adapted to run on a Node server, allowing servers to pre-render web applications, which speeds up page rendering time in the browser and also facilitates search engines.

Finally, if you're considering building a desktop or mobile app, you should try Electron, which is powered by Node. Now that web user interfaces are as rich as desktop experiences, Electron desktop apps can rival native web applications and cut down development time. Electron also supports three major platforms, so you can reuse your code across Windows, Linux, and macOS.

1.6   *Summary*

- Node is an evented and nonblocking platform for building JavaScript applications.
- V8 is used as the JavaScript runtime.
- libuv is the native library that provides fast, cross-platform, nonblocking I/O.
- Node has a small standard library known as the core modules that add network and disk I/O to JavaScript.
- Node comes with a debugger and a dependency manager (npm).
- Node is used for building web applications, command-line tools, and even desktop applications.

Node programming
fundamentals

This chapter covers
- Organizing your code into modules
- Handling one-off events with callbacks
- Handling repeating events with event emitters
- Implementing serial and parallel flow control
- Using flow-control tools

Node, unlike many open source platforms, is easy to set up and doesn't require much in terms of memory and disk space. No complex integrated development environments or build systems are required. Some fundamental knowledge will, however, help you a lot when starting out. In this chapter, we address two challenges that new Node developers face:

- How to organize your code
- How asynchronous programming works

In this chapter, you'll learn important asynchronous programming techniques that will allow you to keep a tight rein on how your application executes. You'll learn

- How to respond to one-time events
- How to handle repeating events
- How to sequence asynchronous logic

19

We'll start, however, with how you can tackle the problem of code organization through the use of *modules*, which are Node's way of keeping code organized and packaged for easy reuse.

2.1 *Organizing and reusing Node functionality*

When creating an application, Node or otherwise, you often reach a point where putting all your code in a single file becomes unwieldy. When this happens, the conventional approach, as represented in figure 2.1, is to take a file containing a lot of code and try to organize it by grouping related logic and moving it into separate files.

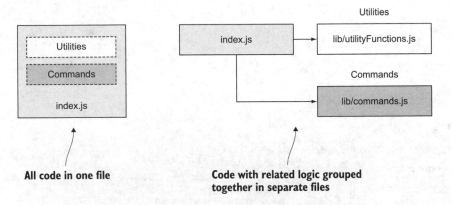

All code in one file

Code with related logic grouped together in separate files

Figure 2.1   Navigating your code is easier if you organize it into directories and separate files rather than keeping your application in one long file.

In some language implementations, such as PHP and Ruby, incorporating the logic from another file (we call this the *included* file) can mean that all the logic executed in that file affects the global scope. Any variables created and functions declared in the included file risk overwriting those created and declared by the application.

Say you're programming in PHP; your application might contain the following logic:

```
function uppercase_trim($text) {
  return trim(strtoupper($text));
}
include('string_handlers.php');
```

If your string_handlers.php file also attempted to define an `uppercase_trim` function, you'd receive the following error:

```
Fatal error: Cannot redeclare uppercase_trim()
```

In PHP you can avoid this by using *namespaces*, and Ruby offers similar functionality through *modules*. Node, however, avoids this potential problem by not offering an easy way to accidentally pollute the global namespace.

PHP NAMESPACES, RUBY MODULES   PHP namespaces are discussed in the PHP language manual at http://php.net/manual/en/language.namespaces.php. Ruby modules are explained in the Ruby documentation: http://ruby-doc.org/core-2.3.1/Module.html.

Node modules bundle up code for reuse, but they don't alter global scope. Suppose, for example, you're developing an open source content management system (CMS) application by using PHP, and you want to use a third-party API library that doesn't use namespaces. This library could contain a class with the same name as one in your application, which would break your application unless you changed the class name either in your application or the library. Changing the class name in your application, however, could cause problems for other developers using your CMS as the basis of their own projects. Changing the class name in the library would require you to remember to repeat this hack each time you update the library in your application's source tree. Naming collisions are a problem best avoided altogether.

Node modules allow you to select which functions and variables from the included file are exposed to the application. If the module is returning more than one function or variable, the module can specify these by setting the properties of an object called `exports`. If the module is returning a single function or variable, the property `module.exports` can instead be set. Figure 2.2 shows how this works.

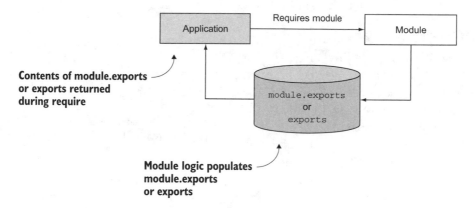

Figure 2.2   The population of the `module.exports` **property or the exports object allows a module to select what should be shared with the application.**

If this seems a bit confusing, don't worry; we run through several examples in this chapter. By avoiding pollution of the global scope, Node's module system avoids naming conflicts and simplifies code reuse. Modules can then be published to the npm (package manager) registry, an online collection of ready-to-use Node modules, and shared with the Node community without those using the modules having to worry about one module overwriting the variables and functions of another.

To help you organize your logic into modules, we cover the following topics:

- How you can create modules
- Where modules are stored in the filesystem
- Things to be aware of when creating and using modules

Let's dive into learning the Node module system by starting a new Node project and then creating a simple module.

2.2   Starting a new Node project

Creating a new Node project is easy: create a folder and then run `npm init`. That's it! The `npm` command will ask you a few questions, and you can answer yes to all of them. Here's a full example:

```
mkdir my_module
cd my_module
npm init -y
```

The `-y` flag means *yes*. That means npm will create a package.json file with default values. If you want more control, leave off the `-y` flag, and npm will run you through a set of questions about the project's license, author name, and so on. After you've done this, look at the contents of package.json. You can manually edit it, but remember, it has to be valid JSON.

Now that you have an empty project, you can create your own module.

2.2.1   Creating modules

Modules can be either single files or directories containing one or more files, as you can see in figure 2.3. If a module is a directory, the file in the module directory that will be evaluated is typically named index.js (although this can be overridden: see section 2.5).

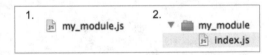

Figure 2.3   Node modules can be created by using either files (example 1) or directories (example 2).

To create a typical module, you create a file that defines properties on the `exports` object with any kind of data, such as strings, objects, and functions.

To show how a basic module is created, let's see how to add some currency conversion functionality to a file named currency.js. This file, shown in the following listing, will contain two functions that convert Canadian dollars to U.S. dollars, and vice versa.

Listing 2.1   Defining a Node module (currency.js)

```
const canadianDollar = 0.91;

function roundTwo(amount) {
  return Math.round(amount * 100) / 100;
}
```

**canadianToUS function is set in exports module
so it can be used by code requiring this module**

```
exports.canadianToUS = canadian => roundTwo(canadian * canadianDollar);
exports.USToCanadian = us => roundTwo(us / canadianDollar);
```

**USToCanadian function is
also set in exports module**

Note that only two properties of the exports object are set. Therefore, only the two functions, canadianToUS and USToCanadian, can be accessed by the application including the module. The variable canadianDollar acts as a private variable that affects the logic in canadianToUS and USToCanadian but can't be directly accessed by the application.

To use your new module, use Node's require function, which takes a path to the module you wish to use as an argument. Node performs a synchronous lookup to locate the module and loads the file's contents. The order in which Node looks for files is first core modules, then the current directory, and finally node_modules.

A note about require and synchronous I/O

require is one of the few synchronous I/O operations available in Node. Because modules are used often and are typically included at the top of a file, having require be synchronous helps keep code clean, ordered, and readable.

Avoid using require in I/O-intensive parts of your application. Any synchronous call will block Node from doing anything until the call has finished. For example, if you're running an HTTP server, you'd take a performance hit if you used require on each incoming request. This is typically why require and other synchronous operations are used only when the application initially loads.

In the next listing, which shows test-currency.js, you require the currency.js module.

Listing 2.2 Requiring a module (test_currency.js)

**Uses currency module's
canadianToUS function**

**Path uses ./ to indicate that module exists
within same directory as application script**

```
const currency = require('./currency');
console.log('50 Canadian dollars equals this amount of US dollars:');
console.log(currency.canadianToUS(50));
console.log('30 US dollars equals this amount of Canadian dollars:');
console.log(currency.USToCanadian(30));
```

**Uses currency module's
USToCanadian function**

Requiring a module that begins with ./ means that if you were to create your application script named test-currency.js in a directory named currency_app, then your currency.js module file, as represented in figure 2.4, would also need to exist in the currency_app directory. When requiring, the .js extension is assumed, so you can omit it if desired. If you don't include .js, Node will also check for a .json file. JSON files are loaded as JavaScript objects.

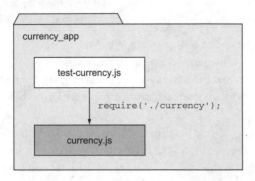

Figure 2.4   **When you put ./ at the beginning of a module `require`, Node will look in the same directory as the program file being executed.**

After Node has located and evaluated your module, the `require` function returns the contents of the `exports` object defined in the module. You're then able to use the two functions returned by the module to perform currency conversion.

If you want to organize related modules, you can put modules into subdirectories. If, for example, you want to put the currency module in a folder called lib/, you can do so by changing the line with `require` to the following:

```
const currency = require('./lib/currency');
```

Populating the `exports` object of a module gives you a simple way to group reusable code in separate files.

2.3   *Fine-tuning module creation by using module.exports*

Although populating the `exports` object with functions and variables is suitable for most module-creation needs, at times you'll want a module to deviate from this model.

The currency converter module created in the previous section, for example, could be redone to return a single `Currency` constructor function rather than an object containing functions. An object-oriented implementation could behave something like the following:

```
const Currency = require('./currency');
const canadianDollar = 0.91;
const currency = new Currency(canadianDollar);
console.log(currency.canadianToUS(50));
```

Returning a function from `require`, rather than an object, will make your code more elegant if it's the only thing you need from the module.

To create a module that returns a single variable or function, you might guess that you need to set `exports` to whatever you want to return. But this won't work, because Node expects `exports` to not be reassigned to any other object, function, or variable. The module code in the next listing attempts to set `exports` to a function.

Listing 2.3   Module won't work as expected

```
class Currency {
  constructor(canadianDollar) {
    this.canadianDollar = canadianDollar;
  }

  roundTwoDecimals(amount) {
    return Math.round(amount * 100) / 100;
  }

  canadianToUS(canadian) {
    return this.roundTwoDecimals(canadian * this.canadianDollar);
  }

  USToCanadian(us) {
    return this.roundTwoDecimals(us / this.canadianDollar);
  }
}
exports = Currency;        ◁── Incorrect; Node doesn't allow
                              exports to be overwritten
```

To get the previous module code to work as expected, you'd need to replace `exports` with `module.exports`. The `module.exports` mechanism enables you to export a single variable, function, or object. If you create a module that populates both `exports` and `module.exports`, `module.exports` will be returned, and `exports` will be ignored.

What really gets exported

What ultimately gets exported in your application is `module.exports`. `exports` is set up as a global reference to `module.exports`, which initially is defined as an empty object that you can add properties to. `exports.myFunc` is shorthand for `module.exports.myFunc`.

As a result, if `exports` is set to anything else, it breaks the *reference* between `module.exports` and `exports`. Because `module.exports` is what gets exported, `exports` will no longer work as expected—it doesn't reference `module.exports` anymore. If you want to maintain that link, you can make `module.exports` reference `exports` again as follows:

```
module.exports = exports = Currency;
```

By using either `exports` or `module.exports`, depending on your needs, you can organize functionality into modules and avoid the pitfall of ever-growing application scripts.

2.4   *Reusing modules by using the node_modules folder*

Requiring modules in the filesystem to exist relative to an application is useful for organizing application-specific code, but isn't as useful for code you'd like to reuse between applications or share with others. Node includes a unique mechanism for code reuse that allows modules to be required without knowing their location in the filesystem. This mechanism is the use of node_modules directories.

In the earlier module example, you required ./currency. If you omit the ./ and simply require currency, Node will follow certain rules, as specified in figure 2.5, to search for this module.

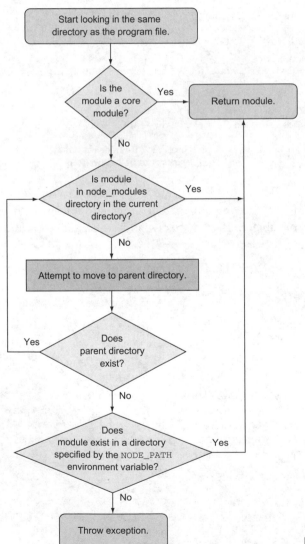

Figure 2.5   Steps to finding a module

The NODE_PATH environmental variable provides a way to specify alternative locations for Node modules. If used, NODE_PATH should be set to a list of directories separated by semicolons in Windows, or colons in other operating systems.

2.5 *Exploring caveats*

Although the essence of Node's module system is straightforward, you should be aware of two points.

First, if a module is a directory, the file in the module directory that will be evaluated must be named index.js, unless specified otherwise by a file in the module directory named package.json. To specify an alternative to index.js, the package.json file must contain JavaScript Object Notation (JSON) data defining an object with a key named main that specifies the path, within the module directory, to the main file. Figure 2.6 shows a flowchart summarizing these rules.

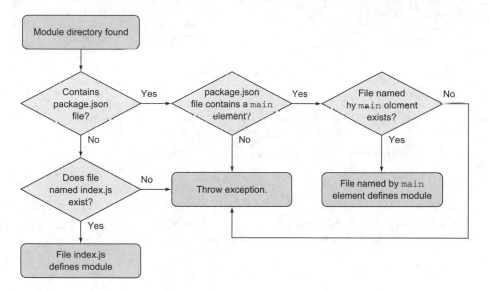

Figure 2.6   The package.json file, when placed in a module directory, allows you to define your module by using a file other than index.js.

Here's an example of a package.json file specifying that currency.js is the main file:

```
{
  "main": "currency.js"
}
```

The other thing to be aware of is Node's capability to cache modules as objects. If two files in an application require the same module, the first require will store the data returned in application memory so the second require won't need to access and evaluate the module's source files. This means loading a module with `require` in the same process returns the same object. Imagine you've built an MVC web application that has a main app object. You can set up that app object, export it, and then `require` it from anywhere within the project. If you've added useful configuration values to the app object, you can then access those values from other files, given a directory structure as follows:

```
project
    app.js
    models
        post.js
```

Figure 2.7 shows how this works.

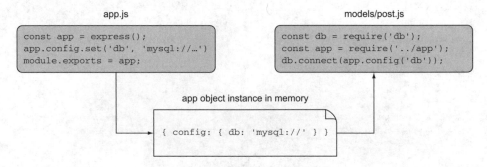

Figure 2.7   Shared app object in a web app

The best way to get comfortable with Node's module system is to play with it, verifying the behavior described in this section yourself. Now that you have a basic understanding of how modules work, let's move on to asynchronous programming techniques.

2.6   *Using asynchronous programming techniques*

If you've done front-end web programming in which interface events (such as mouse clicks) trigger logic, you've done asynchronous programming. Server-side asynchronous programming is no different: events occur that trigger response logic. Two popular models are used in the Node world for managing response logic: callbacks and event listeners.

Callbacks generally define logic for one-off responses. If you perform a database query, for example, you can specify a callback to determine what to do with the query results. The callback may display the database results, perform a calculation based on the results, or execute another callback by using the query results as an argument.

Event listeners, on the other hand, are callbacks associated with a conceptual entity (an *event*). For comparison, a mouse click is an event you would handle in the browser when someone clicks the mouse. As an example, in Node an HTTP server emits a request event when an HTTP request is made. You can listen for that `request` event to occur and add response logic. In the following example, the function `handle-Request` will be called whenever a `request` event is emitted, by using the `Event-Emitter.prototype.on` method to bind an event listener to the server:

```
server.on('request', handleRequest)
```

A Node HTTP server instance is an example of an *event emitter,* a class (`Event-Emitter`) that can be inherited and that adds the ability to emit and handle events. Many aspects of Node's core functionality inherit from `EventEmitter`, and you can also create your own event emitter.

Now that we've established that response logic is generally organized in one of two ways in Node, you're ready to jump into how it all works by learning about the following:

- How to handle one-off events with callbacks
- How to respond to repeating events by using event listeners
- How to handle some of the challenges of asynchronous programming

Let's look first at one of the most common ways asynchronous code is handled: the use of callbacks.

2.7 *Handling one-off events with callbacks*

A *callback* is a function, passed as an argument to an asynchronous function, that describes what to do after the asynchronous operation has completed. Callbacks are used frequently in Node development, more so than event emitters, and they're simple to use.

To demonstrate the use of callbacks in an application, let's see how to make a simple HTTP server that does the following:

- Pulls the titles of recent posts stored as a JSON file asynchronously
- Pulls a basic HTML template asynchronously
- Assembles an HTML page containing the titles
- Sends the HTML page to the user

The results will be similar to figure 2.8.

Figure 2.8   An HTML response from a web server that pulls titles from a JSON file and returns results as a web page

The JSON file (titles.json), shown in the following listing, is formatted as an array of strings containing titles of posts.

Listing 2.4   A list of post titles

```
[
  "Kazakhstan is a huge country... what goes on there?",
  "This weather is making me craaazy",
  "My neighbor sort of howls at night"
]
```

The HTML template file (template.html), shown next, includes just a basic structure to insert the titles of the blog posts.

Listing 2.5   A basic HTML template to render the blog titles

```
<!doctype html>
<html>
  <head></head>
  <body>
    <h1>Latest Posts</h1>
    <ul><li>%</li></ul>            % will be replaced
  </body>                          with title data
</html>
```

The code that pulls in the JSON file and renders the web page is shown next (blog_recent.js).

Listing 2.6   Using callbacks in a simple application

```
const http = require('http');
const fs = require('fs');              Creates HTTP server and uses
http.createServer((req, res) => {      callback to define response logic
  if (req.url == '/') {
    fs.readFile('./titles.json', (err, data) => {      Reads JSON file and uses
      if (err) {                                       callback to define what to
        console.error(err);          If error occurs, logs    do with its contents
        res.end('Server Error');     error and returns
      } else {                       "Server Error" to client
        const titles = JSON.parse(data.toString());
        fs.readFile('./template.html', (err, data) => {      Reads HTML template
          if (err) {                                         and uses callback
            console.error(err);                              when it's loaded
            res.end('Server Error');
          } else {
          const tmpl = data.toString();
            const html = tmpl.replace('%', titles.join('</li><li>'));
            res.writeHead(200, { 'Content-Type': 'text/html' });
            res.end(html);
          }                                          Sends HTML
        });                                          page to user
      }
```

Parses data from JSON text points to `const titles = JSON.parse(data.toString());`

Assembles HTML page showing blog titles points to `const html = tmpl.replace('%', titles.join('</li><li>'));`

```
    });
  }
}).listen(8000, '127.0.0.1');
```

This example nests three levels of callbacks:

```
http.createServer((req, res) => { ...
  fs.readFile('./titles.json', (err, data) => { ...
    fs.readFile('./template.html', (err, data) => { ...
```

Using three levels isn't bad, but the more levels of callbacks you use, the more cluttered your code looks, and the harder it is to refactor and test, so it's good to limit callback nesting. By creating named functions that handle the individual levels of callback nesting, you can express the same logic in a way that requires more lines of code, but that could be easier to maintain, test, and refactor. The following listing is functionally equivalent to listing 2.6.

Listing 2.7 Reducing nesting by creating intermediary functions

```
const http = require('http');
const fs = require('fs');
http.createServer((req, res) => {          ⟵┐ Client request initially
  getTitles(res);                              comes in here
}).listen(8000, '127.0.0.1');              ⟵┐ Control is passed
                                               to getTitles
function getTitles(res) {                  ⟵┐ getTitles pulls titles and passes
  fs.readFile('./titles.json', (err, data) => {  control to getTemplate
    if (err) {
      hadError(err, res);
    } else {
      getTemplate(JSON.parse(data.toString()), res);
    }
  });
}
function getTemplate(titles, res) {        ⟵┐ getTemplate reads template file
  fs.readFile('./template.html', (err, data) => {  and passes control to formatHtml
    if (err) {
      hadError(err, res);
    } else {
      formatHtml(titles, data.toString(), res);
    }
  });                                           ┌ formatHtml takes titles and
}                                               │ template, and renders a
function formatHtml(titles, tmpl, res) {   ⟵┘ response back to client
  const html = tmpl.replace('%', titles.join('</li><li>'));
  res.writeHead(200, {'Content-Type': 'text/html'});
  res.end(html);
}
function hadError(err, res) {              ⟵┐ If an error occurs along the way,
  console.error(err);                          hadError logs error to console and
  res.end('Server Error');                      responds to client with "Server Error"
}
```

You can also reduce the nesting caused by `if/else` blocks with another common idiom in Node development: returning early from a function. The following listing is functionally the same but avoids further nesting by returning early. It also explicitly indicates that the function shouldn't continue executing.

Listing 2.8   Reducing nesting by returning early

```
const http = require('http');
const fs = require('fs');
http.createServer((req, res) => {
  getTitles(res);
}).listen(8000, '127.0.0.1');
function getTitles(res) {
  fs.readFile('./titles.json', (err, data) => {
    if (err) return hadError(err, res);          ◁──  Instead of creating an else branch,
    getTemplate(JSON.parse(data.toString()), res);     you return, because if an error
  });                                                  occurs, you don't need to continue
}                                                      executing this function
function getTemplate(titles, res) {
  fs.readFile('./template.html', (err, data) => {
    if (err) return hadError(err, res);
    formatHtml(titles, data.toString(), res);
  });
}
function formatHtml(titles, tmpl, res) {
  const html = tmpl.replace('%', titles.join('</li><li>'));
  res.writeHead(200, { 'Content-Type': 'text/html'});
  res.end(html);
}
function hadError(err, res) {
  console.error(err);
  res.end('Server Error');
}
```

Now that you've learned how to use callbacks to handle one-off events for such tasks as defining responses when reading files and web server requests, let's move on to organizing events by using event emitters.

The Node convention for asynchronous callbacks

Most Node built-in modules use callbacks with two arguments: the first argument is for an error, should one occur, and the second argument is for the results. The error argument is often abbreviated as `err`.

Here's a typical example of this common function signature:

```
const fs = require('fs');
fs.readFile('./titles.json', (err, data) => {
  if (err) throw err;
  // do something with data if no error has occurred
});
```

2.8 Handling repeating events with event emitters

Event emitters fire events and include the ability to handle those events when triggered. Some important Node API components, such as HTTP servers, TCP servers, and streams, are implemented as event emitters. You can also create your own.

As we mentioned earlier, events are handled through the use of listeners. A *listener* is the association of an event with a callback function that gets triggered each time the event occurs. For example, a TCP socket in Node has an event called `data` that's triggered whenever new data is available on the socket:

```
socket.on('data', handleData);
```

Let's look at using `data` events to create an echo server.

2.8.1 An example event emitter

A simple example of repeated events occurs in an echo server. When you send data to an echo server, it echoes the data back, as shown in figure 2.9.

Listing 2.9 shows the code needed to implement an echo server. Whenever a client connects, a socket is created. The socket is an event emitter to which you can then add a listener, using the on

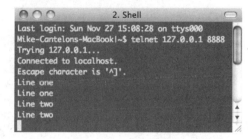

Figure 2.9 An echo server repeating the data sent to it

method, to respond to `data` events. These `data` events are emitted whenever new data is available on the socket.

Listing 2.9 Using the `on` method to respond to events

```
const net = require('net');
const server = net.createServer(socket => {
  socket.on('data', data => {          ← data events handled whenever
    socket.write(data);       ←           new data has been read
  });                            Data is written (echoed
});                              back) to the client
server.listen(8888);
```

You run this echo server by entering the following command:

```
node echo_server.js
```

After the echo server is running, you can connect to it by entering the following command:

```
telnet 127.0.0.1 8888
```

Every time data is sent from your connected telnet session to the server, it will be echoed back into the telnet session.

TELNET ON WINDOWS　If you're using the Microsoft Windows operating system, telnet may not be installed by default, and you'll have to install it yourself. TechNet has instructions for the various versions of Windows: http://mng.bz/egzr.

2.8.2　*Responding to an event that should occur only once*

Listeners can be defined to repeatedly respond to events, as the previous example shows, or listeners can be defined to respond only once. The following listing, using the `once` method, modifies the previous echo server example to echo only the first chunk of data sent to it.

Listing 2.10　Using the `once` method to respond to a single event

```
const net = require('net');
const server = net.createServer(socket => {
  socket.once('data', data => {          ◁─┐ data event will be
    socket.write(data);                     │ handled only once
  });
});
server.listen(8888);
```

2.8.3　*Creating event emitters: a publish/subscribe example*

In the previous example, you used a built-in Node API that uses event emitters. Node's built-in events module, however, allows you to create your own event emitters.

　　The following code defines a `channel` event emitter with a single listener that responds to someone joining the channel. Note that you use on (or, alternatively, the longer form `addListener`) to add a listener to an event emitter:

```
const EventEmitter = require('events').EventEmitter;
const channel = new EventEmitter();
channel.on('join', () => {
  console.log('Welcome!');
});
```

This `join` callback, however, won't ever be called, because you haven't emitted any events yet. You could add a line to the listing that would trigger an event using the emit function:

```
channel.emit('join');
```

EVENT NAMES　Events are keys that can have any string value: `data`, `join`, or `some crazy long` event name. Only one event, called `error`, is special, and you'll look at it soon.

Let's look at how you could implement your own publish/subscribe logic by using `EventEmitter` to make a communication channel. If you run the script in listing 2.11, you'll have a simple chat server. A chat server channel is implemented as an event emitter that responds to `join` events emitted by clients. When a client joins the channel, the join listener logic, in turn, adds an additional client-specific listener to the channel for the broadcast event that will write any message broadcast to the client socket. The names of the event types, such as join and broadcast, are completely arbitrary. You could use other names for these event types if you wished.

Listing 2.11 A simple publish/subscribe system using an event emitter

```
const events = require('events');
const net = require('net');
const channel = new events.EventEmitter();
channel.clients = {};
channel.subscriptions = {};
channel.on('join', function(id, client) {
  this.clients[id] = client;
  this.subscriptions[id] = (senderId, message) => {
    if (id != senderId) {
      this.clients[id].write(message);
    }
  };
  this.on('broadcast', this.subscriptions[id]);
});
const server = net.createServer(client => {
  const id = `${client.remoteAddress}:${client.remotePort}`;
  channel.emit('join', id, client);
  client.on('data', data => {
    data = data.toString();
    channel.emit('broadcast', id, data);
  });
});
server.listen(8888);
```

- Adds a listener for the join event that stores a user's client object, allowing the application to send data back to the user
- Ignores data if it's been directly broadcast by the user
- Adds a listener, specific to the current user, for the broadcast event
- Emits a join event when a user connects to the server, specifying the user ID and client object
- Emits a channel broadcast event, specifying the user ID and message, when any user sends data

---

After you have the chat server running, open a new command line and enter the following code to enter the chat:

```
telnet 127.0.0.1 8888
```

If you open up a few command lines, you'll see that anything typed in one command line is echoed to the others.

The problem with this chat server is that when users close their connections and leave the chat room, they leave behind a listener that will attempt to write to a client that's no longer connected. This will, of course, generate an error. To fix this issue, you need to add the listener in the following listing to the channel event emitter, and add logic to the server's close event listener to emit the channel's leave event. The leave event removes the broadcast listener originally added for the client.

Listing 2.12 Creating a listener to clean up when clients disconnect

```
...
channel.on('leave', function(id) {
  channel.removeListener(
```

- Creates listener for leave event

```
      'broadcast', this.subscriptions[id]
    );
    channel.emit('broadcast', id, `${id} has left the chatroom.\n`);    ◄─────┐
  });                                                                          │
  const server = net.createServer(client => {              Removes broadcast listener
    ...                                                          for specific client
    client.on('close', () => {
      channel.emit('leave', id);              ◄─────  Emits leave event when
    });                                               client disconnects
  });
  server.listen(8888);
```

If you want to prevent a chat for some reason but don't want to shut down the server, you can use the removeAllListeners event emitter method to remove all listeners of a given type. The following code shows how this is implemented for our chat server example:

```
channel.on('shutdown', () => {
  channel.emit('broadcast', '', 'The server has shut down.\n');
  channel.removeAllListeners('broadcast');
});
```

You can then add support for a chat command that triggers the shutdown. To do so, change the listener for the data event to the following code:

```
client.on('data', data => {
  data = data.toString();
  if (data === 'shutdown\r\n') {
    channel.emit('shutdown');
  }
  channel.emit('broadcast', id, data);
});
```

Now when any chat participant enters shutdown into the chat, it'll cause all participants to be kicked off.

> ### Error handling
>
> A convention you can use when creating event emitters is to emit an error type event instead of directly throwing an error. This allows you to define custom event response logic by setting one or more listeners for this event type.
>
> The following code shows how an error listener handles an emitted error by logging on the console:
>
> ```
> const events = require('events');
> const myEmitter = new events.EventEmitter();
> myEmitter.on('error', err => {
>   console.log(`ERROR: ${err.message}`);
> });
> myEmitter.emit('error', new Error('Something is wrong.'));
> ```

(continued)

If no listener for this event type is defined when the `error` event type is emitted, the event emitter will output a stack trace (a list of program instructions that executed up to the point when the error occurred) and halt execution. The stack trace indicates an error of the type specified by the `emit` call's second argument. This behavior is unique to `error` type events; when other event types are emitted, and they have no listeners, nothing happens.

If an `error` type event is emitted without an `error` object supplied as the second argument, a stack trace will indicate an `Uncaught, unspecified 'error'` `event` error, and your application will halt. There is a deprecated method you can use to deal with this error—you can define your own response by defining a global handler via the following code:

```
process.on('uncaughtException', err => {
  console.error(err.stack);
  process.exit(1);
});
```

Alternatives to this, such as domains (http://nodejs.org/api/domain.html), are being developed, but they're not considered production-ready.

If you want to provide users connecting to chat with a count of currently connected users, you can use the following `listeners` method, which returns an array of listeners for a given event type:

```
channel.on('join', function(id, client) {
const welcome = `
  Welcome!
    Guests online: ${this.listeners('broadcast').length}
  `;
  client.write(`${welcome}\n`);
  ...
```

To increase the number of listeners that an event emitter has, and to avoid the warnings Node displays when there are more than 10 listeners, you can use the `setMax-Listeners` method. Using your channel event emitter as an example, you use the following code to increase the number of allowed listeners:

```
channel.setMaxListeners(50);
```

2.8.4 *Extending the event emitter: a file watcher example*

If you want to build upon the event emitter's behavior, you can create a new JavaScript class that inherits from the event emitter. For example, you can create a class called `Watcher` that processes files placed in a specified filesystem directory. You then use this class to create a utility that watches a directory (renaming any files placed in it to lowercase and then copying the files into a separate directory).

After setting up the `Watcher` object, you need to extend the methods inherited from `EventEmitter` with two new methods, as shown in the following listing.

Listing 2.13 Extending the event emitter's functionality

```
const fs = require('fs');
const events = require('events');

class Watcher extends events.EventEmitter {          Extends EventEmitter with
  constructor(watchDir, processedDir) {              method that processes files
    super();
    this.watchDir = watchDir;
    this.processedDir = processedDir;
  }

  watch() {
    fs.readdir(this.watchDir, (err, files) => {      Processes each file
      if (err) throw err;                            in watch directory
      for (var index in files) {
        this.emit('process', files[index]);
      }
    });
  }
  start() {                                          Adds method
    fs.watchFile(this.watchDir, () => {              to start watching
      this.watch();
    });
  }
}

module.exports = Watcher;
```

The `watch` method cycles through the directory, processing any files found. The `start` method starts the directory monitoring. The monitoring uses Node's `fs.watchFile` function, so when something happens in the watched directory, the `watch` method is triggered, cycling through the watched directory and emitting a `process` event for each file found.

Now that you've defined the `Watcher` class, you can put it to work by creating a `Watcher` object with the following code:

```
const watcher = new Watcher(watchDir, processedDir);
```

With your newly created `Watcher` object, you can use the on method, inherited from the event emitter class, to set the logic used to process each file, as shown in this snippet:

```
watcher.on('process', (file) => {
  const watchFile = `${watchDir}/${file}`;
  const processedFile = `${processedDir}/${file.toLowerCase()}`;
  fs.rename(watchFile, processedFile, err => {
    if (err) throw err;
  });
});
```

Now that all the necessary logic is in place, you can start the directory monitor by using the following code:

```
watcher.start();
```

After putting the `Watcher` code into a script and creating watch and done directories, you should be able to run the script by using Node, drop files into the watch directory, and see the files pop up, renamed to lowercase, in the done directory. This is an example of how the event emitter can be a useful class from which to create new classes.

By learning how to use callbacks to define one-off asynchronous logic and how to use event emitters to dispatch asynchronous logic repeatedly, you're one step closer to mastering control of a Node application's behavior. In a single callback or event emitter listener, however, you may want to include logic that performs additional asynchronous tasks. If the order in which these tasks are performed is important, you may be faced with a new challenge: how to control exactly when each task, in a series of asynchronous tasks, executes.

Before we get to controlling when tasks execute—coming up in section 2.10—let's take a look at some of the challenges you'll likely encounter as you write asynchronous code.

2.9 *Challenges with asynchronous development*

When creating asynchronous applications, you have to pay close attention to the way your application flows and keep a watchful eye on application state: the conditions of the event loop, application variables, and any other resources that change as program logic executes.

Node's event loop, for example, keeps track of asynchronous logic that hasn't completed processing. As long as there's uncompleted asynchronous logic, the Node process won't exit. A continually running Node process is desirable behavior for something like a web server, but it isn't desirable to continue running processes that are expected to end after a period of time, such as command-line tools. The event loop keeps track of any database connections until they're closed, preventing Node from exiting.

Application variables can also change unexpectedly if you're not careful. Listing 2.14 shows an example of how the order in which asynchronous code executes can lead to confusion. If the example code was executing synchronously, you'd expect the output to be "The color is blue." Because the example is asynchronous, however, the value of the `color` variable changes before `console.log` executes, and the output is "The color is green."

> **Listing 2.14 How scope behavior can lead to bugs**

```
function asyncFunction(callback) {
  setTimeout(callback, 200);
}
```

```
let color = 'blue';
asyncFunction(() => {                              This is executed last
  console.log(`The color is ${color}`);            (200 ms later)
});
color = 'green';
```

To "freeze" the contents of the color variable, you can modify your logic and use a JavaScript closure. In listing 2.15, you wrap the call to asyncFunction in an anonymous function that takes a color argument. You then execute the anonymous function immediately, sending it the current contents of color. By making color an argument for the anonymous function, it becomes local to the scope of that function, and when the value of color is changed outside the anonymous function, the local version is unaffected.

Listing 2.15   Using an anonymous function to preserve a global variable's value

```
function asyncFunction(callback) {
  setTimeout(callback, 200);
}

let color = 'blue';

(color => {
  asyncFunction(() => {
    console.log('The color is', color);
  });
})(color);

color = 'green';
```

This is but one of many JavaScript programming tricks you'll come across in your Node development.

CLOSURES   For more information on closures, see the Mozilla JavaScript documentation: https://developer.mozilla.org/en-US/docs/JavaScript/Guide/Closures.

Now that you understand how to use closures to control your application state, let's look at sequencing asynchronous logic in order to keep the flow of your application under control.

2.10   *Sequencing asynchronous logic*

During the execution of an asynchronous program, some tasks can happen anytime, independent of what the rest of the program is doing, without causing problems. But some tasks should happen only before or after certain other tasks.

The concept of sequencing groups of asynchronous tasks is called *flow control* by the Node community. There are two types of flow control: *serial* and *parallel*, as figure 2.10 shows.

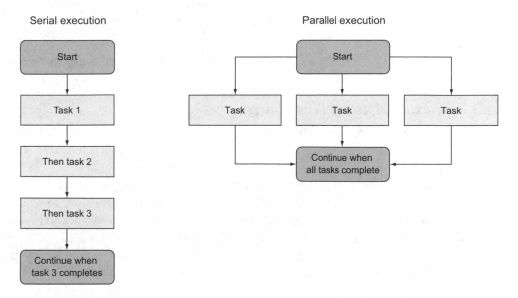

Figure 2.10   Serial execution of asynchronous tasks is similar, conceptually, to synchronous logic: tasks are executed in sequence. Parallel tasks, however, don't have to execute one after another.

Tasks that need to happen one after the other are called *serial.* A simple example is the task of creating a directory and the task of storing a file in it. You can't store the file before creating the directory.

Tasks that don't need to happen one after the other are called *parallel.* It isn't necessarily important when these tasks start and stop relative to one another, but they should all be completed before further logic executes. One example is downloading numerous files that will later be compressed into a zip archive. The files can be downloaded simultaneously, but all of the downloads should be completed before creating the archive.

Keeping track of serial and parallel flow control requires programmatic bookkeeping. When you implement serial flow control, you need to keep track of the task currently executing or maintain a queue of unexecuted tasks. When you implement parallel flow control, you need to keep track of how many tasks have executed to completion.

Flow-control tools handle the bookkeeping for you, which makes grouping asynchronous serial or parallel tasks easy. Although plenty of community-created add-ons deal with sequencing asynchronous logic, implementing flow control yourself demystifies it and helps you gain a deeper understanding of how to deal with the challenges of asynchronous programming.

In the following sections we show you

- When to use serial flow control
- How to implement serial flow control

- How to implement parallel flow control
- How to use third-party modules for flow control

Let's start by looking at when and how you handle serial flow control in an asynchronous world.

2.11   *When to use serial flow control*

To execute numerous asynchronous tasks in sequence, you could use callbacks, but if you have a significant number of tasks, you'll have to organize them. If you don't, you'll end up with messy code due to excessive callback nesting.

The following code is an example of executing tasks in sequence by using callbacks. The example uses `setTimeout` to simulate tasks that take time to execute: the first task takes one second, the next takes half of a second, and the last takes one-tenth of a second. `setTimeout` is only an artificial simulation; in real code you could be reading files, making HTTP requests, and so on. Although this example code is short, it's arguably a bit messy, and there's no easy way to programmatically add another task.

```
setTimeout(() => {
  console.log('I execute first.');
  setTimeout(() => {
    console.log('I execute next.');
    setTimeout(() => {
      console.log('I execute last.');
    }, 100);
  }, 500);
}, 1000);
```

Alternatively, you can use a flow-control tool such as Async (http://caolan.github.io/async/) to execute these tasks. Async is straightforward to use and benefits from having a small codebase (a mere 837 bytes, minified and compressed). You can install Async with the following command:

```
npm install async
```

Now, use the code in the next listing to re-implement the previous code snippet with serial flow control.

Listing 2.16   Serial control using a community-created add-on

```
const async = require('async');
async.series([                          ◁──  Provides an array of functions for
  callback => {                               Async to execute, one after the other
    setTimeout(() => {
      console.log('I execute first.');
      callback();
    }, 1000);
  },
  callback => {
    setTimeout(() => {
```

```
      console.log('I execute next.');
      callback();
    }, 500);
  },
  callback => {
    setTimeout(() => {
      console.log('I execute last.');
      callback();
    }, 100);
  }
]);
```

Although the implementation using flow control means more lines of code, it's generally easier to read and maintain. You're likely not going to use flow control all the time, but if you run into a situation where you want to avoid callback nesting, it's a handy tool for improving code legibility.

Now that you've seen an example of the use of serial flow control with a specialized tool, let's look at how to implement it from scratch.

2.12 Implementing serial flow control

To execute numerous asynchronous tasks in sequence by using serial flow control, you first need to put the tasks in an array, in the desired order of execution. This array, as figure 2.11 shows, acts as a queue: when you finish one task, you extract the next task in sequence from the array.

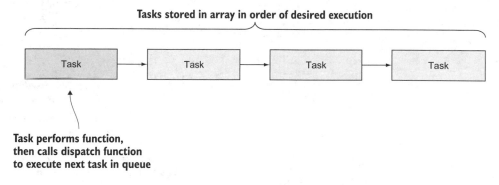

Tasks stored in array in order of desired execution

Task performs function, then calls dispatch function to execute next task in queue

Figure 2.11   How serial flow control works

Each task exists in the array as a function. When a task has completed, the task should call a handler function to indicate error status and results. The handler function in this implementation will halt execution if there's an error. If there isn't an error, the handler will pull the next task from the queue and execute it.

To demonstrate an implementation of serial flow control, you'll make a simple application that displays a single article's title and URL from a randomly chosen RSS feed. The list of possible RSS feeds is specified in a text file. The application's output will look something like the following text:

```
Of Course ML Has Monads!
http://lambda-the-ultimate.org/node/4306
```

Our example requires the use of two helper modules from the npm registry. First, open a command-line prompt, and then enter the following commands to create a directory for the example and install the helper modules:

```
mkdir listing_217
cd listing_217
npm init -y
npm install --save request@2.60.0
npm install --save htmlparser@1.7.7
```

The `request` module is a simplified HTTP client that you can use to fetch RSS data. The `htmlparser` module has functionality that allows you to turn raw RSS data into JavaScript data structures.

Next, create a file named index.js inside your new directory that contains the code shown here.

Listing 2.17   Serial flow control implemented in a simple application

```
const fs = require('fs');
const request = require('request');
const htmlparser = require('htmlparser');          Task 1: Make sure the
const configFilename = './rss_feeds.txt';          file containing the list of
function checkForRSSFile() {                        RSS feed URLs exists
  fs.exists(configFilename, (exists) => {
    if (!exists)
      return next(new Error(`Missing RSS file: ${configFilename}`));
    next(null, configFilename);
  });                                               Whenever there's an
}                                                   error, return early
function readRSSFile(configFilename) {              Task 2: Read and parse the file
  fs.readFile(configFilename, (err, feedList) => {  containing the feed URLs
    if (err) return next(err);
    feedList = feedList                             Converts list of feed URLs to a string
      .toString()                                   and then into an array of feed URLs
      .replace(/^\s+|\s+$/g, '')
      .split('\n');
    const random = Math.floor(Math.random() * feedList.length);
    next(null, feedList[random]);
  });                                               Selects random feed URL
}                                                   from array of feed URLs
function downloadRSSFeed(feedUrl) {
  request({ uri: feedUrl }, (err, res, body) => {   Task 3: Do an HTTP request and
    if (err) return next(err);                      get data for the selected feed
    if (res.statusCode !== 200)
      return next(new Error('Abnormal response status code'));
    next(null, body);
```

```
      });
    }
    function parseRSSFeed(rss) {                    ◁──  Task 4: Parse RSS data
      const handler = new htmlparser.RssHandler();        into the array of items
      const parser = new htmlparser.Parser(handler);
      parser.parseComplete(rss);
      if (!handler.dom.items.length)
        return next(new Error('No RSS items found'));
      const item = handler.dom.items.shift();
      console.log(item.title);                      ◁──  Displays title and URL of
      console.log(item.link);                             the first feed item, if it exists
    }
    const tasks = [
      checkForRSSFile,                    ◁──  Adds each task to be performed
      readRSSFile,                             to an array in execution order
      downloadRSSFeed,
      parseRSSFeed
    ];                                        A function called next
    function next(err, result) {       ◁──    executes each task
      if (err) throw err;                                       ◁──  Throws exception if task
      const currentTask = tasks.shift();    ◁──  Next task comes       encounters an error
      if (currentTask) {                         from array of tasks
        currentTask(result);
      }
    }
    next();                          ◁──  Starts serial execution
                                          of tasks
```

Executes current task

Before trying out the application, create the file rss_feeds.txt in the same directory as the application script. If you don't have any feeds at hand, you can try the Node blog's feed, which is http://blog.nodejs.org/feed/. Put the URLs of RSS feeds into the text file, one on each line of the file. After you've created this file, open a command line and enter the following commands to change to the application directory and execute the script:

```
cd listing_217
node index.js
```

Serial flow control, as this example implementation shows, is a way of putting callbacks into play when they're needed, rather than simply nesting them.

Now that you know how to implement serial flow control, let's look at how to execute asynchronous tasks in parallel.

2.13 *Implementing parallel flow control*

To execute numerous asynchronous tasks in parallel, you again need to put the tasks in an array, but this time the order of the tasks is unimportant. Each task should call a handler function that will increment the number of completed tasks. When all tasks are complete, the handler function should perform some subsequent logic.

For a parallel flow-control example, you'll make a simple application that reads the contents of text files and outputs the frequency of word use throughout the files. Reading the contents of the text files will be done using the asynchronous `readFile`

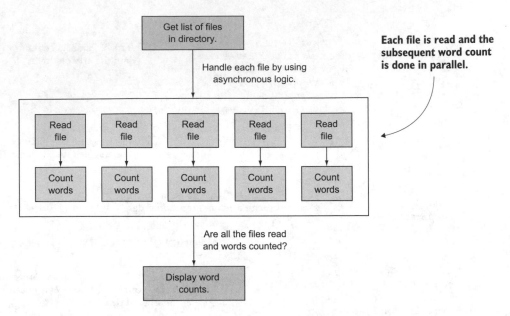

Figure 2.12   Using parallel flow control to implement a frequency count of word use in numerous files

function, so numerous file reads can be done in parallel. Figure 2.12 shows how this application works.

The output looks something like the following text (although it'll likely be much longer):

```
would: 2
wrench: 3
writeable: 1
you: 24
```

Open a command-line prompt and enter the following commands to create two directories—one for the example, and another within that to contain the text files you want to analyze:

```
mkdir listing_218
cd listing_218
mkdir text
```

Next, create a file named word_count.js inside the listing_218 directory that contains the code that follows.

Listing 2.18   Parallel flow control implemented in a simple application

```
const fs = require('fs');
const tasks = [];
const wordCounts = {};
```

```
const filesDir = './text';
let completedTasks = 0;

function checkIfComplete() {
  completedTasks++;
  if (completedTasks === tasks.length) {
    for (let index in wordCounts) {
      console.log(`${index}: ${wordCounts[index]}`);
    }
  }
}

function addWordCount(word) {
  wordCounts[word] = (wordCounts[word]) ? wordCounts[word] + 1 : 1;
}

function countWordsInText(text) {
  const words = text
    .toString()
    .toLowerCase()
    .split(/\W+/)
    .sort();

  words
    .filter(word => word)
    .forEach(word => addWordCount(word));
}

fs.readdir(filesDir, (err, files) => {
  if (err) throw err;
  files.forEach(file => {
    const task = (file => {
      return () => {
        fs.readFile(file, (err, text) => {
          if (err) throw err;
          countWordsInText(text);
          checkIfComplete();
        });
      };
    })(`${filesDir}/${file}`);
    tasks.push(task);
  }
  tasks.forEach(task => task());
});
```

When all tasks have completed, list each word used in the files and the number of times it was used

Counts word occurrences in text

Gets a list of the files in the text directory

Defines a task to handle each file. Each task includes a call to a function that will asynchronously read the file and then count the file's word usage

Adds each task to an array of functions to call in parallel

Starts executing every task in parallel

Before trying out the application, create some text files in the text directory you created earlier. Then open a command line and enter the following commands to change to the application directory and execute the script:

```
cd word_count
node word_count.js
```

Now that you've learned how serial and parallel flow control work under the hood, let's look at how to use community-created tools that allow you to easily benefit from flow control in your applications, without having to implement it yourself.

2.14 *Using community tools*

Many community add-ons provide convenient flow-control tools. Some popular add-ons include Async, Step, and Seq. Although each of these is worth checking out, we'll use Async again for another example.

> **COMMUNITY ADD-ONS FOR FLOW CONTROL** For more information about community add-ons for flow control, see the article "Virtual Panel: How to Survive Asynchronous Programming in JavaScript" by Werner Schuster and Dio Synodinos on InfoQ: http://mng.bz/wKnV.

Listing 2.19 is an example of using Async to sequence tasks in a script that uses parallel flow control to download two files simultaneously and then archive them.

> **THE FOLLOWING EXAMPLE WON'T WORK IN MICROSOFT WINDOWS** Because the Windows operating system doesn't come with the tar and curl commands, the following example won't work in this operating system.

In this example, we use serial control to make sure that the downloading is done before proceeding to archiving.

Listing 2.19   Using a community add-on flow-control tool in a simple application

```
const async = require('async');
const exec = require('child_process').exec;
function downloadNodeVersion(version, destination, callback) {        ◁──────┐
  const url = `http://nodejs.org/dist/v${version}/node-v${version}.tar.gz`;
  const filepath = `${destination}/${version}.tgz`;
  exec(`curl ${url} > ${filepath}`, callback);        Downloads Node source
}                                                       code for given version
async.series([
  callback => {                              ◁──  Executes series of
    async.parallel([                              tasks in sequence
      callback => {
        console.log('Downloading Node v4.4.7...');
        downloadNodeVersion('4.4.7', '/tmp', callback);
      },
      callback => {
        console.log('Downloading Node v6.3.0...');
        downloadNodeVersion('6.3.0', '/tmp', callback);
      }
    ], callback);
  },
  callback => {
    console.log('Creating archive of downloaded files...');        Creates
    exec(                                                           archive file
      'tar cvf node_distros.tar /tmp/4.4.7.tgz /tmp/6.3.0.tgz',
  err => {
  if (err) throw err;
      console.log('All done!');
      callback();
    }
```

Executes downloads in parallel (annotation for `async.parallel`)

```
  );
  }
]);
```

The script defines a helper function that downloads any specified release version of the Node source code. Two tasks are then executed in series: the parallel downloading of two versions of Node and the bundling of the downloaded versions into a new archive file.

2.15 Summary

- Node modules can be organized into reusable modules.
- The `require` function is used to load modules.
- The `module.exports` and `exports` objects are used to share functions and variables from within a module.
- The package.json file is used to specify dependencies and which file is exported as the main file.
- Asynchronous logic can be controlled with nested callbacks, event emitters, and flow-control utilities.

What is a Node web application?

This chapter covers

- Creating a new web application
- Building RESTful services
- Persisting data
- Working with templates

This chapter is all about Node web applications. After reading this chapter, you'll understand what Node web applications look like and how to start building them. You'll do everything a modern web developer does when building an application.

You're going to build a web application called *later* that's inspired by popular read-it-later websites such as Instapaper (www.instapaper.com) and Pocket (getpocket.com). This involves starting a new Node project, managing dependencies, creating a RESTful API, saving data to a database, and making an interface with templates. That might sound like a lot, but you'll explore each of the ideas in this chapter again in subsequent chapters.

Figure 3.1 shows what the result should look like.

The read-it-later page on the left has stripped away all of the navigation from the target website, preserving the main content and title. More significantly, the article is permanently saved to a database, which means you can read it at a future date when the original article may no longer be retrievable.

Figure 3.1   A read-it-later web application

Before building a web application, you should create a fresh project. The next section shows how to create Node projects from scratch.

3.1   Understanding a Node web application's structure

A typical Node web application has the following components:

- package.json—A file that contains a list of dependencies, and the command that runs the application
- public/—A folder of static assets, such as CSS and client-side JavaScript
- node_modules/—The place where the project's dependencies get installed
- One or more JavaScript files that contains your application code

The application code is often further subdivided as follows:

- app.js or index.js—The code that sets up the application
- models/—Database models
- views/—The templates that are used to render the pages in the application
- controllers/ or routes/—HTTP request handlers
- middleware/—Middleware components

There are no rules that dictate how your application should be structured: most web frameworks are flexible and require configuration. But this template is the general outline that you'll find in most projects.

It's much easier to learn how to do this if you practice, so let's see how to create a skeleton web application the way a seasoned Node programmer would.

3.1.1 *Starting a new web app*

To create a new web app, you need to make a new Node project. Refer to chapter 2 if you want to refresh your memory, but to recap, you need to create a directory and run `npm init` with defaults:

```
mkdir later
cd later
npm init -fy
```

Now you have a fresh project; what's next? Most people would add a module from npm that makes web development easier. Node has a built-in http module that has a server, but it's easier to use something that reduces the boilerplate required for command web development tasks. Let's see how to install Express.

ADDING A DEPENDENCY

To add a dependency to a project, use `npm install`. The following command installs Express:

```
npm install --save express
```

Now if you look at package.json, you should see that Express has been added. The following snippet shows the section in question:

```
"dependencies": {
  "express": "^4.14.0"
}
```

The Express module is in the project's node_modules/ folder. If you wanted to uninstall Express from the project, you would run `npm rm express --save`. This removes it from node_modules/ and updates the package.json file.

A SIMPLE SERVER

Express is focused on modeling your application in terms of HTTP requests and responses, and it's built using Node's built-in http module. To make a basic application, you need to make an application instance by using `express()`, add a route handler, and then bind the application to a TCP port. Here's a full example:

```
const express = require('express');
const app = express();

const port = process.env.PORT || 3000;

app.get('/', (req, res) => {
  res.send('Hello World');
});

app.listen(port, () =>
  console.log(`Express web app available at localhost: ${port}`);
};
```

It's not as complicated as it sounds! Save this code to a file called index.js, and run it by typing `node index.js`. Then visit http://localhost:3000 to view the result. To avoid having to remember exactly how to run each application, most people use npm scripts to simplify the process.

NPM SCRIPTS

To save your server start command (`node index.js`) as an npm script, open package.json and add a new property under `scripts` called `start`:

```
"scripts": {
  "start": "node index.js",
  "test": "echo \"Error: no test specified\" && exit 1"
},
```

Now you can run your application by typing `npm start`. If you see an error because port 3000 is already being used on your machine, you can use a different port by running `PORT=3001 npm start`. People use npm scripts for all kinds of things: building client-side bundles, running tests, and generating documentation. You can put anything you like in there; it's basically a mini-script invocation tool.

3.1.2 Comparing other platforms

For comparison, the equivalent PHP Hello World application is shown here:

```
<?php echo '<p>Hello World</p>'; ?>
```

It fits on one line and is easy to understand, so what benefits does the more complex Node example have? The difference is in terms of programming paradigm: with PHP, your application is a *page*; in Node, it's a server. The Node example has complete control over the request and response, so you can do all kinds of things without configuring a server. If you want to use HTTP compression or URL redirection, you can implement these features as part of your application logic. You don't need to separate HTTP and application logic; they become part of your application.

Instead of having a separate HTTP server configuration, you can keep it in the same place, and that means the same directory. This makes Node applications easy to deploy and manage.

Another feature that makes Node applications easy to deploy is npm. Because dependencies are installed per project, you don't get clashes between projects on the same system.

3.1.3 What's next?

Now that you have the hang of creating projects with `npm init` and installing dependencies with `npm install --save`, you can create new projects quickly. This is great, because it means you can try out ideas without messing up other projects. If there's a hot new web framework you want to try, then create a new directory, run `npm init`, and install the module from npm.

With all of this in place, you're ready to start writing code. At this stage, you can add JavaScript files to your project and load modules that you've installed with npm --save by using require. Let's focus on what most web developers would do next: add some RESTful routes. This will help you define your application's API and determine what database models are needed.

3.2 Building a RESTful web service

Your application will be a RESTful web service that allows articles to be created and saved in a similar way to Instapaper or Pocket. It'll use a module that was inspired by the original Readability service (www.readability.com) to turn messy web pages into elegant articles that you can read later.

When designing a RESTful service, you need to think about which operations you need and map them to routes in Express. In this case, you need to be able to save articles, fetch them so they can be read, fetch a list of all of them, and delete articles you no longer want. That maps to these routes:

- POST /articles—Create a new article
- GET /articles/:id—Get a single article
- GET /articles—Get all articles
- DELETE /articles/:id—Delete an article

Before getting into issues such as databases and web interfaces, let's focus on creating RESTful resources with Express. You can use cURL to make requests to a sample application to get the hang of it, and then move on to more complicated operations such as storing data to make it like a real web application.

The following listing is a simple Express app that implements these routes by using a JavaScript array to store the articles.

Listing 3.1 RESTful routes example

```
const express = require('express');
const app = express();
const articles = [{ title: 'Example' }];

app.set('port', process.env.PORT || 3000);

app.get('/articles', (req, res, next) => {     ←  ❶ Gets all articles
  res.send(articles);
});

app.post('/articles', (req, res, next) => {    ←  ❷ Creates an article
  res.send('OK');
});

app.get('/articles/:id', (req, res, next) => {  ←  ❸ Gets a single article
  const id = req.params.id;
  console.log('Fetching:', id);
  res.send(articles[id]);
});
```

```
app.delete('/articles/:id', (req, res, next) => {          ⟵
  const id = req.params.id;                           ❹ Deletes an article
  console.log('Deleting:', id);
  delete articles[id];
  res.send({ message: 'Deleted' });
});

app.listen(app.get('port'), () => {
  console.log('App started on port', app.get('port'));
});

module.exports = app;
```

Save this listing as `index.js` and you should be able to run it with `node index.js`. To use this example, follow these steps:

```
mkdir listing3_1
cd listing3_1
npm init -fy
run npm install --save express@4.12.4
```

Creating new Node projects is explored in more detail in chapter 2.

Running the examples and making changes

To run these examples, make sure you restart the server after editing the code each time. You can do this by pressing Ctrl-C to end the Node process and then type `node index.js` to start it again.

The examples are presented in snippets, so you should be able to combine them sequentially to produce a working app. If you can't get it running, try downloading the book's source code from https://github.com/alexyoung/nodejsinaction.

Listing 3.1 has a built-in array of sample data that's used to respond with JSON for all articles ❶ by using the Express `res.send` method. Express will automatically convert the array to a valid JSON response, so it's perfect for making quick REST APIs.

This example can also respond with a single article by using the same principle ❸. You can even delete an article ❹ by using the standard JavaScript `delete` keyword and a numerical ID specified in the URL. You can get values from the URL by putting them in the route string (`/articles/:id`) and then getting the value with `req.params.id`.

Listing 3.1 can't create articles ❷, because for that it needs a request body parser; you'll look at this in the next section. First, let's look at how you can use this example with cURL (http://curl.haxx.se).

After the example is running with `node index.js`, you can make requests to it with a browser or cURL. To fetch one article, run the following snippet:

```
curl http://localhost:3000/articles/0
```

To fetch all articles, you need to make a request to /articles:

```
curl http://localhost:3000/articles
```

And you can even delete an article:

```
curl -X DELETE http://localhost:3000/articles/0
```

But why did we say you couldn't create articles? The main reason is that implementing a POST request requires *body parsing*. Express used to come with a built-in body parser, but there are so many ways to implement it that the developers opted to make it a separate dependency.

A body parser knows how to accept MIME-encoded (*Multipurpose Internet Mail Extensions*) POST request bodies and turn them into data you can use in your code. Usually, you get JSON data that's easy to work with. Whenever you've submitted a form on a website, a body parser has been involved somewhere in the server-side software.

To add the officially supported body parser, run the following npm command:

```
npm install --save body-parser
```

Now load the body parser in your application, near the top of the file, as shown in the following listing. If you're following along, you can save this to the same folder as listing 3.1 (listing3_1), but we've also saved it in its own folder in the book's source code (ch03-what-is-a-node-web-app/listing3_2).

Listing 3.2   Adding a body parser

```
const express = require('express');
const app = express();
const articles = [{ title: 'Example' }];
const bodyParser = require('body-parser');

app.set('port', process.env.PORT || 3000);

app.use(bodyParser.json());                              ❶ Supports request bodies
app.use(bodyParser.urlencoded({ extended: true }));        encoded as JSON

                                                         ❷ Supports form-
                                                           encoded bodies
app.post('/articles', (req, res, next) => {
  const article = { title: req.body.title };
  articles.push(article);
  res.send(article);
});
```

This adds two useful features: JSON body parsing ❶ and form-encoded bodies ❷. It also adds a basic implementation for creating articles: if you make a POST request with a field called `title`, a new article will be added to the articles array! Here's the cURL command:

```
curl --data "title=Example 2" http://localhost:3000/articles
```

Now you're not too far away from building a real web application. You need just two more things: a way to save data permanently in a database, and a way to generate the readable version of articles found on the web.

3.3 Adding a database

There's no predefined way to add a database to a Node application, but the process usually involves the following steps:

1 Decide on the database you want to use.
2 Look at the popular modules on npm that implement a driver or object-relational mapping (ORM).
3 Add the module to your project with `npm --save`.
4 Create models that wrap database access with a JavaScript API.
5 Add the models to your Express routes.

Before adding a database, let's continue focusing on Express by designing the route-handling code from step 5. The HTTP route handlers in the Express part of the application will make simple calls to the database models. Here's an example:

```
app.get('/articles', (req, res, err) => {
  Article.all(err, articles) => {
    if (err) return next(err);
    res.send(articles);
  });
});
```

Here the HTTP route is for getting all articles, so the model method could be something like `Article.all`. This will vary depending on your database API; typical examples are `Article.find({}, cb)`,[1] and `Article.fetchAll().then(cb)`.[2] Note that in these examples, `cb` is an abbreviation of *callback*.

Given the amazing number of databases out there, how do you decide which one to use? Read on for the reasons that we're going with SQLite for this example.

> **Which database?**
>
> For our project, we're going to use SQLite (www.sqlite.org), with the popular sqlite3 module (http://npmjs.com/package/sqlite3). SQLite is convenient because it's an in-process database: you don't need to install a server that runs in the background on your system. Any data that you add is written to a file that's kept after your application is stopped and started again, so it's a good way to get started with databases.

---

[1] Mongoose: http://mongoosejs.com
[2] Bookshelf.js http://bookshelfjs.org

3.3.1 *Making your own model API*

Articles should be created, retrieved, and deleted. Therefore, you need the following methods for an `Article` model class:

- `Article.all(cb)`—Return all articles.
- `Article.find(id, cb)`—Given an ID, find the corresponding article.
- `Article.create({ title, content }, cb)`—Create an article with a title and content.
- `Article.delete(id, cb)`—Delete an article by ID.

You can implement all of this with the sqlite3 module. This module allows you to fetch multiple rows of results with `db.all`, and single rows with `db.get`. First you need a database connection.

The following listing shows how to do each of these things with SQLite in Node. This code should be saved as `db.js` in the same folder as the code from listing 3.1.

Listing 3.3   An `Article` model

```
const sqlite3 = require('sqlite3').verbose();
const dbName = 'later.sqlite';
const db = new sqlite3.Database(dbName);          ❶ Connects to a
                                                     database file
db.serialize(() => {
const sql = `
  CREATE TABLE IF NOT EXISTS articles
    (id integer primary key, title, content TEXT)
  `;
  db.run(sql);                                    ❷ Creates an "articles"
});                                                  table if there isn't one

class Article {
  static all(cb) {
    db.all('SELECT * FROM articles', cb);         ❸ Fetches all articles
  }

  static find(id, cb) {
    db.get('SELECT * FROM articles WHERE id = ?', id, cb);   ❹ Selects a
  }                                                             specific article

  static create(data, cb) {
    const sql = 'INSERT INTO articles(title, content) VALUES (?, ?)';
    db.run(sql, data.title, data.content, cb);    ❺ Specifies parameters
  }                                                  with question marks

  static delete(id, cb) {
    if (!id) return cb(new Error('Please provide an id'));
    db.run('DELETE FROM articles WHERE id = ?', id, cb);
  }
}

module.exports = db;
module.exports.Article = Article;
```

In this example, an object is created called `Article` that can create, fetch, and delete data by using standard SQL and the sqlite3 module. First, a database file is opened by using `sqlite3.Database` ❶, and then an articles table is created ❷. The `IF NOT EXISTS` SQL syntax is useful here because it means you can rerun the code without accidentally deleting and re-creating the articles table.

When the database and tables are ready, the application is ready to make queries. To fetch all articles, you use the sqlite3 `all` method ❸. To fetch a specific article, use the question mark query syntax with a value ❹; the sqlite3 module will insert the ID into the query. Finally, you can insert and delete data by using the `run` method ❺.

For this example to work, you need to have installed the sqlite3 module with `npm install --save sqlite3`. It's version 3.1.8 at the time of writing.

Now that the basic database functionality is ready, you need to add it to the HTTP routes from listing 3.2.

The next listing shows how to add each method except for POST. (You'll deal with that separately, because it needs to use the readability module, which you haven't yet set up.)

Listing 3.4 Adding the `Article` model to the HTTP routes

```
const express = require('express');
const bodyParser = require('body-parser');
const app = express();
const Article = require('./db').Article;              ◁——
                                                      ❶ Loads the database module

app.set('port', process.env.PORT || 3000);

app.use(bodyParser.json());
app.use(bodyParser.urlencoded({ extended: true }));

app.get('/articles', (req, res, next) => {
  Article.all((err, articles) => {                    ◁——
    if (err) return next(err);                        ❷ Fetches all articles
    res.send(articles);
  });
});

app.get('/articles/:id', (req, res, next) => {
  const id = req.params.id;
  Article.find(id, (err, article) => {                ◁——
    if (err) return next(err);                        ❸ Finds a specific article
    res.send(article);
  });
});

app.delete('/articles/:id', (req, res, next) => {
  const id = req.params.id;
  Article.delete(id, (err) => {                       ◁——
    if (err) return next(err);                        ❹ Deletes an article
    res.send({ message: 'Deleted' });
  });
```

```
});

app.listen(app.get('port'), () => {
  console.log('App started on port', app.get('port'));
});

module.exports = app;
```

Listing 3.4 is written assuming that you've saved listing 3.3 as db.js in the same directory. Node will load that module ❶ and then use it to fetch each article ❷, find a specific article ❸, and delete an article ❹.

The final thing to do is add support for creating articles. To do this, you need to be able to download articles and process them with the magic readability algorithm. What you need is a module from npm.

3.3.2   *Making articles readable and saving them for later*

Now that you've built a RESTful API and data can be persisted to a database, you should add code that converts web pages into simplified "reader view" versions. You won't implement this yourself; instead, you can use a module from npm.

If you search npm for *readability*, you'll find quite a few modules. Let's try using node-readability (which is at version 1.0.1 at the time of this writing). Install it with `npm install node-readability --save`. The module provides an asynchronous function that downloads a URL and turns the HTML into a simplified representation. The following snippet shows how node-readability is used; if you want to try it, add the snippet to index.js in addition to listing 3.5:

```
const read = require('node-readability');
const url = 'http://www.manning.com/cantelon2/';
read(url, (err, result)=> {
  // result has .title and .content
});
```

The node-readability module can be used with your database class to save articles with the `Article.create` method:

```
read(url, (err, result) => {
  Article.create(
    { title: result.title, content: result.content },
    (err, article) => {
      // Article saved to the database
    }
  );
});
```

To use this in the application, open the index.js file and add a new `app.post` route handler that downloads and saves articles. Combining this with everything you learned about HTTP POST in Express and the body parser gives the example in the following listing.

Listing 3.5 Generating readable articles and saving them

```
const read = require('node-readability');

// ... The rest of the index.js from listing 3.4

app.post('/articles', (req, res, next) => {        ① Gets the URL from
  const url = req.body.url;                             the POST body

read(url, (err, result) => {
  if (err || !result) res.status(500).send('Error downloading article');
    Article.create(
      { title: result.title, content: result.content },    Uses the
      (err, article) => {                              readability mode
        if (err) return next(err);                     to fetch the URL ②
        res.send('OK');           ③ After saving the article,
      }                              sends back a 200
    );
  });
});
```

Here you first get the URL from the POST body ① and then use the node-readability module to get the URL ②. You save the article by using your `Article` model class. If an error occurs, you pass handling along the Express middleware stack ③; otherwise, a JSON representation of the article is sent back to the client.

You can make a POST request that will work with this example by using the `--data` option:

```
curl --data "url=http://manning.com/cantelon2/" http://localhost:3000/articles
```

Over the course of the preceding section, you added a database module, created a JavaScript API that wraps around it, and tied it in to the RESTful HTTP API. That's a lot of work, and it will form the bulk of your efforts as a server-side developer. You'll learn more about databases later in this book as you look at MongoDB and Redis.

Now that you can save articles and programmatically fetch them, you'll add a web interface so you can read articles as well.

3.4 Adding a user interface

Adding an interface to an Express project involves several things. The first is the use of a template engine; we'll show you how to install one and render templates shortly. Your application should also serve static files, such as CSS. Before rendering templates and writing any CSS, you need to know how to make the router handlers from the previous examples respond with both JSON and HTML when necessary.

3.4.1 Supporting multiple formats

So far you've used `res.send()` to send JavaScript objects back to the client. You used cURL to make requests, and in this case JSON is convenient because it's easy to read in the console. But to really use the application, it needs to support HTML as well. How can you support both?

The basic technique is to use the `res.format` method provided by Express. It allows your application to respond with the right format based on the request. To use it, provide a list of formats with functions that respond the desired way:

```
res.format({
  html: () => {
    res.render('articles.ejs', { articles: articles });
  },
  json: () => {
    res.send(articles);
  }
});
```

In this snippet, `res.render` will render the articles.ejs template in the views folder. But for this to work, you need to install a template engine and create some templates.

3.4.2   *Rendering templates*

Many template engines are available, and a simple one that's easy to learn is EJS (Embedded JavaScript). Install the EJS module from npm (EJS is at version 2.3.1 at the time of writing):

```
npm install ejs --save
```

Now `res.render` can render HTML files formatted with EJS. If you replace `res.send` `(articles)` in the `app.get('/articles')` route handler from listing 3.4, visiting http://localhost:3000/articles in a browser should attempt to render articles.ejs.

Next you need to create the articles.ejs template in a views folder. The next listing shows a full template that you can use.

Listing 3.6   Article list template

```
<% include head %>                                    ──◄─── ❶ Includes another template
<ul>
  <% articles.forEach((article) => { %>               ◄──┐ Loops over each article
    <li>                                                ❷   and renders it
      <a href="/articles/<%= article.id %>">
        <%= article.title %>                            ◄── Includes the article's
      </a>                                              ❸   title as the link text
    </li>
  <% }) %>
</ul>
<% include foot %>
```

The article list template uses a header ❶ and footer template that are included as snippets in the following code examples. This is to avoid duplicating the header and footer in every template. The article list is iterated over ❷ by using a standard JavaScript forEach loop, and then the article IDs and titles are injected into the template by using the EJS <%= value %> syntax ❸.

Here's an example header template, saved as views/head.ejs:

```html
<html>
  <head>
    <title>Later</title>
  </head>
  <body>
    <div class="container">
```

And this is a corresponding footer (saved as views/foot.ejs):

```html
    </div>
  </body>
</html>
```

The res.format method can be used for displaying specific articles as well. This is where things start to get interesting, because for this application to make sense, articles should look clean and easy to read.

3.4.3 *Using npm for client-side dependencies*

With the templates in place, the next step is to add some style. Rather than creating a style sheet, it's easier to reuse existing styles, and you can even do this with npm! The popular Bootstrap (http://getbootstrap.com/) client-side framework is available on npm (www.npmjs.com/package/bootstrap), so add it to this project:

```
npm install bootstrap --save
```

If you look at node_modules/bootstrap/, you'll see the source for the Bootstrap project. Then, in the dist/css folder, you'll find the CSS files that come with Bootstrap. To use this in your project, you need to be able to serve static files.

SERVING STATIC FILES

When you need to send client-side JavaScript, images, and CSS back to the browser, Express has some built-in middleware called express.static. To use it, you point it at a directory that contains static files, and those files will then be available to the browser.

Near the top of the main Express app file (index.js), there are some lines that load the middleware required by the project:

```
app.use(bodyParser.json());
app.use(bodyParser.urlencoded({ extended: true }));
```

To load Bootstrap's CSS, use express.static to register the file at the right URL:

```
app.use(
  '/css/bootstrap.css',
  express.static('node_modules/bootstrap/dist/css/bootstrap.css')
);
```

Now you can add /css/bootstrap.css to your templates to get some cool Bootstrap styles. Here's what views/head.ejs should look like:

```html
<html>
  <head>
    <title>later;</title>
    <link rel="stylesheet" href="/css/bootstrap.css">
  </head>
  <body>
    <div class="container">
```

This is only Bootstrap's CSS; Bootstrap also comes with other files, including icons, fonts, and jQuery plugins. You could add more of these files to your project, or use a tool to bundle them all up so loading them is easier.

DOING MORE WITH NPM AND CLIENT-SIDE DEVELOPMENT

The previous example is a simple use of a library intended for browsers through npm. Web developers typically download Bootstrap's files and then add them to their project manually, particularly web designers who work on simpler static sites.

But modern front-end developers use npm for both downloading libraries and loading them in client-side JavaScript. With tools such as Browserify (http://browserify.org/) and webpack (http://webpack.github.io/), you get all the power of npm installation and `require` for loading dependencies. Imagine being able to type `const React = require('react')` in not just Node code, but code for front-end development as well! This is beyond the scope of this chapter, but it gives you a hint of the power you can unlock by combining techniques from Node programming with front-end development.

3.5   *Summary*

- You can quickly build a Node web application from scratch with `npm init` and Express.
- The command to install a dependency is `npm install`.
- Express allows you to make web applications with RESTful APIs.
- Selecting the right database and database module requires some up-front investigation and depends on your requirements.
- SQLite is handy for small projects.
- EJS is an easy way to render templates in Express.
- Express supports lots of template engines, including Pug and Mustache.

Part 2

Web development with Node

Now you're ready to learn about server-side development in more depth. Node has found an important niche outside server-side code: front-end build systems. In this part, you'll learn how to start projects with webpack and Gulp. We'll also introduce the most popular web frameworks and compare them from multiple developers' perspectives to help you decide on the perfect framework for your projects.

If you want to learn in detail about Connect and Express, chapter 6 is entirely dedicated to building web applications with these modules. There's also a chapter dedicated to templating and using databases with Node.

To complete the journey of full-stack web development with Node, we've included chapters on testing and deployment, so you can prepare your first Node application.

Front-end build systems

This chapter covers

- Simplifying complex commands with npm scripts
- Using Gulp to manage repetitive tasks
- Bundling client-side web apps with webpack

In modern web development, Node is increasingly used to run tools and services depended on by front-end engineers. As a Node programmer, you may be responsible for setting up and maintaining these tools. As a full-stack developer, you'll want to use these tools to create faster and more reliable web applications. In this chapter, you'll learn how to use npm scripts, Gulp, and webpack to build maintainable projects.

The benefits of using front-end build systems can be huge. They can help you to write more readable and future-proof code. There's no need to worry about ES2015 browser support when you can transpile it with Babel. Also, because you can generate source maps, browser-based debugging is still possible.

The next section provides a brief introduction to front-end development with Node. After that, you'll see some examples of modern front-end technologies such as React that you can use with your own projects.

4.1   *Understanding front-end development with Node*

Recently, front-end and server-side developers have converged on using npm for distributing JavaScript. That means npm is used for front-end modules, such as React, and server-side code, such as Express. But some modules don't neatly fall into either side: lodash is an example of a general-purpose library that can be used in Node and browsers. By packing lodash carefully, the same module can be consumed by Node and browsers, and the dependency within a project can be managed with npm.

You may have seen other module systems dedicated to client-side development, such as Bower (http://bower.io/). You can still use these tools, but as a Node developer, you should consider using npm.

Package distribution isn't the only thing Node gets used for, however. Front-end developers are also increasingly dependent on tools for generating portable, backward-compatible JavaScript. Transpilers such as Babel (https://babeljs.io/) are used to convert modern ES2015 into more widely supported ES5 code. Other tools include minifiers (for example, UglifyJS; https://github.com/mishoo/UglifyJS) and linters (for example, ESLint, http://eslint.org/) for verifying the correctness of your code before shipping it.

Test runners are also often driven by Node. You can run the tests for UI code in a Node process, or use a Node script to drive tests that run in a browser.

It's also typical to use these tools together. When you start juggling a transpiler, minifier, linter, and test runner, you'll need a way to record how the build process works. Some projects use npm scripts; others use Gulp or webpack. You'll look at all of these approaches in this chapter and see some related best practices.

4.2   *Using npm to run scripts*

Node comes with npm, and npm has built-in features for running scripts. Therefore, you can rely on your collaborators or users being able to invoke commands such as `npm start` and `npm test`. To add your own command for npm start, you add it to the `scripts` property of your project's package.json file:

```
{
  ...
  "scripts": {
    "start": "node server.js"
  },
  ...
}
```

Even if you don't define `start`, `node server.js` is the default, so technically you can leave this blank if that's all you need—just remember to create a file called server.js. Defining the `test` property is useful because you can include your test framework as a dependency and run it by typing `npm test`. Let's say you're using Mocha (www.npmjs.com/package/mocha) for tests, and you've installed it with `npm install --save-dev`. To avoid having to install Mocha globally, you can add the following statement to your package.json file:

```
{
  ...
  "scripts": {
    "test": "./node_modules/.bin/mocha test/*.js"
  },
  ...
}
```

Notice that in the previous example, arguments were passed to Mocha. You can also pass arguments when running npm scripts by using two hyphens:

```
npm test -- test/*.js
```

Table 4.1 shows a breakdown of some of the available npm commands.

Table 4.1 npm commands

Command	package.json property	Example uses
start	scripts.start	Start a web application server or an Electron app.
stop	scripts.stop	Stop a web server.
restart		Run stop and then restart.
install, postinstall	scripts.install, scripts.postinstall	Run native build commands after a package is installed. Note that postinstall can be run only with npm **run** postinstall.

More commands are available, including some for cleaning up packages before publishing them, and pre/post version commands for migrating between package versions. But for most web development tasks, start and test are the commands you want.

Plenty of tasks that you may want to define won't fit into the supported command names. For example, let's say you're working on a simple project that's written in ES2015 but you want to transpile it to ES5. You can do this with npm run. In the next section, you'll run through a tutorial that sets up a new project that can build ES2015 files.

4.2.1 Creating custom npm scripts

The npm run command, aliased from npm run-script, is used to define arbitrary scripts that are invoked with npm run script-name. Let's see how to make one for building a client-side script with Babel.

Start by setting up a new project and installing the necessary dependencies:

```
mkdir es2015-example
cd es2015-example
npm init -y
npm install --save-dev babel-cli babel-preset-es2015
echo '{ "presets": ["es2015"] }' > .babelrc
```

Now you should have a new Node project with the basic Babel ES2015 tools and plugins. Next, open the package.json file and add a babel property under scripts.

It should run the script that has been installed into the project's `node_modules/`
`.bin` folder:

```
"babel": "./node_modules/.bin/babel browser.js -d build/"
```

Here's a sample file with ES2015 syntax that you can use; save it to browser.js:

```
class Example {
  render() {
    return '<h1>Example</h1>';
  }
}

const example = new Example();
console.log(example.render());
```

You'll be able to test this by running `npm run babel`. If everything is configured correctly, you should now have a build folder with browser.js. Open browser.js to confirm that it's indeed an ES5 file. It's too long to print, so look for something like `var _createClass` near the top of the file.

   If this is all your project ever does when it builds, you could name it `build` instead of `babel` in the package.json file. But you can go a little further by adding UglifyJS as well:

```
npm i --save-dev uglify-es
```

UglifyJS can be invoked by using node_modules/.bin/uglifyjs, so add it to the package.json under `scripts` with the name `uglify`:

```
./node_modules/.bin/uglifyjs build/browser.js -o build/browser.min.js
```

Now you should be able to invoke `npm run uglify`. You can tie all of this together by combining both of these scripts. Add another `script` property called `build` that invokes both tasks:

```
"build": "npm run babel && npm run uglify"
```

Both scripts are run by typing `npm run build`. People on your team can now combine multiple front-end packaging tools by invoking this simple command. The reason this works is that Babel and UglifyJS can be run as command-line scripts, and both accept command-line arguments, so it's easy to add them as one-liners to a package.json file. In the case of Babel, you can manage complex behavior by defining a .babelrc file, which you did earlier in this chapter.

4.2.2 *Configuring front-end build tools*

In general, you can configure front-end build tools in three ways when used with npm scripts:

- Specifying command-line arguments. For example, `./node_modules/.bin/`
  `uglify --source-map`.

- Creating a project-specific configuration file with options. This is often done for Babel and ESLint.
- Adding configuration options to package.json. Babel supports this as well.

What if your build requirements have more steps, and include things like copying, concatenating, or moving files? You could create a shell script and invoke it with an npm script, but it may help your JavaScript-savvy collaborators if you use JavaScript. Many build systems provide JavaScript APIs for automating builds. In the next section, you'll learn all about one such solution: Gulp.

4.3 Providing automation with Gulp

Gulp (http://gulpjs.com/) is a build system based on streams. You can route streams together to create build processes that do more than just transpile or minify code. Imagine you have a project with an administration area that's built with Angular, but you have a React-based public area; both subprojects share certain build requirements. With Gulp, you can reuse parts of the build process for each stage. Figure 4.1 shows an example of these two build processes that share functionality.

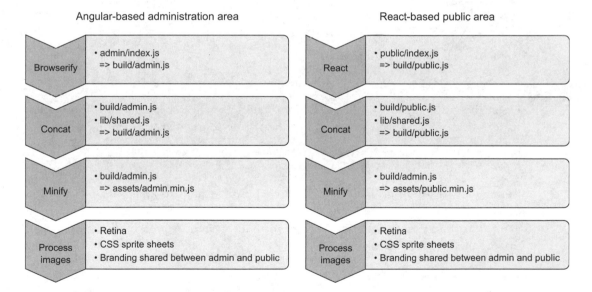

Figure 4.1   Two build processes that share functionality

Gulp helps you achieve a high level of reuse through two techniques: using plugins and defining your own build tasks. As the figure suggests, the build process is a stream, so you can pipe tasks and plugins through each other. For example, you can handle the React part of the previous example with Gulp Babel (www.npmjs.com/package/gulp-babel/) and the built-in gulp.src file globbing method:

```
gulp.src('public/index.jsx')
  .pipe(babel({
    presets: ['es2015', 'react']
  }))
  .pipe(minify())
  .pipe(gulp.dest('build/public.js'));
```

You can even add the concat stage to this chain quite easily. Before looking more closely at this syntax, let's see how to set up a small Gulp project.

4.3.1 Adding Gulp to a project

To add Gulp to a project, you need to install both the gulp-cli and gulp packages with npm. Most people install gulp-cli globally, so Gulp recipes can be run simply by typing `gulp`. Note that you should run `npm rm --global gulp` if you had previously installed the `gulp` package globally. In the next snippet, you install gulp-cli globally and create a new Node project that has a Gulp development dependency:

```
npm i --global gulp-cli
mkdir gulp-example
cd gulp-example
npm init -y
npm i –save-dev gulp
```

Next create a file called gulpfile.js:

```
touch gulpfile.js
```

Open the gulpfile. Now you'll use Gulp to build a small React project. It'll use gulp-babel (www.npmjs.com/package/gulp-babel), gulp-sourcemaps, and gulp-concat:

```
npm i --save-dev gulp-sourcemaps gulp-babel babel-preset-es2015
npm i --save-dev gulp-concat react react-dom babel-preset-react
```

Remember to use npm with `--save-dev` when you want to add Gulp plugins to a project. If you're experimenting with new plugins and decide to remove them, you can use `npm uninstall --save-dev` to remove them from ./node_modules and update the project's package.json file.

4.3.2 Creating and running Gulp tasks

Creating Gulp tasks involves writing Node code with Gulp's API in a file called gulpfile.js. Gulp's API has methods for things like finding files and piping them through plugins that transform them in some way.

To try this for yourself: Open gulpfile.js and set up a build task that uses gulp.src to find JSX files, Babel to process ES2015 and React, and then concat to join each file together, as shown in the following listing.

Listing 4.1   A gulpfile for ES2015 and React with Babel

```
const gulp = require('gulp');
const sourcemaps = require('gulp-sourcemaps');          ◁─── Gulp plugins are loaded like
const babel = require('gulp-babel');                         standard Node modules
const concat = require('gulp-concat');

                                         The built-in gulp.src file globbing utility
                                         is used to find all React jsx files
gulp.task('default', () => {
  return gulp.src('app/*.jsx')          ◁─┘
    .pipe(sourcemaps.init())            ◁────────────────  Starts watching source
    .pipe(babel({                       ◁────────────────  files to build source
      presets: ['es2015', 'react']                         maps for debugging
    }))                           Configures gulp-babel to
    .pipe(concat('all.js'))       use ES2015 and React (JSX)
    .pipe(sourcemaps.write('.'))        ◁────────────────  Writes the source
    .pipe(gulp.dest('dist'));           ◁───                map files separately
});                                  Redirects all files to
                                     the dist/ folder
```

Concats all of the source files together into all.js

Listing 4.1 uses several Gulp plugins to capture, process, and write files. First you find all of the input files by using file globbing, and then you use the gulp-sourcemaps plugin to collect source-map metrics for client-side debugging. Notice that source maps require two stages: one to state that you want to use source maps, and another to write the source-map files. Meanwhile, gulp-babel is configured to process files with ES2015 and React.

This Gulp task can be run by typing gulp in a terminal.

In this example, all of the files are transformed by using a single plugin. It just so happens that Babel is transpiling React JSX code and converting ES2015 to ES5. Once that's done, the files are concatenated using the gulp-concat plugin. Now that all of the transpiling is done, it's safe to write the source maps, and the final build can be placed in the dist folder.

You can try this gulpfile out by creating a JSX file named app/index.jsx. Here's a simple JSX file that you can use to test Gulp:

```
import React from 'react';
import ReactDOM from 'react-dom';

ReactDOM.render(
  <h1>Hello, world!</h1>,
  document.getElementById('example')
);
```

Gulp makes it easy to express build stages in JavaScript, and by using gulp.task(), you can add your own tasks to this file. Tasks usually follow the same pattern:

1 *Source*—Gather input files
2 *Transpile*—Pipe them through a plugin that transforms them
3 *Concat*—Pipe the files together to create a monolithic build
4 *Output*—Set a file destination or move the output files

In the previous example, `sourcemaps` is a special case because it requires two pipes: one for configuration and a final one to output the files. That makes sense because source maps depend on mapping the original line numbers to the transpiled build's line numbers.

4.3.3   Watching for changes

The last thing front-end developers want is a build/refresh cycle. The simplest way to streamline builds is to use a Gulp plugin to watch the filesystem for changes. But alternatives exist. Some libraries work well with hot reloading, and more-generic DOM and CSS-based projects can work well with the LiveReload (http://livereload.com/) project.

As an example, you can add gulp-watch (www.npmjs.com/package/gulp-watch) to the previous project in listing 4.1. Add the package to the project:

```
npm i --save-dev gulp-watch
```

Now remember to load the package in gulpfile.js:

```
const watch = require('gulp-watch');
```

And add a watch task that calls the default task from the previous example:

```
gulp.task('watch', () => {
  watch('app/**.jsx', () => gulp.start('default'));
});
```

This defines a task called `watch`, and then uses `watch()` to watch React JSX files for changes. Whenever a file changes, the default build task will run. With minor modifications, this recipe could be used to build Syntactically Awesome Style Sheets (SASS) files, optimize images, or pretty much anything else you might need for front-end projects.

4.3.4   Using separate files for larger projects

As projects grow, they tend to need more Gulp tasks. Eventually, you'll end up with a long file that's hard to understand. You can fix this, however: break up your code into separate modules.

As you've seen, Gulp uses Node's module system for loading plugins. There's no special plugin-loading system; it just uses standard modules. You can also use Node's module system to split up long gulpfiles, to make your files more maintainable. To use separate files, you need to follow these steps:

1 Create a folder called gulp, and a subfolder called tasks.
2 Define your tasks by using the usual `gulp.task()` syntax in separate files. One file per task is a good rule of thumb.
3 Create a file called gulp/index.js to require each Gulp task file.
4 Require the gulp/index.js file in gulpfile.js.

The file tree should look like the following snippet:

```
gulpfile.js
gulp/
gulp/index.js
gulp/tasks/development-build.js
gulp/tasks/production-build.js
```

This technique can help you organize projects with complex build tasks, but it can also be paired with the gulp-help (www.npmjs.com/package/gulp-help) module. This module allows you to document Gulp tasks; running `gulp help` shows information about each task. This helps when you're working in a team, or if you switch between lots of projects that use Gulp. Figure 4.2 shows what the output looks like.

Gulp is a general-purpose project-automation tool. It's good when adding cross-platform housekeeping scripts to projects—for example, run-

```
~/Projects/world-domination: gulp help
[10:33:38] Using gulpfile ~/Projects/world-domination/gulpfile.js
[10:33:38] Starting 'help'...

Usage
  gulp [TASK] [OPTIONS...]

Available tasks
  help      Display this help text.
  version   prints the version. Aliases: v, V

[10:33:38] Finished 'help' after 1.2 ms
```

Figure 4.2   Sample gulp-help output

ning complex client-side tests or bringing up fixtures for a database. Although it can be used for building client-side assets, there are also tools specifically designed to do that, which means they typically require less code and configuration than Gulp. One such tool is webpack, which focuses on bundling JavaScript and CSS modules. The next section demonstrates how to use webpack for a React project.

4.4   Building web apps with webpack

webpack is specifically designed to build web applications. Imagine that you're working with a designer who has already created a static site for a single-page web app, and you want to adapt it to build more-efficient CSS and ES2015 JavaScript. With Gulp, you write JavaScript code to drive the build system, so this would involve writing a gulpfile and several build tasks. With webpack, you write a configuration file and then bring in new functionality by using plugins and loaders. In some cases, no extra configuration is required: you type `webpack` on the command-line with an argument for the source-file path, and it'll build your project. Skip to section 4.4.4 to see what this looks like.

One of the advantages of webpack is that it's easier to quickly set up a build system that supports incremental builds. If you set it up to automatically build when files change, it won't need to rebuild the entire project when a single file changes. As a result, builds can be faster and easier to understand.

This section shows you how to use webpack for a small React project. First, let's define the terminology webpack uses.

4.4.1   *Using bundles and plugins*

Before setting up a webpack project, some terminology should be clarified. webpack plugins are used to change the behavior of the build process. This can include things like automatically uploading assets to Amazon S3 (https://github.com/MikaAK/s3-plugin-webpack) or removing duplicated files from the output.

In contrast to plugins, loaders are transformations that are applied to resource files. If you need to convert SASS to CSS, or ES2015 to ES5, you need a loader. *Loaders* are functions that transform input source text into output. They can be asynchronous or synchronous. Plugins are instances of classes that can hook into webpack's more low-level APIs.

If you need to convert React code, CoffeeScript, SASS, or any other transpiled languages, you're looking for a *loader*. If you need to instrument your JavaScript, or manipulate sets of files in some way, you'll need a *plugin*.

In the next section you'll see how to use the Babel loader to convert a React ES2015 project to a browser-friendly bundle.

4.4.2   *Configuring and running webpack*

You're going to re-create the React example from listing 4.1 by using webpack. To get started, install React in a new project:

```
mkdir webpack-example
npm init -y
npm install --save react react-dom
npm install --save-dev webpack babel-loader babel-core
npm install --save-dev babel-preset-es2015 babel-preset-react
```

The last line installs Babel's ES2015 plugin and the React transformer for Babel. Now you need to make a file called webpack.config.js that instructs webpack on where to find the input file, where to write the output, and what loaders to use. You're going to use babel-loader with some extra settings for React, as shown in the next listing.

> **Listing 4.2   A webpack.config.js file**

```
const path = require('path');
const webpack = require('webpack');

module.exports = {
  entry: './app/index.jsx',                              Input file
  output: { path: __dirname, filename: 'dist/bundle.js' },   Output file
  module: {
    loaders: [
      {
        test: /.jsx?$/,                                  Matches all
        loader: 'babel-loader',                          JSX files
        exclude: /node_modules/,
        query: {
          presets: ['es2015', 'react']                   Uses the Babel ES2015
        }                                                and React plugins
      }
    }
```

```
    ]
  },
};
```

This configuration file encapsulates everything you need to successfully build a React app with ES2015. The settings are easy to follow: define an `entry`, which is the main file that loads the application. Then specify the directory where the output should be written; this directory will be created if it doesn't yet exist. Next, define a loader and associate it with a file glob search by using the `test` property. Finally, make sure to set any options for the loader. In this example, these options load the ES2015 and React Babel plugins.

You need to include a sample React JSX file in app/index.jsx; use the snippet from section 4.3.2. Now running ./node_modules/.bin/webpack will compile an ES5 version of the file with the React dependencies.

4.4.3 Using webpack development server

If you want to avoid having to rebuild the project whenever a React file changes, you can use the webpack development server (http://webpack.github.io/docs/webpack-dev-server.html). In the book's source code, this can be found under webpack-hotload-example (ch04-front-end/webpack-hotload-example). This small Express server will run webpack with your webpack configuration file when files change, and then serve the changed assets to the browser. You should run it on a different port to your main web server, and this means your script tags will have to include different URLs during development. The server builds assets and stores them in memory rather than in your webpack output folder. You can also use webpack-dev-server for hot module loading, in a similar way to LiveReload servers.

To add webpack-dev-server to a project, follow these steps:

1 Install webpack-dev-server with `npm i --save-dev webpack-dev-server@1.14.1`.
2 Add a `publicPath` option to the `output` property in webpack.config.js.
3 Add an index.html file to your build directory to act as a harness to load your JavaScript and CSS bundles. Ensure that the port is the port specified in the next step.
4 Run the server with the options you want. For example, `webpack-dev-server --hot --inline --content-base dist/ --port 3001`.
5 Visit http://localhost:3001/ and load the app.

Open webpack.config.js from listing 4.2 and change the `output` property to include a `publicPath`:

```
output: {
  path: path.resolve(__dirname, 'dist'),
  filename: 'bundle.js',
  publicPath: '/assets/'
},
```

Create a new file called dist/index.html, as shown in the next listing.

Listing 4.3   An example HTML template for a React web app

```html
<!DOCTYPE html>
<html lang="en">
<head>
  <meta charset="UTF-8">
  <title>Warning: Dev server only</title>
</head>
<body>
  <div id="example"></div>
  <script src="/assets/bundle.js"></script>      The public path of the
</body>                                           webpack-built bundle
</html>
```

Next open package.json and add the command that runs the webpack server under the `scripts` property:

```
"scripts": {
  "server:dev": "webpack-dev-server --hot –inline
     --content-base dist/ --port 3001"
},
```

The `--hot` option makes the dev server use hot module reloading. If you edit the example React file in app/index.jsx, you should see the browser refresh. The refresh mechanism is specified with the `--inline` option. Inline refresh means the dev server will inject code to manage refreshing the bundle. There's also an iframe version that wraps the entire page in an iframe.

Now run the dev server:

```
npm run server:dev
```

Running the webpack development server will trigger the build and start a server listening on port 3001. You can test everything by going to http://localhost:3001 in a browser.

> ### Hot reloading
>
> Because of React and other frameworks including AngularJS, there are framework-specific hot module reloading projects. Some take into account data-flow frameworks such as Redux and Relay, which means code can be refreshed while the current state is maintained. This is the ideal way to perform code reloading, because you don't have to keep running through steps to re-create the UI state that you're working on.
>
> The example we've given you here, however, is less React-specific and is a good way to get you started with webpack dev servers. Be sure to experiment to find the best option for your project.

4.4.4 Loading CommonJS modules and assets

We've been using React and Babel in this chapter, but if you're using webpack with a more vanilla, CommonJS project, then webpack can provide everything you need without a CommonJS browser shim. It's even capable of loading CSS files.

WEBPACK AND COMMONJS

To use CommonJS module syntax with webpack, you don't need to set anything up. Let's say you have a file that uses `require`:

```
const hello = require('./hello');

hello();
```

And another that defines the `hello` function:

```
module.exports = function() {
  return 'hello';
};
```

Then you need only a small webpack config file to define the entry point (the first snippet), and the build destination path:

```
const path = require('path');
const webpack = require('webpack');

module.exports = {
  entry: './app/index.js',
  output: { path: __dirname, filename: 'dist/bundle.js' },
};
```

This example clarifies how different Gulp and webpack are. webpack is entirely focused on building bundles, and as part of that, is capable of generating bundles with CommonJS shims. If you open dist/bundle.js, you'll see the `webpackBootstrap` shim at the top of the file, and then each file from the original source tree is wrapped in closures to simulate the module system. The following snippet is part of the bundle:

```
function(module, exports, __webpack_require__) {

  const hello = __webpack_require__(1);

  hello();


/***/ },
/* 1 */
/***/ function(module, exports) {

module.exports = function() {
  return 'hello';
};
```

The code comments show where the modules are defined, and the files have access to `module` and `exports` objects as arguments to their closures to simulate the CommonJS module API.

USING NPM PACKAGES WITH WEBPACK

You can take this a step further by including modules downloaded from npm. Let's say you want to use jQuery. Rather than making it a `script` tag on the page, you can install it with `npm i --save-dev jquery`, and then load it just like a Node module:

```
const jquery = require('jquery');
```

That means webpack gives you CommonJS modules and access to modules from npm out of the box without any additional configuration!

Finding loaders and plugins

The webpack website has a list of loaders (https://webpack.github.io/docs/list-of-loaders.html) and plugins (https://webpack.github.io/docs/list-of-plugins.html). You can also find webpack tools on npm; the `webpack` keyword is a good place to start (www.npmjs.com/browse/keyword/webpack).

4.5   *Summary*

- If you need to automate simple tasks or invoke scripts, npm scripts are perfect.
- Gulp can be used to write more-complex tasks with JavaScript and is cross-platform.
- When gulpfiles get too long, you can divide the code into separate files.
- webpack can be used to generate client-side bundles.
- If you just need to build a client-side bundle, using webpack might be less work than setting up the equivalent script with Gulp.
- webpack supports hot module reloading, which means you'll see code changes without refreshing your browser.

Server-side frameworks 5

This chapter covers

- Working with popular Node web frameworks
- Choosing the right framework
- Building web apps with web frameworks

This chapter is all about server-side web development. It answers questions including how do I choose the perfect framework for a given project, and what are the advantages and disadvantages of each framework?

Deciding on the right framework is difficult because it's hard to compare them on a level playing field. Most people don't have time to learn all of them, so we tend to make superficial decisions about the frameworks we have experience with. In some cases, you might use different frameworks together. Express, for instance, could be used for larger applications, whereas microservices that support larger applications could be written in hapi.

Imagine you're building a content management system (CMS). It's used to manage legal documents collected by a research firm. It can output PDFs and has an e-commerce component. Such a system could be built with separate frameworks as follows:

- *Document upload, download, and reading*—Express

- *PDF generator microservice*—hapi
- *E-commerce component*—Sails.js

The perfect framework for a given project is dependent on the needs of the project and the team working on it. In this chapter, we use personas—hypothetical people—as a way of exploring which framework is right for a specific type of project. You'll learn about Koa, hapi, Sails.js, DerbyJS, Flatiron, and LoopBack through these imaginary programmers. The personas are defined in the next section.

5.1   Personas

We want to avoid selling a single framework that you'll use for every project. It's much better to be eclectic and use a mix of tools that suit each problem. Using personas to think about design is a widespread practice, in part because it helps designers to empathize with users.

In this chapter, personas are used to help you to think about frameworks in the third person, to see how different classes of projects suit different solutions. The personas are defined in terms of professional situation and development tools. You should be able to identify with at least one of the three people we've invented here.

5.1.1   Phil: agency developer

Phil has been working for three years as a full-stack web developer. He's done a little Ruby, Python, and client-side JavaScript:

- *Job situation*—Employee, full-stack developer
- *Work type*—Front-end engineering, server-side development
- *Computer*—MacBook Pro
- *Tools*—Sublime Text, Dash, xScope, Pixelmator, Sketch, GitHub
- *Background*—High school education; started as a hobbyist programmer

A typical day for Phil involves working with designers and user-experience experts in agile-style meetings to develop or review new features, as well as maintenance and bug fixes.

5.1.2   Nadine: open source developer

Nadine moved to contracting after a successful early career working as a corporate web developer:

- *Job situation*—Contractor, JavaScript specialist
- *Work type*—Server-side programming, occasional high-performance programming in Go and Erlang. Also writes a popular open source, web-based movie catalog app
- *Computer*—High-end PC, Linux
- *Tools*—Vim, tmux, Mercurial, anything in the shell
- Background—Computer science degree

Nadine's day usually involves balancing clocking enough hours for her two major clients with working on her open source projects. Her client work is test-driven, but her open source projects are more feature-driven.

5.1.3 *Alice: product developer*

Alice works on a successful iOS app but also helps with her company's web APIs:

- *Job situation*—Employee, programmer
- *Work type*—iOS development; also responsible for web apps and web services
- *Computer*—MacBook Pro, iPad Pro
- *Tools*—Xcode, Atom, Babel, Perforce
- *Background*—Science degree; one of the first five employees at her current startup

Alice grudgingly works with Xcode, Objective-C, and Swift, but secretly prefers JavaScript and is excited by ES2015 and Babel. She relishes developing new web services to support her company's iOS and desktop apps, and wants to work on React-based web apps more often.

Now that the personas have been defined, let's define the term *framework*.

5.2 *What is a framework?*

Some of the server-side frameworks discussed in this chapter are technically not frameworks at all. The term *framework* is unfortunately overloaded and means different things to different programmers. In the Node community, it's more accurate to call most of these projects *modules*, but a more nuanced definition is useful when directly comparing this family of libraries.

The LoopBack project (http://loopback.io/resources/#compare) uses the following definitions:

- *API framework*—A library for building web APIs, backed by a framework that helps to structure the application. LoopBack itself is defined as this type of framework.
- *HTTP server library*—Anything based on Express falls into this category, including Koa and Kraken.js. These libraries help you build applications that are based around HTTP verbs and routes.
- *HTTP server framework*—A framework for building modular servers that speak HTTP. hapi is an example of this type of framework.
- *Web MVC framework*—Model-View-Controller frameworks including Sails.js fall into this category.
- *Full-stack framework*—These frameworks use JavaScript on the server and browser, and are able to share code between both ends. This is known as *isomorphic code*. DerbyJS is a full-stack MVC framework.

Most Node developers understand *framework* to mean the second term: HTTP server library. The next section introduces Koa, a server library that uses the innovative ES2015 syntax known as *generators* to offer a unique way to handle HTTP middleware.

5.3   *Koa*

Koa (http://koajs.com/) is based on Express, but uses the ES2015 generator syntax to define middleware. That means you can write middleware in an almost synchronous fashion. This partly solves the problem of middleware that depends highly on callbacks. With Koa, you can use the `yield` keyword to exit and then reenter middleware. Table 5.1 is an overview of Koa's main features.

Table 5.1   Koa's main features

Library type	HTTP server library
Features	Generator-based middleware, request/response model
Suggested uses	Lightweight web apps, nonstrict HTTP APIs, serving single-page web app
Plugin architecture	Middleware
Documentation	http://koajs.com/
Popularity	10,000 GitHub stars
License	MIT

The following listing shows how to use Koa to benchmark requests by yielding to the next middleware component and then continuing execution in the callee when it's finished.

Listing 5.1   Koa's middleware ordering

```
const koa = require('koa');
const app = koa();

app.use(function*(next) {
  const start = new Date;
  yield next;
  const ms = new Date - start;
  console.log('%s %s - %s', this.method, this.url, ms);
});

app.use(function*() {
  this.body = 'Hello World';
});

app.listen(3000);
```

2 Yields to run the next middleware component

1 Uses the generator syntax for middleware functions

3 Execution passes back to the original yield here

Listing 5.1 uses generators **1** to switch context between two middleware components. Notice that we use the keyword `function*`—it's not possible to use an arrow function here. By using the `yield` keyword ❷, execution steps down the middleware stack, then back again when the next middleware component returns ❸. An added benefit of using generator functions is you can just set `this.body`. In contrast, Express uses a function to send responses: `res.send(response)`. In Koa middleware, `this` is known as a *context*. A context is created for every request, and it's used to encapsulate Node's HTTP `request` and `response` objects (https://nodejs.org/api/http.html). Whenever you need to access something from the request, such as the GET parameters or cookies, you can use the context. The same is true for the response: as you saw in listing 5.1, you can control what gets sent to the browser by setting values on `this.body`.

If you've used both Express middleware and generator syntax before, Koa should be easy to learn. If either of these things is new to you, Koa might be hard to follow—or at least it might be hard to see why this style is beneficial. Figure 5.1 shows in more detail how `yield` hands off execution between middleware components.

Each of the stages in figure 5.1 corresponds to the numbers in listing 5.1. First, the timer is set up in the first middleware component ❶, and then execution is yielded to the second middleware component that renders the body ❷. After the response has been sent, execution returns to the first middleware component, and the time is calculated ❸. This is displayed in the terminal with `console.log`, and the request is

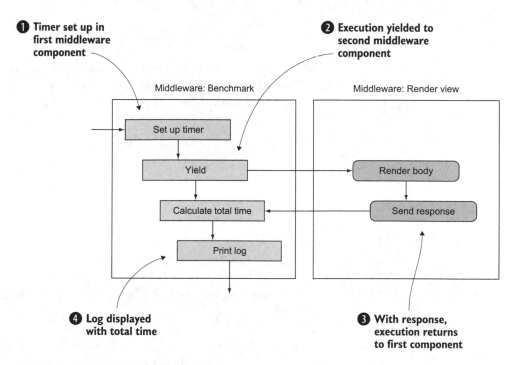

Figure 5.1 Koa middleware execution order

then finished ❹. Note that stage ❹ isn't visible in listing 5.1; it's handled by Koa and Node's HTTP server.

5.3.1 Setting up

Setting up a project with Koa requires installing the module and then defining middleware. If you want more functionality, such as a routing API that makes it easier to define and respond to various types of HTTP request, then you'll need to install router middleware. That means a typical workflow requires planning the middleware your project will use beforehand, so you need to research popular modules first.

> **Persona thoughts**
>
> *Alice*: "As a product developer, I like Koa's minimal feature set—because our project has unique requirements, and we really want to shape the entire stack according to our needs."
>
> *Phil*: "As an agency developer, I find dealing with the middleware research stage too much trouble. I'd prefer this to be handled for me, because many of my projects have similar requirements, and I don't want to keep installing the same modules to do basic things."

The next section demonstrates a third-party module that implements a powerful routing library for Koa.

5.3.2 Defining routes

A popular router middleware component is koa-router (https://www.npmjs.com/package/koa-router). Like Express, it's based on HTTP verbs, but unlike Express, it has a chainable API. The next snippet shows how groups of routes are defined:

```
router
  .post('/pages', function*(next) {
    // Create a page
  })
  .get('/pages/:id', function*(next) {
    // Render the page
  })
  .put('pages-update', '/pages/:id', function*(next) {
    // Update a page
  });
```

Routes can be named by using an additional argument. This is great because you can generate URLs, which not all Node web frameworks support. Here's an example:

```
router.url('pages-update', '99');
```

This module has a unique blend of features from Express and other web frameworks.

> **Persona thoughts**
>
> *Phil*: "This routing library reminds me of some of the things I liked about Ruby on Rails, so Koa could win me over after all!"
>
> *Nadine*: "I can see opportunities for modularizing my existing projects with Koa, and then sharing this code with the community."

5.3.3 REST APIs

Koa doesn't come with the tools necessary to make RESTful APIs without implementing some kind of route-handling middleware. The previous example can be extended to implement a RESTful API in Koa.

5.3.4 Strengths

It would be easy to say that Koa's strengths come from its early adoption of generator syntax, but now that ES2015 is widespread in the Node community, this is no longer as unique as it once was. Currently, Koa's main advantage is that it's streamlined yet has some excellent third-party modules; check out the Koa wiki for more information (https://github.com/koajs/koa/wiki#middleware). Product developers love it, because it has elegant syntax and can be tailored for projects with specific requirements.

5.3.5 Weaknesses

Koa's level of configurability alienates some developers. Creating many small projects with Koa can lead to low levels of code reuse, unless you already have code-sharing strategies in place.

5.4 Kraken

Kraken is based on Express, but adds new functionality through custom modules developed by PayPal. One useful module in particular is Lusca (https://github.com/krakenjs/lusca), which provides an application security layer. Although it's possible to use Lusca without Kraken, one of Kraken's benefits is its predefined project structure. Express and Koa applications don't require any specific project structure, so if you're looking for help with starting new projects, Kraken can help get things going. Table 5.2 shows an overview of Kraken's main features.

Table 5.2 Kraken's main features

Library type	HTTP server library
Features	Strict project structure, models, templates (Dust), security hardening (Lusca), configuration management, internationalization
Suggested uses	Corporate web apps

Table 5.2   Kraken's main features *(continued)*

Plugin architecture	Express middleware
Documentation	https://www.kraken.com/help/api
Popularity	4,000 GitHub stars
License	Apache 2.0

5.4.1   Setting up

If you already have an Express project, you can add Kraken as a middleware component:

```
const express = require('express'),
const kraken = require('kraken-js');

const app = express();
app.use(kraken());
app.listen(3000);
```

But if you want to start a new project, you should try Kraken's Yeoman generator. Yeoman is a tool that helps you to generate new projects. By using Yeoman generators, you can create bootstrapped projects for a variety of frameworks. Here are the steps to create a tailored Kraken project using Yeoman, with Kraken's preferred filesystem layout:

```
$ npm install -g yo generator-kraken bower grunt-cli
$ yo kraken

       ,'"""`.
hh   / _   _ \
    |(@) (@)|      Release the Kraken!
     )  __  (
    /,')) ((`.\
   (( (( )) ))
    `\ `)(' /'

Tell me a bit about your application:

[?] Name: kraken-test
[?] Description: A Kraken application
[?] Author: Alex R. Young
...
```

The generator creates a new directory, so you don't need to do this yourself. After the generator finishes, you should be able to start a server and visit http://localhost:8000 to try it out.

5.4.2   Defining routes

In Kraken, routes are defined alongside the *controller*. Rather than separating out route definitions and route handlers as Express does, Kraken uses an MVC-inspired approach, which is lightweight thanks to the use of ES6 arrow functions:

```
module.exports = (router) => {
  router.get('/', (req, res) => {
    res.render('index');
  });
};
```

Routes can include parameters in the URL:

```
module.exports = (router) => {
  router.get('/people/:id', (req, res) => {
    const people = { alex: { name: 'Alex' } };
    res.render('people/edit', people[req.param.id]);
  });
};
```

Kraken's routing API is express-enrouten (https://github.com/krakenjs/express-enrouten), and it partly infers the route from the directory the file is in. Say you have a file layout like this:

```
controllers
 |-user
     |-create.js
     |-list.js
```

Then Kraken will generate routes such as /user/create and /user/list.

5.4.3   REST APIs

Kraken can be used to make REST APIs but doesn't provide specific support for them. The capabilities of express-enrouten combined with middleware for parsing JSON means you can use Kraken to implement REST APIs.

    Kraken's router has HTTP verbs for DELETE, GET, POST, PUT, and so on, which makes implementing REST similar to Express.

5.4.4   Strengths

Because Kraken comes with a generator, Kraken projects look similar from a high level. Although Express projects can vary wildly in their layout, Kraken projects typically put files and directories in the same places.

    Because Kraken provides both a templating library (Dust) and internationalization (Makara), the two are seamlessly integrated. To write Dust templates with internationalization, you need to specify a key:

```
<h1>{@pre type="content" key="greeting"/}</h1>
```

Then add a .properties file to locales/language-code/view-name.properties. These properties files are simple key/value pairs, so if the previous example was in a view file called public/templates/profile.dust, the .profile file would be locales/US/en/profile.properties.

> **Persona thoughts**
>
> *Phil*: "The fact that Kraken has a filesystem layout and uses controllers for routes appeals to me a lot. Some of my team know Django and Ruby on Rails, so this will be an easy transition for them. Kraken's documentation also seems really good; there's lots of useful stuff on the blog."
>
> *Alice*: "I like the idea of getting better application security with Lusca, but Kraken provides things I don't really need. I'm going to try just using Lusca by itself."

5.4.5   Weaknesses

It takes more effort to learn Kraken than Koa or Express. Some tasks that are done programmatically in Express are done through JSON configuration files, and it's sometimes hard to figure out exactly what JSON properties are needed to get things to work the desired way.

5.5   hapi

hapi (http://hapijs.com/) is a server framework that focuses on web API development. It has its own hapi plugin API, and doesn't come with any client-side support or database model layer. It comes with a routing API and has its own HTTP server wrapper. In hapi, you design APIs by thinking about the server as the main abstraction. The built-in server features for connections and logging make hapi good at scaling and management from a DevOps point of view. Table 5.3 contains an overview of hapi's main features.

Table 5.3   hapi's main features

Library type	HTTP server framework
Features	High-level server container abstraction, security headers
Suggested uses	Single-page web apps, HTTP APIs
Plugin architecture	hapi plugins
Documentation	http://hapijs.com/api
Popularity	6,000 GitHub stars
License	BSD 3 Clause

5.5.1   Setting up

First, create a new Node project and install hapi:

```
mkdir listing5_2
cd listing5_2
npm init -y
npm install --save hapi
```

Then create a new file called server.js. Add the code from the following listing.

Listing 5.2 Basic hapi server

```
const Hapi = require('hapi');
const server = new Hapi.Server();

server.connection({
  host: 'localhost',
  port: 8000
});

server.start((err) => {
  if (err) {
    throw err;
  }
  console.log('Server running at:', server.info.uri);
});
```

You could run this example as it is, but it won't do much without any routes. Read on to learn about how hapi handles routes.

5.5.2 Defining routes

hapi has a built-in API for creating routes. You must provide an object that includes properties for the request method, a URL, and a callback to run, which is known as a *handler.* The next listing shows how to define a route with a handler method.

Listing 5.3 hapi hello world server

```
const Hapi = require('hapi');
const server = new Hapi.Server();

server.connection({
  host: 'localhost',
  port: 8000
});

server.route({
  method: 'GET',
  path:'/hello',
  handler: (request, reply) => {
    return reply('hello world');
  }
});

server.start((err) => {
  if (err) {
    throw err;
  }
  console.log('Server running at:', server.info.uri);
});
```

Add this code to the previous listing to define a route and handler that will respond with the text *hello world*. You can run this example by typing `npm start`. Open http://localhost:8000/hello to see the response.

hapi doesn't come with a predefined folder structure or any MVC features; it's entirely based around servers. In this regard, it's similar to Express. Notice, however, a key difference: the `request, reply` route handler signature is different from Express's `req, res`. hapi's request and reply objects are different from Express's equivalents as well: you must call `reply` rather than manipulate Express's `res` object. Express is more similar to Node's built-in HTTP server.

To go beyond this simple example and get more functionality, such as serving static files, you need plugins.

5.5.3   *Plugins*

hapi has its own plugin architecture, and most projects require several plugins to provide features such as authentication and user input validation. A simple plugin that most projects need is inert (https://github.com/hapijs/inert), which adds static file and directory handlers.

To add inert to a hapi project, you need to first register the plugin with the `server.register` method. This adds the `reply.file` method for sending single files, and a built-in directory handler. Let's look at the directory handler.

Make sure you have a project set up based on listing 5.2. Next, install inert:

```
npm install --save inert
```

Now the plugin can be loaded and registered. Open the server.js file and add the following lines.

Listing 5.4   Adding a plugin with hapi

```
const Inert = require('inert');

server.register(Inert, () => {});

server.route({
  method: 'GET',
  path: '/{param*}',
  handler: {
    directory: {
      path: '.',
      redirectToSlash: true,
      index: true
    }
  }
});
```

Instead of accepting only functions, hapi routes can also accept configuration objects for plugins. In this listing, the `directory` object includes the inert settings to serve files in the current path and show an index of the files in that directory. This is different from Express middleware, and shows how plugins extend the server's behavior in hapi applications.

5.5.4 REST APIs

hapi supports HTTP verbs and URL parameterization, allowing REST APIs to be implemented by using the standard hapi route API. The following snippet is the route required for a generalized delete method:

```
server.route({
  method: 'DELETE',
  path: '/items/{id}',
  handler: (req, reply) => {
    // Delete "item" here, based on req.params.id
    reply(true);
  }
});
```

In addition, plugins make creating RESTful APIs easier. For example, hapi-sequelize-crud (https://www.npmjs.com/package/hapi-sequelize-crud) automatically generates a RESTful API based on Sequelize models (http://docs.sequelizejs.com/en/latest/).

Persona thoughts

Phil: "I would definitely like to try hapi-sequelize-crud because we already have apps that use PostgreSQL and MySQL, so Sequelize might be a good fit. But, because hapi doesn't come with features like this out of the box, I'm worried that this plugin might become unsupported, so I'm not sure if hapi will work well in an agency scenario."

Alice: "As a product developer, I think hapi is interesting because like Express, it's minimal, yet the plugin API is more formal and expressive."

Nadine: "I can see several opportunities for making open source plugins for hapi, and the existing plugins mostly seem well written. hapi seems to have a technically competent audience, which appeals to me."

5.5.5 Strengths

hapi's plugin API is one of the biggest advantages of using hapi. Plugins can extend hapi's server but also add all kinds of other behavior, from data validation to templating. Also, because hapi is based around HTTP servers, it suits certain types of deployment scenarios. If you're deploying many servers that need to be connected together or load balanced, you might prefer hapi's server-based API to Express or Koa.

5.5.6 Weaknesses

hapi has similar weaknesses to Express: it's minimal, so there's no guidance on project structure. You can never be sure whether development on a plugin might cease, so relying on lots of plugins could cause maintenance issues in the future.

5.6   *Sails.js*

The frameworks you've seen so far have been minimal server libraries. Sails (http://sailsjs.org/) is a Model-View-Controller (MVC) framework, which is fundamentally different from a server library. It comes with an object-relational mapping (ORM) library for working with databases, and it can automatically generate REST APIs. It has modern features as well, including built-in WebSocket support. And if you're a fan of React or Angular, you'll be glad to know it's front-end agnostic: it's not a full-stack framework, so you can use it with practically any front-end library or framework. Table 5.4 shows the main features of Sails.

Table 5.4   The main features of Sails

Library type	MVC framework
Features	Database support with an ORM, REST API generation, WebSocket
Suggested uses	Rails-style MVC apps
Plugin architecture	Express middleware
Documentation	http://sailsjs.org/documentation/concepts/
Popularity	6,000 GitHub stars
License	BSD 3 Clause

Persona thoughts

Phil: "This sounds exactly what I'm looking for—what's the catch?!"

Alice: "I thought this wouldn't be for me because we've already invested development time in a React app, but because it's focused on the server, it may work for our product."

5.6.1   *Setting up*

Sails comes with a project generator, so it's best if you install it globally to make creating new projects easier. Install it with npm and then use `sails new` to make a project:

```
npm install -g sails
sails new example-project
```

This creates a new directory with a package.json for the basic Sails dependencies. The new project includes Sails itself, EJS, and Grunt. You can run `npm start` to start the server, or type `sails lift`. When the server is running, you'll be able to see the built-in Getting Started page by visiting http://localhost:1337.

5.6.2   Defining routes

To add routes, known as *custom routes* in Sails, open config/routes.js and add a property to the exported routes. This property is the HTTP verb and partial URL. For example, these are some valid Sails routes:

```
module.exports.routes = {
  'get /example': { view: 'example' },
  'post /items': 'ItemController.create
};
```

The first route expects a file called views/example.ejs. The second route expects a file called api/controllers/ItemController with a method called `create`. You can generate this controller with a method called `create` by running `sails generate controller item create`. A similar command can be used to quickly create RESTful APIs.

5.6.3   REST APIs

Sails combines database models and controllers into APIs, so to quickly stub RESTful APIs, use `sails generate api resource-name`. To use a database, you first need to install a database adapter. Adding MySQL involves finding the name of the Waterline MySQL package (https://github.com/balderdashy/waterline) and then adding it to the project:

```
npm install --save waterline sails-mysql
```

Next, open config/connections.js and fill out the connection details for your MySQL server. Sails model files allow you to specify the database connection, so you can use different models with different databases. That allows situations like a user session database in Redis and other, more permanent resources in a relational database such as MySQL.

Waterline is the database library for Sails, and it has its own documentation repository (https://github.com/balderdashy/waterline-docs). Other than supporting multiple databases, Waterline has useful features: you can define table and column names to support legacy schemas, and the query API supports promises so queries look like modern JavaScript.

Persona thoughts

Phil: "The ease of creating APIs and the fact that Waterline models can support existing database schemas means Sails sounds ideal for us. We have clients that we want to slowly move from MySQL to PostgreSQL, so we may be able to do this with Waterline. Some of our developers and designers have already worked with Ruby on Rails, so I think they'll pick up Sails with Node's modern ES2015 syntax in no time."

Alice: "This framework provides things that I don't need for our product. I feel like Koa or hapi would be a better fit."

5.6.4   *Strengths*

The built-in project creation and API generation means that setting up projects and adding typical REST APIs is fast. It works well for quickly creating new projects and collaborating, because Sails projects have the same filesystem layout. The creators of Sails, Mike McNeil and Irl Nathan, have written a book called *Sails.js in Action* (Manning Publications, 2017), which shows how Sails welcomes to Node beginners as well.

5.6.5   *Weaknesses*

Sails has some of the weaknesses shared by other server-side MVC frameworks: the routing API means you have to design your application with the Sails routing features in mind, and you may find it hard to adapt your schema to suit the Waterline way of handling things.

5.7   *DerbyJS*

DerbyJS is a full-stack framework that supports data synchronization and server rendering of views. It depends on MongoDB and Redis. The data synchronization layer is provided by ShareJS, and it supports automatic conflict resolution. Table 5.5 summarizes DerbyJS' main features.

Table 5.5   DerbyJS features

Library type	Full-stack framework
Features	Database support with an ORM (Racer), isomorphic
Suggested uses	Single-page web apps with server-side support
Plugin architecture	DerbyJS plugins
Documentation	http://derbyjs.com/docs/derby-0.6
Popularity	4,000 GitHub stars
License	MIT

5.7.1   *Setting up*

If you don't have MongoDB or Redis, you need to install both of them to run the DerbyJS examples. The DerbyJS documentation explains how to do this for Mac OS, Linux, and Windows (http://derbyjs.com/started#environment).

To create a new DerbyJS project quickly, install derby and derby-starter. The derby-starter package is used to bootstrap a Derby application:

```
mkdir example-derby-app
cd example-derby-app
npm init -f
npm install --save derby derby-starter derby-debug
```

Derby applications are split into several smaller applications, so create a new app directory with three files: index.js, server.js, and index.html. The following listing shows a simple Derby app that renders a template.

Listing 5.5   Derby app/index.js file

```
const app = module.exports = require('derby')
  .createApp('hello', __filename);
app.loadViews(__dirname);

app.get('/', (page, model) => {
  const message = model.at('hello.message');
  message.subscribe(err => {
    if (err) return next(err);
    message.createNull('');
    page.render();
  });
});
```

The server file needs to load only the derby-starter module, as shown in the following snippet. Save this as app/server.js:

```
require('derby-starter').run(__dirname, { port: 8005 });
```

The app/index.html file renders an input field and the message that the user types:

```
<Body:>
  Holler: <input value="{{hello.message}}">
  <h2>{{hello.message}}</h2>
```

You should be able to run the application from the example-derby-app directory by typing `node derby/server.js`. Once it's running, editing the app/index.html file will cause the application to restart; you automatically get real-time updates when editing code and templates.

5.7.2   *Defining routes*

DerbyJS uses derby-router for routing. Because DerbyJS is powered by Express, the routing API is similar for server-side routes, and the same routing module is used in the browser. When clicking a link in a DerbyJS app, it'll attempt to render the response in the client.

DerbyJS is a full-stack framework, so adding routes isn't quite the same as with the other libraries that you've looked at in this chapter. The most idiomatic way to add a basic route is by adding a view. Open apps/app/index.js and add a route by using `app.get`:

```
app.get('hello', '/hello');
```

Next, open apps/app/views/hello.pug and add a simple Pug template:

```
index:
  h2 Hello
  p Hello world
```

Now open apps/app/views/index.pug and import the template:

```
import:(src="./hello")
```

The project should constantly update if you've run `npm start`, so opening http://localhost:3000/hello will now show the new view.

The line that reads `index:` is the *namespace* for the view. In DerbyJS, view names have colon-separated namespaces, so you just created `hello:index`. The idea behind this is to encapsulate views so they don't clash in larger projects.

5.7.3   REST APIs

In DerbyJS projects, you need to create RESTful APIs by adding routes and route handlers with Express. Your DerbyJS project will have a server.js file that uses Express to create a server. If you open server/routes.js, you'll find an example route, defined by using the standard Express routing API.

In the server routes file, you could use `app.use` to mount another Express application, so you could model a REST API as a completely separate Express app that the main DerbyJS app mounts.

5.7.4   Strengths

DerbyJS has a database model API and a data synchronization API. You can use it to build single-page web apps, and modern real-time applications. Because it comes with WebSocket and synchronization built in, you don't have to worry about which WebSocket library to use, or how to sync data between the client and server.

Persona thoughts

Phil: "We had a client asking about building a data visualization project based on real-time data, so I think DerbyJS could be good for that. But the learning curve seems steep, so I'm not sure I can convince our developers to use it."

Alice: "As a product developer, I find it hard to see how to fit our product's needs to DerbyJS' architecture, so I don't think it's a good fit for my project."

5.7.5   Weaknesses

It's hard to convince people who are already experienced with either server-side or client-side libraries to use DerbyJS. Client-side developers who love React, for example, don't typically want to use DerbyJS. Server-side developers who love making REST APIs or MVC projects and who are comfortable with WebSocket also fail to be motivated to learn DerbyJS.

5.8   *Flatiron.js*

Flatiron is a web framework that includes features for URL routing, data management, middleware, plugins, and logging. Unlike most web frameworks, Flatiron's modules are designed to be decoupled, so you don't have to use all of them. You could even use one or more in your own projects—if you like the logging module, for example, you could drop it into an Express project. Unlike many Node frameworks, Flatiron's URL routing and middleware layers aren't written using Express or Connect, although the middleware is backward-compatible with Connect. Table 5.6 summarizes Flatiron's features.

Table 5.6   Flatiron's features

Library type	Modular MVC framework
Features	Database management layer (Resourceful), decoupled reusable modules
Suggested uses	Lightweight MVC apps, use Flatiron modules in other frameworks
Plugin architecture	Broadway plugin API
Documentation	https://github.com/flatiron
Popularity	1,500 GitHub stars
License	MIT

5.8.1   *Setting up*

Installing Flatiron requires globally installing the command-line tool to create new Flatiron projects:

```
npm install -g flatiron
flatiron create example-flatiron-app
```

After running these commands, you'll find a new directory that contains a package.json file with the necessary dependencies. Run `npm install` to install the dependencies, and then `npm start` to run the app.

The main app.js file looks a lot like a typical Express app:

```
const flatiron = require('flatiron');
const path = require('path');
const app = flatiron.app;

app.config.file({ file: path.join(__dirname, 'config', 'config.json') });

app.use(flatiron.plugins.http);

app.router.get('/', () => {
  this.res.json({ 'hello': 'world' })
});

app.start(3000);
```

Notice, however, that the router is different from both Express and Koa. Responses are returned by using `this.res`, instead of an argument to the responder callback. Let's look at Flatiron's routes in more detail.

5.8.2 *Defining routes*

Flatiron's routing library is called Director. Although it can be used for server routes, it also supports routes in browsers, so it can be used to make single-page apps as well. Director calls Express-style HTTP verb routes ad hoc:

```
router.get('/example', example);
router.post('/example', examplePost);
```

Routes can have parameters, and parameters can be defined with a regular expression:

```
router.param('id', /([\\w\\-]+)/);
router.on('/pages/:id', pageId => {});
```

To generate a response, use `res.writeHead` to send headers, and `res.end` to send the response body:

```
router.get('/',  () => {
  this.res.writeHead(200, { 'content-type': 'text/plain' });
  this.res.end('Hello, World');
});
```

The routing API can also be used as a class, with a routing table object. To use it, instantiate a new router and then use the dispatch method when HTTP requests arrive:

```
const http = require('http');
const director = require('director');
const router = new director.http.Router({
  '/example': {
    get: () => {
      this.res.writeHead(200, { 'Content-Type': 'text/plain' })
      this.res.end('hello world');
    }
  }
});
const server = http.createServer((req, res) =>
  router.dispatch(req, res);
});
```

Using the routing API as a class also means you can hook into the streaming API. This makes dealing with large requests possible in a quick and easy way, which is good for doing things such as parsing uploaded data and exiting early:

```
const director = require('director');
const router = new director.http.Router();

router.get('/', { stream: true }, () => {
  this.req.on('data', (chunk) => {
    console.log(chunk);
  });
});
```

Director has a scoped routing API, which can be useful for creating REST APIs.

5.8.3 *REST APIs*

REST APIs can be created with the standard Express HTTP verb style methods, or Director's scoped routing feature. This allows routes to be grouped together based on URL fragments and URL parameters:

```
router.path(/\/users\/(\w+)/, () => {
  this.get((id) => {});
  this.delete((id) => {});
  this.put((id) => {});
});
```

Flatiron also provides a high-level REST wrapper called Resourceful (https://github.com/flatiron/resourceful), which supports CouchDB, MongoDB, Socket.IO, and data validation.

5.8.4 *Strengths*

It's hard for frameworks to gain traction, which is why Flatiron's decoupled design is a major strength. You can use some of its modules without using the entire framework. For example, the Winston logging module (https://github.com/winstonjs/winston) is used by many projects that don't use the rest of Flatiron. This means some parts of Flatiron receive a good level of open source contributions.

The Director URL-routing API is isomorphic, so you can use it as a solution for both client- and server-side development. Director's API differs from the Express-style routing APIs as well: Director has a simplified streaming API, and the routing object emits events before and after routes are executed.

Unlike most Node web frameworks, Flatiron has a plugin manager. Therefore, it's easier to extend Flatiron projects with community-supported plugins.

> **Persona thoughts**
>
> *Nadine*: "I love Flatiron's modular design, and the plugin manager is great. I can already think of some plugins that I'd like to make."
>
> *Alice*: "I don't like the sound of all of Flatiron's modules, so I'd like to try it with a different ORM and template library."

5.8.5 *Weaknesses*

Flatiron isn't as easy to use for larger MVC-style projects as some other frameworks. For example, Sails is easier to set up. If you're creating several medium-sized traditional web apps, Flatiron may work well. The ability to configure Flatiron is an added bonus, but make sure you evaluate it next to other options first.

One strong competitor is LoopBack, which is the last framework that features in this chapter.

5.9   *LoopBack*

LoopBack was created by StrongLoop, a company offering several commercial services that support the development of Node web apps. It's billed as an API framework,
but has features that make it work well with databases and for MVC apps. It even comes
with a web interface for exploring and managing REST APIs. If you're looking for
something that will help create web APIs for mobile and desktop clients, LoopBack's
features are ideal. See table 5.7 for details about LoopBack.

Table 5.7   LoopBack's features

Library type	API framework
Features	ORM, API user interface, WebSocket, client SDKs (including iOS)
Suggested uses	APIs that support multiple clients (mobile, desktop, web)
Plugin architecture	Express middleware
Documentation	http://loopback.io/doc/
Popularity	6,500 GitHub stars
License	Dual license: MIT and StrongLoop Subscription Agreement

LoopBack is open source, and since StrongLoop's acquisition by IBM, the framework
now has major commercial endorsement. That makes it a unique offering in the Node
community. It comes with Yeoman generators for quickly setting up application scaf-
folds. In the next section, you'll see how to create a fresh LoopBack application.

5.9.1   *Setting up*

To set up a new LoopBack project, you need to use the StrongLoop command-line
tools (www.npmjs.com/package/strongloop). Globally installing the strongloop package makes the command-line tools available through the `slc` command. This package
includes features for process management, but what we're interested in is the Loop-
Back project generator:

```
npm install -g strongloop
slc loopback
```

The StrongLoop command-line tool walks you through the steps necessary to set up a
new project. Type in a name for the project and then select the api-server application
skeleton. When the generator has finished installing the project's dependencies, it
will display some handy tips for working with the new project. Figure 5.2 shows what
this should look like.

To run the project, type `node .`, and to create a model, use `slc loop-
back:model`. You'll use the `slc` command regularly as you set up a new LoopBack
project.

```
● ● ●                    3. alex@Alexs-MacBook-Pro: ~/Documents/Code (zsh)
→ Code slc loopback

    _____
   |     |        .---------------------------.
   |--(o)--|      |   Let's create a LoopBack |
   `---------`    |       application!        |
  ( _'U`_ )       '---------------------------'
  /___A___\
   |  ~  |
 '.___.'.'.'.
      |° 'Y`

? What's the name of your application? loopback-example
? Enter name of the directory to contain the project: loopback-example
   create loopback-example/
      info change the working directory to loopback-example

? What kind of application do you have in mind? api-server (A LoopBack API server with local Use
r auth)
Generating .yo-rc.json


I'm all done. Running                  for you to install the required dependencies. If this fails, t
ry running the command yourself.

   create .editorconfig
   create .jshintignore
   create .jshintrc
   create server/boot/root.js
   create server/middleware.json
   create server/middleware.production.json
```

**Figure 5.2
LoopBack's
project generator**

When the project is running, you should be able to access the API explorer at http://0.0.0.0:3000/explorer/. Click User to expand the User endpoint. You should see a large list of available API methods, including standard RESTful routes such as PUT /Users and DELETE /Users/{id}. Figure 5.3 shows the API explorer.

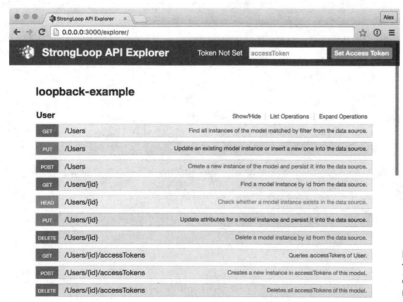

**Figure 5.3
The StrongLoop API
explorer showing
User routes**

5.9.2   Defining routes

In LoopBack, you can add routes at the Express level. Add a new file called server/boot/routes.js, and add a route by accessing the LoopBack Router instance:

```
module.exports = (app) => {
  const router = app.loopback.Router();
  router.get('/hello', (req, res) => {
    res.send('Hello, world');
  });
  app.use(router);
};
```

Visiting http://localhost:3000/hello will now respond with *Hello, world*. Adding routes this way, however, isn't typical in a LoopBack project. It may be required for certain unusual API endpoints, but in general, routes are added automatically when models are generated.

5.9.3   REST APIs

The easiest way to create REST APIs in a LoopBack project is by using the model generator. This is part of the `slc` command's features. If you want to add a new model called *product*, for example, run `slc loopback:model`:

```
slc loopback:model product
```

The `slc` command walks you through the steps to create a model, allowing you to select whether the model is server-only, and set up some properties and validators. After you add a model, take a look at the corresponding JSON file—it should be in common/models/product.json. This JSON file is a lightweight way of defining how models behave, including all of the properties you specified in the previous step.

   If you want to add more properties, type `slc loopback:property`. You can add properties to models at any time.

> **Persona thoughts**
>
> *Phil*: "Our teams love the sound of LoopBack, mainly because of the ability to quickly add RESTful resources and browse them with the API explorer. But I like it because it looks like it's flexible enough to support our legacy MVC web apps. We could hook into the older database and move these projects over to Node."
>
> *Alice*: "This is the only framework that really targets iOS and Android, as well as rich web clients. LoopBack has client libraries for iOS and Android, so this is a big deal for us as product developers who depend on mobile apps."

5.9.4   Strengths

Even from this short introduction, it should be clear that one of the strengths of LoopBack is it removes the need to write boilerplate code. The command-line tool generates almost everything you need for lightweight RESTful web APIs, even database models and validation. At the same time, LoopBack doesn't dictate too much about the front-end code. It also enables you to think about which models should be accessible to the browser and which are server-side only. Some frameworks get this wrong and push everything to the browser.

If you have mobile apps that need to talk to your web APIs, take a look at Loop-Back's client SDKs (http://loopback.io/doc/en/lb2/Client-SDKs.html). LoopBack supports API integration and push messages for both iOS and Android.

5.9.5   Weaknesses

LoopBack's JSON-based model API is different from most JavaScript database APIs. It can take a while to learn how to map it to an existing project's database schema. And because the HTTP layer is based on Express, it's partly limited to what Express supports. Although Express is a solid HTTP server library, newer libraries are available for Node with more-modern APIs. LoopBack doesn't have a specific plugin API. You can use Express middleware, but this isn't as convenient as Flatiron or hapi's plugin APIs.

This concludes the frameworks that are covered in this chapter. Before moving on to the next chapter, let's compare the frameworks to help you decide which is the right choice for your next project.

5.10   Comparison

If you've been following the persona thoughts throughout this chapter, you may already have decided which framework to use. If not, the rest of this chapter compares the benefits of each framework. And, if you're still lost, figure 5.4 will help you pick the right framework by answering some questions.

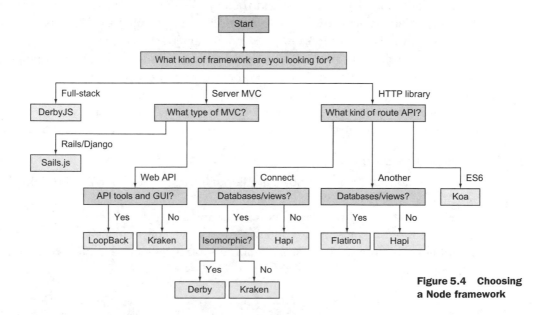

Figure 5.4   Choosing a Node framework

If you glance through Node's popular server-side frameworks, they all sound similar. They offer lightweight HTTP APIs, and they use the server model instead of PHP's page model. But the differences in their design have big implications for projects made with them, so to compare these frameworks, we'll start at the HTTP level.

5.10.1 HTTP servers and routes

The majority of Node frameworks are based on Connect or Express. In this chapter, you've seen three that aren't based on Express at all, and have their own solutions to HTTP APIs: Koa, hapi, and Flatiron.

Koa was created by the same author as Express, but offers a fresh approach by using more-modern JavaScript features. If you like Express but want to use ES2015 generator syntax, Koa may work for you.

hapi's server and routing APIs are highly modular and feel different from those of Express. If you find Express's syntax awkward, you should give hapi a try. hapi makes it easier to reason about HTTP servers, so if you need to do things such as connect servers or cluster them, you may prefer hapi to Express descendants.

Flatiron's router is backward-compatible with Express but has extra features. The router emits events and uses a routing table. That's different from the Express-style stack of middleware components. You can pass an object literal to Flatiron's router. The router also works in browsers, so if you have server-side developers trying to tackle modern client-side development, they might be more at home with Flatiron than going all out with something like React Router.

5.11 Writing modular code

Not all of the frameworks covered here directly support plugins, but they're all extensible in some way. The Express-based frameworks can use Connect middleware, but hapi and Flatiron have their own plugin APIs. Well-defined plugin APIs are useful because they make it easier for new users of a framework to extend it.

If you're using a larger MVC framework such as Sails.js or LoopBack, a plugin API makes it much easier to set up a new project. LoopBack partly sidesteps needing a plugin API by providing a highly capable project management tool. If you look at StrongLoop's npm account (www.npmjs.com/~strongloop), you'll see lots of loopback-related projects that add support for things like Angular and several databases.

5.12 Persona choices

The personas in this chapter now have enough background to make the right choice for their next project:

Phil: "In the end I decided to go with LoopBack. It was a difficult choice because Sails and Kraken both have excellent features that my team liked, but we felt like LoopBack has stronger long-term support and reduces so much effort on server-side development."

Nadine: "As an open source developer, I've opted for Flatiron. It'll adapt to the various projects that I'm working on. For example, some projects will just use Winston and Director, but others will use the whole stack."

Alice: "I've chosen hapi for my next project. It's minimal, so I can adapt it to the project's unique requirements. Most of the code will be Node and not rely on any specific framework, so I feel this works well with hapi."

5.13 *Summary*

- Koa is lightweight, minimal, and uses ES2015 generator syntax for middleware. It's good for hosting single-page web apps that depend on external web APIs.
- hapi is focused on HTTP servers and routes. It's good for lightweight back ends composed of lots of small services.
- Flatiron is a set of decoupled modules that can be used like either a web MVC framework or a more lightweight Express library. Flatiron is compatible with Connect middleware.
- Kraken is based on Express, with added security features. It can be used for MVC.
- Sails.js is a Rails/Django-inspired MVC framework. It has an ORM and a template system.
- DerbyJS is an isomorphic framework that's good for real-time applications.
- LoopBack removes the need to write boilerplate code for quickly generating REST APIs complete with database support and an API explorer.

Connect and
Express in depth

This chapter covers

- Understanding what Connect and Express are for
- Using and creating middleware
- Creating and configuring an Express application
- Using key Express techniques for error handling, rendering views, and forms
- Using Express architectural techniques for routes, REST APIs, and authentication

In chapter 3, you saw how to build a simple Express application. This chapter provides a more in-depth study of Express and Connect. These two popular Node modules are used by many web developers. This chapter shows you how to build web apps and REST APIs with the most commonly used patterns.

Connect and Express

The concepts discussed in the following section are directly applicable to the higher-level framework Express because it extends and builds upon Connect with additional higher-level sugar. After reading this section, you'll have a firm understanding

108

of how Connect middleware works and how to compose components together to create an application. Other Node web frameworks work in a similar way, so learning Connect will give you a head start when learning new frameworks.

To start, let's see how to create a basic Connect application. Later in the chapter, you'll see how to build a more complex Express application by using popular Express techniques.

6.1 Connect

In this section, you'll learn about *Connect*. You'll see how its middleware can be used to build simple web applications, and how middleware ordering matters. This will help you to build more-modular Express applications later.

6.1.1 Setting up a Connect application

Express is built with Connect, but do you know you can make a fully functionally web app with Connect alone? You can download and install Connect from the npm registry by using the command shown here:

```
$ npm install connect@3.4.0
```

Here's what a minimal Connect application looks like:

```
const app = require('connect')();
app.use((req, res, next) => {
  res.end('Hello, world!');
});
app.listen(3000);
```

This simple application (found under ch06-connect-and-express/hello-world in the sample code) will respond with *Hello, world!* The function passed to app.use is a middleware component that ends the request by sending back the *Hello, world!* text as a response. Middleware components form the basis of all Connect and Express apps. Let's look at them in more detail.

6.1.2 Understanding how Connect middleware works

In Connect, a *middleware component* is a JavaScript function that by convention accepts three arguments: a request object, a response object, and an argument commonly named next, which is a callback function indicating that the component is done and the subsequent middleware component can be executed.

Before your middleware runs, Connect uses a dispatcher that takes in requests and then hands them off to the first middleware component that you've added to your application. Figure 6.1 shows a typical Connect application, which is composed of the

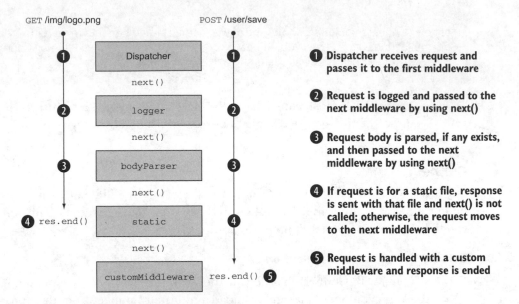

Figure 6.1   The life cycle of two HTTP requests making their way through a Connect server

dispatcher as well as an arrangement of middleware including a logger, a body parser, a static file server, and custom middleware.

As you can see, the design of the middleware API means that more-complex behavior can be composed of smaller building blocks. In the next section, you'll see how to do this by combining components.

6.1.3   *Combining middleware*

Connect provides a method called use for combining middleware components. Let's define two middleware functions and add them both to the application. One is the simple Hello World function from earlier, and the other is a logger.

Listing 6.1   Using multiple Connect middleware components

```
const connect = require('connect');
function logger(req, res, next) {
  console.log('%s %s', req.method, req.url);     ◁──  Prints HTTP method and
  next();                                              requests URL and calls next()
}
function hello(req, res) {
  res.setHeader('Content-Type', 'text/plain');   ◁──  Ends response to HTTP
  res.end('hello world');                              request with "hello world"
}
connect()
  .use(logger)
  .use(hello)
  .listen(3000);
```

This middleware has two signatures: one with `next`, and one without. That's because this component finishes the HTTP response and never needs to give control back to the dispatcher.

The `use()` function returns an instance of a Connect application to support method chaining, as shown previously. Note that chaining the `.use()` calls isn't required, as shown in the following snippet:

```
const app = connect();
app.use(logger);
app.use(hello);
app.listen(3000);
```

Now that you have a simple Hello World application working, we'll look at why the ordering of middleware `.use()` calls is important, and how to strategically use that ordering to alter the way your application works.

6.1.4 *Ordering middleware*

The ordering of middleware in your application can dramatically affect the way it behaves. Execution can be stopped by omitting `next()`, and middleware can be combined to implement features such as authentication.

What happens when middleware components don't call `next`? Consider the previous Hello World example, where the `logger` middleware component is used first, followed by the `hello` component. In that example, Connect logs to stdout and then responds to the HTTP request. But consider what would happen if the ordering were switched, as follows.

Listing 6.2 Wrong: `hello` middleware component before `logger` component

```
const connect = require('connect');
function logger(req, res, next) {            ← Always calls next(), so subsequent
  console.log('%s %s', req.method, req.url);    middleware is invoked
  next();
}
function hello(req, res) {                    ← Doesn't call next(), because
  res.setHeader('Content-Type', 'text/plain');  component responds to request
  res.end('hello world');
}
const app = connect()
  .use(hello)                                 ← logger will never be invoked
  .use(logger)                                  because hello doesn't call next().
  .listen(3000);
```

In this example, the `hello` middleware component is called first and responds to the HTTP request as expected. But `logger` is never called because `hello` never calls `next()`, so control is never passed back to the dispatcher to invoke the next middleware component. The moral here is that when a component doesn't call `next()`, no remaining middleware in the chain of command will be invoked.

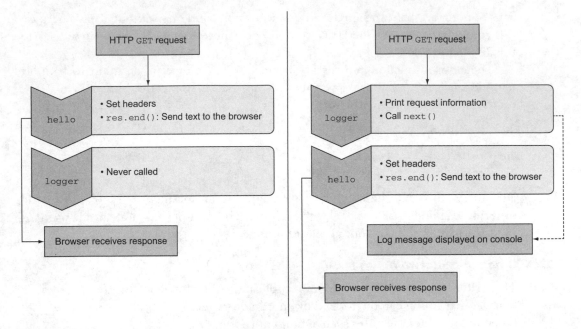

Figure 6.2 Middleware ordering is important.

Figure 6.2 shows how this example would skip the logger, and how to correct it.

As you can see, placing `hello` in front of `logger` is rather useless, but when used properly, ordering can be to your benefit.

6.1.5 *Creating configurable middleware*

You've learned some middleware basics; now we'll go into detail and look at how to create more-generic and reusable middleware.

Middleware commonly follows a simple convention in order to provide configuration capabilities to developers: using a function that returns another function (a closure). The basic structure for configurable middleware of this kind looks like this:

```
function setup(options) {
  // setup logic

  return function(req, res, next) {
    // middleware logic

  }
}
```

Additional middleware initialization here

Options still accessible even though outer function has returned

This type of middleware is used as follows:

```
app.use(setup({ some: 'options' }));
```

Notice that the `setup` function is invoked in the `app.use` line, whereas in previous examples you were just passing a reference to the function.

In this section, you'll apply this technique to build three reusable, configurable middleware components:

- A logger component with a configurable printing format
- A router component that invokes functions based on the requested URL
- A URL rewriter component that converts URL slugs to IDs

You'll start by expanding your logger component to make it more configurable. The `logger` middleware component you created earlier in this chapter wasn't configurable. It was hardcoded to print out the request's `req.method` and `req.url` when invoked. But what if you want to change what the logger displays at some point in the future?

In practice, using configurable middleware is just like using any of the middleware you've created so far, except that you can pass additional arguments to the middleware component to alter its behavior. Using the configurable component in your application might look a little like the following example, where `logger` can accept a string that describes the format that it should print out:

```
const app = connect()
  .use(logger(':method :url'))
  .use(hello);
```

To implement the configurable `logger` component, you first need to define a `setup` function that accepts a single string argument (in this example, you'll name it `format`). When `setup` is invoked, a function is returned, and it's the middleware component Connect will use. The returned component retains access to the `format` variable, even after the `setup` function has returned, because it's defined within the same JavaScript closure. The `logger` then replaces the tokens in the `format` string with the associated request properties on the `req` object, logs to stdout, and calls `next()`, as shown in the following listing.

Listing 6.3 A configurable `logger` middleware component for Connect

```
function setup(format) {            ◁─┐  Setup function can be called multiple
  const regexp = /:(\w+)/g;         ◁── times with different configurations

                                        Logger component uses a regexp
                                        to match request properties

  return function createLogger(req, res, next) {      ◁───  Logger
    const str = format.replace(regexp, (match, property) => {   ◁──  component
      return req[property];                                          that Connect
    });                                                              will use

                          Uses regexp to format
                          log entry for request
```

```
        console.log(str);
        next();
    }
}
module.exports = setup;
```

Prints request log entry to console

Passes control to next middleware component

Directly exports logger setup function

Because you've created this `logger` middleware component as configurable middleware, you can `.use()` the logger multiple times in a single application with different configurations or reuse this logger code in any number of future applications you might develop. This simple concept of configurable middleware is used throughout the Connect community, and it's used for all core Connect middleware to maintain consistency.

To use the logger middleware in listing 6.3, you need to pass it a string that includes some of the properties found on the request object. For example, `.use(setup(':method   :url'))` prints the HTTP method (`GET`, `POST`, and so forth) and URL of each request.

Before moving on to Express, let's look at how Connect supports error handling.

6.1.6 *Using error-handling middleware*

All applications have errors, whether at the system level or the user level, and being well prepared for error situations—even ones you aren't anticipating—is a smart thing to do. Connect implements an error-handling variant of middleware that follows the same rules as regular middleware but accepts an error object along with the request and response objects.

Connect's error handling is intentionally minimal, allowing the developer to specify the way errors should be handled. For example, you could pass only system and application errors through the middleware (for example, *foo is undefined*) or user errors (*password is invalid*) or a combination of both. Connect lets you choose which is best for your application.

In this section, you'll use both types, and you'll learn how error-handling middleware works. You'll also learn some useful patterns that can be applied while we look at the following:

- Using Connect's default error handler
- Handing application errors yourself
- Using multiple error-handling middleware components

Let's jump in with a look at how Connect handles errors without any configuration.

USING CONNECT'S DEFAULT ERROR HANDLER

Consider the following middleware component, which will throw a `ReferenceError` error because the function `foo()` isn't defined by the application:

```
const connect = require('connect')
connect()
  .use((req, res) => {
```

```
    foo();
    res.setHeader('Content-Type', 'text/plain');
    res.end('hello world');
  })
.listen(3000)
```

By default, Connect will respond with a 500 status code, a response body containing the text *Internal Server Error*, and more information about the error itself. This is fine, but in any kind of real application, you'd probably want to do more-specialized things with those errors, such as send them off to a logging daemon.

HANDLING APPLICATION ERRORS YOURSELF

Connect also offers a way for you to handle application errors yourself, using error-handling middleware. For instance, in development you might want to respond to the client with a JSON representation of the error for quick and easy reporting, whereas in production you'd want to respond with a simple *Server error*, so as not to expose sensitive internal information (such as stack traces, filenames, and line numbers) to a potential attacker.

An error-handling middleware function must be defined to accept four arguments—err, req, res, and next—as shown in listing 6.4, whereas regular middleware takes the arguments req, res, and next. The following listing shows an example error middleware. For a full example with a server, look at ch06-connect-and-express/listing6_4 in the book's source code.

Listing 6.4 Error-handling middleware in Connect

```
const env = process.env.NODE_ENV || 'development';

function errorHandler(err, req, res, next) {
    res.statusCode = 500;
    switch (env) {
      case 'development':
        console.error('Error:');
        console.error(err);
        res.setHeader('Content-Type', 'application/json');
        res.end(JSON.stringify(err));
        break;
      default:
        res.end('Server error');
    }
}

module.exports = errorHandler;
```

> Error-handling middleware uses four arguments

> errorHandler middleware component behaves differently, depending on value of NODE_ENV

USE NODE_ENV TO SET THE APPLICATION'S MODE A common Connect convention is to use the NODE_ENV environment variable (process.env.NODE_ENV) to toggle the behavior between server environments, such as production and development.

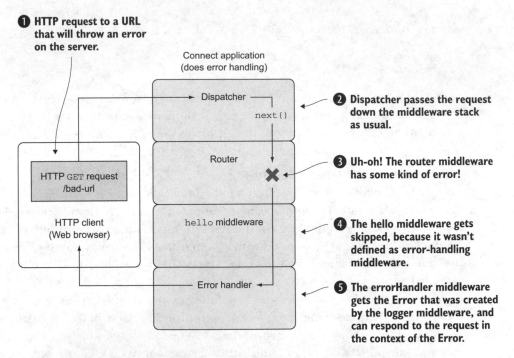

Figure 6.3   The life cycle of an HTTP request causing an error in a Connect server

When Connect encounters an error, it'll switch to invoking only error-handling middleware, as you can see in figure 6.3.

Imagine you have an application that allows people to authenticate to an administration area for a blog. If the routing middleware component for the user routes causes an error, both the blog and admin middleware components will be skipped, because they don't act as error-handling middleware—they only define three arguments. Connect will then see that errorHandler accepts the error argument and will invoke it. The middleware components could look something like this:

```
connect()
  .use(router(require('./routes/user')))
  .use(router(require('./routes/blog'))) // Skipped
  .use(router(require('./routes/admin'))) // Skipped
  .use(errorHandler);
```

Short-circuiting functionality based on middleware execution is a fundamental concept used to organize Express applications. Now that you've learned the basics of Connect, it's time to go into more detail about Express.

6.2   Express

Express is a popular web framework formerly built on Connect but still compatible with Connect middleware. Although Express comes with basic functionality, such as serving static files, URL routing, and application configuration, it's still minimal. It provides enough structure so you can compose reusable chunks without being too restrictive of your development practices.

Over the next few sections, you'll implement a new Express application by using the Express skeleton app generator. This process is more detailed than the brief overview in chapter 3, so by the end of this chapter you should have enough knowledge of Express to build your own Express web apps and RESTful APIs. As the chapter continues, you'll keep adding functionality to the skeleton to produce a full app by the end.

6.2.1 *Generating the application skeleton*

Express doesn't force application structure on the developer. You can place routes in as many files as you want, public assets in any directory you want, and so on. A minimal Express application can be as small as the following listing, which implements a fully functional HTTP server.

Listing 6.5   A minimal Express application

```
const express = require('express');
const app = express();

app.get('/', (req, res) => {                 Responds to any
  res.send('Hello');                         web request to /
});                           Sends "Hello" as
                              response text
app.listen(3000);       Listens on port 3000
```

The `express(1)` command-line tool available in the express-generator package (www.npmjs.com/package/express-generator) can set up an application skeleton for you. Using the generated application is a good way to get started if you're new to Express, as it sets up an application complete with templates, public assets, configuration, and more.

The default application skeleton that `express(1)` generates consists of only a few directories and files, as shown in figure 6.4. This structure is designed to get developers up and running with Express in seconds, but the application's structure is entirely up to you and your team to create.

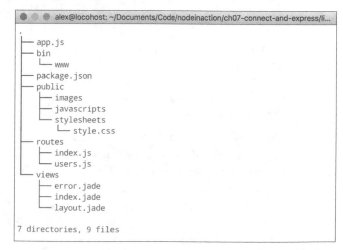

**Figure 6.4
Default application skeleton
structure using EJS templates**

```
alex@locohost: ~/Documents/Code/nodeinaction/ch07-connect-and-express/li...
.
├── app.js
├── bin
│   └── www
├── package.json
├── public
│   ├── images
│   ├── javascripts
│   └── stylesheets
│       └── style.css
├── routes
│   ├── index.js
│   └── users.js
└── views
    ├── error.jade
    ├── index.jade
    └── layout.jade

7 directories, 9 files
```

This chapter's example uses Embedded JavaScript (EJS) templates, which are similar in structure to HTML. EJS is similar to PHP, JSP (for Java), and ERB (for Ruby), because server-side JavaScript is embedded in an HTML document and executed prior to being sent to the client. You'll look at EJS more closely in chapter 7.

In this section, you'll do the following:

- Install Express globally with npm
- Generate the application
- Explore the application and install dependencies

Let's get started.

INSTALLING THE EXPRESS EXECUTABLE

First, install express-generator globally with npm:

```
$ npm install -g express-generator
```

Next, you can use the `--help` flag to see the options available, as shown in figure 6.5.

```
● ● ●   alex@locohost: ~/Documents/Code/nodeinaction/ch07-connect-and-express/li...
❯ express --help

 Usage: express [options] [dir]

 Options:

   -h, --help          output usage information
   -V, --version       output the version number
   -e, --ejs           add ejs engine support (defaults to jade)
       --hbs           add handlebars engine support
   -H, --hogan         add hogan.js engine support
   -c, --css <engine>  add stylesheet <engine> support (less|stylus
|compass|sass) (defaults to plain css)
       --git           add .gitignore
   -f, --force         force on non-empty directory
```

Figure 6.5   Express help

Some of these options will generate small portions of the application for you. For example, you can specify a template engine to generate a dummy template file for the chosen template engine. Similarly, if you specify a CSS preprocessor by using the `--css` option, a dummy template file will be generated for it.

Now that the executable is installed, let's see how to generate what will become the photo application.

GENERATING THE APPLICATION

For this application, you use the `-e` (or `--ejs`) flag to use the EJS templating engine. Execute `express -e shoutbox`. If you want to duplicate the code samples in our GitHub repository, use `express -e listing6_6`.

A fully functional application is created in the shoutbox directory. It contains a package.json file to describe the project and dependencies, the application file itself, the public file directories, and a directory for route handlers.

EXPLORING THE APPLICATION

Let's take a closer look at what was generated. Open the package.json file in your editor to see the application's dependencies, as shown in figure 6.6. Express can't guess which version of the dependencies you'll want, so it's good practice to supply the major, minor, and patch levels of the module so you don't introduce any surprise bugs. For example, `"express":` `"~4.13.1"` is explicit and will provide you with identical code on each installation.

Now look at the application file generated by `express(1)`, shown in the following listing. For now, you'll leave this file as is. You should be familiar with these middleware components from the Connect sections earlier in this chapter, but it's worth taking a look at how the default middleware configuration is set up.

```
1   {
2     "name": "listing6_6",
3     "version": "0.0.0",
4     "private": true,
5     "scripts": {
6       "start": "node ./bin/www"
7     },
8     "dependencies": {
9       "body-parser": "~1.13.2",
10      "cookie-parser": "~1.3.5",
11      "debug": "~2.2.0",
12      "express": "~4.13.1",
13      "jade": "~1.11.0",
14      "morgan": "~1.6.1",
15      "serve-favicon": "~2.3.0"
16    }
17  }
```

Figure 6.6 Generated package.json contents

Listing 6.6 Generated Express application skeleton

```
var express = require('express');
var path = require('path');
var favicon = require('serve-favicon');        Serves default
var logger = require('morgan');                 favicon
var cookieParser = require('cookie-parser');
var bodyParser = require('body-parser');
var routes = require('./routes/index');
var users = require('./routes/users');
var app = express();

app.set('views', path.join(__dirname, 'views'));
app.set('view engine', 'ejs');
                                               Outputs development-
app.use(logger('dev'));                        friendly colored logs
app.use(bodyParser.json());
app.use(bodyParser.urlencoded({ extended: false }));    Parses request bodies
app.use(cookieParser());
app.use(express.static(path.join(__dirname, 'public')));    Serves static
                                                            files from ./public
app.use('/', routes);
app.use('/users', users);            Specifies
                                     application
app.use(function(req, res, next) {   routes
  let err = new Error('Not Found');
  err.status = 404;
  next(err);
});

if (app.get('env') === 'development') {    Displays styled HTML error
  app.use(function(err, req, res, next) {  pages in development
```

```
    res.status(err.status || 500);
    res.render('error', {
      message: err.message,
      error: err
    });
  });
}

app.use(function(err, req, res, next) {
  res.status(err.status || 500);
  res.render('error', {
    message: err.message,
    error: {}
  });
});

module.exports = app;
```

You have the package.json and app.js files, but the application won't run yet because the dependencies haven't been installed. Whenever you generate a package.json file from express(1), you need to install the dependencies. Execute npm install to do this, and then execute npm start to run the application.

Check out the application by visiting http://localhost:3000 in your browser. The default application looks like the one in figure 6.7.

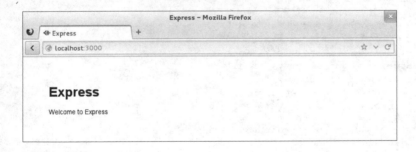

Figure 6.7   Default Express application

Now that you've seen the generated skeleton, you can start building a real Express application. The application will be a shoutbox that allows people to post messages. When building applications like this, most seasoned Express developers start by planning their API and hence the required routes and resources that will be required.

PLANNING THE SHOUTBOX APPLICATION

Here are the requirements for the shoutbox application:

1   It should allow users to register accounts, sign in, and sign out.
2   Users should be able to post messages (entries).
3   Site visitors should be able to paginate through entries.
4   There should be a simple REST API that supports authentication.

You need to store data and handle authentication. You also need to validate user input. The necessary routes look something like this:

- API routes
- GET /api/entries: Get a list of entries
- GET /api/entries/page: Get a single page of entries
- POST /api/entry: Create a new shoutbox entry
- Web UI routes
- GET /post: The form for a new entry
- POST /post: Post a new entry
- GET /register: Show the registration form
- POST /register: Create a new account
- GET /login: Show the sign-in form
- POST /login: Sign in
- GET /logout: Sign out

This layout is similar to that of most web applications. Hopefully, you'll be able to use the example from this chapter as a template for your own applications in the future.

In the previous listing, you may have noticed some calls to `app.set`:

```
app.set('views', path.join(__dirname, 'views'));
app.set('view engine', 'ejs');
```

This is how Express applications are configured. The next section explains Express configuration in more detail.

6.2.2 Configuring Express and your application

Your application's requirements will depend on the environment in which it's running. For example, you may want verbose logging when your product is in development, but a leaner set of logs and gzip compression when it's in production. In addition to configuring environment-specific functionality, you may want to define some application-level settings so Express knows what template engine you're using and where it can find the templates. Express also lets you define custom configuration key/value pairs.

Setting environment variables

To set an environment variable in UNIX systems, you can use this command:

```
$ NODE_ENV=production node app
```

In Windows, you can use this code:

```
$ set NODE_ENV=production
$ node app
```

These environment variables will be available in your application on the `process.env` object.

Express has a minimal environment-driven configuration system, consisting of several methods, all driven by the NODE_ENV environment variable:

- app.set()
- app.get()
- app.enable()
- app.disable()
- app.enabled()
- app.disabled()

In this section, you'll see how to use the configuration system to customize the way Express behaves, as well as how to use this system for your own purposes throughout development.

Let's take a closer look at what *environment-based configuration* means. Although the NODE_ENV environment variable originated in Express, many other Node frameworks have adopted it as a means to notify the Node application which environment it's operating within, defaulting to development.

The app.configure() method accepts optional strings representing the environment, and a function. When the environment matches the string passed, the callback is immediately invoked; when only a function is given, it's invoked for all environments. These environment names are completely arbitrary. For example, you may have development, stage, test, and production, or prod for short:

```
if (app.get('env') === 'development') {
  app.use(express.errorHandler());
}
```

Express uses the configuration system internally, allowing you to customize the way Express behaves, but it's also available for your own use.

Express also provides Boolean variants of app.set() and app.get(). For example, app.enable(setting) is equivalent to app.set(setting, true), and app.enabled (setting) can be used to check whether the value was enabled. The methods app.disable (setting) and app.disabled(setting) complement the truthful variants.

A useful setting for developing APIs with Express is the json spaces option. If you add it to your app.js file, your JSON will be printed in a more readable format:

```
app.set('json spaces', 2);
```

Now that you've seen how to take advantage of the configuration system for your own use, let's look at rendering views in Express.

6.2.3   *Rendering views*

In this chapter's application, you'll use EJS templates, though as previously mentioned, almost any template engine in the Node community can be used. If you're not familiar with EJS, don't worry. It's similar to templating languages found in other web development platforms (PHP, JSP, ERB). We cover some basics of EJS in this chapter, but we discuss EJS and several other template engines in greater detail in chapter 7.

Whether it's rendering an entire HTML page, an HTML fragment, or an RSS feed, rendering views is crucial for nearly every application. The concept is simple: you pass data to a *view*, and that data is transformed, typically to HTML for web applications. You're likely familiar with the idea of views,

```
{ name: 'Tobi', species: 'ferret', age: 2 }




<h1>Tobi</h1>
<p>Tobi is a 2 year old ferret.</p>
```

Figure 6.8   HTML template plus data = HTML view of data

because most frameworks provide similar functionality; figure 6.8 illustrates how a view forms a new representation for the data.

The template that generates template 6.8 can be found in the following snippet:

```
<h1><%= name %></h1>
<p><%- name %> is a 2 year old <%= species %>.</p>
```

Express provides two ways to render views: at the application level with `app.render()`, and at the response with `res.render()`, which uses the former internally. In this chapter, you'll use only `res.render()`. If you look in ./routes/index.js, a function is defined that invokes `res.render('index')` in order to render the ./views/index.ejs template, as shown in the following code (found in listing6_8):

```
router.get('/', (req, res, next) => {
  res.render('index', { title: 'Express' });
});
```

Before looking at `res.render()` more closely, let's see how to configure the view system.

CONFIGURING THE VIEW SYSTEM

Configuring the Express view system is simple. But even though `express(1)` generated the configuration for you, it's still useful to know what's going on behind the scenes so you can make changes. We'll focus on three areas:

- Adjusting the view lookup
- Configuring the default template engine
- Enabling view caching to reduce file I/O

First up is the `views` setting.

CHANGING THE LOOKUP DIRECTORY

The following snippet shows the `views` setting that the Express executable created:

```
app.set('views', __dirname + '/views');
```

This specifies the directory that Express will use during view lookup. It's a good idea to use __dirname so that your application isn't dependent on the current working directory being the application's root.

> ### __dirname
> __dirname (with two leading underscores) is a global variable in Node that identifies the directory in which the currently running file *exists*. Often in development this directory will be the same as your current working directory (CWD), but in production the Node executable may run from another directory. Using __dirname helps keep paths consistent across environments.

The next setting is view engine.

USING THE DEFAULT TEMPLATE ENGINE

When express(1) generated the application, the view engine setting was assigned ejs because EJS was the template engine selected by the -e command-line option. This setting enables you to render index rather than index.ejs. Otherwise, Express requires the extension in order to determine which template engine is to be used.

You might be wondering why Express even considers extensions. The use of extensions allows you to use multiple template engines within a single Express application, while providing a clean API for common use cases, because most applications will use one template engine.

Suppose, for example, you find writing RSS feeds easier with another template engine, or perhaps you're migrating from one template engine to another. You might use Pug as the default, and EJS for the /feed route, as indicated in the following code by the .ejs extension:

```
app.set('view engine', 'pug');
app.get('/', function(){
  res.render('index');
 });
app.get('/feed', function(){
  res.render('rss.ejs');
});
```

> **KEEPING PACKAGE.JSON IN SYNC**   Keep in mind that any additional template engines you wish to use should be added to your package.json dependencies object. Try to remember to install packages with npm install --save package-name. Remove them with npm uninstall --save package-name to delete them from node_modules and package.json. This makes experimenting with different template engines easier when you're still trying to figure out which one you want to use.

VIEW CACHING

The view cache setting is enabled by default in the production environment and prevents subsequent render() calls from performing disk I/O. The contents of the templates are saved in memory, greatly improving performance. The side effect of enabling this setting is that you can no longer edit the template files without restarting the server, which is why it's disabled in development. If you're running a staging environment, you'll likely want to enable this option.

As illustrated in figure 6.9, when `view cache` is disabled, the template is read from disk on every request. This is what allows you to make changes to a template without restarting the application. When `view cache` is enabled, the disk is hit only once per template.

You've seen how the view-caching mechanism helps improve performance in a nondevelopment environment. Now let's see how Express locates views in order to render them.

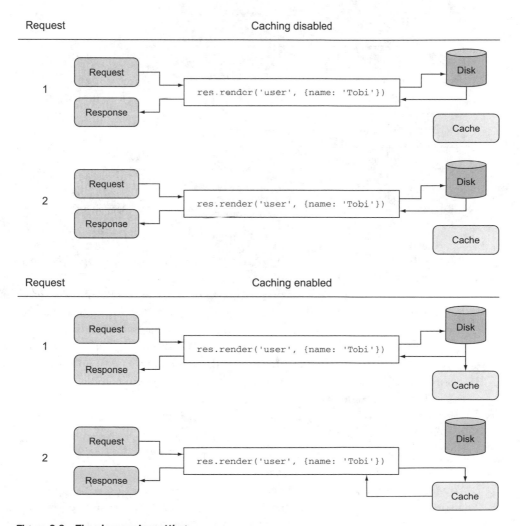

Figure 6.9   The view cache setting

VIEW LOOKUP

The process of looking up a view is similar to the way Node's `require()` works. When `res.render()` or `app.render()` is invoked, Express first checks whether a file exists at an absolute path. Next, Express looks relative to the views directory. Finally, Express tries an index file. This process is represented as a flowchart in figure 6.10.

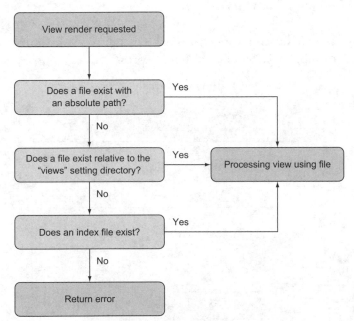

Figure 6.10   Express view lookup process

Because `ejs` is set as the default engine, the render call omits the .ejs extension, and the template file will still be resolved correctly.

As the application evolves, you'll need more views, and sometimes several for a single resource. Using `view lookup` can help with organization—for example, you can use subdirectories related to the resource and create views within them.

Adding subdirectories allows you to eliminate redundant parts of names (such as edit-entry.ejs and show-entry.ejs). Express then adds the `view engine` extension and resolves `res.render('entries/edit')` to ./views/entries/edit.ejs.

Express checks to see whether a file named *index* resides in subdirectories of the view directory. When files are named with a pluralized resource, such as *entries*, this typically implies a resource listing. This means you can use `res.render('entries')` to render the file in views/entries/index.ejs.

METHODS OF EXPOSING DATA TO VIEWS

You've seen how to pass local variables directly to `res.render()` calls, but you can also use a few other mechanisms for this. For example, you can use `app.locals` for application-level variables, and `res.locals` for request-level local variables that are typically set by middleware components prior to the final route-handling method where views are rendered.

The values passed directly to `res.render()` take precedence over values set in `res.locals` and `app.locals`, as figure 6.11 shows.

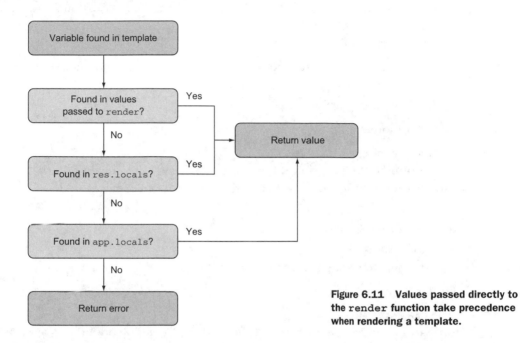

Figure 6.11 Values passed directly to the `render` function take precedence when rendering a template.

By default, Express exposes only one application-level variable, `settings`, to views, which is the object containing all of the values set with `app.set()`. For example, using `app.set('title', 'My Application')` would expose `settings.title` in the template, as shown in the following EJS snippet:

```
<html>
  <head>
    <title><%= settings.title %></title>
  </head>
  <body>
    <h1><%= settings.title %></h1>
    <p>Welcome to <%= settings.title %>.</p>
  </body>
```

Internally, Express exposes this object with the following JavaScript:

```
app.locals.settings = app.settings;
```

That's all there is to it! Now that you've seen how to render views and send data to them, let's look at how routes are defined and see how to write route handlers that can render views for the shoutbox application. You'll also set up database models to persist data.

6.2.4 *Express routing 101*

The primary function of Express routes is to pair a URL pattern with response logic. But routes also can pair a URL pattern with middleware. This allows you to use middleware to provide reusable functionality to certain routes.

In this section, you'll do the following:

- Validate user-submitted content by using route-specific middleware
- Implement route-specific validation
- Implement pagination

Let's explore some of the ways to use route-specific middleware.

VALIDATING USER CONTENT SUBMISSION

To give you something to apply validation to, you're going to finally add the ability to post to the shoutbox application. To add the ability to post, you need to do a few things:

- Create an entry model
- Add entry-related routes
- Create an entry form
- Add logic to create entries using submitted form data

You'll start by creating an entry model.

CREATING AN ENTRY MODEL

Before moving on, you need to install the Node redis module into the project. Install it with `npm install --save redis`. If you don't have Redis installed, go to http://redis.io/ to learn how to install it; if you're using macOS, you can easily install it with Homebrew (http://brew.sh/), and Windows has a Redis Chocolatey package (https://chocolatey.org/).

We're using Redis to cheat a little bit: the features of Redis and ES6 make creating lightweight models without a complex database library easy. If you're feeling ambitious, you could use another database library (see chapter 8 for more about databases in Node).

Let's see how to create a lightweight model to store your shoutbox entries. Create a file to contain the entry model definition at models/entry.js. Add the code contained in the following listing to this file. The entry model will be a simple ES6 class that saves data in a Redis list.

Listing 6.7 A model for entries

```
const redis = require('redis');
const db = redis.createClient();          ◁──┐ Instantiates
                                              │ Redis client
class Entry {
  constructor(obj) {
```

```
      for (let key in obj) {                  ◁───  Iterates keys in
        this[key] = obj[key];                        the object passed
      }
    }

  save(cb) {                                         Converts saved entry
    const entryJSON = JSON.stringify(this);   ◁───   data to JSON string
    db.lpush(                            ◁─────
      'entries',
      entryJSON,                               Saves JSON
      (err) => {                               string to Redis list
        if (err) return cb(err);
        cb();
      }
    );
  }
}
```

Merges values

```
module.exports = Entry;
```

With the basic model fleshed out, you now need to add a function called `getRange`, using the contents of the following listing. This function will allow you to retrieve entries.

Listing 6.8 Logic to retrieve a range of entries

```
class Entry {
  static getRange(from, to, cb) {
    db.lrange('entries', from, to, (err, items) => {    ◁───  Redis lrange function is
      if (err) return cb(err);                                used to retrieve entries
      let entries = [];
      items.forEach((item) => {
        entries.push(JSON.parse(item));      ◁───  Decodes entries previously
      });                                          stored as JSON
      cb(null, entries);
    });
  }
  ...
}
```

With a model created, you can now add routes to create and list entries.

CREATING AN ENTRY FORM

The app has the ability to list entries, but no way to add them. You'll add this capability next, starting by adding the following lines to the routing section of app.js:

```
app.get('/post', entries.form);
app.post('/post', entries.submit);
```

Next, add the following route to routes/entries.js. This route logic will render a template containing a form:

```
exports.form = (req, res) => {
  res.render('post', { title: 'Post' });
};
```

Next, use the EJS template in the following listing to create a template for the form and save it to views/post.ejs.

Listing 6.9   A form for entering post data

```html
<!DOCTYPE html>
<html>
  <head>
    <title><%= title %></title>
    <link rel='stylesheet' href='/stylesheets/style.css' />
  </head>
  <body>
    <% include menu %>
    <h1><%= title %></h1>
    <p>Fill in the form below to add a new post.</p>
    <form action='/post' method='post'>
      <p>
        <input type='text' name='entry[title]' placeholder='Title' />
      </p>
      <p>
        <textarea name='entry[body]' placeholder='Body'></textarea>
      </p>
      <p>
        <input type='submit' value='Post' />
      </p>
    </form>
  </body>
</html>
```

Entry title text

Entry body text

This form uses input names such as entry[title], so extended body parsing is required. To change the body parser, open app.js, and move to the line that reads

```
app.use(bodyParser.urlencoded({ extended: false }));
```

Change this to use extended parsing:

```
app.use(bodyParser.urlencoded({ extended: true }));
```

With form display taken care of, let's move on to creating entries from the submitted form data.

IMPLEMENTING ENTRY CREATION

To add the capability to create entries from submitted form data, add the logic in the next listing to the file routes/entries.js. This logic will add entries when form data is submitted.

Listing 6.10   Add an entry using submitted form data

```
exports.submit = (req, res, next) => {
  const data = req.body.entry;
  const user = res.locals.user;
  const username = user ? user.name : null;
```

Comes from name="entry[…]" in the form

The middleware for loading users will be added in listing 6.28

```
const entry = new Entry({
  username: username,
  title: data.title,
  body: data.body
});
entry.save((err) => {
  if (err) return next(err);
  res.redirect('/');
});
};
```

Now when you use a browser to access /post on your application, you'll be able to add entries. You'll take care of forcing the user to sign in first in listing 6.21.

With posting content taken care of, it's time to render lists of entries.

ADDING FRONT-PAGE DISPLAY OF ENTRIES

Start by creating the file routes/entries.js. Then add the code in the following listing to require the entry model and export a function for rendering a list of entries.

Listing 6.11   Listing entries

```
const Entry = require('../models/entry');
exports.list = (req, res, next) => {
  Entry.getRange(0, -1, (err, entries) => {          // Retrieves entries
    if (err) return next(err);
    res.render('entries', {                           // Renders HTTP response
      title: 'Entries',
      entries: entries,
    });
  });
};
```

With route logic defined for listing entries, you now need to add an EJS template to display them. In the views directory, create a file named entries.ejs and put the following EJS in it.

Listing 6.12   The entries.ejs view

```
<!DOCTYPE html>
<html>
  <head>
    <title><%= title %></title>
    <link rel='stylesheet' href='/stylesheets/style.css' />
  </head>
  <body>
    <% include menu %>
    <% entries.forEach((entry) => { %>
      <div class='entry'>
        <h3><%= entry.title %></h3>
        <p><%= entry.body %></p>
        <p>Posted by <%= entry.username %></p>
      </div>
```

```
    <% }) %>
  </body>
</html>
```

Before running the application, run `touch views/menu.ejs` to create a temporary file that will hold the menu at a later stage. When the views and routes are ready, you need to tell the application where to find the routes.

ADDING ENTRY-RELATED ROUTES

Before you add entry-related routes to the application, you need to make modifications to app.js. First, add the following `require` statement to the top of your app.js file:

```
const entries = require('./routes/entries');
```

Next, also in app.js, change the line containing the text `app.get('/'` to the following to make any requests to the path / to return the entry listing:

```
app.get('/', entries.list);
```

When you run the application, the front page will display a list of entries. Now that entries can be created and listed, let's move on to using route-specific middleware to validate form data.

USING ROUTE-SPECIFIC MIDDLEWARE

Suppose you want the entry text field in the post entry form to be required. The first way you might think of to address this problem is to add it straight in your route call-back, as shown in the following snippet. This approach isn't ideal, however, because it tightly ties the validation logic to this particular form. In many cases, validation logic can be abstracted into reusable components, making development easier, faster, and more declarative:

```
...
exports.submit = (req, res, next) => {
  let data = req.body.entry;
  if (!data.title) {
    res.error('Title is required.');
    res.redirect('back');
    return;
  }
  if (data.title.length < 4) {
    res.error('Title must be longer than 4 characters.');
    res.redirect('back');
    return;
  }
...
```

Express routes can optionally accept middleware of their own, applied only when that route is matched, before the final route callback. The route callbacks themselves that you've been using throughout the chapter aren't treated specially. These are the same as any other middleware, even the ones you're about to create for validation!

Let's get started with route-specific middleware by looking at a simple, but inflexible, way to implement validation as route-specific middleware.

PERFORMING FORM VALIDATION WITH ROUTE-SPECIFIC MIDDLEWARE

The first possibility is to write a few simple, yet specific, middleware components to perform validation. Extending the POST /post route with this middleware might look something like the following:

```
app.post('/post',
  requireEntryTitle,
  requireEntryTitleLengthAbove(4),
  entries.submit
);
```

Note that this route definition, which normally has only a path and routing logic as arguments, has two additional arguments specifying validation middleware.

The two example middleware components in the following listing illustrate how the original validations can be abstracted out. But they're still not modular and work only for the single field entry[title].

Listing 6.13   Two more potential, but imperfect, attempts at validation middleware

```
function requireEntryTitle(req, res, next) {
  const title = req.body.entry.title;
  if (title) {
    next();
  } else {
    res.error('Title is required.');
    res.redirect('back');
  }
}
function requireEntryTitleLengthAbove(len) {
  return (req, res, next) => {
    const title = req.body.entry.title;
    if (title.length > len) {
      next();
    } else {
      res.error(`Title must be longer than ${len}.`);
      res.redirect('back');
    }
  };
}
```

A more viable solution is to abstract the validators and pass the target field name. Let's take a look at approaching it this way.

BUILDING FLEXIBLE VALIDATION MIDDLEWARE

You can pass the field name, as shown in the following snippet. This allows you to reuse validation logic, lessening the amount of code you need to write:

```
app.post('/post',
        validate.required('entry[title]'),
        validate.lengthAbove('entry[title]', 4),
        entries.submit);
```

Swap the line app.post('/post', entries.submit); in the routing section of app.js with this snippet. It's worth noting that the Express community has created many similar libraries for public consumption, but understanding how validation middleware works, and how to author your own, is invaluable.

Let's get on with it. Create a file named ./middleware/validate.js by using the program code in listing 6.14. In validate.js, you'll export several middleware components—in this case, validate.required() and validate.lengthAbove(). The implementation details aren't important; the point of this example is that a small amount of effort can go a long way if the code is common within the application.

Listing 6.14   Validation middleware implementation

```
function parseField(field) {            ⟵    Parses entry[name]
  return field                                notation
    .split(/\[|\]/)
    .filter((s) => s);
}                                             Looks up property based
function getField(req, field) {         ⟵    on parseField() results
  let val = req.body;
  field.forEach((prop) => {
    val = val[prop];
  });
  return val;
}                                        Parses field
exports.required = (field) => {          once
  field = parseField(field);       ⟵
  return (req, res, next) => {                On each request, checks
    if (getField(req, field)) {       ⟵     whether field has a value
      next();                         ⟵
    } else {                                 If it does, moves on
      res.error(`${field.join(' ')} is required`);   ⟵   to next middleware
      res.redirect('back');                                component
    }
  };                                   If it doesn't,
};                                     displays an error
exports.lengthAbove = (field, len) => {
  field = parseField(field);
  return (req, res, next) => {
    if (getField(req, field).length > len) {
      next();
    } else {
      const fields = field.join(' ');
      res.error(`${fields} must have more than ${len} characters`);
      res.redirect('back');
    }
  };
};
```

To make this middleware available to your application, add the following line at the top of app.js:

```
const validate = require('./middleware/validate');
```

If you try the application now, you'll find that the validation will be in effect. This validation API could be made even more fluent, but we'll leave that for you to investigate.

6.2.5 Authenticating users

In this section, you'll create an authentication system for the application from scratch. You'll go through the following steps:

- Implement logic to store and authenticate registered users
- Add account registration functionality
- Allow people to sign in
- Create and use middleware to load users

You'll continue using Redis to implement user accounts. Now let's see how to create a user model to make working with Redis easier in our Node code.

SAVING AND LOADING USER RECORDS

In this section, you'll implement user loading, saving, and authentication. You'll do the following:

- Define application dependencies by using a package.json file
- Create a user model
- Add logic to load and save user data by using Redis
- Secure user passwords by using bcrypt
- Add logic to authenticate attempts to log in

Bcrypt is a salted hashing function that's available as a third-party module designed specifically for hashing passwords. Bcrypt is great for passwords because it incorporates an iteration count argument to make it slower over time.

Before continuing, add bcrypt to your shoutbox project:

```
npm install --save redis bcrypt
```

CREATING A USER MODEL

You now need to create a user model. Add a file named user.js to the models/ directory.

Listing 6.15 is the user model. In this code, the `redis` and `bcrypt` dependencies are required, and then a Redis connection is opened with `redis.createClient()`. The `User` function accepts an object and merges this object's properties into its own. For example, `new User({ name: 'tobi' })` creates an object and sets the object's `name` property to `Tobi`.

Listing 6.15 Starting to create a user model

```
const redis = require('redis');
const bcrypt = require('bcrypt');
const db = redis.createClient();          ◁─── Creates long-running
                                                 Redis connection
class User {
  constructor(obj) {
```

```
    for (let key in obj) {                                              Iterates over the
      this[key] = obj[key];                                            passed-in object
    }                                       Sets each property
  }                                         on the current class
}

module.exports = User;          Exports the
                                User class
```

At the moment, the user mode is just a stub. You'll need to add methods for creating and updating user records as well.

SAVING A USER INTO REDIS

The next functionality you need is the ability to save a user, storing the user's data with Redis. The `save` method shown in listing 6.16 checks whether the user already has an ID, and if so, `save` invokes the `update` method, indexing the user ID by name, and populating a Redis hash with the object's properties. Otherwise, a user who doesn't have an ID is considered a new user; the `user:ids` value is then incremented, which gives the user a unique ID, and the password is hashed before saving into Redis with the same `update` method.

Add the code in the following listing to models/user.js.

Listing 6.16   Updating user records

```
class User {
  // ...
  save(cb) {                          The user already exists
    if (this.id) {                    if an ID is set
      this.update(cb);
    } else {
      db.incr('user:ids', (err, id) => {          Creates a
        if (err) return cb(err);                  unique ID
        this.id = id;
        this.hashPassword((err) => {              Hashes the
          if (err) return cb(err);                password
          this.update(cb);
        });                              Saves the user
      });                               properties
    }
  }

  update(cb) {
    const id = this.id;
    db.set(`user:id:${this.name}`, id, (err) => {          Indexes users
      if (err) return cb(err);                             by name
      db.hmset(`user:${id}`, this, (err) => {              Uses Redis to store the
        cb(err);                                           current class's properties
      });
    });
  }
}
```

Sets the ID so it'll be saved

SECURING USER PASSWORDS

When the user is first created, you need to set a `.pass` property to the user's password. The user-saving logic then replaces the `.pass` property with a hash generated by using the password.

The hash is *salted*. Per-user salting helps to protect against rainbow table attacks: the salt acts as a private key for the hashing mechanism. You can use bcrypt to generate a 12-character salt for the hash with `genSalt()`.

> **RAINBOW TABLE ATTACKS** Rainbow table attacks use precomputed tables to break hashed passwords. You can read more about this topic in Wikipedia: http://en.wikipedia.org/wiki/Rainbow_table.

After the salt is generated, `bcrypt.hash()` is called, which hashes the `.pass` property and the salt. This final `hash` value then replaces the `.pass` property before `.update()` stores it in Redis, ensuring that plain-text passwords aren't saved, only the hash.

The following listing, which you'll add to models/user.js, defines a function that creates the salted hash and stores it in the user's `.pass` property.

Listing 6.17 Adding bcrypt encryption to the user model

```
class User {
  // ...

  hashPassword(cb) {                              Generates a
    bcrypt.genSalt(12, (err, salt) => {    ◁─┘    12-character salt
      if (err) return cb(err);
      this.salt = salt;                           Generates
      bcrypt.hash(this.pass, salt, (err, hash) => {  ◁─┘ hash
        if (err) return cb(err);
        this.pass = hash;        ◁─┐ Sets hash so it'll be
        cb();                      │ saved by update()
      });
    });
  }
}
```

Sets salt so it'll be saved

That's all there is to it.

TESTING THE USER-SAVING LOGIC

To try out saving users, start the Redis server by entering `redis-server` on the command line. Then add the code in the following listing, which creates an example user, to the bottom of models/user.js. You can then run `node models/user.js` on the command line to execute the creation of the example user.

Listing 6.18 Testing the user model

```
const User = require('./models/user');
const user = new User({ name: 'Example', pass: 'test' });  ◁─┘ Creates new user
```

```
user.save((err) => {                         Saves user
  if (err) console.error(err);
  console.log('user id %d', user.id);
});
```

You should see output indicating that the user has been created: user id 1, for example. After testing the user model, remove the code in listing 6.18 from models/user.js.

When you use the redis-cli tool that comes with Redis, you can use the HGETALL command to fetch each key and value of the hash, as the following command-line session demonstrates.

Listing 6.19   Querying with the Redis command-line tool

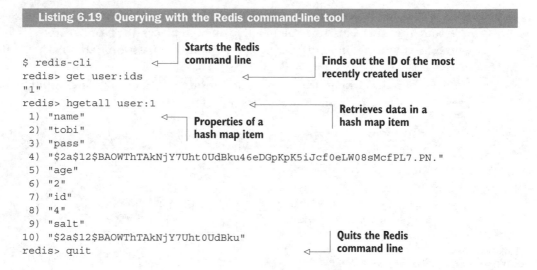

```
$ redis-cli                          Starts the Redis
                                     command line
redis> get user:ids                              Finds out the ID of the most
"1"                                              recently created user
redis> hgetall user:1
 1) "name"                           Properties of a    Retrieves data in a
 2) "tobi"                           hash map item      hash map item
 3) "pass"
 4) "$2a$12$BAOWThTAkNjY7Uht0UdBku46eDGpKpK5iJcf0eLW08sMcfPL7.PN."
 5) "age"
 6) "2"
 7) "id"
 8) "4"
 9) "salt"
10) "$2a$12$BAOWThTAkNjY7Uht0UdBku"               Quits the Redis
redis> quit                                       command line
```

Having defined logic to save a user, you now need to add logic to retrieve user information.

> **OTHER REDIS COMMANDS YOU CAN RUN IN THE REDIS-CLI TOOL**   For more information about Redis commands, see the Redis command reference at http://redis.io/commands.

RETRIEVING USER DATA

When a user attempts to log in to a web application, the user usually enters a username and password into a form, and this data is then submitted to the application for authentication. Once the login form is submitted, you need a method for fetching the user via name.

This logic is defined in the following listing as User.getByName(). The function first performs an ID lookup with User.getId() and then passes the ID that it finds to User.get(), which gets the Redis hash data for that user. Add the following methods to models/user.js.

Listing 6.20 Fetching a user from Redis

```
class User {
  // ...
  static getByName(name, cb) {              Looks up user
    User.getId(name, (err, id) => {          ID by name
      if (err) return cb(err);
      User.get(id, cb);                      Grabs user
    });                                      with the ID
  }

  static getId(name, cb) {                   Gets ID indexed
    db.get(`user:id:${name}`, cb);           by name
  }

  static get(id, cb) {                                   Fetches plain-
    db.hgetall(`user:${id}`, (err, user) => {            object hash
      if (err) return cb(err);
      cb(null, new User(user));              Converts plain object
    });                                      to a new User object
  }
}
```

If you want to try fetching a user, you can try code like this:

```
User.getByName('tobi', (err, user) => {
  console.log(user);
});
```

Having retrieved the hashed password, you can now proceed with authenticating the user.

AUTHENTICATING USER LOGINS

The final component needed for user authentication is a method, defined in the following listing, that takes advantage of the functions defined earlier for user data retrieval. Add this logic to models/user.js.

Listing 6.21 Authenticating a user's name and password

```
static authenticate(name, pass, cb) {
  User.getByName(name, (err, user) => {              Looks up user by name
    if (err) return cb(err);
    if (!user.id) return cb();                        User doesn't exist
    bcrypt.hash(pass, user.salt, (err, hash) => {
      if (err) return cb(err);
      if (hash == user.pass) return cb(null, user);   Match found
      cb();
    });                                    Invalid password
  });
}
```

Hashes the given password

The authentication logic begins by fetching the user by name. If the user isn't found, the callback function is immediately invoked. Otherwise, the user's stored salt and the password submitted are hashed to produce what should be identical to the stored `user.pass` hash. If the submitted and stored hashes don't match, the user has entered invalid credentials. When looking up a key that doesn't exist, Redis will give you an empty hash, which is why the check for `!user.id` is used instead of `!user`.

Now that you're able to authenticate users, you need a way for users to register.

6.2.6 *Registering new users*

To allow users to create new accounts and then sign in, you need both registration and login capabilities.

In this section, you'll do the following to implement registration:

- Map registration and login routes to URL paths
- Add route logic to display a registration form
- Add logic to store user data submitted from the form

The form will look like figure 6.12.

This form is displayed when a user visits /register with a web browser. Later you'll create a similar form that allows users to log in.

Figure 6.12   User registration form

ADDING REGISTRATION ROUTES

To get the registration form to show up, you first want to create a route to render the form and return it to the user's browser for display.

Listing 6.22 shows how you should alter app.js, using Node's module system to import a module defining registration route behavior from the routes directory, and associating HTTP methods and URL paths to route functions. This forms a sort of "front controller." As you can see, there are both GET and POST register routes.

Listing 6.22   Adding registration routes

```
...
const register = require('./routes/register');   ⟵── Requires route logic
...
app.get('/register', register.form);      ⟵┐
app.post('/register', register.submit);   ⟵┴ Adds routes
```

Next, to define the route logic, create an empty file in the routes directory called register.js. Start defining registration route behavior by exporting the following function from routes/register.js—a route that renders the registration template:

```
exports.form = (req, res) => {
  res.render('register', { title: 'Register' });
};
```

This route uses an EJS template, which you'll create next, to define the registration form's HTML.

CREATING A REGISTRATION FORM

To define the registration form's HTML, create a file in the views directory called regis-ter.ejs. You can define this form by using the HTML/EJS detailed in the following listing.

Listing 6.23   A view template that provides a registration form

```
<!DOCTYPE html>
<html>
  <head>
    <title><%= title %></title>
    <link rel='stylesheet' href='/stylesheets/style.css' />
  </head>
  <body>
    <% include menu %>                          Navigation links
    <h1><%= title %></h1>                       will be added later
    <p>Fill in the form below to sign up!</p>   Display of messages
    <% include messages %>                      will be added later
    <form action='/register' method='post'>
      <p>
        <input type='text' name='user[name]' placeholder='Username' />
      </p>
      <p>
        <input type='password' name='user[pass]'
          placeholder='Password' />               User must enter
      </p>                                         a password
      <p>
        <input type='submit' value='Sign Up' />
      </p>
    </form>
  </body>
</html>
```

User must enter a username

Note the use of `include messages`, which includes another template: messages.ejs. This template, which you'll define next, is used to communicate with the user.

RELAYING FEEDBACK TO USERS

During user registration, and in many other parts of a typical application, it can be necessary to relay feedback to the user. A user, for example, may attempt to register with a username that someone else is already using. In this case, you need to tell the user to choose another name.

In your application, the messages.ejs template will be used to display errors. Numerous templates throughout the application will include the messages.ejs template.

To create the messages template, create a file in the views directory called mes-sages.ejs and put the logic in the following snippet into that file. The template logic checks whether the `locals.messages` variable is set. If so, the template cycles through the variable, displaying message objects. Each message object has a `type` property (allowing you to use messages for nonerror notifications if need be) and a `string` property (the message text). Application logic can queue an error for display by adding to the `res.locals.messages` array. After messages are displayed, `removeMessages` is called to empty the messages queue:

```
<% if (locals.messages) { %>
  <% messages.forEach((message) => { %>
    <p class='<%= message.type %>'><%= message.string %></p>
  <% }) %>
  <% removeMessages() %>
<% } %>
```

Figure 6.13 shows the registration form when displaying an error message.

Figure 6.13 Registration form error reporting

Adding a message to `res.locals.messages` is a simple way to communicate with the user, but because `res.locals` doesn't persist across redirects, you need to make it more robust by using sessions to store messages between requests.

STORING TRANSIENT MESSAGES IN SESSIONS

A common web application design pattern is the Post/Redirect/Get (PRG) pattern. In this pattern, a user requests a form, the form data is submitted as an HTTP POST request, and the user is then redirected to another web page. Where the user is redirected to depends on whether the form data was considered valid by the application. If the form data isn't considered valid, the application redirects the user back to the form page. If the form data is valid, the user is redirected to a new web page. The PRG pattern is primarily used to prevent duplicate form submissions.

In Express, when a user is redirected, the content of `res.locals` is reset. If you're storing messages to the user in `res.locals`, the messages are lost before they can be displayed. By storing messages in a session variable, however, you can work around this. Messages can then be displayed on the final redirect page.

To accommodate the ability to queue messages to the user in a session variable, you need to add a module to your application. Create a file named ./middleware/messages.js, and add the following code:

```
const express = require('express');

function message(req) {
  return (msg, type) => {
    type = type || 'info';
    let sess = req.session;
    sess.messages = sess.messages || [];
    sess.messages.push({ type: type, string: msg });
  };
};
```

The `res.message` function provides a way to add messages to a session variable from any Express request. The `express.response` object is the prototype that Express uses for the response objects. Adding properties to this object means they'll then be available to all middleware and routes alike. In the preceding snippet, express.response is assigned to a variable named res to make it easier to add properties on the object and to improve readability.

This feature requires session support. To add support for sessions, you need an Express-compatible middleware module. There's an officially supported package called express-session. Install it with npm install --save express-session, and then add the middleware to app.js, like this:

```
const session = require('express-session');
...
app.use(session({
  secret: 'secret',
  resave: false, saveUninitialized: true
}));
```

It's best to place the middleware after the cookie middleware is inserted (it should be around line 26).

To make it even easier to add messages, add the code in the following snippet. The res.error function allows you to easily add a message of type error to the message queue. Use the res.message function you previously defined in the module:

```
res.error =  msg => this.message(msg, 'error');
```

The last step is to expose these messages to the templates for output. If you don't do this, you have to pass req.session.messages to every res.render() call in the application, which isn't exactly ideal.

To address this, you'll create middleware that populates res.locals.messages with the contents of res.session.messages on each request, effectively exposing the messages to any templates that are rendered. So far, ./middleware/messages.js extends the response prototype, but it doesn't export anything. But adding the following snippet to this file exports the middleware you need:

```
module.exports = (req, res, next) => {
  res.message = message(req);
  res.error = (msg) => {
    return res.message(msg, 'error');
  };
  res.locals.messages = req.session.messages || [];
  res.locals.removeMessages = () => {
    req.session.messages = [];
  };
  next();
};
```

First, a messages template variable is defined to store the session's messages; it's an array that may or may not exist from the previous request (remember that these are session-persisted messages). Next, you need a way to remove the messages from the session; otherwise, they'll build up, because nothing is clearing them.

Now, all you need to do to integrate this new feature is to `require()` the file in app.js. You should mount this middleware below the session middleware because it depends on `req.session` being defined. Note that because this middleware was designed not to accept options and doesn't return a second function, you can call `app.use(messages)` instead of `app.use(messages())`. For future-proofing, it's typically best for third-party middleware to use `app.use(messages())`, regardless of whether it accepts options:

```
...
const register = require('./routes/register');
const messages = require('./middleware/messages');
...
app.use(express.methodOverride());
app.use(express.cookieParser());
   app.use(session({
     secret: 'secret',
     resave: false,
     saveUninitialized: true
   }));
app.use(messages);
...
```

Now you're able to access `messages` and `removeMessages()` within any view, so messages.ejs should work perfectly when included in any template.

With the display of the registration form completed and a way to relay any necessary feedback to the user worked out, let's move on to handling registration submissions.

IMPLEMENTING USER REGISTRATION

You need to create the route function to handle HTTP `POST` requests to /register. This function is called `submit`.

When form data is submitted, the `bodyParser()` middleware populates `req.body` with the submitted data. The registration form uses the object notation `user[name]`, which translates to `req.body.user.name` after parsing by the body parser. Likewise, `req.body.user.pass` is used for the password field.

You need only a small amount of code in the submission route to handle validation, such as ensuring that the username isn't already taken, and to save the new user, as listing 6.24 shows.

Once registration is complete, the `user.id` is assigned to the user's session, which you'll later check to verify that the user is authenticated. If validation fails, a message is exposed to templates as the `messages` variable, via `res.locals.messages`, and the user is redirected back to the registration form.

To add this functionality, add the contents of the following listing to routes/register.js.

Listing 6.24   Creating a user with submitted data

```
const User = require('../models/user');
...
exports.submit = (req, res, next) => {
  const data = req.body.user;
```

```
User.getByName(data.name, (err, user) => {        ◁─┐  Checks whether
  if (err) return next(err);                          username is unique
  // redis will default it
  if (user.id) {                                    ◁─  Username is
    res.error('Username already taken!');               already taken
    res.redirect('back');
  } else {
    user = new User({                          ◁─  Creates a user
      name: data.name,                             with POST data
      pass: data.pass
    });
    user.save((err) => {
      if (err) return next(err);               ┌  Stores uid
      req.session.uid = user.id;             ◁─┘  for authentication
      res.redirect('/');                     ◁─  Redirects to entry
    });                                          listing page
  }
});
};
```

Defers database connection errors and other errors

Saves new user

You can now fire up the application, visit /register, and register a user. The next thing you need is a way for returning registered users to authenticate, via the /login form.

6.2.7 Logging in registered users

Adding login functionality is even simpler than registration, because the bulk of the necessary logic is already in `User.authenticate()`, the general-purpose authentication method defined earlier. In this section, you'll add the following:

- Route logic to display a login form
- Logic to authenticate user data submitted from the form

The form will look like figure 6.14.

You'll start by modifying app.js so login routes are required and the route paths are established:

```
...
const login = require('./routes/login');
...
app.get('/login', login.form);
app.post('/login', login.submit);
app.get('/logout', login.logout);
...
```

Next, you'll add functionality to display a login form.

Figure 6.14   User login form

DISPLAYING A LOGIN FORM

The first step in implementing a login form is creating a file for login- and logout-related routes: routes/login.js. The route logic you need to add to display the login form is nearly identical to the logic used earlier to display the registration form; the only differences are the name of the template displayed and the page title:

```
exports.form = (req, res) => {
  res.render('login', { title: 'Login' });
};
```

The EJS login form that you'll define in ./views/login.ejs, shown in the following listing, is extremely similar to register.ejs as well; the only differences are the instruction text and the route that data is submitted to.

Listing 6.25   A view template for a login form

```
<!DOCTYPE html>
<html>
  <head>
    <title><%= title %></title>
    <link rel='stylesheet' href='/stylesheets/style.css' />
  </head>
  <body>
    <% include menu %>
    <h1><%= title %></h1>
    <p>Fill in the form below to sign in!</p>
    <% include messages %>
    <form action='/login' method='post'>
      <p>
        <input type='text' name='user[name]' placeholder='Username' />     <-- User must enter a username
      </p>
      <p>
        <input type='password' name='user[pass]'
        ➥ placeholder='Password' />     <-- User must enter a password
      </p>
      <p>
        <input type='submit' value='Login' />
      </p>
    </form>
  </body>
</html>
```

Now that you've added the route and template needed to display the login form, the next step is to add logic to handle login attempts.

AUTHENTICATING LOGINS

To handle login attempts, you need to add route logic that will check the submitted username and password and, if they're correct, set a session variable to the user's ID and redirect the user to the home page. The following listing contains this logic, which you should add to routes/login.js.

Listing 6.26   A route to handle logins

```
const User = require('../models/user');
...
exports.submit = (req, res, next) => {                         Checks credentials
  const data = req.body.user;
  User.authenticate(data.name, data.pass, (err, user) => {   <--
    if (err) return next(err);          Delegates errors
    if (user) {                         <-- Handles a user with valid credentials
```

Redirects to entry listing

```
        req.session.uid = user.id;          Stores uid for authentication
        res.redirect('/');
    } else {                                                       Exposes an error
        res.error('Sorry! invalid credentials. ');                message
        res.redirect('back');           Redirects back
    }                                    to login form
  });
};
```

Here, if the user is authenticated by using `User.authenticate()`, `req.session` `.uid` is assigned in the same way as in the `POST /register` route: the session will persist this value, which you can use later to retrieve the `User` or other associated user data. If a match isn't found, an error is set and the form is redisplayed.

Users may also prefer to explicitly log out, so you should provide a link for this somewhere in the application. In app.js, set up the route with this:

```
const login = require('./routes/login');
…
app.get('/logout', login.logout);
```

Then in ./routes/login.js, the following function will remove the session, which is detected by the `session()` middleware, causing the session to be assigned for subsequent requests:

```
exports.logout = (req, res) => {
  req.session.destroy((err) => {
    if (err) throw err;
    res.redirect('/');
  })
};
```

Now that the registration and login pages have been created, the next thing you need to add is a menu so users can reach them. Let's see how to create one.

CREATING A MENU FOR AUTHENTICATED AND ANONYMOUS USERS

In this section, you'll create a menu for both anonymous and authenticated users, allowing them to sign in, register, submit entries, and log out. Figure 6.15 shows the menu for an anonymous user.

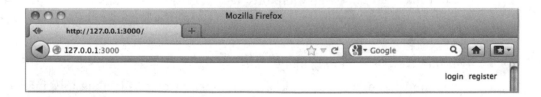

Figure 6.15   User login and registration menu used to access the forms you created

When the user is authenticated, you'll display a different menu showing that user's username, as well as a link to a page for posting messages to the shoutbox and a link allowing the user to log out. Figure 6.16 shows this menu.

Figure 6.16   Menu when the user is authenticated

Each EJS template you've created, representing an application page, has contained the code `<% include menu %>` after the `<body>` tag. This includes the ./views/ menu.ejs template, which you'll create next with the contents of the following listing.

Listing 6.27   Anonymous and authenticated user menu template

```
<% if (locals.user) { %>
  <div id='menu'>
    <span class='name'><%= user.name %></span>          ◁─┐ Menu for
    <a href='/post'>post</a>                               │ logged-in users
    <a href='/logout'>logout</a>
  </div>
<% } else { %>
  <div id='menu'>
    <a href='/login'>login</a>                          ◁─┐ Menu for
    <a href='/register'>register</a>                       │ anonymous users
  </div>
<% } %>
```

In this application, you can assume that if a `user` variable is exposed to the template, a user is authenticated, because you won't be exposing the variable otherwise; you'll see this next. When this variable is present, you can display the username along with the entry submission and logout links. When an anonymous user is visiting, the site login and register links are displayed.

You may be wondering where this `user` local variable comes from—you haven't written it yet. Next you'll write some code to load the logged-in user's data for each request and make this data available to templates.

6.2.8   *Working with user-loading middleware*

A common task when you work with a web application is loading user information from a database, typically represented as a JavaScript object. Having this data readily available makes interacting with the user simpler. For this chapter's application, you'll load the user data on every request, using middleware.

You'll place this middleware script in ./middleware/user.js, requiring the `User` model from the directory above (../models). The middleware function is first exported, and then it checks the session for the user ID. When the user ID is present, a user is authenticated, so it's safe to fetch the user data from Redis.

Because Node is single-threaded, there's no thread-local storage. In the case of an HTTP server, the request and response variables are the only contextual objects available. High-level frameworks could build upon Node to provide additional objects to store the authenticated user, but Express made the choice to stick with the original objects that Node provides. As a result, contextual data is typically stored on the request object, as shown in listing 6.28, where the user is stored as `req.user`; subsequent middleware and routes can access the user object by using the same property.

You may wonder what the assignment to `res.locals.user` is for. `res.locals` is the request-level object that Express provides to expose data to templates, much like `app.locals`. It's also a function that can be used to merge existing objects into itself.

Listing 6.28 Middleware that loads a logged-in user's data

```
const User = require('../models/user');
module.exports = (req, res, next) => {
  const uid = req.session.uid;          // Gets logged-in user
  if (!uid) return next();              // ID from session
  User.get(uid, (err, user) => {        // Gets logged-in user's
    if (err) return next(err);          // data from Redis
    req.user = res.locals.user = user;  // Exposes user data to
    next();                             // response object
  });
};
```

To use this new middleware, first delete all lines in app.js containing the text `user`. You can then require the module as usual and pass it to `app.use()`. In this application, `user` is used above the router, so only the routes and middleware following `user` have access to `req.user`. If you're using middleware that loads data, as this middleware does, you may want to move the `express.static` middleware above it; otherwise, each time a static file is served, a needless round-trip to the database takes place to fetch the user.

The following listing shows how to enable this middleware in app.js.

Listing 6.29 Enabling user-loading middleware

```
const user = require('./middleware/user');
...
app.use(express.session());
app.use(express.static(__dirname + '/public'));
app.use(user);                          // Adds the middleware
app.use(messages);                      // to the application
app.use(app.router);
...
```

If you fire up the application again and visit either the /login or /register pages in your browser, you should see the menu. If you want to style the menu, add the following lines of CSS to public/stylesheets/style.css.

Listing 6.30   CSS that can be added to style.css to style application menus

```
#menu {
  position: absolute;
  top: 15px;
  right: 20px;
  font-size: 12px;
  color: #888;
}
#menu .name:after {
  content: ' -';
}
#menu a {
  text-decoration: none;
  margin-left: 5px;
  color: black;
}
```

With the menu in place, you should be able to register yourself as a user. Then you should see the authenticated user menu with the Post link.

In the next section, you'll learn how to create a public REST API for the application.

6.2.9   *Creating a public REST API*

In this section, you'll implement a RESTful public API for the shoutbox application, so that third-party applications can access and add to publication data. REST enables application data to be queried and changed using verbs and nouns, represented by HTTP methods and URLs, respectively. A REST request typically returns data in a machine-readable form, such as JSON or XML.

To implement an API, you'll do the following:

- Design an API that allows users to show, list, remove, and post entries
- Add Basic authentication
- Implement routing
- Provide JSON and XML responses

Various techniques can be used to authenticate and sign API requests, but implementing the more complex solutions are beyond the scope of this book. To illustrate how to integrate authentication, you'll use the basic-auth package.

DESIGNING THE API

Before proceeding with the implementation, it's a good idea to rough out the routes involved. For this application, you'll prefix the RESTful API with the /api path, but this is a design choice you can alter. For example, you may wish to use a subdomain such as http://api.myapplication.com.

The following snippet illustrates why it can be a good choice to move the callback functions into separate Node modules, versus defining them inline with the `app.VERB()` calls. A single list of routes gives you a clear picture of what you and the rest of your team have implemented, and where the implementation callback lives:

```
app.get('/api/user/:id', api.user);
app.get('/api/entries/:page?', api.entries);
app.post('/api/entry', api.add);
```

ADDING BASIC AUTHENTICATION

As previously mentioned, there are many ways to approach API security and restrictions that fall outside the scope of this book. But it's worth illustrating the process with Basic authentication.

The `api.auth` middleware will abstract this process, because the implementation will live in the soon-to-be-created ./routes/api.js module. The `app.use()` method can be passed a pathname, which is known in Express as a *mount point*. With this mount point, pathnames beginning with /api and any HTTP verb will cause this middleware to be invoked.

The line `app.use('/api', api.auth)`, as shown in the following snippet, should be placed before the middleware that loads user data. This is so that you can later modify the user-loading middleware to load data for authenticated API users:

```
...
const api = require('./routes/api');
...
app.use('/api', api.auth);
app.use(user);
...
```

To perform Basic authentication, install the basic-auth module: `npm install --save basic-auth`. Next, create the ./routes/api.js file, and require both Express and the user model, as shown in the following snippet. The basic-auth package accepts a function to perform the authentication, taking the function signature `(username, password, callback)`. Your `User.authenticate` method is a perfect fit:

```
const auth = require('basic-auth');
const express = require('express');
const User = require('../models/user');

exports.auth = (req, res, next) => {
  const { name, pass } = auth(req);
  User.authenticate(name, pass, (err, user) => {
    if (user) req.remoteUser = user;
    next(err);
  });
};
```

Authentication is ready to roll. Let's move on to implementing the API routes.

IMPLEMENTING ROUTING

The first route you'll implement is GET /api/user/:id. The logic for this route has to first fetch the user by ID, responding with a *404 Not Found* code if the user doesn't exist. If the user exists, the user data will be passed to res.send() to be serialized, and the application will respond with a JSON representation of this data. Add the logic in the following snippet to routes/api.js:

```
exports.user = (req, res, next) => {
  User.get(req.params.id, (err, user) => {
    if (err) return next(err);
    if (!user.id) return res.sendStatus(404);
    res.json(user);
  });
};
```

Next, add the following route path to app.js:

```
app.get('/api/user/:id', api.user);
```

You're now ready to test it.

TESTING USER DATA RETRIEVAL

Fire up the application and test it with the cURL command-line tool. The following snippet shows how to test the application's REST authentication. Credentials are provided in the URL tobi:ferret, which cURL uses to produce the Authorization header field:

```
$ curl http://tobi:ferret@127.0.0.1:3000/api/user/1 -v
```

The following listing shows the result of a successful test. To perform a similar test, you need to make sure you know the ID of a user. Try using redis-cli and GET user:ids if 1 doesn't work and you've registered a user.

Listing 6.31 Test output

```
* About to connect() to local port 80 (#0)
*   Trying 127.0.0.1... connected
* Connected to local (127.0.0.1) port 80 (#0)
* Server auth using Basic with user 'tobi'              Display of HTTP
> GET /api/user/1 HTTP/1.1                              headers sent
> Authorization: Basic Zm9vYmFyYmF6Cg==
> User-Agent: curl/7.21.4 (universal-apple-darwin11.0) libcurl/7.21.4
  ➥ OpenSSL/0.9.8r zlib/1.2.5
> Host: local
> Accept: */*
>                                                       Display of HTTP
< HTTP/1.1 200 OK                                       headers received
< X-Powered-By: Express
< Content-Type: application/json; charset=utf-8         Display of JSON
< Content-Length: 150                                   data received
< Connection: keep-alive
<
{"id":"1","name":"tobi"}
```

REMOVING SENSITIVE USER DATA

As you can see by the JSON response, both the user's password and salt are provided in the response. To alter this, you can implement `.toJSON()` on the `User` in models/user.js:

```
class User {
  // ...
  toJSON() {
    return {
      id: this.id,
      name: this.name
    };
  }
}
```

If `.toJSON` exists on an object, it will be used by `JSON.stringify` calls to get the JSON format. If the cURL request shown earlier was to be issued again, you'd now receive only the ID and name properties:

```
{
  "id": "1",
  "name": "tobi"
}
```

The next thing you'll add to the API is the ability to create entries.

ADDING ENTRIES

The processes for adding an entry via the HTML form and through an API are nearly identical, so you'll likely want to reuse the previously implemented `entries.submit()` route logic.

When adding entries, however, the route logic stores the name of the user, adding the entry in addition to the other details. For this reason, you need to modify the user-loading middleware to populate `res.locals.user` with the user data loaded by the `basic-auth` middleware. The `basic-auth` middleware returns this data, and you set it to `req.remoteUser`. Adding a check for this in the user-loading middleware is straightforward; change the `module.exports` definition in middleware/user.js as follows to make the user-loading middleware work with the API:

```
...
module.exports = (req, res, next) => {
  if (req.remoteUser) {
    res.locals.user = req.remoteUser;
  }
  const uid = req.session.uid;
  if (!uid) return next();
  User.get(uid, (err, user) => {
    if (err) return next(err);
    req.user = res.locals.user = user;
    next();
  });
};
```

With this change made, you're now able to add entries via the API.

One more change to implement, however, is an API-friendly response, rather than redirection to the application's home page. To add this functionality, change the `entry.save` call in routes/entries.js to the following:

```
...
  entry.save(err => {
    if (err) return next(err);
    if (req.remoteUser) {
      res.json({ message: 'Entry added.' });
    } else {
      res.redirect('/');
    }
  });
...
```

Finally, to activate the entry-adding API in your application, add the contents of the following snippet to the routing section of app.js:

```
app.post('/api/entry', entries.submit);
```

By using the following cURL command, you can test adding an entry via the API. Here the title and body data is sent using the same field names that are in the HTML form:

```
$ curl -X POST -d "entry[title]='Ho ho ho'&entry[body]='Santa loves you'"
    http://tobi:ferret@127.0.0.1:3000/api/entry
```

Now that you've added the ability to create entries, you need to add the ability to retrieve entry data.

ADDING ENTRY LISTING SUPPORT

The next API route to implement is `GET /api/entries/:page?`. The route implementation is nearly identical to the existing entry list route in ./routes/entries.js. You also need to add pagination middleware, which is `page()` in the following snippets. You'll add `page()` shortly.

Because the routing logic will be accessing entries, you require the `Entry` model at the top of routes/api.js by using the following line:

```
const Entry = require('../models/entry');
```

Next, add the lines in the following snippet to app.js:

```
const Entry = require('./models/entry');
...
app.get('/api/entries/:page?', page(Entry.count), api.entries);
```

Now add the routing logic in the following snippet to routes/api.js. The difference between this route logic and the similar logic in routes/entries.js reflects the fact that you're no longer rendering a template, but JSON instead:

```
exports.entries = (req, res, next) => {
  const page = req.page;
  Entry.getRange(page.from, page.to, (err, entries) => {
```

```
    if (err) return next(err);
    res.json(entries);
  });
};
```

IMPLEMENTING PAGINATION MIDDLEWARE

For pagination, you use the query-string ?page=N value to determine the current page. Add the following middleware function to ./middleware/page.js.

Listing 6.32   Pagination middleware

```
module.exports = (cb, perpage) => {          ◀── Defaults to
  perpage = perpage || 10;                        10 per page
  return (req, res, next) => {                          ◀── Returns middleware
    let page = Math.max(                                    function
      parseInt(req.params.page || '1', 10),
      1                                          ◀── Parses page param
    ) - 1;                                           as a base 10 integer
    cb((err, total) => {                                  ◀── Invokes the
      if (err) return next(err);                              function passed
      req.page = res.locals.page = {        ◀──
        number: page,                         Stores page properties
        perpage: perpage,                     for future reference
        from: page * perpage,
        to: page * perpage + perpage - 1,
        total: total,
        count: Math.ceil(total / perpage)
      };
      next();                          ◀── Passes control to next
    });                                    middleware component
  }
};
```

Delegates errors (pointing to `if (err) return next(err);`)

This middleware grabs the value assigned to ?page=N; for example, ?page=1. It then fetches the total number of results and exposes the page object with precomputed values to any views that may later be rendered. These values are computed outside the template to allow for a cleaner template containing less logic.

TESTING THE ENTRIES ROUTE

The following cURL command requests entry data from the API:

```
$ curl http://tobi:ferret@127.0.0.1:3000/api/entries
```

This cURL command should result in output similar to the following JSON:

```
[
  {
    "username": "rick",
    "title": "Cats can't read minds",
    "body": "I think you're wrong about the cat thing."
  },
  {
    "username": "mike",
```

```
        "title": "I think my cat can read my mind",
        "body": "I think cat can hear my thoughts."
    },
...
```

With basic API implementation covered, let's move on to how APIs can support multiple response formats.

6.2.10 *Enabling content negotiation*

Content negotiation enables a client to specify the formats that it's willing to accept, and which it prefers. In this section, you'll provide JSON and XML representations of the API content so that the API consumers can decide what they want.

HTTP provides the content negotiation mechanism via the `Accept` header field. For example, a client who prefers HTML but is willing to accept plain text could set the following request header:

```
Accept: text/plain; q=0.5, text/html
```

The *qvalue,* or *quality value* (q=0.5 in this example), indicates that even though text/html is specified second, it's favored by 50% over text/plain. Express parses this information and provides a normalized `req.accepted` array:

```
[{ value: 'text/html', quality: 1 },
 { value: 'text/plain', quality: 0.5 }]
```

Express also provides the `res.format()` method, which accepts an array of MIME types and callbacks. Express will determine what the client is willing to accept and what you're willing to provide, and it'll invoke the appropriate callback.

IMPLEMENTING CONTENT NEGOTIATION

Implementing content negotiation for the `GET /api/entries` route, in routes/api.js, might look something like listing 6.33. JSON is supported as it was before—you serialize the entries as JSON with `res.send()`. The XML callback iterates the entries and writes to the socket as it does so. Note that there's no need to set the `Content-Type` explicitly; `res.format()` sets it to the associated type automatically.

Listing 6.33 Implementing content negotiation

```
exports.entries = (req, res, next) => {
  const page = req.page;                                          Fetches entry
  Entry.getRange(page.from, page.to, (err, entries) => {   ◁──┘   data
    if (err) return next(err);
    res.format({                                   ◁── Responds differently, based
      'application/json': () => {                        on Accept header value
        res.send(entries);
      },
      'application/xml': () => {                   ◁── XML response
        res.write('<entries>\n');
        entries.forEach((entry) => {
          res.write(```
```

JSON response →

```
            <entry>
              <title>${entry.title}</title>
              <body>${entry.body}</body>
              <username>${entry.username}</username>
            </entry>
            ```
          );
        });
        res.end('</entries>');
      }
    })
  });
};
```

If you set a default response format callback, this will execute if a user hasn't requested a format you've explicitly handled.

The `res.format()` method also accepts an extension name that maps to an associated MIME type. For example, `json` and `xml` can be used in place of `application/json` and `application/xml`, as the following snippet shows:

```
...
res.format({
  json: () => {
    res.send(entries);
  },
  xml: () => {
    res.write('<entries>\n');
    entries.forEach((entry) => {
      res.write(```
        <entry>
            <title>${entry.title}</title>
          <body>${entry.body}</body>
          <username>${entry.username}</username>
        </entry>
        ```
      );
    });
    res.end('</entries>');
  }
})
...
```

RESPONDING WITH XML

Writing a bunch of custom logic in the route in order to respond with XML may not be the cleanest way to go, so let's see how to use the view system to clean this up.

Create a template named ./views/entries/xml.ejs with the following EJS iterating the entries to generate `<entry>` tags.

Listing 6.34 Using an EJS template to generate XML

```
<entries>
<% entries.forEach(entry => { %>          ⟵──┐ Cycles through
                                               each entry
```

```
  <entry>
    <title><%= entry.title %></title>          ⟵⎯⎤  Outputs the fields
    <body><%= entry.body %></body>                  ⎦
    <username><%= entry.username %></username>
  </entry>
<% }) %>
</entries>
```

The XML callback can now be replaced with a single `res.render()` call, passing the `entries` array, as shown in the following code:

```
...
  xml: () => {
    res.render('entries/xml', { entries: entries });
  }
})
...
```

You're now ready to test the XML version of the API. Enter the following in the command line to see the XML output:

```
curl -i -H 'Accept: application/xml'
➥ http://tobi:ferret@127.0.0.1:3000/api/entries
```

6.3   *Summary*

- Connect is an HTTP framework that lets you stack middleware components before and after requests are processed.
- Connect middleware components are functions that accept Node's request and response objects, as well as a function that calls the next middleware and an optional error object.
- Express web applications are also built with middleware components.
- You can build REST APIs with Express by using HTTP verbs to define routes.
- Express routes can respond with JSON, HTML, or other data formats.
- Express has a simple template engine API that supports many engines.

Web application templating

7

This chapter covers

- Organizing applications with templating
- Creating templates by using Embedded JavaScript
- Learning minimalist templating with Hogan
- Using Pug to create templates

In chapters 3 and 6, you learned some basics about templates in Express applications in order to create views. In this chapter, you'll focus exclusively on templating, learning how to use three popular template engines, and how to use templating to keep any web application's code clean by separating logic from presentation markup.

If you're familiar with templating and the Model-View-Controller (MVC) pattern, you can skim through to section 7.2, where you'll start learning about the template engines detailed in this chapter, which include Embedded JavaScript, Hogan, and Pug. If you're not familiar with templating, keep reading—you'll explore it conceptually in the next few sections.

7.1   Using templating to keep code clean

You can use the MVC pattern to develop conventional web applications in Node as well as in nearly every other web technology. One of the key concepts in MVC is the separation of logic, data, and presentation. In MVC web applications, the user typically requests a resource from the server, which causes the *controller* to request application data from the *model* and then pass the data to the *view*, which finally formats the data for the end user. This view portion of the MVC pattern is often implemented by using one of various templating languages. When an application uses templating, the view relays selected values, returned by the model, to a *template engine*, and specifies the template file that defines how to display the provided values.

Figure 7.1 shows how templating logic fits into the overall architecture of an MVC application. Template files typically contain placeholders for application values as well as HTML, CSS, and sometimes small bits of client-side JavaScript to implement dynamic behavior, including displaying third-party widgets such as Facebook's Like button, or to trigger interface behavior, such as hiding or revealing parts of the page. Because template files focus on presentation rather than logic, front-end developers and server-side developers can work on them, which can help with a project's division of labor.

In this section, we'll render HTML with, and without, a template to show you the difference. But first, let's start with an example of templating in action.

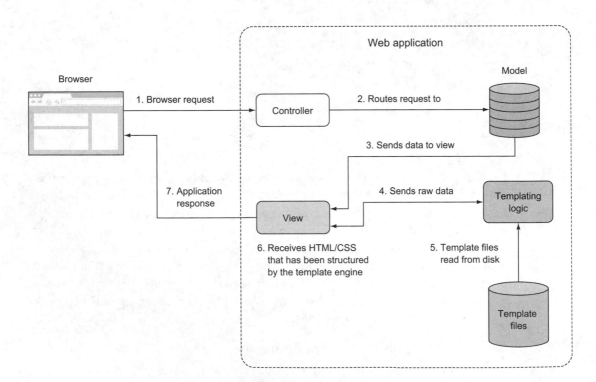

Figure 7.1 The flow of an MVC application and its interaction with the template layer

7.1.1 Templating in action

As a quick illustration of applying templating, let's look at the problem of elegantly outputting HTML from a simple blogging application. Each blog entry has a title, date of entry, and body text. The blog looks similar to figure 7.2 in a web browser.

Blog entries are read from a text file formatted like the following snippet from entries.txt. The - - - in the following listing indicates where one entry stops and another begins.

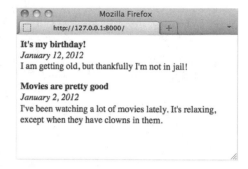

Figure 7.2 Example blog application browser output

Listing 7.1 Blog entries text file

```
title: It's my birthday!
date: January 12, 2016
I am getting old, but thankfully I'm not in jail!
---
title: Movies are pretty good
date: January 2, 2016
I've been watching a lot of movies lately. It's relaxing,
except when they have clowns in them.
```

The blog application code in blog.js starts by requiring necessary modules and reading in the blog entries, as shown in the following listing.

Listing 7.2 Blog entry file-parsing logic for a simple blogging application

```
const fs = require('fs');
const http = require('http');
function getEntries() {                                    ← Function to read and
  const entries = [];                                        parse blog entry text
  let entriesRaw = fs.readFileSync('./entries.txt', 'utf8'); ← Reads blog entry
  entriesRaw = entriesRaw.split('---');                        data from file
  entriesRaw.map((entryRaw) => {                             ← Parses text into individual
    const entry = {};                                          blog entries
    const lines = entryRaw.split('\n');                      ← Parses entry text
    lines.map((line) => {                                      into individual lines
      if (line.indexOf('title: ') === 0) {
        entry.title = line.replace('title: ', '');
      } else if (line.indexOf('date: ') === 0) {
        entry.date = line.replace('date: ', '');
      } else {
        entry.body = entry.body || '';
        entry.body += line;
      }
    });
    entries.push(entry);
```

Parses lines into entry properties

```
  });
  return entries;
}
const entries = getEntries();
console.log(entries);
```

The following code, when added to the blog application, defines an HTTP server. When the server receives an HTTP request, it returns a page containing all blog entries. This page is rendered using a function called `blogPage`, which you'll define next:

```
const server = http.createServer((req, res) => {
  const output = blogPage(entries);
  res.writeHead(200, {'Content-Type': 'text/html'});
  res.end(output);
});
server.listen(8000);
```

Now you need to define the `blogPage` function, which renders the blog entries into a page of HTML that can be sent to the user's browser. You'll implement this by trying two approaches:

- Rendering HTML without a template
- Rendering HTML using a template

Let's look at rendering without a template first.

7.1.2 *Rendering HTML without a template*

The blog application could output the HTML directly, but including the HTML with the application logic would result in clutter. In the following listing, the `blogPage` function illustrates a nontemplated approach to displaying blog entries.

> **Listing 7.3   Template engines separate presentation details from application logic**

```
function blogPage(entries) {
  let output = `
    <html>
    <head>
      <style type="text/css">
        .entry_title { font-weight: bold; }
        .entry_date { font-style: italic; }
        .entry_body { margin-bottom: 1em; }
      </style>
    </head>
    <body>
  `;
  entries.map(entry => {                          ⟵─┐ Too much HTML
    output += `                                       │ interspersed with logic
      <div class="entry_title">${entry.title}</div>
      <div class="entry_date">${entry.date}</div>
      <div class="entry_body">${entry.body}</div>
    `;
  });
```

```
  output += '</body></html>';
  return output;
}
```

Note that all of this presentation-related content, CSS definitions, and HTML adds many lines to the application.

RENDERING HTML BY USING A TEMPLATE

Rendering HTML by using templating allows you to remove the HTML from the application logic, cleaning up the code considerably.

To try the demos in this section, you need to install the Embedded JavaScript (EJS) module into your application directory. You can do this by entering the following on the command line:

```
npm install ejs
```

The following snippet loads a template from a file and then defines a new version of the `blogPage` function, this time using the EJS template engine, which we'll show you how to use in section 7.2:

```
const fs = require('fs');
const ejs = require('ejs');
const template = fs.readFileSync('./templatess/blog_page.ejs', 'utf8');
function blogPage(entries) {
  const values = { entries };
  return ejs.render(template, values);
}
```

The full listing can be found in this book's listings under ch07-templates/listing7_4/. The EJS template file contains HTML markup (keeping it out of the application logic) and placeholders that indicate where data passed to the template engine should be put. The EJS template file that shows the blog entries contains the HTML and placeholders shown in the following listing.

Listing 7.4 An EJS template for displaying blog entries

```
<html>
  <head>
    <style type="text/css">
      .entry_title { font-weight: bold; }
      .entry_date { font-style: italic; }
      .entry_body { margin-bottom: 1em; }
    </style>
  </head>
  <body>
    <% entries.map(entry => { %>                    ◁———  Placeholder that loops
      <div class="entry_title"><%= entry.title %></div>    through blog entries
      <div class="entry_date"><%= entry.date %></div>  ◁——— Placeholders for bits
      <div class="entry_body"><%= entry.body %></div>       of data in each entry
    <% }); %>
  </body>
</html>
```

Community-contributed Node modules also provide template engines, and a wide variety of them exist. If you consider HTML and/or CSS inelegant, because HTML requires closing tags and CSS requires opening and closing braces, take a closer look at template engines. They allow template files to use special languages (such as the Pug language, which we cover later in this chapter) that provide a shorthand way of specifying HTML, CSS, or both.

These template engines can make your templates cleaner, but you may not want to take the time to learn an alternative way of specifying HTML and CSS. Ultimately, what you decide to use comes down to a matter of personal preference.

In the rest of this chapter, you'll learn how to incorporate templating in your Node applications through the lens of three popular template engines:

- The Embedded JavaScript (EJS) engine
- The minimalist Hogan engine
- The Pug template engine

Each engine allows you to write HTML in an alternative way. Let's start with EJS.

7.2 Templating with Embedded JavaScript

Embedded JavaScript (https://github.com/visionmedia/ejs) takes a fairly straightforward approach to templating, and it will be familiar territory for folks who've used template engines in other languages, such as Java Server Pages (JSP), Smarty (PHP), Embedded Ruby (ERB), and so on. EJS allows you to embed EJS tags as placeholders for data within HTML. EJS also lets you execute raw JavaScript logic in your templates for tasks such as conditional branching and iteration, much as PHP does.

In this section, you'll learn how to do the following:

- Create EJS templates
- Use EJS filters to provide commonly needed, presentation-related functionality, such as text manipulation, sorting, and iteration
- Integrate EJS with your Node applications
- Use EJS for client-side applications

Let's dive deeper into the world of EJS templating.

7.2.1 Creating a template

In the world of templating, the data sent to the template engine for rendering is sometimes called the *context*. The following is a bare-bones example of Node using EJS to render a simple template in a context:

```
const ejs = require('ejs');
const template = '<%= message %>';
const context = { message: 'Hello template!' };
console.log(ejs.render(template, context));
```

Note the use of `locals` in the second argument sent to `render`. The second argument can include rendering options as well as context data, which means the use of `locals` ensures that individual bits of context data aren't interpreted as EJS options. But it's possible in most cases to pass the context itself as the second option, as the following render call illustrates:

```
console.log(ejs.render(template, context));
```

If you pass a context to EJS directly as the second argument to render, make sure you don't name context values by using any of the following terms: `cache`, `client`, `close`, `compileDebug`, `debug`, `filename`, `open`, or `scope`. These values are reserved to allow the changing of template engine settings.

CHARACTER ESCAPING

When rendering, EJS escapes any special characters in context values, replacing them with HTML entity codes. This is intended to prevent cross-site scripting (XSS) attacks, in which malicious web application users attempt to submit JavaScript as data in the hopes that when displayed, it'll execute in some other user's browser. The following code shows EJS's escaping at work:

```
const ejs = require('ejs');
const template = '<%= message %>';
const context = {message: "<script>alert('XSS attack!');</script>"};
console.log(ejs.render(template, context));
```

The previous code displays the following output:

```
&lt;script&gt;alert('XSS attack!');&lt;/script&gt;
```

If you trust the data being used in your template and don't want to escape a context value in an EJS template, you can use `<%-` instead of `<%=` in your template tag, as the following code demonstrates:

```
const ejs = require('ejs');
const template = '<%- message %>';
const context = {
  message: "<script>alert('Trusted JavaScript!');</script>"
};
console.log(ejs.render(template, context));
```

Note that if you don't like the characters used by EJS to specify tags, you can customize them, like so:

```
const ejs = require('ejs');
ejs.delimiter = '$'
const template = '<$= message $>';
const context = { message: 'Hello template!' };
console.log(ejs.render(template, context));
```

Now that you know the basics of EJS, let's look at some more detailed examples.

7.2.2   *Integrating EJS into your application*

Because it's awkward to store templates in files along with application code, and doing so clutters up your code, we'll show you how to use Node's filesystem API to read them from separate files.

Move to a working directory and create a file named app.js containing the code in the following listing.

Listing 7.5   Storing template code in files

```
const ejs = require('ejs');
const fs = require('fs');
const http = require('http');
const filename = './templates/students.ejs';          Notes location
                                                      of template file
const students = [                          Data to pass to
  { name: 'Rick LaRue', age: 23 },          template engine
  { name: 'Sarah Cathands', age: 25 },
  { name: 'Bob Dobbs', age: 37 }
];

const server = http.createServer((req, res) => {      Creates HTTP
  if (req.url === '/') {                               server
    fs.readFile(filename, (err, data) => {             Reads template
      const template = data.toString();                from file
      const context = { students: students };
      const output = ejs.render(template, context);    Renders
      res.setHeader('Content-type', 'text/html');      template
      res.end(output);
    });                                     Sends HTTP
  } else {                                  response
    res.statusCode = 404;
    res.end('Not found');
  }
});

server.listen(8000);
```

Next, create a child directory called templates. You'll keep your templates in this directory. Create a file named students.ejs in the templates directory. Enter the code in the following listing into templates/students.ejs.

Listing 7.6   EJS template that renders an array of students

```
<% if (students.length) { %>
  <ul>
    <% students.forEach((student) => { %>
      <li><%= student.name %> (<%= student.age %>)</li>
    <% }) %>
  </ul>
<% } %>
```

CACHING EJS TEMPLATES

EJS supports optional, in-memory caching of template functions: after parsing your template file once, EJS will store the function that's created by the parsing. Rendering a cached template will be faster because the parsing step can be skipped.

If you're doing initial development of a Node web application, and you want to see any changes you make to your template files reflected immediately, don't enable caching. But if you're deploying an application to production, enabling caching is a quick, easy win. Caching is conditionally enabled via the NODE_ENV environment variable.

To try out caching, change the call to EJS's render function in the previous example to the following:

```
const cache = process.env.NODE_ENV === 'production';
const output = ejs.render(
  template,
  { students, cache, filename }
);
```

Note that the filename option doesn't necessarily have to be a file; you can use a unique value that identifies whichever template you're rendering.

Now that you've learned how to integrate EJS with your Node applications, let's look at how EJS can be used in a different way: in web browsers.

7.2.3 Using EJS for client-side applications

To use EJS on the client side, you first need to download the EJS engine to your working directory, as shown by the following commands:

```
cd /your/working/directory
curl -O https://raw.githubusercontent.com/tj/ejs/master/lib/ejs.js
```

After you download the ejs.js file, you can use EJS in your client-side code. The following listing shows a simple client-side application of EJS. If you save this file as index.html, you should be able to open it in a browser to see the results.

Listing 7.7 Using EJS to add templating capabilities to the client side

```html
<html>
  <head>
  <title>EJS example</title>
    <script src="ejs.js"></script>
    <script
      src="http://ajax.googleapis.com/ajax/libs/jquery/1.8/jquery.js">
    </script>
  </head>
  <body>
    <div id="output"></div>
    <script>
      const template = "<%= message %>";
```

Includes jQuery library for DOM manipulation

Placeholder for rendered template output

Template to use to render content

Data to use with template →

```
        const context = { message: 'Hello template!' };
        $(document).ready(() => {                                    ← Waits until browser
          $('#output').html(                                            loads page
            ejs.render(template, context)        ←
          );                                      ┐ Renders template to
        });                                         div with ID "output"
      </script>
    </body>
</html>
```

You've now learned how to use a fully featured Node template engine, so it's time to look at the Hogan template engine, which deliberately limits the functionality available to templating code.

7.3 *Using the Mustache templating language with Hogan*

Hogan.js (https://github.com/twitter/hogan.js) is a template engine that was created by Twitter for its templating needs. Hogan is an implementation of the popular Mustache (http://mustache.github.com/) template language standard, which was created by GitHub's Chris Wanstrath.

Mustache takes a minimalist approach to templating. Unlike EJS, the Mustache standard deliberately doesn't include conditional logic, or any built-in content-filtering capabilities other than escaping content to prevent XSS attacks. Mustache advocates that template code should be kept as simple as possible.

In this section you'll learn

- How to create and implement Mustache templates in your application
- How to use the various template tags in the Mustache standard
- How to organize your templates by using partials
- How to fine-tune Hogan with your own delimiters and other options

Let's look at the alternative approach Hogan provides for templating.

7.3.1 *Creating a template*

To use Hogan in an application, or to try the demos in this section, you need to install Hogan in your application directory (ch07-templates/hogan-snippet). You can do this by entering the following command on the command line:

```
npm i --save hogan.js
```

The following is a bare-bones example of Node using Hogan to render a simple template in a context. Running it outputs the text *Hello template!*

```
const hogan = require('hogan.js');
const templateSource = '{{message}}';
const context = { message: 'Hello template!' };
const template = hogan.compile(templateSource);
console.log(template.render(context));
```

Now that you know how to process Mustache templates with Hogan, let's look at what tags Mustache supports.

7.3.2 *Using Mustache tags*

Mustache tags are conceptually similar to EJS's tags. Mustache tags serve as placeholders for variable values, indicate where iteration is needed, and allow you to augment Mustache's functionality and add comments to your templates.

DISPLAYING SIMPLE VALUES

To display a context value in a Mustache template, include the name of the value in double braces. Braces, in the Mustache community, are known as *mustaches*. If you want to display the value for context item name, for example, you use the Hogan tag {{name}}.

Like most template engines, Hogan escapes content by default to prevent XSS attacks. But to display an unescaped value in Hogan, you can either add a third mustache or prepend the name of the context item with an ampersand. Using the previous name example, you could display the context value unescaped by either using the {{{name}}} or {{&name}} tag formats.

If you want to add a comment in a Mustache template, you can use this format: {{! This is a comment }}.

SECTIONS: ITERATING THROUGH MULTIPLE VALUES

Although Hogan docsn't allow the inclusion of logic in templates, it does include an elegant way to iterate through multiple values in a context item by using Mustache *sections*. The following context, for example, contains an item with an array of values:

```
const context = {
  students: [
    { name: 'Jane Narwhal', age: 21 },
    { name: 'Rick LaRue', age: 26 }
  ]
};
```

If you want to create a template that displays each student in a separate HTML paragraph, with output similar to the following, it's a straightforward task using a Hogan template:

```
<p>Name: Jane Narwhal, Age: 21 years old</p>
<p>Name: Rick LaRue, Age: 26 years old</p>
```

The following template produces the desired HTML:

```
{{#students}}
  <p>Name: {{name}}, Age: {{age}} years old</p>
{{/students}}
```

INVERTED SECTIONS: DEFAULT HTML WHEN VALUES DON'T EXIST

What if the value of the students item in the context data isn't an array? If the value is a single object, for example, the template will display it. But sections won't display if the corresponding item's value is undefined or false, or is an empty array.

If you want your template to output a message indicating that values don't exist for a section, Hogan supports what Mustache calls *inverted sections*. The following template code, if added to the previous student display template, would display a message when no student data exists in the context:

```
{{^students}}
  <p>No students found.</p>
{{/students}}
```

SECTION LAMBDAS: CUSTOM FUNCTIONALITY IN SECTION BLOCKS

In order to allow developers to augment Mustache's functionality, the Mustache standard lets you define section tags that process template content through a function call, rather than iterating through arrays. This is called a *section lambda*.

Listing 7.8 shows an example of using a section lambda to add Markdown support when rendering a template. Note that the example uses the github-flavored-markdown module, which you install by entering npm install github-flavored-markdown --dev on your command line. If you're using the book's source code, run npm install from ch07-templates/listing7_8 to run the example.

In the following listing, the **Name** in the template gets rendered to Name when passing through the Markdown parser called by the section lambda logic.

Listing 7.8   Using a lambda in Hogan

```
const hogan = require('hogan.js');
const md = require('github-flavored-markdown');      ⊲——| Requires Markdown parser
const templateSource = `
  {{#markdown}}**Name**: {{name}}{{/markdown}}       ⊲——| Mustache template also
`;                                                         contains Markdown formatting
const context = {
  name: 'Rick LaRue',
  markdown: () => text => md.parse(text)             ⊲——| Template context includes a
};                                                         section lambda to parse
const template = hogan.compile(templateSource);            Markdown in the template
console.log(template.render(context));
```

Section lambdas allow you to easily implement features such as caching and translation mechanisms in your templates.

PARTIALS: REUSING TEMPLATES WITHIN OTHER TEMPLATES

When writing templates, you want to avoid unnecessarily repeating the same code in multiple templates. One way to avoid this is to create partials. *Partials* are templates used as building blocks that are included in other templates. Another use of partials is to break up complicated templates into simpler templates.

The following listing, for example, uses a partial to separate the template code used to display student data from the main template.

Listing 7.9   Using partials in Hogan

```
const hogan = require('hogan.js');
const studentTemplate = `                 ⊲——| Template code used for partial
  <p>
```

```
      Name: {{name}},
      Age: {{age}} years old
    </p>
`;
const mainTemplate = `                    ←——|  Main template code
  {{#students}}
    {{>student}}
  {{/students}}
`;
const context = {
  students: [{
    name: 'Jane Narwhal',
    age: 21
  }, {
    name: 'Rick LaRue',
    age: 26
  }]
};
const template = hogan.compile(mainTemplate);     ←—
const partial = hogan.compile(studentTemplate);
const html = template.render(context, {student: partial });  ←—
console.log(html);
```

Compiling the main
and partial templates

Rendering the
main template
and partial

7.3.3 *Fine-tuning Hogan*

Hogan is fairly simple to use—after you've learned its vocabulary of tags, you should be off and running. You may need to tweak only a couple of options as you use it.

If you don't like Mustache-style braces, you can change the delimiters Hogan uses by passing the `compile` method an option to override them. The following example shows compiling in Hogan using EJS-style delimiters:

```
hogan.compile(text, { delimiters: '<% %>' });
```

In addition to Mustache, other template languages are available. One that attempts to eliminate as much of HTML's noise as possible is Pug.

7.4 *Templating with Pug*

Pug (http://pugjs.org), formerly known as Jade, offers an alternative way to specify HTML. It's the default template engine in Express. The key difference between Pug and the majority of other templating systems is the use of meaningful whitespace. When creating a template in Pug, you use indentation to indicate HTML tag nesting. HTML tags also don't have to be explicitly closed, which eliminates the problem of accidentally closing tags prematurely or not at all. Using indentation also results in templates that are less visually dense and easier to maintain.

For a quick example of this at work, let's look at how you'd represent this snippet of HTML:

```
<html>
  <head>
    <title>Welcome</title>
  </head>
  <body>
```

```
    <div id="main" class="content">
      <strong>"Hello world!"</strong>
    </div>
  </body>
</html>
```

This HTML could be represented using the following Pug template:

```
html
  head
    title Welcome
  body
    div.content#main
      strong "Hello world!"
```

Pug, like EJS, allows you to embed JavaScript, and you can use it on the server or client side. But Pug offers additional features, such as support for template inheritance and mixins. Mixins allow you to define easily reusable mini-templates to represent the HTML used for commonly occurring visual elements, such as item lists and boxes. Mixins are similar in concept to the Hogan.js partials, which you learned about in the previous section. Template inheritance makes it easy to organize the Pug templates needed to render a single HTML page into multiple files. You'll learn about these features in detail later in this section. To install Pug in a Node application directory, enter the following on the command line:

```
npm install pug --save
```

In this section, you'll learn

- Pug basics, such as specifying class names, attributes, and block expansion
- How to add logic to your Pug templates by using built-in keywords
- How to organize your templates by using inheritance, blocks, and mixins

To get started, let's look at the basics of Pug usage and syntax.

7.4.1   *Pug basics*

Pug uses the same tag names as HTML, but it lets you lose the opening and closing < and > characters and instead uses indentation to express tag nesting. A tag can have one or more CSS classes associated with it by adding `.<classname>`. A `div` element with the content and sidebar classes applied to it would be represented like this:

```
div.content.sidebar
```

CSS IDs are assigned by adding `#<ID>` to the tag. You add a CSS ID of `featured _content` to the previous example by using the following Pug representation:

```
div.content.sidebar#featured_content
```

USING DIV TAG SHORTHAND

Because the `div` tag is commonly used in HTML, Pug offers a shorthand way of specifying it. The following example renders to the same HTML as the previous example:

```
.content.sidebar#featured_content
```

Now that you know how to specify HTML tags and their CSS classes and IDs, let's look at how to specify HTML tag attributes.

SPECIFYING TAG ATTRIBUTES

You can specify tag attributes by enclosing the attributes in parentheses, separating the specification of each attribute from the next with a comma. You can specify a hyperlink that'll open in a different tab by using the following Pug representation:

```
a(href='http://nodejs.org', target='_blank')
```

Because the specification of tag attributes can lead to long lines of Pug, the template engine provides you with some flexibility. The following Pug is valid and equivalent to the previous example:

```
a(href='http://nodejs.org',
  target='_blank')
```

You can also specify attributes that don't require a value. The next Pug example shows the specification of an HTML form that includes a `select` element with an option preselected:

```
strong Select your favorite food:
form
  select
    option(value='Cheese') Cheese
    option(value='Tofu', selected) Tofu
Specifying tag content
```

In the previous code snippet, you can also see examples of tag content: `Select your favorite food:` after the `strong` tag; `Cheese` after the first `option` tag; and `Tofu` after the second `option` tag.

This is the normal way to specify tag content in Pug, but it's not the only way. Although this style is great for short bits of content, it can result in Pug templates with overly long lines if a tag's content is lengthy. Luckily, as the following example shows, Pug allows you to specify tag content by using the | character:

```
textarea
  | This is some default text
  | that the user should be
  | provided with.
```

If the HTML tag, such as the `style` and `script` tags, accepts only text (meaning it doesn't allow nested HTML elements), then the | characters can be left out entirely, as the following example shows:

```
style
  h1 {
    font-size: 6em;
    color: #9DFF0C;
  }
```

Having two separate ways to express long tag content and short tag content helps you keep your Pug templates looking elegant. Pug also supports an alternative way to express nesting, called *block expansion.*

KEEPING IT ORGANIZED WITH BLOCK EXPANSION

Pug normally expresses nesting through indentation, but sometimes indentation can lead to excess whitespace. For example, here's a Pug template that uses indentation to define a simple list of links:

```
ul
  li
    a(href='http://nodejs.org/') Node.js homepage
  li
    a(href='http://npmjs.org/') NPM homepage
  li
    a(href='http://nodebits.org/') Nodebits blog
```

A more compact way to express the previous example is by using Pug block expansion. With block expansion, you add a colon after your tag to indicate nesting. The following code generates the same output as the previous listing, but in four lines instead of seven:

```
ul
  li: a(href='http://nodejs.org/') Node.js homepage
  li: a(href='http://npmjs.org/') NPM homepage
  li: a(href='http://nodebits.org/') Nodebits blog
```

Now that you've had a good look at how to represent markup using Pug, let's look at how to integrate Pug with your web application.

INCORPORATING DATA IN PUG TEMPLATES

Data is relayed to the Pug engine in the same basic way as in EJS. The template is first compiled into a function that's then called with a context in order to render the HTML output. The following is an example of this:

```
const pug = require('pug');
const template = 'strong #{message}';
const context = { message: 'Hello template!' };
const fn = pug.compile(template);
console.log(fn(context));
```

Here, the #{message} in the template specifies a placeholder to be replaced by a context value.

Context values can also be used to supply values for attributes. The next example renders <a href="http://google.com"></a>:

```
const pug = require('pug');
const template = 'a(href = url)';
const context = { url: 'http://google.com' };
const fn = pug.compile(template);
console.log(fn(context));
```

Now that you've learned how HTML is represented using Pug, and how to provide Pug templates with application data, let's look at how to incorporate logic in Pug.

7.4.2 Logic in Pug templates

After you supply Pug templates with application data, you need logic to deal with that data. Pug allows you to directly embed lines of JavaScript code into your templates, which is how you define logic in your templates. Code such as `if` statements, `for` loops, and `var` declarations are common. Before we dive into the details, here's an example for template rendering a contact list, to give you a practical feel for how you might use Pug logic in an application:

```
h3.contacts-header My Contacts
if contacts.length
  each contact in contacts
    - var fullName = contact.firstName + ' ' + contact.lastName
    .contact-box
      p fullName
      if contact.isEditable
        p: a(href='/edit/'+contact.id) Edit Record
      p
        case contact.status
          when 'Active'
            strong User is active in the system
          when 'Inactive'
            em User is inactive
          when 'Pending'
            | User has a pending invitation
else
  p You currently do not have any contacts
```

Let's first look at the various ways Pug handles output when embedding JavaScript code.

USING JAVASCRIPT IN PUG TEMPLATES

Prefixing a line of JavaScript logic with `-` will execute the JavaScript without including any value returned from the code in the template's output. Prefixing JavaScript logic with `=` will include a value returned from the code, escaped to prevent XSS attacks. But if your JavaScript generates code that shouldn't be escaped, you can prefix it with `!=`. Table 7.1 summarizes the output resulting from these prefixes.

Table 7.1 Prefixes used to embed JavaScript in Pug

Prefix	Output
=	Escaped output (for untrusted or unpredictable values, XSS safe)
!=	Output without escaping (for trusted or predictable values)
-	No output

Pug includes commonly used conditional and iterative statements that can be written without prefixes: `if`, `else`, `case`, `when`, `default`, `until`, `while`, `each`, and `unless`.

Pug also allows you to define variables. The following shows two ways to assign values that are equivalent in Pug:

```
- count = 0
count = 0
```

The unprefixed statements have no output, just like the - prefix discussed previously.

ITERATING THROUGH OBJECTS AND ARRAYS

Values passed in a context are accessible to JavaScript in Pug. In the next example, you'll read a Pug template from a file and pass the Pug template a context containing a couple of messages that you intend to display in an array:

```
const pug = require('pug');
const fs = require('fs');
const template = fs.readFileSync('./template.pug');
const context = { messages: [
  'You have logged in successfully.',
  'Welcome back!'
]};
const fn = pug.compile(template);
console.log(fn(context));
```

The Pug template contains the following:

```
- messages.forEach(message => {
  p= message
- })
```

The final HTML output looks like this:

```
<p>You have logged in successfully.</p><p>Welcome back!</p>
```

Pug also supports a non-JavaScript form of iteration: the each statement, which allows you to cycle through arrays and object properties with ease.

The following is equivalent to the previous example, but using each instead:

```
each message in messages
  p= message
```

You can cycle through object properties by using a slight variation, like this:

```
each value, key in post
  div
    strong #{key}
    p value
```

CONDITIONALLY RENDERING TEMPLATE CODE

Sometimes templates need to make decisions about how data is displayed, depending on the value of the data. The next example illustrates a conditional in which, roughly half the time, the script tag is outputted as HTML:

```
- n = Math.round(Math.random() * 1) + 1
- if (n == 1) {
```

```
  script
    alert('You win!');
- }
```

Conditionals can also be written in Pug by using a cleaner, alternative form:

```
- n = Math.round(Math.random() * 1) + 1
  if n == 1
    script
      alert('You win!');
```

If you're writing a negated conditional, such as if (n != 1), you can use Pug's unless keyword:

```
- n = Math.round(Math.random() * 1) + 1
  unless n == 1
    script
      alert('You win!');
```

USING CASE STATEMENTS IN PUG

Pug also supports a non-JavaScript form of conditional similar to a switch: the case statement, which allows you to specify an outcome based on various template scenarios.

The following example template shows how the case statement can be used to display results from the search of a blog in three ways. If the search finds nothing, a message is shown indicating that. If a single blog post is found, it's displayed in detail. If multiple blog posts are found, an each statement is used to iterate through the posts, displaying their titles:

```
case results.length
  when 0
    p No results found.
  when 1
    p= results[0].content
  default
    each result in results
      p- result.title
```

7.4.3 Organizing Pug templates

With your templates defined, you next need to know how to organize them. As with application logic, you don't want to make your template files overly large. A single template file should correspond to a conceptual building block: a page, a sidebar, or blog post content, for example.

In this section, you'll learn a few mechanisms that allow template files to work together to render content:

- Structuring multiple templates with template inheritance
- Implementing layouts by using block prepending/appending
- Template including
- Reusing template logic with mixins

Let's begin by looking at template inheritance in Pug.

STRUCTURING MULTIPLE TEMPLATES WITH TEMPLATE INHERITANCE

Template inheritance is one means of structuring multiple templates. The concept treats templates, conceptually, like classes in the object-oriented programming paradigm. One template can extend another, which can in turn extend another. You can use as many levels of inheritance as makes sense.

As a simple example, let's look at using template inheritance to provide a basic HTML wrapper that you can use to wrap page content. In a working directory, create a folder called templates in which you'll put the example's Pug file. For a page template, you'll create a file called layout.pug containing the following Pug:

```
html
  head
    block title
  body
    block content
```

The layout.pug template contains the bare-bones definition of an HTML page as well as two *blocks*. Blocks are used in template inheritance to define where a descendant template can provide content. In layout.pug, there's a `title` block, allowing a descendant template to set the title, and a `content` block, allowing a descendant template to set what's to be displayed on the page.

Next, in your working directory's templates directory, create a file named page.pug. This template file will populate the `title` and `content` blocks:

```
extends layout
block title
  title Messages
block content
  each message in messages
    p= message
```

Finally, add the logic in the following listing (a modification of an earlier example in this section), which will display the template results, showing inheritance in action.

Listing 7.10   Template inheritance in action

```
const pug = require('pug');
const fs = require('fs');
const templateFile = './templates/page.pug';
const iterTemplate = fs.readFileSync(templateFile);
const context = { messages: [
  'You have logged in successfully.',
  'Welcome back!'
]};
const iterFn = pug.compile(
  iterTemplate,
  { filename: templateFile }
);
console.log(iterFn(context));
```

Now let's look at another template inheritance feature: block prepending and appending.

IMPLEMENTING LAYOUTS BY USING BLOCK PREPENDING/APPENDING

In the previous example, the blocks in layout.pug contain no content, which makes setting the content in the page.pug template straightforward. But if a block in an inherited template *does* contain content, this content can be built upon, rather than replaced, by descendant templates using block prepending and appending. This allows you to define common content and add to it, rather than replace it.

The following layout.pug template contains an additional block, `scripts`, which contains content—a `script` tag that loads the jQuery JavaScript library:

```
html
  head
    - const baseUrl = "http://ajax.googleapis.com/ajax/libs/jqueryui/1.8/"
    block title
    block style
    block scripts
  body
    block content
```

If you want the page.pug template to additionally load the jQuery UI library, you can do this by using the template in the following listing.

Listing 7.11 Using `block appending` to load an additional JavaScript file

```
extends layout                              ◁──   This template extends
block title                                       the layout template
  title Messages
block style                                                      Defines style block
  link(rel="stylesheet", href=baseUrl+"themes/flick/jquery-ui.css")  ◁
block scripts                               ◁
  script(src=baseUrl+"jquery-ui.js")              Defines scripts block
block content
  - count = 0
  each message in messages
    - count = count + 1
    script
      $(() => {
        $("#message_#{count}").dialog({
          height: 140,
          modal: true
        });
      });
    != '<div id="message_' + count + '">' + message + '</div>'
```

Template inheritance isn't the only way to integrate multiple templates. You also can use the `include` Pug command.

TEMPLATE INCLUDING

Another tool for organizing templates is Pug's `include` command. This command incorporates the contents of another template. If you add the line `include footer` to the layout.pug template from the earlier example, you end up with the following template:

```
html
  head
    block title
    block style
    block scripts
      script(src='//ajax.googleapis.com/ajax/libs/jquery/1.8/jquery.js')
  body
    block content
    include footer
```

This template includes the contents of a template named footer.pug in the rendered output of layout.pug, as illustrated in figure 7.3.

This can be used, for example, to add information about the site or design elements to layout.pug. You can also include non-Pug files by specifying the file extension (for example, `include twitter_widget.html`).

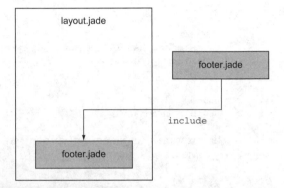

Figure 7.3   Pug's `include` mechanism provides a simple way to include the contents of one template in another template during rendering.

REUSING TEMPLATE LOGIC WITH MIXINS

Although Pug's `include` command is useful for bringing in previously created chunks of code, it's not ideal for creating a library of reusable functionality that you can share between pages and applications. For this, Pug provides the `mixin` command, which lets you define reusable Pug snippets.

A Pug mixin is analogous to a JavaScript function. A mixin can, like a function, take arguments, and these arguments can be used to generate Pug code.

Let's say, for example, your application handles a data structure similar to the following:

```
const students = [
  { name: 'Rick LaRue', age: 23 },
  { name: 'Sarah Cathands', age: 25 },
  { name: 'Bob Dobbs', age: 37 }
];
```

If you want to define a way to output an HTML list derived from a given property of each object, you could define a mixin like the following one to accomplish this:

```
mixin list_object_property(objects, property)
  ul
    each object in objects
      li= object[property]
```

You could then use the mixin to display the data using this line of Pug:

```
mixin list_object_property(students, 'name')
```

By using template inheritance, `include` statements, and mixins, you can easily reuse presentation markup and can prevent your template files from becoming larger than they need to be.

7.5 Summary

- Templating engines help keep application logic and presentation organized.
- Node has several popular template engines, including EJS, Hogan.js, and Pug.
- EJS supports simple control flow and escape or unescaped interpolation.
- Hogan.js is a simple template engine that doesn't support control flow, but does support the Mustache standard.
- Pug is a more complex template language that can output HTML, but doesn't use angled brackets.
- Pug relies on whitespace for embedding tags.

Storing application data

8

Node.js serves an incredibly diverse set of developers with equally diverse needs. No single database or storage solution solves the number of use cases tackled by Node. This chapter provides a broad overview of the data storage possibilities, along with some important high-level concepts and terminology.

8.1 Relational databases

For most of the history of the web, relational databases have been the dominant choice for application data storage. This topic has been covered at length in many other texts and university programs, so we don't spend too much time elaborating on this topic in this chapter.

Relational databases, built upon the mathematical ideas of relational algebra and set theory, have been around since the 1970s. A *schema* specifies the format of various data types and the relationships that exist among those types. For example, if you're building a social network, you may have `User` and `Post` data types, and define a one-to-many relationship between `User` and `Post`. Then using Structured Query Language (SQL), you can issue queries on this data, such as, "Give me all posts belonging to a user with ID 123," or in SQL: `SELECT * FROM post WHERE user_id=123`.

8.2 PostgreSQL

Both MySQL and PostgreSQL (Postgres) are popular relational database choices for Node applications. The differences between relational databases are mostly aesthetic, so for the most part, this section also applies to using other relational databases such as MySQL in Node. First, let's look at how to install Postgres on your development machine.

8.2.1 Performing installation and setup

Postgres needs to be installed on your system. You can't simply npm install it. Installation instructions vary from platform to platform. On macOS, installation is as simple as this:

```
brew update
brew install postgres
```

You may run into upgrade issues if you already have a Postgres installation. Follow the instructions for your platform to migrate your existing databases, or wipe the database directory:

```
# WARNING: will delete existing postgres configuration & data
rm -rf /usr/local/var/postgres
```

Then initialize and start Postgres:

```
initdb -D /usr/local/var/postgres
pg_ctl -D /usr/local/var/postgres -l logfile start
```

This starts a Postgres daemon. This daemon needs to be started every time you boot your computer. You may want to automatically boot the Postgres daemon on startup, and many online guides detail this process for your particular operating system.

Similarly, most Linux systems have a package for installing Postgres. With Windows, you should download the installer from postgresql.org (www.postgresql.org/download/windows/).

Several command-line administration utilities are installed with Postgres. You may want to familiarize yourself with some of them by reading their man pages.

8.2.2 Creating the database

After the Postgres daemon is running, you need to create a database to use. This needs to be done only once. The simplest way is to use `createdb` from the command line. Here you create a database named *articles*:

```
createdb articles
```

There is no output if this succeeds. If a database with this name already exists, this command does nothing and reports a failure.

Most applications connect to only a single database at a time, though multiple databases may be configured, depending on the *environment* the database is running in. Many applications have at least two environments: development and production.

To drop all the data from an existing database, you can run the `dropdb` command from a terminal, passing the database name as an argument:

```
dropdb articles
```

You need to run `createdb` before using this database again.

8.2.3 *Connecting to Postgres from Node*

The most popular package for interfacing with Postgres from node is `pg`. You can install `pg` by using `npm`:

```
npm install pg --save
```

With the Postgres server running, a database created, and the `pg` package installed, you're ready to start using the database from Node. Before you can issue any commands against the server, you need to establish a connection to it, as shown in the next listing.

Listing 8.1   Connecting to the database

```
const pg = require('pg');
const db = new pg.Client({ database: 'articles' });        ◁——  Configuration parameters
                                                                  for the connection
db.connect((err, client) => {
  if (err) throw err;
  console.log('Connected to database', db.database);         Closes database connection,
  db.end();                                            ◁——┘  allows the node process to exit
});
```

Comprehensive documentation for `pg.Client` and other methods can be found on the `pg` package's wiki page on GitHub: https://github.com/brianc/node-postgres/wiki.

8.2.4 *Defining tables*

In order to store data in PostgreSQL, you first need to define some tables and the shape of the data to be stored within them, as shown in the following listing (ch08-databases/listing8_3 in the book's source code).

Listing 8.2   Defining a schema

```
db.query(`
  CREATE TABLE IF NOT EXISTS snippets (
    id SERIAL,
```

```
    PRIMARY KEY(id),
    body text
  );
`, (err, result) => {
  if (err) throw err;
  console.log('Created table "snippets"');
  db.end();
});
```

8.2.5 Inserting data

After your table is defined, you can insert data into it by using INSERT queries, as shown in the next listing. If you don't specify the id value, PostgreSQL will select an ID for you. To learn which ID was chosen for a particular row, you append RETURNING id to your query, and it appears in the rows of the result passed to the callback.

Listing 8.3 Inserting data

```
const body = 'hello world';
db.query(`
  INSERT INTO snippets (body) VALUES (
    '${body}'
  )
  RETURNING id
`, (err, result) => {
  if (err) throw err;
  const id = result.rows[0].id;
  console.log('Inserted row with id %s', id);
  db.query(`
    INSERT INTO snippets (body) VALUES (
      '${body}'
    )
    RETURNING id
  `, () => {
    if (err) throw err;
    const id = result.rows[0].id;
    console.log('Inserted row with id %s', id);
  });
});
```

8.2.6 Updating data

After data is inserted, you can update the data by using an UPDATE query, as shown in the next listing. The number of affected rows will be available in the rowCount property of the query result. You can find the full example for this listing in ch08-databases/listing8_4.

Listing 8.4 Updating data

```
const id = 1;
const body = 'greetings, world';
db.query(`
  UPDATE snippets SET (body) = (
```

```
      '${body}'
    ) WHERE id=${id};
`, (err, result) => {
  if (err) throw err;
  console.log('Updated %s rows.', result.rowCount);
});
```

8.2.7 Querying data

One of the most powerful features of a relational database is the ability to perform complex ad hoc queries on your data. Querying is performed by using `SELECT` statements, and the simplest example of this is shown in the following listing.

Listing 8.5   Querying data

```
db.query(`
  SELECT * FROM snippets ORDER BY id
`, (err, result) => {
  if (err) throw err;
  console.log(result.rows);
});
```

8.3   Knex

Many developers prefer to not work with SQL statements directly in their applications, instead using an abstraction over the top. This is understandable, given that concatenating strings into SQL statements can be a clunky process and that queries can grow hard to understand and maintain. This has been particularly true for JavaScript, which didn't have a syntax for representing multiline strings until ES2015 introduced template literals (see https://developer.mozilla.org/en/docs/Web/JavaScript/Reference/Template_literals). Figure 8.1 shows Knex's statistics, including the number of downloads, which demonstrates its popularity.

Figure 8.1   Knex's usage statistics

Knex is a Node package implementing a type of lightweight abstraction over SQL, known as a *query builder*. A query builder constructs SQL strings though a declarative API that closely resembles the generated SQL. The Knex API is intuitive and unsurprising:

```
knex({ client: 'mysql' })
  .select()
  .from('users')
  .where({ id: '123' })
  .toSQL();
```

This produces a parameterized SQL query in the MySQL dialect of SQL:

```
select * from `users` where `id` = ?
```

8.3.1 jQuery for databases

Despite ANSI and ISO SQL standards existing since the mid-1980s, most databases still speak their own SQL dialects. PostgreSQL is a notable exception; it prides itself on adhering to the SQL:2008 standard. A query builder can normalize differences across SQL dialects, providing a single, unified interface for SQL generation for multiple technologies. This has clear benefits for teams that regularly context-switch between various database technologies.

Knex.js currently supports the following databases:

- PostgreSQL
- MSSQL
- MySQL
- MariaDB
- SQLite3
- Oracle

Table 8.1 compares the ways Knex generates an insert statement, depending on which database is selected.

Table 8.1   Comparing Knex-generated SQL for various databases

Database	SQL
PostgreSQL, SQLite, and Oracle	`insert into "users" ("name", "age") values (?, ?)`
MySQL and MariaDB	`insert into `users` (`name`, `age`) values (?, ?)`
Microsoft SQL Server	`insert into [users] ([name], [age]) values (?, ?)`

Knex supports promises and Node-style callbacks.

8.3.2 Connecting and running queries with Knex

Unlike many other query builders, Knex can also connect and execute queries for you against the selected database driver:

```
db('articles')
  .select('title')
  .where({ title: 'Today's News' })
  .then(articles => {
    console.log(articles);
  });
```

Knex queries return promises by default, but can also support Node's callback convention with .asCallback:

```
db('articles')
  .select('title')
  .where({ title: 'Today's News' })
  .asCallback((err, articles) => {
    if (err) throw err;
    console.log(articles);
  });
```

In chapter 3, you interacted with a SQLite database by using the sqlite3 package directly. This API can be rewritten using Knex. To run this example, first ensure that both the knex and sqlite3 packages are installed from npm:

```
npm install knex@~0.12.0 sqlite3@~3.1.0 --save
```

The next listing uses sqlite3 to implement a simple Article model. Save this file as db.js; you'll use it in listing 8.7 to interact with the database.

Listing 8.6   Using Knex to connect and query sqlite3

```
const knex = require('knex');

const db = knex({
  client: 'sqlite3',
  connection: {
    filename: 'tldr.sqlite'
  },
  useNullAsDefault: true          ◁── Setting this as a default works
});                                    better when changing back ends

module.exports = () => {
  return db.schema.createTableIfNotExists('articles', table => {
    table.increments('id').primary();        ◁──┐
    table.string('title');                       Define a primary key named
    table.text('content');                       "id" that autoincrements
  });                                            upon insertion
};

module.exports.Article = {
  all() {
    return db('articles').orderBy('title');
  },

  find(id) {
    return db('articles').where({ id }).first();
  },

  create(data) {
    return db('articles').insert(data);
  },
```

```
  delete(id) {
    return db('articles').del().where({ id });
  }
};
```

Now `Article` entries can be added by using `db.Article`. The following listing can be used with the previous one to create articles and then print them. See ch08-databases/listing8_7/index.js for the full example.

Listing 8.7 Interacting with the Knex-powered API

```
db().then(() => {
  db.Article.create({
    title: 'my article',
    content: 'article content'
  }).then(() => {
    db.Article.all().then(articles => {
      console.log(articles);
      process.exit();
    });
  });
})
.catch(err => { throw err });
```

SQLite requires minimal configuration: you don't need to boot up a server daemon or create databases from outside the application. SQLite writes everything into a single file. If you run the preceding code, you'll find an articles.sqlite file in your current directory. Wiping a SQLite database is as simple as deleting this one file:

```
rm articles.sqlite
```

SQLite also has an in-memory mode, which avoids writing to disk entirely. This mode is commonly used to decrease the running time of automated tests. You can configure in-memory mode by using the special `:memory:` filename. Opening multiple connections to the `:memory:` file gives each connection its own private database:

```
const db = knex({
  client: 'sqlite3',
  connection: {
    filename: ':memory:'
  },
  useNullAsDefault: true
});
```

8.3.3 Swapping the database back end

Because you're using Knex, it's trivial to change listings 8.6 and 8.7 to use PostgreSQL over sqlite3. Knex needs the pg package installed to talk to the PostgreSQL server, which you'll need to have installed and running. Install the pg package into the folder with listing 8.7 (ch08-databases/listing8_7 in the book's code) and remember to create the appropriate database by using PostgreSQL's `createdb` command-line utility:

```
npm install pg --save
createdb articles
```

The only code changes required to use this new database are in the Knex configuration; otherwise, the consumer API and usage are identical:

```
const db = knex({
  client: 'pg',
  connection: {
    database: 'articles'
  }
})
```

Note that in a real-world scenario, you'd also need to migrate any existing data.

8.3.4   *Beware of leaky abstractions*

Query builders can normalize SQL syntax, but can do little to normalize behavior. Some features are supported in only particular databases, and some databases may exhibit entirely different behavior given identical queries. For example, the following are two methods of defining a primary key when using Knex:

- `table.increments('id').primary();`
- `table.integer('id').primary();`

Both options work as expected in SQLite3, but the second option will cause an error in PostgreSQL when inserting a new record:

```
"null value in column "id" violates not-null constraint"
```

Values inserted into SQLite with a `null` primary key will be assigned an automatically incremented ID, regardless of whether the primary-key column was explicitly configured to autoincrement. PostgreSQL, on the other hand, requires autoincrement columns to be defined explicitly. Many such behavioral differences exist between databases, and some differences may be subtle without visible errors. Thorough testing needs to be applied if you do choose to transition to a different database.

8.4   *MySQL vs. PostgreSQL*

Both MySQL and PostgreSQL are mature and powerful databases, and for many projects, there will be minimal differences when selecting one over the other. Many distinctions, which won't be significant until the project needs to scale, exist below or at the edge of the interface exposed to the application developer.

An exhaustive comparison between relational databases is mostly beyond the scope of this book, as the topic is complicated. Some notable distinctions are listed here:

- PostgreSQL supports more-expressive data types, including arrays, JSON, and user-defined types.

- PostgreSQL has built-in full-text search.
- PostgreSQL supports the full ANSI SQL:2008 standard.
- PostgreSQL's replication support isn't as powerful or battle-tested as MySQL's.
- MySQL is older and has a bigger community. More compatible tools and resources are available for MySQL.
- The MySQL community has more fragmentation through subtly different forks (for example, MariaDB and WebScaleSQL from Facebook, Google, Twitter, and so forth).
- MySQL's pluggable storage engine can make it more complicated to understand, administer, and tune. On the other hand, this can be seen as an opportunity for more fine-grained control over performance.

MySQL and PostgreSQL express different performance characteristics at scale, depending on the type of workload. The subtleties of your workload may not become obvious until the project matures.

Many online resources provide far more in-depth comparisons between relational databases:

- www.digitalocean.com/community/tutorials/sqlite-vs-mysql-vs-postgresql-a-comparison-of-relational-database-management-systems
- https://blog.udemy.com/mysql-vs-postgresql/
- https://eng.uber.com/mysql-migration/

Which relational database you initially choose is unlikely to be a significant factor in the success of your project, so don't worry about this decision too much. You can migrate to another database later, but Postgres should be powerful enough to provide most of the features and scalability that you'll ever need. But if you're in a position to evaluate several databases, you should familiarize yourself with the idea of ACID guarantees.

8.5   ACID guarantees

ACID describes a set of desirable properties for database transactions: atomicity, consistency, isolation, and durability. The exact definitions of these terms can vary. As a general rule, the more strictly a system guarantees ACID properties, the greater the performance compromise. This ACID categorization is a common way for developers to quickly communicate the trade-offs of a particular solution, such as those found in NoSQL systems.

8.5.1   Atomicity: transactions either succeed or fail in entirety

An *atomic* transaction can't be partially executed: either the entire operation completes, or the database is left unchanged. For example, if a transaction is to delete all comments by a particular user, either all comments will be deleted, or none of them will be deleted. There is no way to end up with some comments deleted and some not. Atomicity should apply even in the case of system error or power failure. *Atomic* is used here with its original meaning of *indivisible*.

8.5.2   *Consistency: constraints are always enforced*

The completion of a successful transaction must maintain all data-integrity constraints defined in the system. Some example constraints are that primary keys must be unique, data conforms to a particular schema, or foreign keys must reference entities that exist. Transactions that would lead to inconsistent state typically result in transaction failures, though minor issues may be resolved automatically; for example, coercing data into the correct shape. This isn't to be confused with the C of *consistency* in the CAP theorem, which refers to guaranteeing a single view of the data being presented to all readers of a distributed store.

8.5.3   *Isolation: concurrent transactions don't interfere*

Isolated transactions should produce the same result, whether the same transactions are executed concurrently or sequentially. The level of isolation a system provides directly affects its ability to perform concurrent operations. A naïve isolation scheme is the use of a *global lock*, whereby the entire database is locked for the duration of a transaction, thus effectively processing all transactions in series. This gives a strong isolation guarantee but it's also pathologically inefficient: transactions operating on entirely disjointed datasets are needlessly blocked (for example, a user adding a comment ideally doesn't block another user updating their profile). In practice, systems provide various levels of isolation using more fine-grained and selective locking schemes (for example, by table, row, or field). More-sophisticated systems may even optimistically attempt all transactions concurrently with minimal locking, only to retry transactions by using increasingly coarse-grained locks in cases where conflicts are detected.

8.5.4   *Durability: transactions are permanent*

The *durability* of a transaction is the degree to which its effects are guaranteed to persist, even after restarts, power failures, system errors, or even hardware failures. For example, an application using the SQLite in-memory mode has no transaction durability; all data is lost when the process exits. On the other hand, SQLite persisting to disk will have good transaction durability, because data persists even after the machine is restarted.

This may seem like a no-brainer: just write the data to disk—and voila, you have durable transactions. But disk I/O is one of the slowest operations your application can perform and can quickly become a significant bottleneck in your application, even at moderate levels of scale. Some databases offer different durability trade-offs that can be employed to maintain acceptable system performance.

8.6   *NoSQL*

The umbrella term for data stores that don't fit in the relational model is *NoSQL*. Today, because some NoSQL databases do speak SQL, the term NoSQL has a meaning closer to *nonrelational* or as the backronym *not only SQL*.

Here's a subset of paradigms and example databases that can be considered NoSQL:

- *Key-value/tuple*—DynamoDB, LevelDB, Redis, etcd, Riak, Aerospike, Berkeley DB
- *Graph*—Neo4J, OrientDB
- *Document*—CouchDB, MongoDB, Elastic (formerly Elasticsearch)
- *Column*—Cassandra, HBase
- *Time series*—Graphite, InfluxDB, RRDtool
- *Multiparadigm*—Couchbase (document database, key/value store, distributed cache)

For a more comprehensive list of NoSQL databases, see http://nosql-database.org/.

NoSQL concepts can be difficult to digest if you've worked only with relational databases, because NoSQL usage often goes directly against well-established best practices: No defined schemas. Duplicate data. Loosely enforced constraints. NoSQL systems take responsibilities normally assigned to the database and place them in the realm of the application. It can all seem dirty.

Usually, only a small set of access patterns create the bulk of the workload for the database, such as the queries that generate the landing screen of your application, where multiple domain objects need to be fetched. A common technique for improving read performance in a relational database is denormalization, whereby domain queries are preprocessed and shaped into a form that reduces the number of reads required for consumption by the client.

NoSQL data is more frequently denormalized by default. The domain modeling step may be entirely skipped. This can discourage overengineering of the data model, allow changes to be executed more quickly, and lead to an overall simpler, better-performing design.

8.7 Distributed databases

An application can scale vertically by increasing the capacity of the machines running it, or horizontally by adding more machines. Vertical scaling is usually the less complicated option, but constraints borne by the hardware limit how far one machine can scale. Vertical scaling also tends to get expensive quickly. Horizontal scaling, on the other hand, has a far higher capacity for growth as you add capacity by adding more processes and more machines. This comes at the cost of complexity in orchestrating many more moving parts. All growing systems eventually reach a point where they must scale horizontally.

Distributed databases are designed from the outset with horizontal scaling as the premise. Data stored across multiple machines improves the durability of the data by removing any single point of failure. Many relational systems have some capacity to perform horizontal scaling in the form of sharding, master/slave, master/master replication, though even with these capacities, relational systems aren't designed to scale beyond a few hundred nodes. For example, the upper limit for a MySQL cluster is 255 nodes. Distributed databases, on the other hand, can scale into the thousands of nodes by design.

8.8   *MongoDB*

MongoDB is a document-oriented, distributed database that's hugely popular among Node developers. It's the *M* in the fashionable MEAN stack (MongoDB, Express, Angular, Node) and is often one of the first databases people encounter when they start working with Node. Figure 8.2 shows how popular the mongodb module is on npm.

```
npm install mongodb
3 dependencies      version 2.2.0
1,893 dependents    updated 6 hours ago
1,807,134 downloads in the last month
download rank: top 1% of 296,000 packages
```

Figure 8.2   MongoDB's usage statistics

MongoDB attracts more than its fair share of criticism and controversy; despite this, it remains a staple data store for many developers. MongoDB has known deployments in prominent companies including Adobe, LinkedIn, and eBay and is even used in a component of the Large Hadron Collider at the European Organization for Nuclear Research (CERN).

A MongoDB database stores documents in schemaless *collections*. Documents don't need to have a predefined schema, and documents in a single collection needn't share the same schema. This grants a lot of flexibility to MongoDB, though the burden is now upon the application to ensure that documents maintain a predictable structure (guaranteeing consistency—the *C* in ACID).

8.8.1   *Performing installation and setup*

MongoDB needs to be installed on your system. Installation varies between platforms. On macOS, installation is as simple as this:

```
brew install mongodb
```

The MongoDB server is started by using the mongod executable:

```
mongod --config /usr/local/etc/mongod.conf
```

The most popular MongoDB driver is the official mongodb package by Christian Amor Kvalheim:

```
npm install mongodb@^2.1.0 --save
```

Windows users should note that driver installation requires msbuild.exe, which is installed by Microsoft Visual Studio.

8.8.2 Connecting to MongoDB

After installing the mongodb package and starting the mongod server, you can connect as a client from Node, as shown in the following listing.

Listing 8.8 Connecting to MongoDB

```
const { MongoClient } = require('mongodb');

MongoClient.connect('mongodb://localhost:27017/articles')
  .then(db => {
    console.log('Client ready');
    db.close();
  }, console.error);
```

The connection's success handler is passed a database client instance, from which all database commands are executed.

Most interactions with the database are via the collection API:

- `collection.insert(doc)`—Insert one or more documents
- `collection.find(query)`—Find documents matching the query
- `collection.remove(query)`—Remove documents matching the query
- `collection.drop()`—Remove the entire collection
- `collection.update(query)`—Update documents matching the query
- `collection.count(query)`—Count documents matching the query

Operations such as `find`, `insert`, and `delete` come in a few flavors, depending on whether you're operating on one or many values. For example:

- `collection.insertOne(doc)`—Insert a single document
- `collection.insertMany([doc1, doc2])`—Insert many documents
- `collection.findOne(query)`—Find a single document matching the query
- `collection.updateMany(query)`—Update all documents matching the query

8.8.3 Inserting documents

`collection.insertOne` places a single object into the collection as a document, as shown in the next listing. The success handler is passed an object containing metadata about the state of the operation.

Listing 8.9 Inserting a document

```
const article = {
  title: 'I like cake',
  content: 'It is quite good.'
};
db.collection('articles')
  .insertOne(article)
```

```
.then(result => {
  console.log(result.insertedId);
  console.log(article._id);   B
});
```

If the document has no _id, a new ID is created. insertedId will be that ID

The original object defining the document is mutated, adding an _id property

The `insertMany` call is similar, except it takes an array of multiple documents. The `insertMany` response will contain an array of `insertedIds`, in the order the documents were supplied, instead of a singular `insertedId`.

8.8.4 Querying

Methods that read documents from the collection (such as `find`, `update`, and `remove`) take a query argument that's used to match documents. The simplest form of a query is an object with which MongoDB will match documents with the same structure and same values. For example, this finds all articles with the title "I like cake":

```
db.collection('articles')
  .find({ title: 'I like cake' })
  .toArray().then(results => {
    console.log(results);
  });
```

An array of documents matching the query

Queries can be used to match objects by their unique `_id`:

```
collection.findOne({ _id: someID })
```

Or match based on a *query operator*:

```
db.collection('articles')
  .find({title: { $regex:  /cake$/I })
```

Title ends with 'cake', case-insensitive

Many *query operators* exist in the MongoDB query language—for example:

- `$eq`—Equal to a particular value
- `$neq`—Not equal to a particular value
- `$in`—In array
- `$nin`—Not in array
- `$lt, $lte, $gt, $gte`—Greater/less than or equal to comparison
- `$near`—Geospatial value is near a certain coordinate
- `$not, $and, $or, $nor`—Logical operators

These can be combined to match almost any condition and create a highly readable, sophisticated, and expressive query language. See https://docs.mongodb.com/manual/reference/operator/query/ for more information on queries and query operators.

The next listing shows an example that the previous Articles API implemented by using MongoDB, while maintaining a nearly identical external interface. Save this file as db.js (it's listing8_10/db.js in the book's sample code).

Listing 8.10   Implementing the Article API with MongoDB

```
const { MongoClient, ObjectID } = require('mongodb');

let db;

module.exports = () => {
  return MongoClient
    .connect('mongodb://localhost:27017/articles')
    .then((client) => {
      db = client;
    });
};

module.exports.Article = {
  all() {
    return db.collection('articles2').find().sort({ title: 1 }).toArray();
  },

  find(_id) {
    if (typeof _id !== 'object') _id = ObjectID(_id);      ◁──┐ Adds support for
    return db.collection('articles2').findOne({ _id });         passing _id as a
  },                                                             String or ObjectID

  create(data) {
    return db.collection('articles2').insertOne(data, { w: 1 });
  },

  delete(_id) {
    if (typcof _id !== 'object') _id = ObjectID(_id);
    return db.collection('articles2').deleteOne({ _id }, { w: 1 });
  }
};
```

The following snippet shows how to use listing 8.10 (listing 8_10/index.js in the sample code):

```
const db = require('./db');

db().then(() => {
  db.Article.create({ title: 'An article!' }).then(() => {
    db.Article.all().then(articles => {
      console.log(articles);
      process.exit();
    });
  });
});
```

This uses a promise from listing 8.10 to connect to the database, then creates an article using Article's create method. After that, it loads all articles and logs them out.

8.8.5   *Using MongoDB identifiers*

Identifiers from MongoDB are encoded in *Binary JSON* (BSON) format. The _id property on a document is a JavaScript Object that wraps a BSON-formatted ObjectID value. MongoDB uses BSON to represent documents internally and as a transmission format. BSON is more space-efficient than JSON and can be parsed more quickly, which means faster database interactions using less bandwidth.

A BSON `ObjectID` isn't just a random sequence of bytes; it encodes metadata about where and when the ID was generated. For example, the first four bytes of an `ObjectID` are a timestamp. This removes the need to have to store a `createdAt` timestamp property in your documents:

```
const id = new ObjectID(61bd7f57bf1532835dd6174b);
id.getTimestamp();
```
getTimestamp returns a JavaScript Date: 2016-07-08TI4:49:05.000Z

See https://docs.mongodb.com/manual/reference/method/ObjectId/ for more information about the `ObjectID` format.

`ObjectID`s may superficially appear to be strings because of the way they're printed in the terminal, but they're objects. `ObjectID`s suffer from classic object comparison gotchas: seemingly totally equivalent values are reported as inequivalent because they reference different objects.

In the following snippet, we extract the same value twice. Using the node's built-in assert module, we try to assert that the objects or the IDs are equivalent, but both result in failure:

```
const Articles = db.collection('articles');
Articles.find().then(articles => {
  const article1 = articles[0];
  return Articles
    .findOne({_id: article1._id})
    .then(article2 => {
      assert.equal(article2._id, article1._id);
    });
});
```

These assertions produce error messages that at first seem confusing, as the actual values appear to match the expected values:

```
operator: equal
expected: 577f6b45549a3b991e1c3c18
actual:   577f6b45549a3b991e1c3c18
operator: equal
expected:
  { _id: 577f6b45549a3b991e1c3c18, title: 'attractive-money' ... }
actual:
  { _id: 577f6b45549a3b991e1c3c18, title: 'attractive-money' ... }
```

Equivalence can be detected correctly by using the `ObjectID`'s `equal` method that's available on every `_id`. Alternatively, you can coerce the identifiers and compare them as strings, or use a `deepEquals` method such as that found on Node's built-in assert module:

```
article1._id.equals(article2._id);
String(article1._id) === String(article2._id);
assert.deepEqual(article1._id, article2._id);
```
Note that this will throw if the assertion doesn't hold true

Identifiers passed to the Node mongodb driver must be a BSON-formatted `ObjectID`. A string can be converted into an `ObjectID` by using the `ObjectID` constructor:

```
const { ObjectID } = require('mongodb');
const stringID = '577f6b45549a3b991e1c3c18';
const bsonID = new ObjectID(stringID);
```

Where possible, the BSON form should be maintained; the cost of marshalling to and from strings works against the potential performance gains MongoDB hopes to achieve by serving client identifiers as BSON. See http://bsonspec.org/ for detailed information about the BSON format.

8.8.6　*Using replica sets*

The distributed features of MongoDB are mostly beyond the scope of this book, but in this section we quickly cover the basics of replica sets. Many mongod processes can be run as nodes/members of a replica set. A *replica set* consists of a single primary node and numerous secondary nodes. Each member of a replica set needs to be allocated a unique port and directory to store its data. Instances can't share ports or directories, and the directories must already exist before startup.

In the following listing, you create a unique directory for each member and start them on a sequential port number starting from 27017. You may want to run each of the mongod commands in a new terminal tab without backgrounding them (without the trailing &).

Listing 8.11　Starting a replica set

```
mkdir -p ./mongodata/db0 ./mongodata/db1 ./mongodata/db2

pkill mongod
sleep 3

mongod --port 27017 --dbpath ./rs0-data/db0 --replSet rs0 &
mongod --port 27018 --dbpath ./rs0-data/db1 --replSet rs0 &
mongod --port 27019 --dbpath ./rs0-data/db2 --replSet rs0 &
```

Ensures no other mongod instances are running

Gives existing instances a moment to shut down

After the replica set is running, MongoDB needs to perform some initiation. You need to connect to the port of the instance that you want to become the first *primary* node (27017 by default) and call `rs.initiate()`, as shown in the following listing. Then you need to add each instance as a member of the replica set. Note that you need to supply the hostname of the machine you're connecting to.

Listing 8.12　Initiating a replica set

```
mongo --eval "rs.initiate()"
mongo --eval "rs.add('`hostname`:27017')"
mongo --eval "rs.add('`hostname`:27018')"
mongo --eval "rs.add('`hostname`:27019')"
```

The hostname UNIX command prints the current machine's hostname

MongoDB clients need to know about all the possible replica set members when they connect, though not all members need to currently be online. After connecting, you may use the MongoDB client as usual. Listing 8.13 shows how to create a replica set with three members.

Listing 8.13 Connecting to a replica set

```
const os = require('os');
const { MongoClient } = require('mongodb');
const hostname = os.hostname();

const members = [
  `${hostname}:27018`,
  `${hostname}:27017`,
  `${hostname}:27019`
];

MongoClient.connect(`mongodb://${members.join(',')}/test?replSet=rs0`)      ⟵  test is the name of the database; rs0 is the name of the replica set
.then(db => {
  db.admin().replSetGetStatus().then(status => {      ⟵  replSetGetStatus prints the members and metadata about the replica set
    console.log(status);
    db.close();
  });
});
```

If any of the mongod nodes crash, the system will continue working, as long as at least two instances are running. If the primary node crashes, a secondary node will automatically be elected to be promoted into the primary.

8.8.7 *Understanding write concerns*

MongoDB gives the developer fine-grained control over which performance and safety trade-offs are acceptable for various areas of your application. It's important to understand the concepts of both write and read concerns in order to use MongoDB without surprises, especially as the number of nodes in your replica set increases. In this section, we touch only on write concerns, as they're the most important.

Write concerns dictate the number of mongod instances that the data needs to be successfully written to before the overall operation responds with a success. If not explicitly specified, the default write concern is 1, which ensures that the data has been written to at least one node. It may not provide an adequate level of assurance for critical data; data may be lost if the node goes down before replicating to other nodes.

It's possible and often desirable to set a zero write concern, whereby the application doesn't wait for any response:

```
db.collection('data').insertOne(data, { w: 0 });
```

A zero write concern grants the highest performance but provides the least durability assurances, and is typically used for only temporary or unimportant data (such as the writing of logs or caches).

If you're connected to a replica set, you can indicate a write concern greater than 1. Replicating to more nodes decreases the likelihood of data loss, at the expense of more latency when performing operations:

```
db.collection('data').insertOne(data, { w: 2 });
db.collection('data').insertOne(data, { w: 5 });
```

You may want to scale the write concern as the number of nodes in the cluster changes. This can be done dynamically by MongoDB itself if you set the write concern to `major-ity`. This ensures that data is written to more than 50% of the available nodes:

```
db.collection('data').insertOne(data, { w: 'majority' });
```

The default write concern of 1 may not provide an adequate level of assurance for critical data. Data may be lost if the node goes down before replicating to other nodes.

Setting a write concern higher than 1 ensures that the data exists across multiple mongod instances before continuing. Running multiple instances on the same machine adds protection but doesn't help in the case of systemwide failures such as running out of disk space or RAM. You can protect against machine failure by running instances across multiple machines and ensuring that writes propagate to these nodes, but this again will be slower and doesn't protect against datacenter-wide failure. Running nodes across different datacenters protects against datacenter outage, but ensuring that data is replicated across datacenters will greatly impact performance.

As always, the more assurances you add, the slower and more complicated the system becomes. This isn't an issue specific to MongoDB; it's an issue with any and all data storage. No perfect solution exists, and you'll need to decide the acceptable level of risk for the various parts of your application.

For more information about how MongoDB replication works, see the following resources:

- https://docs.mongodb.com/manual/faq/replica-sets/
- https://docs.mongodb.com/manual/faq/concurrency/

8.9 Key/value stores

Each record in a key/value store comprises a single key and a single value. In many key/value systems, values can be of any data type, of any length or structure. From the perspective of the database, values are opaque atoms: the database doesn't know or care about the type of the data and can't be subdivided or accessed other than in its entirety. Contrast this with value storage in a relational database: data is stored in a series of tables, which contain rows of data separated into predefined columns. In a key/value store, the responsibility of managing the format of the data is handed to the application.

Key/value stores can often be found in performance-critical paths of an application. Ideally, values are laid out in a manner such that the absolute minimum number of reads is required to fulfill a task. Key/value stores come with simpler querying capabilities than other database types. Ideally, complex queries are precalculated; otherwise, they need to be performed within the application rather than the database. This constraint can lead to easily understood and predictable performance characteristics.

The most popular key/value stores, such as Redis and Memcached, are often used for volatile storage (if the process exits, the data is lost). Avoiding writing to disk is one of the best ways to improve performance. This can be an acceptable trade-off for features when data can be regenerated or loss is of little concern; for example, caches and user sessions.

Key/value stores may carry a stigma that they can't be used for primary storage, but this isn't always true. Many key/value stores provide just as much durability as a "real" database.

8.10   *Redis*

Redis is a popular in-memory, data-structure store. Although many consider Redis to be a key/value store, keys and values represent only a subset of the features Redis supports across a variety of useful, basic data structures. Figure 8.3 shows the usage statistics for the redis package on npm.

Figure 8.3   The redis package's statistics on npm

The data structures built into Redis include the following:

- Strings
- Hashes
- List
- Set
- Sorted set

Redis also comes with many other useful features out of the box:

- *Bitmap data*—Direct bit manipulation in values.
- *Geospatial indexes*—Storing geospatial data with radius queries.
- *Channels*—A publish/subscribe data-delivery mechanism.
- *TTLs*—Values can be configured with an expiry time, after which they're automatically removed.
- *LRU eviction*—Optionally removes values that haven't been recently used in order to maintain maximum memory usage.
- *HyperLogLog*—High-performing approximation of set cardinality, while maintaining a low-memory footprint (doesn't need to store every member).

- *Replication, clustering, and partitioning*—Horizontal scaling and data durability.
- *Lua scripting*—Extend Redis with custom commands.

In this section, you'll find several bulleted lists of Redis commands. They're not intended to be a reference, but rather to give some insight into what's possible with Redis. It's an incredibly powerful and versatile tool. See http://redis.io/commands for more details.

8.10.1 Performing installation and setup

Redis can be installed through your system's package management tool. On macOS, you can easily install it with Homebrew:

```
brew install redis
```

Starting the server is done using the `redis-server` executable:

```
redis-server /usr/local/etc/redis.conf
```

The server listens on port 6379 by default.

8.10.2 Performing initialization

A Redis client instance is created with the `createClient` function from the redis npm package:

```
const redis = require('redis');
const db = redis.createClient(6379, '127.0.0.1');
```

This function takes the port and a host as arguments. But if you're running the Redis server on the default port on your local machine, you don't need to supply any arguments at all:

```
const db = redis.createClient();
```

The Redis client instance is an `EventEmitter`, so you can attach listeners for various Redis status events, as shown in the next listing. You can immediately start issuing commands to the client, and they'll be buffered until the connection is ready.

Listing 8.14   Connecting to Redis and listening for status events

```
const redis = require('redis');

const db = redis.createClient();
db.on('connect', () => console.log('Redis client connected to server.'));
db.on('ready', () => console.log('Redis server is ready.'));
db.on('error', err => console.error('Redis error', err));
```

The error handler will fire if a connection or client problem occurs. If an `error` event is fired and no error handler is attached, the application process will throw the error and crash; this is a feature of all `EventEmitters` in Node. If the connection fails and an error handler is supplied, the Redis client will attempt to retry the connection.

8.10.3 *Working with key/value pairs*

Redis can be used as a generic key/value store for strings and arbitrary binary data. Reading and writing a key/value pair can be done using the set and get methods, respectively:

```
db.set('color', 'red', err => {
  if (err) throw err;
});

db.get('color', (err, value) => {
  if (err) throw err;
  console.log('Got:', value);
});
```

If you set an existing key, the value will be overwritten. If you try to get a key that doesn't exist, the value will be null; it's not considered an error.

The following commands can be used to retrieve and manipulate values:

- append
- decr
- decrby
- get
- getrange
- getset
- incr
- incrby
- incrbyfloat
- mget
- mset
- msetnx
- psetex
- set
- setex
- setnx
- setrange
- strlen

8.10.4 *Working with keys*

You can check whether a key exists by using exists. This works with any data type:

```
db.exists('users', (err, doesExist) => {
  if (err) throw err;
      console.log('users exists:', doesExist);
});
```

Along with exists, the following commands can all be used with any key, regardless of the type of the value (these commands work with strings, sets, lists, and so forth):

- del
- exists

- rename
- renamex
- sort
- scan
- type

8.10.5 *Encoding and data types*

The Redis server stores keys and values as binary objects; it's not dependent on the encoding of the value passed to the client. Any valid JavaScript string (UCS2/UTF16) can be used as a valid key or value:

```
db.set('greeting', '你好', redis.print);
db.get('greeting', redis.print);
db.set('icon', '?', redis.print);
db.get('icon', redis.print);
```

By default, keys and values are coerced to strings as they're written. For example, if you set a key with a number, it will be a string when you try to get that same key:

```
db.set('colors', 1, (err) => {
  if (err) throw err;
});

db.get('colors', (err, value) => {
  if (err) throw err;
  console.log('Got: %s as %s', value, typeof value);    ⟵  Value will be
});                                                          of type string
```

The Redis client silently coerces numbers, Booleans, and dates into strings, and it also happily accepts buffer objects. Trying to set any other JavaScript type as a value (for example, Object, Array, RegExp) prints a warning that should be heeded:

```
db.set('users', {}, redis.print);
```

```
Deprecated: The SET command contains a argument of type Object.
This is converted to "[object Object]" by using .toString() now
  and will return an error from v.3.0 on.
Please handle this in your code to make sure everything works
  as you intended it to.
```

In the future, this will be an error, so the calling application *must* be responsible for ensuring that the correct types are passed to the Redis client.

GOTCHA: SINGLE VS. MULTIPLE VALUE ARRAYS

The client produces a cryptic error, "ReplyError: ERR syntax error," if you try to set an array of values:

```
db.set('users', ['Alice', 'Bob'], redis.print);
```

But note that no error occurs when the array contains only a single value:

```
db.set('user', ['Alice'], redis.print);
db.get('user', redis.print);
```

This type of bug may show symptoms only when you're running it in production, as it can easily elude detection if the test suite happens to produce only single-valued arrays, which is common for stripped-down test data. Be aware!

BINARY DATA WITH BUFFERS

Redis is capable of storing arbitrary byte data, which means you can store any type of data in it. The Node client supports this feature with special handling for Node's Buffer type. When a buffer is passed to the Redis client as a key or value, the bytes are sent unmodified to the Redis server. This avoids accidental data corruption and performance penalties of unnecessary marshalling between strings and buffers. For example, if you want to write data from disk or network directly into Redis, it's more efficient to write the buffers directly to Redis than to convert them into strings first.

> **Buffers**
>
> *Buffers* are what you receive from Node's core file and network APIs by default. They're a container around contiguous blocks of binary data, and were introduced in Node before JavaScript had its own native binary data types (Uint8Array, Float32Array, and so forth). Today, buffers are implemented in Node as a specialized subclass of Uint8Array. The Buffer API is available globally in Node; you don't need to require anything to use it.
>
> See https://github.com/nodejs/node/blob/master/lib/buffer.js

Redis has recently added commands for manipulating individual bits of string values, which can be of use when working with buffers:

- bitcount
- bitfield
- bitop
- setbit
- bitpos

8.10.6 *Using hashes*

A *hash* is a collection of key/value pairs. The hmset command takes a key and an object representing the key/value pairs of the hash. You can get the key/value pairs back as an object by using hmget, as shown in the next listing.

Listing 8.15 Storing data in elements of Redis hashes

```
db.hmset('camping', {              ◁─── Sets hash
  shelter: '2-person tent',             key/value pairs
  cooking: 'campstove'
}, redis.print);

db.hget('camping', 'cooking', (err, value) => {    ◁─── Gets the
  if (err) throw err;                                    "camping.cooking" value
```

```
    console.log('Will be cooking with:', value);
});

db.hkeys('camping', (err, keys) => {          ⟵——— Gets hash keys
  if (err) throw err;                                  as an array
  keys.forEach(key => console.log(`  ${key}`));
});
```

You can't store nested objects in a Redis hash. It provides only a single level of keys and values.

The following commands operate on hashes:

- hdel
- hexists
- hget
- hgetall
- hincrby
- hincrbyfloat
- hkeys
- hlen
- hmget
- hmset
- hset
- hsetnx
- hstrlen
- hvals
- hscan

8.10.7 Using lists

A *list* is an ordered collection of string values. A list can contain multiple copies of the same value. Lists are conceptually similar to arrays. Lists are best used for their ability to behave as a stack (LIFO: last in, first out) or queue (FIFO: first in, first out) data structures.

The following code shows the storage and retrieval of values in a list. The lpush command adds a value to a list. The lrange command retrieves a range of values, using start and end indices. The -1 argument in the following code signifies the last item of the list, so this use of lrange retrieves all list items:

```
client.lpush('tasks', 'Paint the bikeshed red.', redis.print);
client.lpush('tasks', 'Paint the bikeshed green.', redis.print);
client.lrange('tasks', 0, -1, (err, items) => {
  if (err) throw err;
  items.forEach(item => console.log(`  ${item}`));
});
```

Lists don't contain any built-in means to determine whether a value is in the list, or any means of discovering the index of a particular value in the list. You can manually iterate over the list to obtain this information, but this is a highly inefficient approach that should be avoided. If you need these types of features, you should consider a different data structure, such as a set, perhaps even used in addition to a list. Duplicating data across multiple data structures is often desirable in order to take advantage of various performance characteristics.

The following commands operate on lists:

- `blpop`
- `brpop`
- `lindex`
- `linsert`
- `llen`
- `lpop`
- `lpush`
- `lpushx`
- `lrange`
- `lrem`
- `lset`
- `ltrim`
- `rpop`
- `rpush`
- `rpushx`

8.10.8 *Using sets*

A *set* is an unordered collection of unique values. Testing membership, and adding and removing items from a set can be performed in O(1) time, making it a high-performing structure suitable for many tasks:

```
db.sadd('admins', 'Alice', redis.print);
db.sadd('admins', 'Bob', redis.print);
db.sadd('admins', 'Alice', redis.print);
db.smembers('admins', (err, members) => {
  if (err) throw err;
  console.log(members);
});
```

The following commands operate on Redis sets:

- `sadd`
- `scard`
- `sdiff`
- `sdiffstore`
- `sinter`
- `sinterstore`
- `sismember`
- `smembers`
- `spop`

- srandmember
- srem
- sunion
- sunionstore
- sscan

8.10.9 *Providing pub/sub with channels*

Redis goes beyond the traditional role of a data store by providing channels. *Channels* are a data-delivery mechanism that provides publish/subscribe functionality, as shown conceptually in figure 8.4. They can be useful for real-time applications such as chat and gaming.

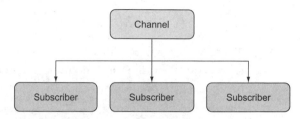

Figure 8.4   Redis channels provide an easy solution to a common data-delivery scenario.

A Redis client can subscribe or publish to a channel. A message published to a channel will be delivered to all subscribers. A publisher doesn't need to know about the subscribers, nor the subscribers about the publishers. This decoupling of publishers and subscribers is what makes this a powerful and clean pattern.

The following listing shows an example of how Redis's publish/subscribe functionality can be used to implement a TCP/IP chat server.

Listing 8.16   A simple chat server implemented with Redis pub/sub functionality

```
const net = require('net');
const redis = require('redis');

const server = net.createServer(socket => {            ◁──  Defines setup logic for each
  const subscriber = redis.createClient();                  user connecting to chat server
  subscriber.subscribe('main');            ◁── Creates subscriber
  subscriber.on('message', (channel, message) => {      client for each user
    socket.write(`Channel ${channel}: ${message}`);
  });

  const publisher = redis.createClient();            ◁──  Creates publisher
  socket.on('data', data => {                              client for each user
    publisher.publish('main', data);
  });

  socket.on('end', () => {
    subscriber.unsubscribe('main');            ◁── If user disconnects,
    subscriber.end(true);                          ends client connections
    publisher.end(true);
  });
});

server.listen(3000);
```

Subscribes to a channel

When a message is received from a channel, shows it to user

When user enters a message, publishes it

8.10.10 *Improving Redis performance*

The hiredis npm package is a native binding from JavaScript to the protocol parser in the official Hiredis C library. Hiredis can significantly improve the performance of Node Redis applications, particularly if you're using `sunion`, `sinter`, `lrange`, and `zrange` operations with large datasets.

To use hiredis, simply install it alongside the redis package in your application, and the Node redis package will detect it and use it automatically the next time it starts:

```
npm install hiredis --save
```

There are few downsides to using hiredis, but because it's compiled from C code, some complications or limitations may arise when building hiredis for some platforms. As with all native add-ons, you may need to rebuild hiredis with `npm rebuild` after updating Node.

8.11 *Embedded databases*

An embedded database doesn't require the installation or administration of an external server. It runs *embedded* within your application process itself. Communication with an embedded database usually occurs via direct procedure calls in your application, rather than across an interprocess communication (IPC) channel or a network.

In many situations, an application needs to be self-contained, so an embeddable database is the only option (for example, mobile or desktop applications). Embedded databases can also be used on web servers, often found powering high-throughput features such as user sessions or caching, and sometimes even as the primary storage.

Some embeddable databases commonly used in Node and Electron apps are as follows:

- SQLite
- LevelDB
- RocksDB
- Aerospike
- EJDB
- NeDB
- LokiJS
- Lowdb

NeDB, LokiJS, and Lowdb are all written in pure JavaScript, which by nature makes them embeddable into Node/Electron applications. Most embedded databases are simple key/value or document stores, though SQLite is a notable exception as an embeddable *relational* store.

8.12 *LevelDB*

LevelDB is an embeddable, persistent key/value store developed in early 2011 by Google, initially for use as the backing store for the IndexedDB implementation in

Chrome. LevelDB's design is built on concepts from Google's Bigtable database. LevelDB is comparable to databases such as Berkley DB, Tokyo/Kyoto Cabinet, and Aerospike, but in the context of this book, you can think of LevelDB as an embeddable Redis with only the bare minimum of features. Like many embedded databases, LevelDB isn't multithreaded and doesn't support multiple instances using the same underlying file storage, so it doesn't work in a distributed setting without a wrapping application.

LevelDB stores arbitrary byte arrays, sorted lexicographically by key. Values are compressed by using Google's Snappy compression algorithm. Data is always persisted to disk; the total data capacity isn't constrained by the amount of RAM on the machine, unlike an in-memory store such as Redis.

Only a small set of self-explanatory operations are provided with LevelDB: `Get`, `Put`, `Del`, and `Batch`. LevelDB can also capture snapshots of the current database state and create bidirectional iterators for moving forward or backward through the dataset. Creating an iterator creates an implicit snapshot; the data an iterator can see can't be changed by subsequent writes.

LevelDB forms the foundation for other databases, in the form of LevelDB forks. The number of significant LevelDB offshoots could be attributed to the simplicity of LevelDB itself:

- RocksDB by Facebook
- HyperLevelDB by Hyperdex
- Riak by Basho
- leveldb-mcpe by Mojang (creators of Minecraft)
- bitcoin/leveldb for the bitcoind project

For more information about LevelDB, see http://leveldb.org/.

8.12.1 LevelUP and LevelDOWN

LevelDB support in Node is provided by the LevelUP and LevelDOWN packages written by Node foundation chair and prolific Australian developer Rod Vagg. LevelDOWN is a simple, sugar-free C++ binding to LevelDB for Node, and it's unlikely you'll interface with it directly. LevelUP wraps the LevelDOWN API with a more convenient, idiomatic node interface, adding support for key/value encodings, JSON, buffering writes until the database is open, and wrapping the LevelDB iterator interface in a Node stream. Figure 8.5 shows levelup's popularity on npm.

Figure 8.5 The levelup package's statistics on npm

8.12.2   *Installation*

A major convenience of using LevelDB in your Node application is that it's *embedded*: you can install everything you need solely with npm. You don't need to install any additional software; just issue the following command and you're ready to start using LevelDB:

```
npm install level --save
```

The level package is a simple convenience wrapper around the LevelUP and Level-DOWN packages, providing a LevelUP API preconfigured to use a LevelDown back end. Documentation for the LevelUP API exposed by the level package can be found on the LevelUP readme:

- www.npmjs.com/package/levelup
- www.npmjs.com/package/leveldown

8.12.3   *API overview*

The LevelDB client's main methods for storing and retrieving values are as follows:

- db.put(key, value, callback—Store a value under key
- db.get(key, callback)—Get the value under key
- db.del(key, callback)—Remove the value under key
- db.batch().write()—Perform batch operations
- db.createKeyStream(options)—Stream of keys in database
- db.createValueStream(options)—Stream of values in database

8.12.4   *Initialization*

When you initialize level, you need to provide a path to the directory that will store the data, as shown in the following listing; the directory will be created if it doesn't already exist. There's a loose community convention of giving this directory a .db extension (for example, ./app.db).

> **Listing 8.17   Initializing a level database**

```
const level = require('level');

const db = level('./app.db', {
  valueEncoding: 'json'
});
```

After level() is called, the returned LevelUP instance is immediately ready to start accepting commands, synchronously. Commands issued before the LevelDB store is open will be buffered until the store is open.

8.12.5   *Key/value encodings*

Because LevelDB can store arbitrary data of any type for both keys and values, it's up to the calling application to handle data serialization and deserialization. LevelUp can be configured to encode keys and values by using the following data types out of the box:

- `utf8`
- `json`
- `binary`
- `id`
- `hex`
- `ascii`
- `base64`
- `ucs2`
- `utf16le`

By default, both keys and values are encoded as UTF-8 strings. In listing 8.17, keys will remain as UTF-8 strings, but values are encoded/decoded as JSON. JSON encoding permits storage and retrieval of structured values such as objects or arrays in a somewhat similar fashion to that of a document store such as MongoDB. But note that unlike a real document store, there's no way to access keys within values with vanilla LevelDB; values are opaque. Users can also supply their own custom encodings—for example, to support a different structured data format such as MessagePack.

8.12.6 *Reading and writing key/value pairs*

The core API is simple: use `put(key, value)` to write a value, `get(key)` to read a value, and `del(key)` to delete a value, as shown in the next listing. The code in listing 8.18 should be appended to the code in listing 8.17; for a full example, see ch08-databases/listing8_18/index.js in the book's sample code.

Listing 8.18   Reading and writing values

```
const key = 'user';
const value = {
  name: 'Alice'
};

db.put(key, value, err => {
  if (err) throw err;
  db.get(key, (err, result) => {
    if (err) throw err;
    console.log('got value:', result);
    db.del(key, (err) => {
      if (err) throw err;
      console.log('value was deleted');
    });
  });
});
```

If you `put` a value on a key that already exists, the old value will be overwritten. Trying to `get` a key that doesn't exist will result in an error. This error object will be of a particular type, `NotFoundError`, and has a special property, `err.notFound`, that can be used to differentiate it from other types of errors. This may seem unusual, but because LevelDB doesn't have a built-in method to check for existence, LevelUp needs to be able to disambiguate nonexistent values and values that are undefined. Unlike with get, trying to del a nonexistent key will not cause an error.

Listing 8.19   Getting keys that don't exist

```
db.get('this-key-does-not-exist', (err, value) => {
  if (err && !err.notFound) throw err;
  if (err && err.notFound) return console.log('Value was not found.');
  console.log('Value was found:', value);
});
```

All data reading and writing operations take an optional options argument for overriding the encoding options of the current operation, as shown in the next listing.

Listing 8.20   Overriding encoding for specific operations

```
const options = {
  keyEncoding: 'binary',
  valueEncoding: 'hex'
};

db.put(new Uint8Array([1, 2, 3]), '0xFF0099', options, (err) => {
  if (err) throw err;
  db.get(new Uint8Array([1, 2, 3]), options, (err, value) => {
    if (err) throw err;
    console.log(value);
  });
});
```

8.12.7 *Pluggable back ends*

A happy side effect of the separation of LevelUP/LevelDOWN is that LevelUP isn't restricted to using LevelDB as the storage back end. Anything you can wrap with the MemDown API can be used as a storage back end for LevelUP, allowing you to use the exact same API to interface with many data stores.

Some examples of alternative back ends are as follows:

- MySQL
- Redis
- MongoDB
- JSON files
- Google spreadsheets
- AWS DynamoDB
- Windows Azure table storage
- Browser web storage (IndexedDB/localStorage)

This ability to easily swap out the storage medium or even write your own custom back end means you can use a single, consistent set of database APIs and tooling across many situations and environments. One database API to rule them all!

A commonly used alternative back end is *memdown*, which stores values entirely in memory rather than disk, akin to using SQLite in-memory mode. This can be particularly useful in a test environment to reduce the cost of test setup and teardown.

To run the following listing, make sure you have the LevelUP and memdown packages installed:

```
npm install --save levelup memdown
```

Listing 8.21   Using memdown with LevelUP

```
const level = require('levelup')
const memdown = require('memdown')

const db = level('./level-articles.db', {     ← For memdown, the "path" here can be
  keyEncoding: 'json',                           any string, since it doesn't use the disk
  valueEncoding: 'json',                ← The only real difference is in passing
  db: memdown                              memdown as the db parameter
});
```

In this sample, you could've used the same level package you used before, because it's just a wrapper for LevelUP. But if you're not using the LevelDB-backed LevelDOWN that comes bundled with level, you can just use LevelUP and avoid the binary dependency on LevelDB via LevelDOWN.

8.12.8   *The modular database*

LevelDB's performance and minimalism resonate with many Node developers, and it has fostered a modular database movement within the Node community. The concept is to be able to pick and choose exactly which features your application needs and tailor a database for your specific use case.

Here are just a few examples of modular LevelDB functionality available through npm packages:

- Atomic updates
- Autoincrementing keys
- Geospatial queries
- Live update streams
- LRU eviction
- Map/reduce jobs
- Master/master replication
- Master/slave replication
- SQL queries

- Secondary indexes
- Triggers
- Versioned data

The LevelUP wiki maintains a fairly comprehensive overview of the LevelDB ecosystem: https://github.com/Level/levelup/wiki/Modules, or you can search for *leveldb* on npm, for which there are 898 packages at the time of this writing. Figure 8.6 shows how popular LevelDB is on npm.

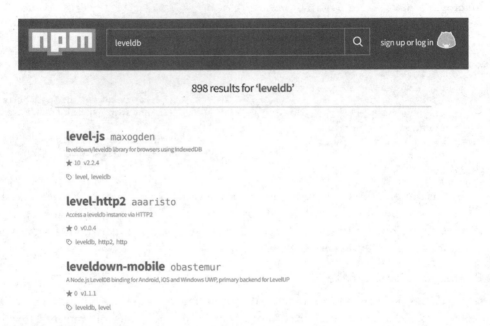

Figure 8.6   Examples of third-party LevelDB packages on npm

8.13 *Serialization and deserialization are expensive*

It's important to remember that the built-in JSON operations are both expensive and blocking; your process can't do anything else while it's marshalling data to and from JSON. The same goes for most other serialization formats. It's common for serialization to be a key bottleneck on a web server. The best way to reduce its impact is to minimize how often it's performed and how much data it needs to handle.

You may experience some speed improvement by using a different serialization format (for example, MessagePack or Protocol Buffers), but alternative formats should be considered only after you've squeezed the possible gains out of reducing the payload sizes and unnecessary serialization/deserialization steps.

`JSON.stringify` and `JSON.parse` are native functions and have been thoroughly optimized, but they can easily be overwhelmed when needing to handle megabytes of data. To demonstrate, the following listing benchmarks serializing and deserializing about 10 MB of data.

Listing 8.22 Serialization benchmarking

```
const bytes = require('pretty-bytes');
const obj = {};
for (let i = 0; i < 200000; i++) {
  obj[i] = {
    [Math.random()]: Math.random()
  };
}

console.time('serialise');
const jsonString = JSON.stringify(obj);
console.timeEnd('serialise');
console.log('Serialised Size', bytes(Buffer.byteLength(jsonString)));
console.time('deserialise');
const obj2 = JSON.parse(jsonString);
console.timeEnd('deserialise');
```

On a 2015 3.1 GHz Intel Core i7 MacBook Pro running Node 6.2.2, it takes roughly 140 ms to serialize, and 335 ms to deserialize, the approximately 10 MB of data. This would be a disaster if such a load were to occur on a web server, because these steps are totally blocking and have to be processed in series. Such a server would be able to handle only about a dismal seven requests a second when serializing, and about three requests a second when deserializing.

8.14 In-browser storage

The asynchronous programming model used in Node works well for many use cases because the assumption holds that I/O is the single biggest bottleneck for most web applications. The single most significant thing you can do to simultaneously reduce server workload and improve user experience is to take advantage of client-side data storage. A happy user is one who doesn't have to wait for a full network round-trip to get results. Client-side storage can also facilitate improved application availability by allowing your application to remain at least semifunctional while the user or your service is offline.

8.14.1 Web storage: localStorage and sessionStorage

Web storage defines a simple key/value store and has great support across both desktop and mobile browsers. Using web storage, a domain can persist a moderate amount of data in the browser and retrieve it at a later time, even after the website has been refreshed, the tab closed, or the browser shut down. Web storage is your first resort for client-side persistence. Its winning feature is its bare simplicity.

There are two web storage APIs: localStorage and sessionStorage. sessionStorage implements an identical API to localStorage, though it differs in its persistence behavior. Like localStorage, data stored in sessionStorage is persisted across page reloads, but unlike localStorage, all sessionStorage data expires when the page session ends (when the tab or browser is closed). sessionStorage data can't be accessed from different browser windows.

The web storage APIs were developed to overcome limitations with browser cookies. Specifically, cookies aren't well suited for sharing data between multiple active tabs on the same domain. If a user is performing an activity across multiple tabs, sessionStorage can be used for sharing state between those tabs, without requiring the use of the network.

Cookies are also ill-suited for handling more long-term data that should live across multiple sessions, tabs, and windows; for example, user-authored documents or email. This is the use case that localStorage was designed to handle. Depending on the particular browser, varying upper limits exist for the amount of data that can be stored in web storage. Mobile browsers are limited to just 5 MB of storage.

API OVERVIEW

The localStorage API provides the following methods for working with keys and values:

- `localStorage.setItem(key, value)`—Store a value under key
- `localStorage.getItem(key)`—Get the value under key
- `localStorage.removeItem(key)`—Remove the value under key
- `localStorage.clear()`—Remove all keys and values
- `localStorage.key(index)`—Get value at index
- `localStorage.length`—Total number of keys in localStorage

8.14.2 *Reading and writing values*

Both keys and values must be strings. If you pass a value that isn't a string, it'll be coerced into a string for you. This conversion doesn't produce JSON strings; instead, it's a naïve conversion using `.toString`. Objects will end up serialized as the string `[object Object]`. The application must serialize values to and from strings in order to store more-complicated data types in web storage. The next listing shows how to store JSON in localStorage.

Listing 8.23   Storing JSON in web storage

```
const examplePreferences = {
  temperature: 'Celcius'
};

// serialize on write
localStorage.setItem('preferences', JSON.stringify(examplePreferences));

// deserialize on read
const preferences = JSON.parse(localStorage.getItem('preferences'));
console.log('Loaded preferences:', preferences);
```

Access to web storage data is reasonably fast, though it's also synchronous. Web storage blocks the UI thread while performing read and write operations. For small workloads, this overhead will be unnoticeable, but care should be taken to avoid excessive reads or writes, especially with large quantities of data. Unfortunately, web storage is also unavailable from web workers, so all reads and writes must happen on the main UI thread. For a detailed analysis of the performance impact of various client-side storage technologies, see this post by Nolan Lawson, author of PouchDB: http://nolanlawson .com/2015/09/29/indexeddb-websql-localstorage-what-blocks-the-dom/.

Web storage APIs provide no built-in facilities to perform queries, select keys by range, or search through values. You're limited to accessing items key by key. To perform searches, you can set up and maintain your own indexes; or if your dataset is small enough, you can iterate over it in its entirety. The following listing iterates over all the keys in localStorage.

Listing 8.24   Iterating over entire dataset in localStorage

```
function getAllKeys() {
  return Object.keys(localStorage);
}

function getAllKeysAndValues() {
  return getAllKeys()
    .reduce((obj, str) => {
      obj[str] = localStorage.getItem(str);
      return obj;
    }, {});
}

// Get all values
const allValues = getAllKeys().map(key => localStorage.getItem(key));

// As an object
console.log(getAllKeysAndValues());
```

As in most key/value stores, there's only a single namespace for keys. For example, if you have posts and comments, there's no way to create separate stores for posts and comments. It's easy enough to create your own "namespace" by using a prefix on each key to delineate namespaces, as shown in the next listing.

Listing 8.25   Namespacing keys

```
localStorage.setItem(`/posts/${post.id}`, post);
localStorage.setItem(`/comments/${comment.id}`, comment);
```

To get all items within a namespace, you can filter through all items using the preceding getAllKeys function, as shown in the next listing.

Listing 8.26   Getting all items in a namespace

```
function getNamespaceItems(namespace) {
  return getAllKeys().filter(key => key.startsWith(namespace));
}
console.log(getNamespaceItems('/exampleNamespace'));
```

Note that this loops over every single key in localStorage, so be wary of performance when iterating over many items.

As a result of the localStorage API being synchronous, a few restrictions exist on when and where it can be used. For example, you could use localStorage to permanently memoize the result of any function that takes and returns JSON-serializable data, as shown in the following listing.

Listing 8.27 Using localStorage for persistent memoization

```
// subsequent calls with the same argument will fetch the memoized result
function memoizedExpensiveOperation(data) {
  const key = `/memoized/${JSON.stringify(data)}`;
  const memoizedResult = localStorage.getItem(key);
  if (memoizedResult != null) return memoizedResult;
  // do expensive work
  const result = expensiveWork(data);
  // save result to localStorage, never calculate again
  localStorage.setItem(key, result);
  return result;
}
```

Note that an operation would need to be particularly slow in order for the memoization benefits to outweigh the overhead of the serialization/deserialization process (for example, a cryptographic algorithm). As such, localStorage works best when it's saving time spent moving data across a network.

Web storage does have limitations, but for the right tasks, it can be a powerful and simple tool. Other in-browser storage topics to investigate are as follows:

- IndexedDB
- Service workers
- Offline-first

8.14.3 *localForage*

Web storage's main drawbacks are its blocking, synchronous API and limited storage capacity in some browsers. In addition to web storage, most modern browsers also support one or both of WebSQL and IndexedDB. Both data stores are nonblocking and can reliably hold far more data than web storage.

But using either of these databases directly, as we did with the web storage APIs, is inadvisable. WebSQL is deprecated, and its successor, IndexedDB, has a particularly unfriendly and verbose API, not to mention patchier browser support. To conveniently and reliably store data in the browser without blocking, we're relegated to using a nonstandard tool to "normalize" the landscape. The localForage library from Mozilla (http://mozilla.github.io/localForage/) is one such normalizing tool.

API OVERVIEW

Conveniently, the localForage interface closely mirrors that of web storage, though in an asynchronous, nonblocking form:

- `localforage.setItem(key, value, callback)`—Store a value under key
- `localforage.getItem(key, callback)`—Get the value under key
- `localforage.removeItem(key, callback)`—Remove the value under key
- `localforage.clear(callback)`—Remove all keys and values
- `localforage.key(index, callback)`—Get value at index
- `localforage.length(callback)`—Number of keys in localForage

The localForage API also includes useful additions with no web storage equivalent:

- `localforage.keys(callback)`—Remove all keys and values
- `localforage.iterate(iterator, callback)`—Iterate over keys and values

8.14.4 Reading and writing

The localForage API supports both promises and Node's error-first callback convention.

Listing 8.28 Comparison of getting data with localStorage vs. localForage

```
const value = localStorage.getItem(key);          ◁─┐  localStorage: blocking,
console.log(value);                                   synchronous

localforage.getItem(key)                          ◁─┐  localForage: nonblocking,
  .then(value => console.log(value));                 asynchronous using promises

localforage.getItem(key, (err, value) => {        ◁─┐  localForage: nonblocking,
  console.log(value);                                 asynchronous call using
});                                                   node callback-style
```

Under the hood, localForage utilizes the best storage mechanism available in the current browser environment. If IndexedDB is available, localForage will use that. Otherwise, it'll try to fall back to WebSQL or even using web storage if required. You can configure the order in which the stores will be tried and even blacklist certain options:

```
                                                          This will never fall back
                                                          to using localStorage
// e.g. will not use localStorage
localforage.setDriver([localforage.INDEXEDDB, localforage.WEBSQL]);    ◁─
```

Unlike localStorage, localForage isn't limited to storing just strings. It supports most JavaScript primitives such as arrays and objects, as well as binary data types: `Typed-Arrays`, `ArrayBuffers`, and `Blobs`. Note that IndexedDB is the only back end that can store binary data natively: the WebSQL and localStorage back ends will incur marshalling overheads:

```
Promise.all([
  localforage.setItem('number', 3),
  localforage.setItem('object', { key: 'value' }),
  localforage.setItem('typedarray', new Uint32Array([1,2,3]))
]);
```

Mirroring the web storage APIs makes localForage intuitive to use, while also overcoming many of the shortcomings and compatibility issues when trying to store data in the browser.

8.15   Hosted storage

Hosted storage is another tactic you can use to avoid managing your own server-side storage. Hosted infrastructure services such as those provided by Amazon Web Services (AWS) are often considered as only a scaling and performance optimization, but smart usage of hosted services early on can save a lot of time implementing unnecessary infrastructure poorly.

Many, if not all, of the databases listed in this chapter have a hosted offering. Hosted services allow you to try tools quickly and even deploy publicly accessible production applications without the hassles of setting up your own database hosting. But hosting your own is becoming increasingly easy. Many cloud services provide prebuilt server images, loaded with all the right software and configurations needed to run a machine hosting the database of your choosing.

8.15.1   Simple Storage Service

Amazon Simple Storage Service (S3) is a remote file-hosting service provided as a part of the popular AWS suite. S3 is a cost-effective means of storing and hosting network-accessible files. It's a filesystem in the cloud. Using RESTful HTTP calls, files can be uploaded into buckets, along with up to 2 KB of metadata. Bucket contents can then be accessed via HTTP GET or the BitTorrent protocol.

Buckets and their contents can be configured with various permissions, including time-based access. You can also specify a time to live (TTL) on bucket contents themselves, after which they'll become inaccessible and be removed from your bucket. It's easy to promote your S3 data up to a content delivery network (CDN). AWS provides the CloudFront CDN, which can be easily connected to your files and will be accessible with low latency from around the world.

Not all data needs to be or should be stored in a database. Are there components of your data that could be treated as files? After you've generated the results of an expensive calculation for a user, perhaps you can push those results up to S3 then forever step out of the way.

A common and obvious use for S3 is the hosting of user-uploaded assets such as images. Uploaded assets live in a temporary directory on the application machine, processed by using a tool such as ImageMagick to reduce the file size, and then uploaded to S3 for hosting to web browsers. This process can be simplified even further by streaming uploads directly to S3, where they can trigger further processing. The client-side applications can also upload to S3 directly. Some more developer-centric services even opt for providing absolutely zero storage, requiring users to provide access tokens so the application can use their S3 buckets.

S3 ISN'T LIMITED TO THE STORAGE OF IMAGES
S3 can be used to store any type of file, up to 5 terabytes in size, of any format. S3 works best for large blobs of data that change infrequently and need to be accessed as a single atom.

Storing data in S3 steps around the complications and complexity of setting up and maintaining a server for the hosting and storage of files. It's great for instances where writes are infrequent, large chunks of data need to be accessed as a single atom, and there are many reads and potentially many read locations.

8.16 *Which database?*

In this chapter, we've covered just a few of the many databases commonly used in Node applications. Successful applications can be and have been built using any of these databases. Within a single application, there's not always one ideal data storage solution; there's no silver bullet. Each database presents its own unique set of trade-offs, and it's up to the developer to evaluate which trade-offs make sense for the current state of the project. A hybrid of technologies is frequently the most appropriate.

Rather than asking, "What database should I use?" you could be asking, "How far can I go without using a database at all?" How much of your project can you build with the fewest long-lasting decisions? It's often best to defer decisions; you'll always be able to make a better decision later, when you have more information.

8.17 *Summary*

- Both relational and NoSQL databases can be used with Node.
- The simple pg Node module is great for working with the SQL language.
- The Knex module allows you to use several databases with Node.
- ACID is a set of properties for database transactions and ensures safety.
- MongoDB is a NoSQL database that uses JavaScript.
- Redis is a data-structure store that can be used as a database and cache.
- LevelDB is a fast key/value store by Google that maps from strings to values.
- LevelDB is a modular database.
- Web-based storage, including localForage and localStorage, can be used to save data in browsers.
- Storage services, such as Amazon S3, can be used to persist data to cloud providers.

Testing Node applications

9

This chapter covers

- Testing logic with Node's assert module
- Using other assertion libraries
- Using Node unit-testing frameworks
- Simulating and controlling web browsers using Node
- Getting more details when tests fail

As features are added to your application, the risk of introducing bugs is increased. An application isn't complete if it's not tested, and because manual testing is tedious and prone to human error, automated testing has become increasingly popular with developers. Automated testing involves writing logic to test your code, rather than running through application functionality by hand.

If the idea of automated testing is new to you, think of it as a robot doing all of the boring stuff while you focus on the interesting work. Every time you make a change to the code, the robot ensures that bugs haven't crept in. Although you may not have completed or started your first Node application yet, it's good to get a handle on how to implement automated testing because you'll be able to write tests as you develop.

224

In this chapter, you'll look at two types of automated testing: unit testing and acceptance testing. *Unit testing* is used to verify logic, typically at a function or method level, and it's applicable to all types of applications. Unit-testing methodologies can be divided into two major forms: test-driven development (TDD) and behavior-driven development (BDD). Practically speaking, TDD and BDD are largely the same thing, but they differ stylistically. This can be important, depending on who needs to read your tests. Other differences between TDD and BDD exist, but they're beyond the scope of this book. *Acceptance testing* is an additional layer of testing most commonly used for web applications. Acceptance testing involves scripting control of a browser and attempting to trigger web application functionality with it.

This chapter covers established solutions for both unit and acceptance testing. For unit testing, we cover Node's assert module; the Mocha, Vows, and Should.js frameworks; and Chai. For acceptance testing, we look at using Selenium with Node. Figure 9.1 places the tools alongside their respective testing methodologies and flavors.

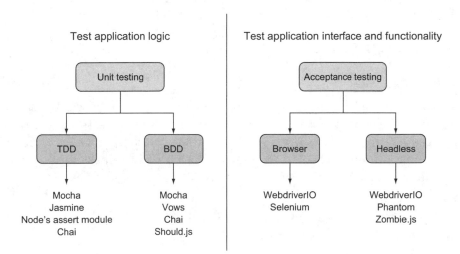

Figure 9.1   Test framework overview

Let's start with unit testing.

9.1   *Unit testing*

Unit testing is a type of automated testing in which you write logic to test discrete parts of your application. Writing tests helps you think more critically about your application design choices and helps you avoid pitfalls early on. The tests also give you confidence that your recent changes haven't introduced errors. Although unit tests take a bit of work up front to write, they can save you time by lessening the need to manually retest every time you make a change to an application.

Unit testing can be tricky, and testing asynchronous logic can present its own challenges. Asynchronous unit tests can run in parallel, so you have to be careful to ensure that tests don't interfere with each other. For example, if your tests create temporary files on disk, you have to be careful that when you delete the files after a test, you don't delete the working files of another test that hasn't yet finished. For this reason, many unit-testing frameworks include flow control to sequence the running of tests.

In this section, we show you how to use the following:

- *Node's built-in assert module*—A good building block for TDD-style automated testing
- *Mocha*—A relatively new testing framework that can be used for TDD- or BDD-style testing
- *Vows*—A widely used BDD-style testing framework
- *Should.js*—A module that builds on Node's assert module to provide BDD-style assertions

The next section demonstrates how to test business logic with the assert module, which is included with Node.

9.1.1 *The assert module*

The basis for most Node unit testing is the built-in assert module, which tests a condition and, if the condition isn't met, throws an error. Node's assert module is used by many third-party testing frameworks. Even without a testing framework, you can do useful testing with it. If you're trying out a quick idea, you can use the assert module by itself to write a quick test.

A SIMPLE EXAMPLE

Suppose you have a simple to-do application that stores items in memory, and you want to assert that it's doing what you think it's doing.

The following listing defines a module containing the core application functionality. Module logic supports creating, retrieving, and deleting to-do items. It also includes a simple doAsync method, so you can look at testing asynchronous methods too. Save this file as todo.js.

> **Listing 9.1   A model for a to-do list**

```
class Todo {
  constructor() {
    this.todos = [];          Defines to-do
  }                           database

  add(item) {                                 Adds a to-do item
    if (!item) throw new Error('Todo.prototype.add requires an item');
```

```
      this.todos.push(item);
  }

  deleteAll() {                          Deletes all
    this.todos = [];                     to-do items
  }

  get length() {                         Gets count of
    return this.todos.length;            to-do items
  }

  doAsync(cb) {                          Calls back with
    setTimeout(cb, 2000, true);          "true" after 2 secs
  }
}
                                         Exports Todo
                                         function
module.exports = Todo;
```

Now you can use Node's assert module to test the code. In a file called test.js, enter the following code to load the necessary modules, set up a new to-do list, and set a variable that tracks the number of completed tests.

Listing 9.2 Set up necessary modules

```
const assert = require('assert');
const Todo = require('./todo');
const todo = new Todo();
let testsCompleted = 0;
```

USING EQUAL TO TEST THE CONTENTS OF A VARIABLE

Next, you can add a test of the to-do application's delete functionality. Add the function in the following listing to the end of test.js.

Listing 9.3 Test to make sure that no to-do items remain after deletion

```
                                    Adds some data in
                                    order to test delete
function deleteTest() {                                         Asserts data was
  todo.add('Delete Me');                                        added correctly
  assert.equal(todo.length, 1, '1 item should exist');
  todo.deleteAll();
  assert.equal(todo.length, 0, 'No items should exist');
  testsCompleted++;                Notes that test          Asserts record
}                                  has completed            was deleted
```

Deletes all records →

This test adds a todo item and then deletes it. Because there should be no to-dos at the end of this test, the value of todo.length should be 0 if the application logic is working properly. If a problem occurs, an exception is thrown. If the value returned by todo.length isn't set to 0, the assertion will result in a stack trace showing an error message, "No items should exist," outputted to the console. After the assertion, testsCompleted is incremented to note that a test has completed.

USING NOTEQUAL TO FIND PROBLEMS IN LOGIC

Next, add the code in the following listing to test.js. This code is a test of the to-do application's add functionality.

Listing 9.4 Test to make sure adding a to-do works

```
function addTest() {
  todo.deleteAll();               ◁──┐ Deletes any
  todo.add('Added');                  │ existing items
  assert.notEqual(todo.getCount(), 0, '1 item should exist');  ◁── Adds item
  testsCompleted++;               ◁──┐
}                                      │ Notes that test
                                       │ has completed
```

Deletes any existing items

Adds item

Asserts that items exist

Notes that test has completed

The assert module also allows `notEqual` assertions. This type of assertion is useful when the generation of a certain value by application code indicates a problem in logic. Listing 9.4 shows the use of a `notEqual` assertion. All to-do items are deleted, an item is added, and the application logic then gets all items. If the number of items is `0`, the assertion will fail and an exception will be thrown.

USING ADDITIONAL FUNCTIONALITY: STRICTEQUAL, NOTSTRICTEQUAL, DEEPEQUAL, NOTDEEPEQUAL

In addition to `equal` and `notEqual` functionality, the assert module offers strict versions of assertions called `strictEqual` and `notStrictEqual`. These use the strict equality operator (`===`) rather than the more permissive version (`==`).

To compare objects, the assert module offers `deepEqual` and `notDeepEqual`. The *deep* in the names of these assertions indicates that they recursively compare two objects, comparing two object's properties, and if the properties are themselves objects, comparing these as well.

USING OK TO TEST FOR AN ASYNCHRONOUS VALUE BEING TRUE

Now it's time to add a test of the to-do application's `doAsync` method, as shown in listing 9.5. Because this is an asynchronous test, you're providing a callback function (cb) to signal to the test runner when the test has completed; you can't rely on the function returning to tell you, as you can with synchronous tests. To see whether the result of `doAsync` is the value `true`, use the `ok` assertion. The `ok` assertion provides an easy way to test a value for being `true`.

Listing 9.5 Test whether the doAsync callback is passed true

```
function doAsyncTest(cb) {
  todo.doAsync(value => {                              ◁── Callback will fire
    assert.ok(value, 'Callback should be passed true');      2 secs later
    testsCompleted++;                     ◁──┐ Notes that test
    cb();                    ◁──┐               has completed
  });                            │ Triggers callback
}                                │ when done
```

Asserts value is true

Callback will fire 2 secs later

Triggers callback when done

Notes that test has completed

TESTING THAT THROWN ERRORS ARE CORRECT

You can also use the assert module to check that thrown error messages are correct, as the following listing shows. The second argument in the `throws` call is a regular expression that looks for the text *requires* in the error message.

> **Listing 9.6 Test whether `add` throws when missing a parameter**

```
function throwsTest(cb) {
  assert.throws(todo.add, /requires/);          todo.add called with
  testsCompleted++;            Notes that test   no arguments
}                              has completed
```

ADDING LOGIC TO RUN YOUR TESTS

Now that you've defined the tests, you can add logic to the file to run each of the tests. The logic in the following listing runs each test, and then prints the number of tests that were run and completed.

> **Listing 9.7 Running the tests and reporting test completion**

```
deleteTest();
addTest();
throwsTest();
doAsyncTest(() => {                                        Indicates
  console.log(`Completed ${testsCompleted} tests`);        completion
});
```

You can run the tests with the following command:

```
$ node chapter09-testing/listing_09_1-7/test.js
```

If the tests don't fail, the script informs you of the number of tests completed. It also can be smart to keep track of when tests start execution as well as when they complete, to protect against flaws in individual tests. For example, a test may execute without reaching the assertion.

In order to use Node's built-in functionality, each test case has to include a lot of boilerplate to set up the test (such as deleting all items) and to keep track of progress (the `completed` counter). All this boilerplate shifts the focus away from the primary concern of writing test cases, and it's better left to a dedicated framework that can do the heavy lifting while you focus on testing business logic. Let's look at making things easier by using Mocha, a third-party unit-testing framework.

9.1.2 *Mocha*

Mocha, a popular testing framework, is easy to grasp. Although it defaults to a BDD style, you can also use it in a TDD style. Mocha has a wide variety of features, including global variable leak detection and client-side testing.

> **Global variable leak detection**
>
> You should have little need for global variables that are readable application-wide, and it's considered a programming best practice to minimize your use of them. But in ES5, it's easy to inadvertently create global variables by forgetting to include the `var` keyword when declaring a variable. Mocha helps detect accidental global variable leaks by throwing an error when you create a global variable during testing.
>
> If you want to disable global leak detection, run `mocha` with the `--ignored-leaks` command-line option. Alternatively, if you want to allow a select number of globals to be used, you can specify them by using the `--globals` command-line option followed by a comma-delimited list of allowable global variables.

By default, Mocha tests are defined and their logic is set up by using BDD-flavored functions called `describe`, `it`, `before`, `after`, `beforeEach`, and `afterEach`. Alternatively, you can use Mocha's TDD interface, which replaces the use of `describe` with `suite`, `it` with `test`, `before` with `setup`, and `after` with `teardown`. For our example, you'll stick with the default BDD interface.

TESTING NODE APPLICATIONS WITH MOCHA

Let's dive right in and see how to create a small project called *memdb*—a small in-memory database—and use Mocha to test it. First, you need to create the directories and files for the project:

```
$ mkdir -p memdb/test
$ cd memdb
$ touch index.js
$ touch test/memdb.js
$ npm init -y
$ npm install --save-dev mocha
```

Open package.json and add a `scripts` property that defines how the tests are run:

```
"scripts": {
  "test": "mocha"
},
```

The *test* directory is where the tests will live. By default, Mocha uses the BDD interface. The following listing shows what it looks like (chapter09-testing/memdb in the book's sample code).

Listing 9.8   Basic structure for a Mocha test

```
const memdb = require('..');
describe('memdb', () => {
  describe('.saveSync(doc)', () => {
    it('should save the document', () => {
    });
  });
});
```

Mocha also supports TDD and qunit, and exports style interfaces, which are detailed on the project's site (https://mochajs.org/). To illustrate the concept of interfaces, here's the `exports` interface:

```
module.exports = {
  'memdb': {
    '.saveSync(doc)': {
      'should save the document': () => {
      }
    }
  }
}
```

All of these interfaces provide the same functionality, but for now you'll stick to the BDD interface and write the first test, shown in the following listing, in test/memdb.js. This test uses Node's assert module to perform the assertions.

Listing 9.9 Describing the memdb `.save` functionality

```
const memdb = require('..');
const assert = require('assert');
describe('memdb', () => {                          ← Describes memdb functionality
  describe('.saveSync(doc)', () => {               ← Describes .save() method's functionality
    it('should save the document', () => {
      const pet = { name: 'Tobi' };
      memdb.saveSync(pet);
      const ret = memdb.first({ name: 'Tobi' });
      assert(ret == pet);                           ← Ensures the pet was found
    });
  });
});
```

Describes the expectation

To run the tests, all you need to do is execute `npm test`. Mocha looks in the ./test directory by default for JavaScript files to execute. Because you haven't implemented the `.saveSync()` method yet, you'll see that the single defined test fails, as shown in figure 9.2.

```
wavded@dev: ~/Projects/memdb
wavded@dev ~/Projects/memdb» mocha


  ✱ 1 of 1 test failed:

  1) memdb .save(doc) should save the document:
     TypeError: Object #<Object> has no method 'save'
       at Context.<anonymous> (/home/wavded/Projects/memdb/test/memdb.js:8:13)
       at Test.Runnable.run (/usr/local/lib/node_modules/mocha/lib/runnable.js:184:32)
       at Runner.runTest (/usr/local/lib/node_modules/mocha/lib/runner.js:300:10)
       at Runner.runTests.next (/usr/local/lib/node_modules/mocha/lib/runner.js:346:12)
       at next (/usr/local/lib/node_modules/mocha/lib/runner.js:228:14)
       at Runner.hooks (/usr/local/lib/node_modules/mocha/lib/runner.js:237:7)
       at next (/usr/local/lib/node_modules/mocha/lib/runner.js:185:23)
       at Runner.hook (/usr/local/lib/node_modules/mocha/lib/runner.js:205:5)
       at process.startup.processNextTick.process._tickCallback (node.js:244:9)

wavded@dev ~/Projects/memdb» _
```

Figure 9.2 Failing test in Mocha

Let's make it pass! Add the code in the following listing to index.js.

Listing 9.10   Added save functionality

```
const db = [];
exports.saveSync = (doc) => {          ⟵  Adds the doc to
  db.push(doc);                             database array
};
exports.first = (obj) => {             ⟵  Selects docs that match
  return db.filter((doc) => {              every property in obj
    for (let key in obj) {
      if (doc[key] != obj[key]) {      ⟵  Not a match; returns false
        return false;                      and doesn't select this doc
      }
    }
    return true;                       ⟵  They all matched; returns
  }).shift();                              and selects the doc
};                                     ⟵  Wants only the
                                           first doc or null
```

Run the tests again with npm, and the results should be similar to figure 9.3.

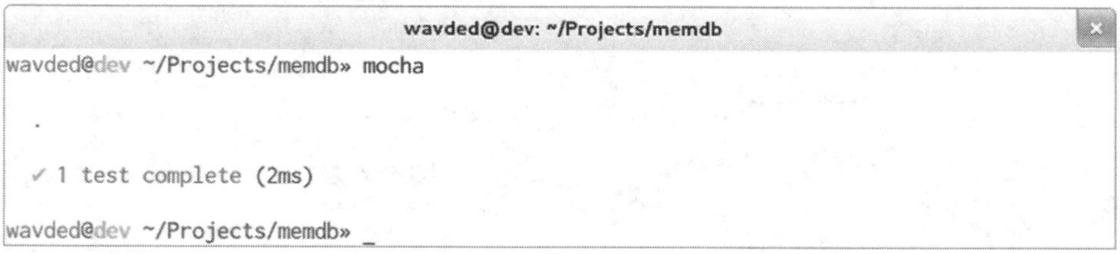

wavded@dev: ~/Projects/memdb

```
wavded@dev ~/Projects/memdb» mocha


  .

  ✓ 1 test complete (2ms)

wavded@dev ~/Projects/memdb» _
```

Figure 9.3   Successful test in Mocha

DEFINING SETUP AND CLEANUP LOGIC BY USING MOCHA HOOKS

The test case in listing 9.10 makes the assumption that `memdb.first()` works correctly, so you'll want to add a few test cases for that as well. The revised test file, listing 9.11, includes a new concept—the concept of Mocha *hooks*. The BDD interface exposes `beforeEach()`, `afterEach()`, `before()`, and `after()`, which take callbacks for defining setup and cleanup logic.

Listing 9.11   Adding a `beforeEach` hook

```
const memdb = require('..');
const assert = require('assert');
describe('memdb', () => {
  beforeEach(() => {                   ⟵  Clears database before each test
    memdb.clear();                         case to keep tests stateless
  });
  describe('synchronous .saveSync(doc)', () => {
```

```
  it('should save the document', () => {
    const pet = { name: 'Tobi' };
    memdb.saveSync(pet);
    const ret = memdb.first({ name: 'Tobi' });
    assert(ret == pet);
  });
});
describe('.first(obj)', () => {                          ⟵───  The first expectation
  it('should return the first matching doc', () => {  ⟵───    for .first()
    const tobi = { name: 'Tobi' };
    const loki = { name: 'Loki' };
    memdb.saveSync(tobi);
    memdb.saveSync(loki);                                     Makes sure each one
    let ret = memdb.first({ name: 'Tobi' });    ⟵───          can be returned properly
    assert(ret == tobi);
    ret = memdb.first({ name: 'Loki' });
    assert(ret == loki);
  });
  it('should return null when no doc matches', () => {  ⟵───  The second
    const ret = memdb.first({ name: 'Manny' });               expectation
    assert(ret == null);                                      for .first()
  });
});
});
```

Saves two documents (annotation pointing to the two `memdb.saveSync` lines)

Ideally, test cases share no state whatsoever. To achieve this with memdb, you need to remove all the documents by implementing the `.clear()` method in index.js:

```
exports.clear = () => {
  db.length = 0;
};
```

Running Mocha again should show you that three tests have passed.

TESTING ASYNCHRONOUS LOGIC

One thing we haven't yet looked at in Mocha is testing asynchronous logic. To see how this is done, you'll make a small change to one of the functions defined earlier in index.js. By changing the save function to the following, a callback can be optionally provided that will execute after a small delay (meant to simulate some sort of asynchronous operation):

```
exports.save = (doc, cb) => {
  db.push(doc);
  if (cb) {
    setTimeout(() => {
      cb();
    }, 1000);
  }
};
```

Mocha test cases can be defined as asynchronous by adding an argument to a function defining testing logic. The argument is commonly named done. The following listing shows how to write a test for the asynchronous save method.

Listing 9.12   Testing asynchronous logic

```
describe('asyncronous .save(doc)', () => {
  it('should save the document', (done) => {
    const pet = { name: 'Tobi' };
    memdb.save(pet, () => {                          ◁──┐  Saves doc
      const ret = memdb.first({ name: 'Tobi' });
      assert(ret == pet);                            ◁──── Asserts document
      done();                    ◁──┐                       saved properly
    });                             │ Tells Mocha you're
  });                               │ done with this test case
});
```

Invokes callback with first doc (label pointing to `memdb.save(pet, () => {` line)

This same rule applies to all of the hooks. For example, the `beforeEach()` hook to clear the database could add a callback, and Mocha could wait until it's called in order to move on. If `done()` is invoked with an error as the first argument, Mocha will report the error and mark the hook or test case as a failure:

```
beforeEach((done) => {
  memdb.clear(done);
});
```

For more about Mocha, check out its full online documentation: http://mochajs.org. Mocha also works for client-side JavaScript.

Mocha's use of nonparallel testing

Mocha executes tests one after another rather than in parallel, which makes test suites execute more slowly but makes writing tests easier. But Mocha won't let any test run for an inordinately long time. Mocha, by default, allows any given test to run for only 2,000 milliseconds before failing it. If you have tests that take longer, you can run Mocha with the `--timeout` command-line option and then specify a larger number.

For most testing, running tests serially is fine. If you find this problematic, other frameworks, such as Vows, execute in parallel, and are covered in the next section.

9.1.3 Vows

The tests you can write using the Vows unit-testing framework are more structured than those of many other frameworks, with the structure intended to make the tests easy to read and maintain.

Vows uses its own BDD-flavored terminology to define test structure. In the realm of Vows, a test suite contains one or more batches. A *batch* can be thought of as a group of related *contexts*, or conceptual areas of concern that you want to test. The batches and contexts run in parallel. A context may contain a *topic*, one or more *vows*, and/or one or more related contexts (inner contexts also run in parallel). A *topic* is testing logic that's related to a context. A *vow* is a test of the result of a topic. Figure 9.4 shows how Vows structures tests.

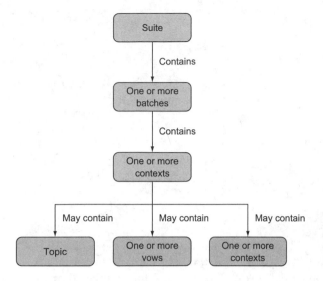

Figure 9.4 **Vows can structure tests in a suite using batches, contexts, topics, and vows.**

Vows, like Mocha, is geared toward automated application testing. The difference is primarily in flavor and parallelism, with Vows tests requiring a specific structure and terminology. In this section, we run through an example application test and explain how to use a Vows test to run multiple tests at the same time.

Add Vows to the to-do project by installing it using npm:

```
mkdir -p vows-todo/test
cd vows-todo
touch todo.js
touch test/todo-test.js
npm init -y
npm install --save-dev -g vows
```

You need to add Vows to the test property in package.json so you can run the tests by typing npm test:

```
"scripts": {
  "test": "vows test/*.js"
},
```

TESTING APPLICATION LOGIC WITH VOWS

You can trigger testing in Vows either by running a script containing test logic or by using the vows command-line test runner. The following example of a standalone test script (which can be run like any other Node script) uses one of the tests of the to-do application's core logic.

Listing 9.13 creates a batch. Within the batch, you define a context. Within the context, you define a topic and a vow. Note how the code uses the callback to deal with asynchronous logic in the topic. If a topic isn't asynchronous, a value can be returned rather than being sent via a callback. Save the file as test/todo-test.js.

Listing 9.13   Using Vows to test the to-do application

```
const vows = require('vows');
const assert = require('assert');
const Todo = require('./../todo');
vows.describe('Todo').addBatch({                          ⟵——— A batch
  'when adding an item': {                    ⟵——— A context
    topic: () => {                                  ⟵——— A topic
      const todo = new Todo();
      todo.add('Feed my cat');
      return todo;
    },
    'it should exist in my todos': (er, todo) => {   ⟵——— A vow
      assert.equal(todo.length, 1);
    }
  }
}).export(module);
```

You should be able to run this test by typing `npm test`. If you install Vows globally with `npm i -g vows`, you can also run all tests in a folder named *test* by entering the following command:

```
$ vows test/*
```

For more about Vows, check out the project's online documentation (http://vowsjs.org/), as shown in figure 9.5.

Vows offers a comprehensive testing solution, but you can mix and match test library features by using a different assertion library. Perhaps you like Mocha but don't like Node's assertion library. The next section introduces Chai, an assertion library that you can use in place of Node's assert module.

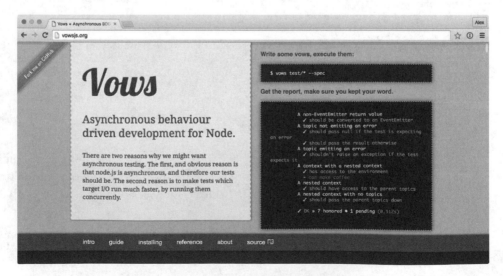

Figure 9.5   Vows combines full-featured BDD testing with macros and flow control.

9.1.4 Chai

Chai (http://chaijs.com/) is a popular assertion library that comes with three interfaces: *should, expect,* and *assert.* The `assert` interface, shown in the following listing, looks like Node's built-in assertion module, but it comes with useful tools for comparing objects, arrays, and their properties. For example, `typeOf` can be used to compare types, and `property` checks that an object has the desired property.

Listing 9.14 Chai's `assert` interface

```
const chai = require('chai');
const assert = chai.assert;                                    ◁──────── Selects assertion
const foo = 'bar';                                                       interface
const tea = { flavors: ['chai', 'earl grey', 'pg tips'] };

assert.typeOf(foo, 'string');

assert.equal(foo, 'bar');
assert.lengthOf(foo, 3);

assert.property(tea, 'flavors');
assert.lengthOf(tea.flavors, 3);
```

The main reason you might want to try Chai is the `should` and `expect` interfaces. They provide fluent APIs that are more like BDD-style libraries. Here's the `expect` interface:

```
const chai = require('chai');
const expect = chai.expect;
const foo = 'bar';
expect(foo).to.be.a('string');
expect(foo).to.equal('bar');
```

This API reads more like an English sentence—the declarative style is more verbose but easier to read aloud. The `should` interface switches this around: objects are decorated to have extra properties, so you don't need to wrap assertions in a call as with `expect`:

```
const chai = require('chai');
chai.should();
const foo = 'bar';
foo.should.be.a('string');
foo.should.equal('bar');
```

Deciding which interface to use depends on the project. If you're writing tests first and using them to document the project, the verbose `expect` and `should` interfaces will work well. JavaScript purists prefer `expect` because it doesn't change prototypes, but those with Ruby experience may be familiar with APIs such as `should`.

The main advantage of using Chai is the range of plugins. This includes handy things such as chai-as-promised (http://chaijs.com/plugins/chai-as-promised/), which helps test code that uses promises, and chai-stats (http://chaijs.com/plugins/chai-stats/), a library for comparing numbers according to statistical methods. Note that Chai is an assertion library, so you should use it alongside a test runner like Mocha.

Another BDD assertion library like Chai is Should.js. The next section introduces Should.js and demonstrates how to write tests with it.

9.1.5 *Should.js*

Should.js is an assertion library that can help make your tests easier to read by allowing you to express assertions in a BDD-like style. It's designed to be used in conjunction with other testing frameworks, which lets you continue to use your own preferred framework. In this section, you'll learn how to write assertions with Should.js and, as an example, you'll write a test for a custom module.

Should.js is easy to use with other frameworks because it augments `Object.-prototype` with a single property: `should`. This allows you to write expressive assertions such as `user.role.should.equal('admin')`, or `users.should.include('rick')`.

Let's say you're writing a Node command-line tip calculator that you want to use to figure out who should pay what amount when you split a bill with friends. You'd like to write tests for your calculation logic in a way that's easily understood by your nonprogrammer friends, because then they won't think you're cheating them.

To set up your tip calculator application, enter the following commands, which set up a folder for the application, and then install Should.js for testing:

```
mkdir -p tips/test
cd tips
touch index.js
touch test/tips.js
```

Now you can install Should.js by running the following commands:

```
npm init -y
npm install --save-dev should
```

Next, edit the index.js file, which will contain the logic defining the application's core functionality. Specifically, the tip calculator logic includes four helper functions:

- `addPercentageToEach`—Increases each number in an array by a given percentage
- `sum`—Calculates the sum of each element in an array
- `percentFormat`—Formats a percentage for display
- `dollarFormat`—Formats a dollar value for display

Add this logic by populating index.js with the contents of the following listing.

Listing 9.15 Logic for calculating tips when splitting a bill

```
exports.addPercentageToEach = (prices, percentage) => {      ◁──  Adds percentage
  return prices.map((total) => {                                   to array elements
    total = parseFloat(total);
    return total + (total * percentage);
```

```
    });
  };
exports.sum = (prices) => {                              ┐  Calculates sum of
  return prices.reduce((currentSum, currentValue) => {  ←┘  array elements
    return parseFloat(currentSum) + parseFloat(currentValue);
  });
};
exports.percentFormat = (percentage) => {                ┐  Formats percentage
  return parseFloat(percentage) * 100 + '%';            ←┘  for display
};
exports.dollarFormat = (number) => {                     ┐  Formats dollar value
  return `$${parseFloat(number).toFixed(2)}`;           ←┘  for display
};
```

Now edit the test script in test/tips.js, as shown in the following listing. The script loads the tip logic module; defines a tax, tip percentage, and the bill items to test; tests the addition of a percentage to each array element; and tests the bill total.

> **Listing 9.16 Logic that calculates tips when splitting a bill**

```
const tips = require('..');                           ←──── Uses tip logic module
const should = require('should');
const tax = 0.12;                                     ←──── Defines tax and tip rates
const tip = 0.15;
const prices = [10, 20];                              ←──── Defines bill items to test

const pricesWithTipAndTax = tips.addPercentageToEach(prices, tip + tax);
pricesWithTipAndTax[0].should.equal(12.7);            ┐
pricesWithTipAndTax[1].should.equal(25.4);            ┘  Tests tax and tip addition

const totalAmount = tips.sum(pricesWithTipAndTax).toFixed(2);
totalAmount.should.equal('38.10');                    ←──── Tests bill totaling

const totalAmountAsCurrency = tips.dollarFormat(totalAmount);
totalAmountAsCurrency.should.equal('$38.10');

const tipAsPercent = tips.percentFormat(tip);
tipAsPercent.should.equal('15%');
```

Run the script by using the following command. If all is well, the script should generate no output, because no assertions have been thrown, and your friends will be reassured of your honesty:

```
$ node test/tips.js
```

To make this easier to run, add it as the test property under scripts in package.json:

```
"scripts": {
  "test": "node test/tips.js"
}
```

Should.js supports many types of assertions—everything from assertions that use regular expressions to assertions that check object properties—allowing comprehensive testing of data and objects generated by your application. The project's GitHub page (https://github.com/shouldjs/should.js) provides comprehensive documentation of Should.js's functionality.

Spies, stubs, and mocks are often used in addition to assertion libraries to control the way that code under tests is executed. The next section demonstrates how to do these with Sinon.JS.

9.1.6   *Spies and stubs with Sinon.JS*

The final tool for your testing toolbox is a mock and stub library. The reason we write unit tests is to isolate parts of a system to test, but sometimes this is difficult. For example, imagine you're testing code that resizes images. You don't want to write to real image files, so how do you write tests? The code shouldn't have special test branches that avoid touching the filesystem, because then you wouldn't be truly testing the code. In cases like this, you need to *stub* the filesystem functionality. The practice of writing stubs also helps you do true TDD, because you can stub dependencies that aren't ready yet.

In this section, you'll learn how to use Sinon.JS (http://sinonjs.org/) to write test spies, stubs, and mocks. Before you get started, create a new project and install Sinon:

```
mkdir sinon-js-examples
cd sinon-js-examples
npm init -y
mkdir test
npm i --save-dev sinon
```

Next create a sample file to test. The example we use is a simple JSON key/value database. Our goal is to be able to stub the filesystem API so it doesn't create real files on the filesystem. This will allow us to test only our database code rather than the file-handling code, as shown in the next listing.

Listing 9.17   Database class

```
const fs = require('fs');

class Database {
  constructor(filename) {
    this.filename = filename;
    this.data = {};
  }

  save(cb) {
    fs.writeFile(this.filename, JSON.stringify(this.data), cb);
  }

  insert(key, value) {
    this.data[key] = value;
  }
}

module.exports = Database;
```

Save the listing as db.js. Now you'll try testing it with Sinon's spies.

SPIES

Sometimes you just want to see whether a method has been called. Spies are perfect for this. The API lets you replace a method with something you can use to make assertions on. To mock the `fs.writeFile` call in db.js, use Sinon's method replacement, `spy`:

```
sinon.spy(fs, 'writeFile');
```

When the test is finished, you can get the original method back with `restore`:

```
fs.writeFile.restore();
```

In a test library like Mocha, you'd place these calls in the `beforeEach` and `afterEach` blocks. The following listing shows a full example of using spies. Save this file as spies.js.

Listing 9.18 Using spies

```
const sinon = require('sinon');
const Database = require('./db');
const fs = require('fs');
const database = new Database('./sample.json');

const fsWriteFileSpy = sinon.spy(fs, 'writeFile');    ❶ Replaces original fs method
const saveDone = sinon.spy();

database.insert('name', 'Charles Dickens');
database.save(saveDone);
                                                      ❷ Ensures writeFile is called only once
sinon.assert.calledOnce(fsWriteFileSpy);
                                                      ❸ Restores the original method
fs.writeFile.restore();
```

After setting up the spy ❶, the code under test is run. Then you ensure that the expected method was called with `sinon.assert` ❷. The original method is then restored ❸. In this test, restoring it isn't strictly necessary, but it's best practice to always restore methods that you've changed.

STUBS

Sometimes you need to control code flow. For example, you might want to force an error branch to be executed so you can test error handling in your code. The preceding example could be rewritten to use a stub instead of a spy to cause `writeFile` to execute its callback. Note that you still want to avoid calling the original method, but instead force the code under test to run the supplied callback. The next listing shows how to use stubs to replace functions. Save it as stub.js.

Listing 9.19 Using stubs

```
const sinon = require('sinon');
const Database = require('./db');
```

```
const fs = require('fs');
const database = new Database('./sample.json');

const stub = sinon.stub(fs, 'writeFile', (file, data, cb) => {    ◁———
  cb();
});
const saveDone = sinon.spy();

database.insert('name', 'Charles Dickens');
database.save(saveDone);

sinon.assert.calledOnce(stub);                   ◁———
sinon.assert.calledOnce(saveDone);                  ◁———

fs.writeFile.restore();
```

Replaces writeFile with your own function

Ensures writeFile was called

Ensures database.save's callback was run

Using a combination of stubs and spies is ideal for testing Node code that makes heavy use of user-supplied functions, callbacks, and promises. Now that you've looked at tools designed for unit testing, let's move on to an altogether different style of testing: functional testing.

9.2   *Functional testing*

In most web development projects, *functional tests* work by driving the browser and then checking for various DOM transformations against a list of user-specific requirements. Imagine you're building a content management system. A functional test for the image library upload feature would upload an image, check that it gets added, and then check that it's added to a corresponding list of images.

The choice of tools to implement functional testing in Node is bewildering. From a high level, however, they fall into two broad groups: headless and browser-based tests. *Headless tests* typically use something like PhantomJS to provide a terminal-friendly browser environment, but lighter solutions use libraries such as Cheerio and JSDOM. *Browser-based tests* use a browser automation tool such as Selenium (www.seleniumhq.org) so you can write scripts that drive a real browser. Both approaches can use the same under-

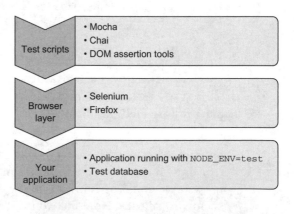

Figure 9.6   Testing with browser automation

lying Node test tools, so you could use Mocha, Jasmine, or even Cucumber to drive Selenium against your application. Figure 9.6 shows an example test environment.

In this section, you'll learn about functional testing solutions for Node, so you can set up test environments based on your own requirements.

9.2.1 *Selenium*

Selenium is a popular Java-based browser automation library. With the aid of a language-specific driver, you can connect to a Selenium server and run tests against a real browser. In this section, you'll learn how to use WebdriverIO (http://webdriver.io/), a Node Selenium driver.

Getting Selenium running is trickier than pure Node test libraries, because you need to install Java and download the Selenium JAR file. Download Java for your operating system, and then go to the Selenium download site (http://docs.seleniumhq.org/download/) to download the JAR file. You can then run a Selenium server like this:

```
java -jar selenium-server-standalone-2.53.0.jar
```

Note that your exact Selenium version may be different. You may also have to supply a path to the browser binary. For example, in Windows 10 with Firefox set as the browserName, you can specify Firefox's full path like this:

```
java -jar -Dwebdriver.firefox.driver="C:\path\to\firefox.exe" selenium-
    server-standalone-3.0.1.jar
```

The exact path will depend on how Firefox is installed on your machine. For more about the Firefox driver, read the SeleniumHQ documentation (https://github.com/SeleniumHQ/selenium/wiki/FirefoxDriver). Drivers for Chrome and Microsoft Edge are configured in similar ways.

Now create a new Node project and install WebdriverIO:

```
mkdir -p selenium/test/specs
cd selenium
npm init -y
npm install --save-dev webdriverio
npm install --save express
```

WebdriverIO comes with a friendly config file generator. To run it, run `wdio config`:

```
./node_modules/.bin/wdio config
```

Follow the questions and accept the defaults. Figure 9.7 shows my session.

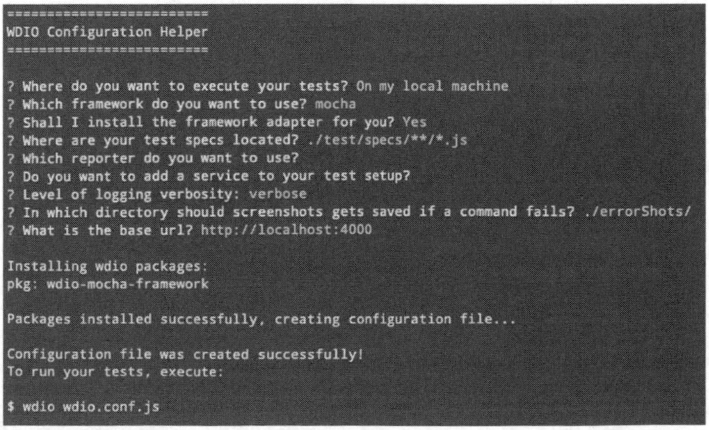

Figure 9.7 Using `wdio` to configure Selenium tests

```
==========================
WDIO Configuration Helper
==========================

? Where do you want to execute your tests? On my local machine
? Which framework do you want to use? mocha
? Shall I install the framework adapter for you? Yes
? Where are your test specs located? ./test/specs/**/*.js
? Which reporter do you want to use?
? Do you want to add a service to your test setup?
? Level of logging verbosity: verbose
? In which directory should screenshots gets saved if a command fails? ./errorShots/
? What is the base url? http://localhost:4000

Installing wdio packages:
pkg: wdio-mocha-framework

Packages installed successfully, creating configuration file...

Configuration file was created successfully!
To run your tests, execute:

$ wdio wdio.conf.js
```

Update the package.json file with the `wdio` command so tests can be run with `npm test`:

```
"scripts": {
  "test": "wdio wdio.conf.js"
},
```

Now add something to the test. A basic Express server will suffice. The example in the following listing will be used in the subsequent listing for testing. Save this listing as index.js (it's c09-testing/selenium/index.js in the book's sample code).

Listing 9.20 Sample Express project

```
const express = require('express');
const app = express();
const port = process.env.PORT || 4000;

app.get('/', (req, res) => {
  res.send(`
<html>
  <head>
    <title>My to-do list</title>
  </head>
  <body>
    <h1>Welcome to my awesome to-do list</h1>
  </body>
</html>
  `);
});

app.listen(port, () => {
  console.log('Running on port', port);
});
```

The good thing about WebdriverIO is it provides a simple, fluent API for writing Selenium tests. The syntax is clear and easy to learn—you can even write tests with CSS selectors. The next listing (found in test/specs/todo-test.js in the book's sample code) shows a simple test that sets up a WebdriverIO client and then checks the title on the page.

Listing 9.21 A WebdriverIO test

```
const assert = require('assert');
const webdriverio = require('webdriverio');

describe('todo tests', () => {
  let client;

  before(() => {                              ❶ Sets up WebdriverIO
    client = webdriverio.remote();                client
    return client.init();
  });
```

```
        it('todo list test', () => {
          return client
            .url('/')
            .getTitle()
              .then(title => assert.equal(title, 'My to-do list'));
        });
      });
```

Gets home page ❷

Gets title from head

Asserts title is expected

After WebdriverIO is connected ❶, you can use an instance of the client to fetch pages from your app ❷. Then you can query the current state of the document in the browser—this example uses `getTitle` to get the `title` element from the document's `head`. If you want to query the document for CSS elements, you can use `.elements` instead (http://webdriver.io/api/protocol/elements.html). There are all kinds of methods for manipulating the document, forms, and even cookies.

This test, which looks like the other Mocha tests in this chapter, is capable of running a real browser against a Node web app. To run it, start the server on port 4000:

```
PORT=4000 node index.js
```

Then type `npm test`. You should see Firefox open and the tests run in the command line. If you want to use Chrome, open wdio.conf.js and change the `browserName` property.

More-advanced testing with Selenium

If you use WebdriverIO and Selenium to test a more complex web app that uses something like React or Angular, you'll want to check out the `utility` methods. Some of the methods will pause the test until certain elements are available, which is great for React apps that may asynchronously render the document, updating it several times based on when remote data is available.

Take a look at the `waitFor*` methods, such as `waitForVisible` (http://webdriver.io/api/utility/waitForVisible.html) to learn more.

9.3 Dealing with failing tests

When you're working on an established project, there will come a point when tests begin to fail. Node provides several tools for getting more detail on failed tests, and in this section you'll learn about how to enrich the output generated when debugging failing tests.

The first thing to do when tests fail is to generate more-verbose logging output. The next section demonstrates how to do that with `NODE_DEBUG`.

9.3.1 Getting more-detailed logs

When tests fail, it's useful to get information on what the program is doing. Node has two ways to do this: one for Node's internals, and another for npm modules. To debug Node's core modules, use `NODE_DEBUG`.

USING NODE_DEBUG

To see how NODE_DEBUG works, imagine you have a deeply nested filesystem call where you've forgotten to use a callback. For example, the following example will throw an exception:

```
const fs = require('fs');

function deeplyNested() {
fs.readFile('/');
}

deeplyNested();
```

The stack trace shows only a limited amount of detail about the exception, and in particular doesn't include full information on the call site where the exception originated:

```
fs.js:60
      throw err;  // Forgot a callback but don't know where? Use
    NODE_DEBUG=fs
      ^

Error: EISDIR: illegal operation on a directory, read
    at Error (native)
```

Without the helpful comment, many programmers see a trace like this and blame Node for the unhelpful error. But, as the comment points out, NODE_DEBUG=fs can be used to get more information on the fs module. Run the script like this instead:

```
NODE_DEBUG=fs node node-debug-example.js
```

Now you'll see a more detailed trace that helps debug the issue:

```
fs.js:53
        throw backtrace;
        ^

Error: EISDIR: illegal operation on a directory, read
    at rethrow (fs.js:48:21)
    at maybeCallback (fs.js:66:42)
    at Object.fs.readFile (fs.js:227:18)
    at deeplyNested (node-debug-example.js:4:6)
    at Object.<anonymous> (node-debug-example.js:7:1)
    at Module._compile (module.js:435:26)
    at Object.Module._extensions..js (module.js:442:10)
    at Module.load (module.js:356:32)
    at Function.Module._load (module.js:311:12)
    at Function.Module.runMain (module.js:467:10)
```

It's clear from this trace that the problem lies in our file, inside a function on line 4 that was originally called from line 7. This makes debugging any code that uses core modules much easier, and that includes not only the filesystem, but also network libraries such as Node's HTTP client and server modules.

Using DEBUG

The public alternative to NODE_DEBUG is DEBUG. Many packages on npm look for the DEBUG environment variable. It mimics the parameter style used by NODE_DEBUG, so you can specify a list of modules to debug or see all of them with DEBUG='*'. Figure 9.8 shows the project from chapter 4 running with DEBUG='*'.

```
→ tldr git:(master) X DEBUG="*" npm start

> tldr@1.0.0 start /Users/alex/Documents/Code/nodeinaction/ch04-what-is-a-node-web-app/tldr
> node index.js

  express:application set "x-powered-by" to true +0ms
  express:application set "etag" to 'weak' +3ms
  express:application set "etag fn" to [Function: wetag] +2ms
  express:application set "env" to 'development' +1ms
  express:application set "query parser" to 'extended' +0ms
  express:application set "query parser fn" to [Function: parseExtendedQueryString] +0ms
  express:application set "subdomain offset" to 2 +0ms
  express:application set "trust proxy" to false +0ms
  express:application set "trust proxy fn" to [Function: trustNone] +1ms
  express:application booting in development mode +0ms
  express:application set "view" to [Function: View] +0ms
  express:application set "views" to '/Users/alex/Documents/Code/nodeinaction/ch04-what-is-a-node-web-app/tldr/views' +0ms
  express:application set "jsonp callback name" to 'callback' +0ms
  express:router use / query +429ms
```

Figure 9.8 Running an Express application with DEBUG='*'

If you want to incorporate the NODE_DEBUG functionality into your own projects, use the built-in util.debuglog method:

```
const debuglog = require('util').debuglog('example');
debuglog('You can only see these messages by setting NODE_DEBUG=example!');
```

To make custom debug loggers that are configured with DEBUG, you need to use the debug package from npm (www.npmjs.com/package/debug). You can create as many loggers as you want. Imagine you're building an MVC web application. You could create separate loggers for models, views, and controllers. Then, when tests fail, you'll be able to specify the debug logs that are necessary to debug the specific part of the application. The following listing (found in ch09-testing/debug-example/index.js) demonstrates how to use the debug module.

Listing 9.22 Using the debug package

```
const debugViews = require('debug')('debug-example:views');
const debugModels = require('debug')('debug-example:models');

debugViews('Example view message');
debugModels('Example model message');
```

To run this example and see the view logs, set DEBUG to debug-example:views:

```
DEBUG=debug-example:views node index.js
```

One final feature of debug logging is that you can prefix a debug section with a hyphen to remove it from logs:

```
DEBUG='* -debug-example:views' node index.js
```

Hiding certain modules means you can still use the wildcard, but omit unneeded or noisy sections from the output.

9.3.2 *Getting better stack traces*

If you're using asynchronous operations, and that includes anything you've written using asynchronous callbacks or promises, then you may run into problems when stack traces aren't detailed enough. Packages on npm can help you in such cases. For example, when callbacks run asynchronously, Node won't keep the call stack from when the operation was queued. To test this, create two files, one called async.js that defines an asynchronous function, and another called index.js that requires async.js. This snippet is aync.js (found in ch09-testing/debug-stacktraces/async.js in the book's sample code):

```
module.exports = () => {
  setTimeout(() => {
    throw new Error();
  })
};
```

And index.js just needs to require async.js:

```
require('./async.js')();
```

Now if you run index.js with `node index.js`, you'll get a short stack trace that doesn't show the caller of the failed function, only the location of the thrown exception:

```
    throw new Error();
    ^

Error
    at null._onTimeout (async.js:3:11)
    at Timer.listOnTimeout (timers.js:92:15)
```

To improve this reporting, install the trace package (www.npmjs.com/package/trace) and run it with `node -r trace index.js`. The `-r` flag tells Node to require the trace module before loading anything else.

Another problem with stack traces is they can be *too* detailed. This happens when the trace includes too much detail about Node's internals. To clear up your stack traces, use `clarify` (www.npmjs.com/package/clarify). Again, you can run it with the `-r` flag:

```
$ node -r clarify index.js
    throw new Error();
    ^
```

```
Error
    at null._onTimeout (async.js:3:11)
```

`clarify` is particularly useful if you want to include stack traces in error alert emails for a web application.

If you're running code intended for browsers in Node, perhaps as part of an isomorphic web application, then you can get better stack traces by using source-map-support (www.npmjs.com/package/source-map-support). This can be run with `-r`, but it also works with some test frameworks:

```
$ node -r source-map-support/register index.js
$ mocha --require source-map-support/register index.js
```

The next time you're struggling with a stack trace generated by asynchronous code, look for tools such as `trace` and `clarify` to make sure you're getting the best out of what V8 and Node can offer.

9.4 *Summary*

- Writing unit tests requires a test runner such as Mocha.
- Node has a built-in assertion library called assert.
- There are other assertion libraries, including Chai and Should.js.
- If you don't want to run certain code, such as network requests, you can use Sinon.JS.
- Sinon.JS also allows you to spy on code and verify that certain functions or methods were run.
- Selenium can be used to write browser tests by scripting real browsers.

10

Deploying Node applications and maintaining uptime

This chapter covers

- Choosing where to host your Node application
- Deploying a typical application
- Maintaining uptime and maximizing performance

Developing a web application is one thing, but putting it into production is another. For every web technology, tips and tricks are available that can increase stability and maximize performance, and Node is no different. In this chapter, you'll get an overview of how to choose the right deployment environment for your application, and you'll also learn about how to maintain uptime.

The following section outlines the main types of environments you'll deploy to. Then you'll look at ways to maintain high uptimes.

10.1 Hosting Node applications

The web applications you've developed in this book use a Node-based HTTP server. A browser can talk to your application without a dedicated HTTP server such as Apache or Nginx. It's possible to sit a server such as Nginx in front of your application, however, so Node can often be hosted anywhere you've previously been able to run a web server.

Cloud providers, including Heroku and Amazon, also support Node. As a result, you have three ways to run your application in a reliable and scalable way:

- *Platform as a service*—Run your application on Amazon, Azure, or Heroku
- *Server or virtual machine*—Run your application on a UNIX or Windows server in the cloud, a private hosting company, or internally at your place of business
- *Container*—Run your application and any other associated services by using a software container such as Docker

Choosing which of these three approaches to use can be difficult, particularly because trying them out first isn't always easy. Note that each option isn't tied to a particular vendor: Amazon and Azure are both capable of providing all of these deployment strategies, for example. To understand which option is right for you, this section explains their requirements as well as their advantages and disadvantages. Fortunately, every option has free or affordable options, so they should all be accessible to hobbyists and professionals alike.

10.1.1 *Platform as a service*

With platform as a service (PaaS), you typically prepare an application for deployment by signing up for the service, creating a new app, and then adding a Git remote to your project. Pushing to that remote deploys your application. By default, it'll run on a single container—the exact definition of container varies among vendors—and the service will attempt to restart the application if it crashes. You'll get limited access to logs, and web and command-line interfaces for managing your app. To scale, you'll run more instances of your application, which carries an additional fee. Table 10.1 contains an overview of the features of a typical PaaS offering.

Table 10.1   PaaS features

Ease of use	High
Features	Git push to deploy, simple horizontal scalability
Infrastructure	Abstracted/black box
Commercial suitability	Good: applications are typically network isolated
Pricing[a]	Low traffic: $$; Popular site: $$$$
Vendors	Heroku, Azure, AWS Elastic Beanstalk

[a] $: Cheap, $$$$$: Expensive

PaaS providers support their own preferred database and third-party databases. For Heroku, this is PostgreSQL; and for Azure, it's SQL Database. The database connection details will be in environment variables, so you can connect without adding database credentials to your project's source code. PaaS is great for hobbyists, because it can be cheap or even sometimes free to run small projects with low traffic.

Some vendors are easier to use than others: Heroku is extremely easy for programmers familiar with Git, even with little or no sysadmin or DevOps knowledge. PaaS systems typically know how to run projects made with popular tools such as Node, Rails, and Django, so they're almost plug-and-play.

EXAMPLE: NODE ON HEROKU IN 10 MINUTES

In this section, you'll deploy an application to Heroku. Using Heroku's default settings, you'll deploy the application to a single lightweight Linux container, known as a *dyno* in Heroku's terminology, to serve your application. To deploy a basic Node app to Heroku, you need the following prerequisites:

- An app to deploy
- An account with Heroku: https://signup.heroku.com/
- The Heroku CLI: https://devcenter.heroku.com/articles/heroku-cli

After you have these elements, sign in to Heroku on the command-line:

```
heroku login
```

Heroku then prompts you to enter your email address and Heroku password. Next, make a simple Express app:

```
mkdir heroku-example
npm i -g express-generator
express
npm i
```

You can run `npm start` and visit http://localhost:3000 to ensure that everything is running correctly. The next step is to make a Git repository and create a Heroku application:

```
git init
git add .
git commit -m 'Initial commit'
heroku create
git push heroku master
```

This displays a randomly generated URL for your application, and a Git remote. Whenever you want to deploy, commit your changes with Git and push to `heroku master`. You can change the URL and the name of the application with `heroku rename`.

Now visit the herokuapp.com URL from the previous step to see your basic Express app. To see the application logs, run `heroku logs`, and to get a shell in the application's dyno, run `heroku run bash`.

Heroku is a quick and easy way to run a Node application. Notice that you don't have to do any Node-specific tailoring—Heroku runs basic Node apps out of the box without extra configuration. Sometimes you need more control over the environment, however, so in the next section we introduce using servers for hosting Node apps.

10.1.2 Servers

Getting your own server has some advantages over PaaS. Instead of worrying about where to run the database, you can install PostgreSQL, MySQL, or even Redis on the same server if you want. You can install anything you like: custom logging software, HTTP servers, caching layers—it's up to you. Table 10.2 summarizes the main characteristics of running your own servers.

Table 10.2   Server features

Ease of use	Low
Features	Complete control over the whole stack, run your own database and caching layer
Infrastructure	Open to the developer (or sysadmin/DevOps)
Commercial suitability	Good if you have staff capable of maintaining the server
Pricing	Small VM: $; Large hosted server: $$$$$
Vendors	Azure, Amazon, hosting companies

You can obtain and maintain a server in various ways. You can get a cheap virtual machine from a company such as Linode or Digital Ocean; this will be a full server that you can configure however you like, but it'll share resources with other virtual machines on the same hardware. You can also buy your own hardware or rent a server. Some hosting companies offer managed hosting, whereby they'll help maintain the server's operating system.

You have to decide which operating system you want to use. Debian has several flavors, and Node also works well in Windows and Solaris, so the choice is more difficult than it seems.

Another critical decision is how to expose your app to the world: traffic can be redirected from port 80 and 443 to your app, but you could also sit Nginx in front of it to proxy requests and potentially handle static files.

You have various ways to move your code from your repository to the server as well. You can manually copy files with scp, sftp, or rsync, or you can use Chef to control multiple servers and manage releases. Some people set up a Heroku-like Git hook that will automatically update the app on the server, based on pushes to a certain Git branch.

The important thing to realize is that managing your own server is difficult. Configuration takes a lot of work, and the server also has to be maintained with the latest OS bug fixes and security updates. If you're a hobbyist, this may put you off—but you'll learn a lot and may discover an interest in DevOps.

Running Node apps on a virtual machine or full server doesn't require anything special. If you want to see some of the techniques used to run a Node app on a server and keep it running for long periods of time, skip forward to section 10.2, Understanding deployment basics. Otherwise, continue reading to learn about Node and Docker.

10.1.3 Containers

Using software containers is a kind of OS virtualization that automates the deployment of applications. The most well-known project is Docker, which is open source but also has commercial services that help you deploy production applications. Table 10.3 shows the main features of containers.

Table 10.3 Server features

Ease of use	Medium
Features	Complete control over the whole stack, run your own database and caching layer, redeploy to various providers and local machines
Infrastructure	Open to the developer (or sysadmin/DevOps)
Commercial suitability	Great: deploy to a managed host, Docker host, or your own datacenter
Pricing	$$$
Vendors	Azure, Amazon, Docker Cloud, Google Cloud Platform (with Kubernetes), hosting companies that allow you to run Docker containers

Docker allows you to define your application in terms of images. If you've built a typical content management system that has a microservice for image processing, a main service for storing application data, and then a back-end database, you could deploy it with four separate Docker images:

- *Image 1*—Microservice for resizing images that are uploaded to the CMS
- *Image 2*—PostgreSQL
- *Image 3*—Your main CMS web application with the administration interface
- *Image 4*—The public front-end web application

Because Docker is open source, you're not limited to a single vendor for deploying Dockerized applications. You can use Amazon's Elastic Beanstalk to deploy your images, Docker Cloud, or even Microsoft's Azure. Amazon also offers EC2 Container Service (ECS), and AWS CodeCommit for cloud Git repositories, which can be deployed to Elastic Beanstalk in a similar fashion to Heroku.

The amazing thing about using containers is that after you've containerized your app, you can bring up a fresh instance of it with a single command. If you get a new computer, you just need to check out your app's repository, install Docker locally, and then run the script to start your app. Because your application has a well-defined recipe for deployment, it's easier for you and your collaborators to understand how your application is supposed to run outside the local development environment.

EXAMPLE: RUNNING NODE APPS WITH DOCKER

Example: https://nodejs.org/en/docs/guides/nodejs-docker-webapp/

To run a Node app with Docker, you need to do a few things first:

1 Install Docker: https://docs.docker.com/engine/installation/.

2 Create a Node app. Refer to section 10.1.1, Platform as a service, for details on how to quickly make an example Express app.

3 Add a new file to the project called Dockerfile.

The Dockerfile tells Docker how to build your application's image, and how to install the app and run it. You'll use the official Node Docker image (https://hub.docker .com/_/node/) by specifying `FROM node:boron` in the Dockerfile, and then `run npm install` and `npm start` with the `RUN` and `CMD` instructions. The following snippet is a full Dockerfile that works for simple Node apps:

```
FROM node:argon

RUN mkdir -p /usr/src/app
WORKDIR /usr/src/app

COPY package.json /usr/src/app/
RUN npm install

COPY . /usr/src/app

EXPOSE 3000
CMD ["npm", "start"]
```

After you've created the Dockerfile, run the `docker build` (https://docs.docker .com/engine/reference/commandline/build/) command in the terminal to create an application image. You need to specify only the directory to build, so if you're in the example Express app, you should be able to type `docker build .` to build the image and send it to the Docker daemon.

Run `docker images` to see a list of images. Get the image ID, and then run `docker run -p 8080:3000 -d <image ID>` to run the app. We've bound the internal port (3000) to 8080 on localhost, so to access the app, we used http://localhost:8080 in a browser.

10.2 Understanding deployment basics

Suppose you've created a web application that you want to show off, or maybe you've created a commercial application and need to test it before putting it into full production. You'll likely start with a simple deployment, and then do some work later to maximize uptime and performance. In this section, we walk you through a simple, temporary Git deployment, as well as details on how to keep the application up and running with Forever. Temporary deployments don't persist beyond reboots, but they have the advantage of being quick to set up.

10.2.1 Deploying from a Git repository

Let's quickly go through a basic deployment using a Git repository to give you a feel for the fundamental steps. Deployment is most commonly done by following these steps:

1 Connect to a server by using SSH.

2 Install Node and version-control tools (such as Git or Subversion) on the server if needed.

3 Download application files, including Node scripts, images, and CSS style sheets, from a version-control repository to the server.

4 Start the application.

Here's an example of an application starting after downloading the application files using Git:

```
git clone https://github.com/Marak/hellonode.git
cd hellonode
node server.js
```

Like PHP, Node doesn't run as a background task. Because of this, the basic deployment we've outlined requires keeping the SSH connection open. As soon as the SSH connection closes, the application will terminate. Luckily, it's fairly easy to keep your application running by using a simple tool.

> **Automating deployment**
>
> You can automate deployment of your Node application in various ways. One is to use a tool such as Fleet (https://github.com/substack/fleet), which allows you to deploy to one or more servers by using `git push`. A more traditional approach is to use Capistrano, as detailed in the "Deploying node.js applications with Capistrano" post on Evan Tahler's Bricolage blog (https://blog.evantahler.com/deploying-node-js-applications-with-capistrano-af675cdaa7c6#.8r9v0kz3l).

10.2.2 *Keeping Node running*

Let's say you've created a personal blog by using the Ghost blogging application (https://ghost.org/), and you want to deploy it, making sure that it stays running even if you disconnect from SSH.

The most popular tool in the Node community for dealing with this is Nodejitsu's Forever (https://github.com/foreverjs/forever). It keeps your application running after you disconnect from SSH and, additionally, restarts it if it crashes. Figure 10.1 shows, conceptually, how Forever works.

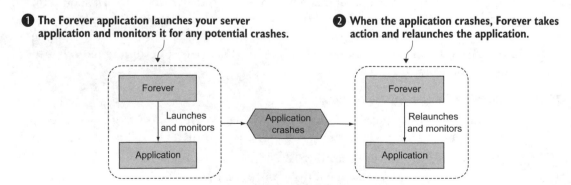

❶ The Forever application launches your server application and monitors it for any potential crashes.

❷ When the application crashes, Forever takes action and relaunches the application.

Figure 10.1   **The Forever tool helps you keep your application running, even if it crashes.**

You can install Forever globally by using the sudo command.

> **THE SUDO COMMAND** Sometimes when installing an npm module *globally* (with the -g flag), you need to prefix the npm command with the sudo command (www.sudo.ws) in order to run npm with superuser privileges. The first time you use the sudo command, you'll be prompted to enter your password. Then the command specified after it will be run.

If you're following along, install Forever now by using this command:

```
npm install -g forever
```

After you've installed Forever, you can use it to start your blog and keep it running with the following command:

```
forever start server.js
```

If you want to stop your blog for some reason, you can use Forever's stop command:

```
forever stop server.js
```

When using Forever, you can get a list of applications that the tool is managing by using its list command:

```
forever list
```

Another useful capability of Forever is that it can optionally restart your application when any source files have changed. This frees you from having to manually restart each time you add a feature or fix a bug.

To start Forever in this mode, use the -w flag:

```
forever -w start server.js
```

Although Forever is an extremely useful tool for deploying applications, you may want to use something more full-featured for long-term deployments. In the next section, you'll look at some industrial-strength monitoring solutions and see how to maximize application performance.

10.3 *Maximizing uptime and performance*

When a Node application is release-worthy, you'll want to make sure it starts and stops when the server starts and stops, and that it automatically restarts when the server crashes. It's easy to forget to stop an application before a reboot or to forget to restart an application afterward.

You'll also want to make sure you're taking steps to maximize performance. For example, it makes sense when you're running your application on a server with a quad-core CPU to not use only a single core. If you're using only a single core and your web application's traffic increases significantly, a single core may not have the processing capability to handle the traffic, and your web application won't be able to consistently respond.

In addition to using all CPU cores, you'll want to avoid using Node to host static files for high-volume production sites. Node is geared toward interactive applications, such as web applications and TCP/IP protocols, and it can't serve static files as efficiently as software optimized to do only that. For serving static files, you should use technologies such as Nginx (http://nginx.org/en/), which specializes in serving static files. Alternatively, you could upload all your static files to a content delivery network (CDN), such as Amazon S3 (http://aws.amazon.com/s3/), and reference those files in your application.

This section covers some server uptime and performance tips:

- Using Upstart to keep your application up and running through restarts and crashes
- Using Node's cluster API for multicore processors
- Serving Node application static files using Nginx

Let's start by looking at a powerful and easy-to-use tool for maintaining uptime: Upstart.

10.3.1   *Maintaining uptime with Upstart*

Let's say you're happy with an application and want to market it to the world. You want to make dead sure that if you restart a server, you don't then forget to restart your application. You also want to make sure that if your application crashes, it's not only automatically restarted, but the crash is logged and you're notified, which allows you to diagnose any underlying issues.

Upstart (http://upstart.ubuntu.com) is a project that provides an elegant way to manage the starting and stopping of any Linux application, including Node applications. Modern versions of Ubuntu and CentOS support the use of Upstart. An alternative for macOS is to create launchd files (node-launchd on npm can do this), and the Windows equivalent is to use Windows Services, which is supported by the node-windows package on npm.

You can install Upstart on Ubuntu, if it's not already installed, with this command:

```
sudo apt-get install upstart
```

You can install Upstart on CentOS, if it's not already installed, with this command:

```
sudo yum install upstart
```

After you install Upstart, you need to add an Upstart configuration file for each of your applications. These files are created in the /etc/init directory and are named something like my_application_name.conf. The configuration files don't need to be marked as executable.

The following creates an empty Upstart configuration file for this chapter's example application:

```
sudo touch /etc/init/hellonode.conf
```

Now add the contents of the following listing to your config file. This setup will run the application when the server starts and will stop the application upon shutdown. The exec section gets executed by Upstart.

Listing 10.1   A typical Upstart configuration file

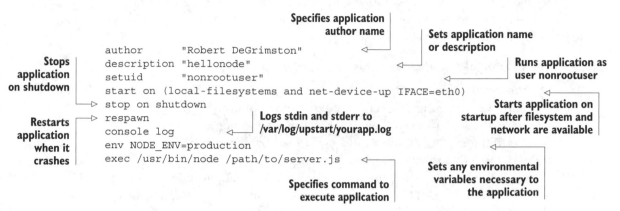

This configuration will keep your process up and running after the server restarts and even after it crashes unexpectedly. All the application-generated output will be sent to /var/log/upstart/hellonode.log, and Upstart will manage the log rotation for you.

Now that you've created an Upstart configuration file, you can start your application by using the following command:

```
sudo service hellonode
```

If your application was started successfully, you'll see a line like this:

```
hellonode start/running, process 6770
```

Upstart is highly configurable. Check out the online cookbook (http://upstart.ubuntu.com/cookbook/) for all the available options.

UPSTART AND RESPAWNING

When the respawn option is used, Upstart will by default continually reload your application on crashes *unless* the application is restarted 10 times within 5 seconds. You can change this limit by using the respawn limit COUNT INTERVAL option, where COUNT is the number of times within the INTERVAL, which is specified in seconds. For example, you set a limit of 20 times in 5 seconds like this:

```
respawn
respawn limit 20 5
```

If your application is reloaded 10 times within 5 seconds (the default limit), typically there's something wrong in the code or configuration, and it will never start successfully. Upstart won't try to restart after reaching the limit, in order to save resources for other processes.

It's a good idea to do health checks outside Upstart that provide alerts to the development team through email or some other means of quick communication. A health check, for a web application, can simply involve hitting the website and seeing whether you get a valid response. You could roll your own methods or use tools such as Monit (http://mmonit.com/monit/) or Zabbix (www.zabbix.com) for this.

Now that you know how to keep your application running regardless of crashes and server reboots, the next logical concern is performance. Node's cluster API can help with this.

10.3.2 The cluster API: taking advantage of multiple cores

Most modern computer CPUs have multiple cores, but a Node process uses only one of them when running. If you're hosting a Node application on a server and want to maximize the server's usage, you can manually start multiple instances of your application on different TCP/IP ports and use a load balancer to distribute web traffic to these instances, but that's laborious to set up.

To make it easier to use multiple cores for a single application, the cluster API was added to Node. This API makes it easy for your application to simultaneously run multiple workers on different cores that each do the same thing and respond to the same TCP/IP port. Figure 10.2 shows how an application's processing would be organized using the cluster API on a four-core processor.

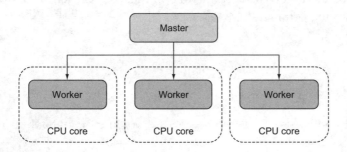

Figure 10.2   A master spawning three workers on a four-core processor

The following listing automatically spawns a master process and a worker for each additional core.

Listing 10.2   A demonstration of Node's cluster API

```
const cluster = require('cluster');
const http = require('http');
const numCPUs = require('os').cpus().length;       Determines the server's
if (cluster.isMaster) {                             number of cores
  for (let i = 0; i < numCPUs; i++) {
    cluster.fork();                                 Creates a fork
  }                                                 for each core
  cluster.on('exit', (worker, code, signal) => {
```

```
    console.log('Worker %s died.', worker.process.pid);
  });
} else {
  http.Server((req, res) => {                          ⟵──  Defines work to be
    res.writeHead(200);                                     done by each worker
    res.end('I am a worker running in process: ' + process.pid);
  }).listen(8000);
}
```

Because masters and workers run in separate operating system processes, which is necessary if they're to run on separate cores, they can't share state through global variables. But the cluster API does provide a means for the master and workers to communicate.

The following listing shows an example in which messages are passed between the master and the workers. A count of all requests is kept by the master, and whenever a worker reports handling a request, it's relayed to each worker.

> **Listing 10.3   A demonstration of Node's cluster API**

```
const cluster = require('cluster');
const http = require('http');
const numCPUs = require('os').cpus().length;
const workers = {};
let requests = 0;

if (cluster.isMaster) {
  for (let i = 0; i < numCPUs; i++) {
    workers[i] = cluster.fork();
    ((i) => {                                               Listens for messages
      workers[i].on('message', (message) => {       ⟵──    from worker
        if (message.cmd == 'incrementRequestTotal') {
          requests++;                                       Sends new request
          for (var j = 0; j < numCPUs; j++) {        ⟵──    total to each worker
            workers[j].send({
              cmd: 'updateOfRequestTotal',
              requests: requests
            });
          }
        }
      });                                      Uses closure to preserve
    })(i);                                ⟵──  the value of worker
  }
  cluster.on('exit', (worker, code, signal) => {
    console.log('Worker %s died.', worker.process.pid);
  });
} else {                                                    Listens for messages
  process.on('message', (message) => {              ⟵──    from master
    if (message.cmd === 'updateOfRequestTotal') {
      requests = message.requests;             ⟵──  Updates request count
    }                                                using master's message
  });
  http.Server((req, res) => {
```

Increases request total (annotation pointing to `requests++;`)

```
        res.writeHead(200);
        res.end(`Worker ${process.pid}: ${requests} requests.`);
        process.send({ cmd: 'incrementRequestTotal' });      ◁──┐   Lets master know request
    }).listen(8000);                                              total should increase
}
```

Using Node's cluster API is a simple way of creating applications that take advantage of modern hardware.

10.3.3 Hosting static files and proxying

Although Node is an effective solution for serving dynamic web content, it's not the most efficient way to serve static files such as images, CSS style sheets, or client-side JavaScript. Serving static files over HTTP is a specific task for which specific software projects are optimized, because they've focused primarily on this task for many years.

Fortunately, Nginx (http://nginx.org/en/), an open source web server optimized for serving static files, is easy to set up alongside Node to serve those files. In a typical Nginx/Node configuration, Nginx initially handles each web request, relaying requests that aren't for static files back to Node. Figure 10.3 illustrates this configuration.

The configuration in the following listing, which would be put in the Nginx configuration file's `http` section, implements this setup. The configuration file is conventionally stored in a Unix server's /etc directory at /etc/nginx/nginx.conf.

Listing 10.4   A configuration file that uses Nginx to proxy Node.js and serve static files

```
http {
  upstream my_node_app {
    server 127.0.0.1:8000;          ◁──┐   IP and port of Node
  }                                        application
  server {
    listen 80;                      ◁──┐   Port on which proxy
    server_name localhost domain.com;      will receive requests
    access_log /var/log/nginx/my_node_app.log;      ◁──┐  Handles file requests for URL
    location ~ /static/ {                                  paths starting with /static/
      root /home/node/my_node_app;
      if (!-f $request_filename) {
        return 404;
      }
    }
    location / {                    ◁──┐   Defines URL path the
      proxy_pass http://my_node_app;      proxy will respond to
      proxy_redirect off;
      proxy_set_header X-Real-IP $remote_addr;
      proxy_set_header X-Forwarded-For $proxy_add_x_forwarded_for;
      proxy_set_header Host $http_host;
      proxy_set_header X-NginX-Proxy true;
    }
  }
}
```

By using Nginx to handle your static web assets, you ensure that Node is dedicated to doing what it does best.

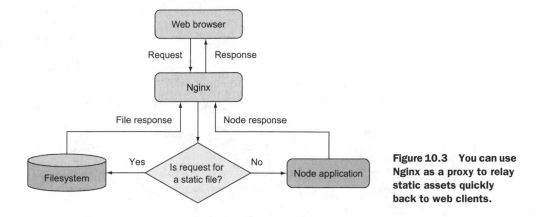

Figure 10.3 **You can use Nginx as a proxy to relay static assets quickly back to web clients.**

10.4 *Summary*

- Node applications can be hosted by PaaS providers, dedicated services, virtual private servers, and cloud hosting.
- You can quickly deploy Node applications to Linux servers by using Forever and Upstart.
- To make your application perform better, Node's cluster module lets you run multiple processes.

Part 3

Beyond web development

Millions of people depend on apps that are built with Node. If you've ever used Slack or Visual Studio Node, you've used applications that are powered by Node. This part introduces both Electron and modules for writing command-line tools with Node. If you've ever wanted to make an app for Linux, macOS, or Windows, now you can.

Writing command-line applications

Node command-line utilities are used everywhere, from project automation tools, such as Gulp and Yeoman, to XML and JSON parsers. If you've ever wondered how to build command-line tools with Node, this chapter will show you everything you need to know to get started. You'll learn how Node programs accept command-line arguments and how to handle I/O with pipes. We've also included shell tips that will help you use the command line more effectively.

Although writing command-line tools with Node isn't hard, it's important to follow community conventions. This chapter includes many of these conventions so you'll be able to write tools that other people can use, without too much documentation.

11.1   *Understanding conventions and philosophy*

A big part of command-line development is understanding the conventions used by established programs. As a real-world example, take a look at Babel:

```
Usage: babel [options] <files ...>

Options:

  -h, --help                         output usage information
  -f, --filename [filename]          filename to use when reading from
   stdin
[ ... ]
  -q, --quiet                        Don't log anything
  -V, --version                      output the version number
```

Several points are worth noting here. The first is the use of both -h and --help for printing help: this is a flag that many programs use. The second flag is -f for file-name—this is an easy mnemonic to learn. Lots of flags are based on mnemonics. Using -q for quiet output is also a popular convention, and so is -v for showing the program's version. Your applications should include these flags.

This user interface isn't merely a convention, however. The use of the hyphen and double hyphen (--) is recognized by the Open Group's Utility Conventions.[1] This document even specifies how they should be used:

- *Guideline 4*—All options should be preceded by the - delimiter character.
- *Guideline 10*—The first -- argument that's not an option-argument should be accepted as a delimiter indicating the end of options. Any following arguments should be treated as operands, even if they begin with the - character.

Another aspect of command-line application design is philosophy. This dates back to the creators of UNIX, who wanted to design "small, sharp tools" that could be used together with a simple, text-based interface.

> *This is the UNIX philosophy: Write programs that do one thing and do it well. Write programs to work together. Write programs to handle text streams, because that is a universal interface.*
>
> —Doug McIlroy[2]

In this chapter, we provide a broad overview of shell techniques and UNIX conventions so you can design command-line tools that other people can use. We offer guidance for Windows-specific usage as well, but for the most part, your Node tools should be cross-platform by default.

---

[1] "The Open Group Base Specifications Issue 7," http://pubs.opengroup.org/onlinepubs/9699919799/basedefs/V1_chap11.html.

[2] "Basics of the Unix Philosophy", www.catb.org/~esr/writings/taoup/html/ch01s06.html.

> **Shell tips: getting help**
>
> If you get stuck when using the shell, try typing `man <cmd>`. This loads the manual page for the command.
>
> If you can't remember the command's name, you can use `apropos <cmd>` to search the database of system commands.

11.2 Introducing parse-json

For JavaScript programmers, one of the simplest useful applications reads JSON and prints it if it's valid. By following this chapter, you'll re-create this tool.

Let's start with what a command line for this application should look like. The following snippet shows how to invoke such a program:

```
node parse-json.js -f my.json
```

The first thing you need to do is figure out how to grab `-f my.json` from the command line; these are the program's arguments. You also need to read input from stdin. Read on to learn how to do both of these things.

11.3 Using command-line arguments

Most—but not all—command-line programs accept arguments. Node has a built-in way to handle these arguments, but third-party modules on npm offer extra features. You need these features in order to implement some widely used conventions. Read on to learn more.

11.3.1 Parsing command-line arguments

Command-line arguments can be accessed by using the `process.argv` array. The items in the array are the strings passed to the shell when running a command. So if you split up the command, you can figure out what each item in the array is. The item at `process.argv[0]` is `node`, the item at `process.argv[1]` is `parse-json.js`, `[2]` is `-f`, and so forth.

If you've ever used command-line applications before, you may have seen arguments with `-` or `--`. These prefixes are special conventions for passing options to applications: `--` denotes a full string for an option name, and `-` denotes a single character for an option name. The npm command-line binary is a great example of this with `-h` and `--help`.

> **Argument conventions**
>
> Other argument conventions are as follows:
>
> - `--version` to print the version of your application
> - `-y` or `--yes` to use default values for any missing options

Adding aliases for arguments, such as -h and --help, makes parsing awkward after you add support for several options, but luckily there's a module for parsing arguments called *yargs*. The following snippet shows how yargs works in the simplest case. All you need to do is require yargs, and then access the argv property to inspect the arguments that were passed to the script:

```
const argv = require('yargs').argv;
console.log({ f: argv.f });
```

Figure 11.1 shows how Node's built-in version of the command-line arguments differs from the object generated by yargs.

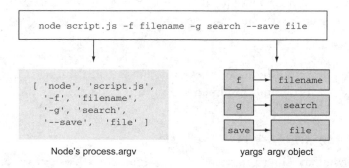

Node's process.argv   yargs' argv object

Figure 11.1   Node's argv compared to yargs

Although an options object is useful, it doesn't provide much structure for validating arguments and generating usage text. The next section shows how to describe and validate arguments.

11.3.2 Validating arguments

The yargs module includes methods for validating the arguments. The following listing shows how to use yargs to parse the -f argument that your JSON parser will need, and it uses the describe and nargs methods to enforce the expected argument format.

Listing 11.1   Using yargs to parse command-line arguments

```
const readFile = require('fs').readFile;
const yargs = require('yargs');
const argv = yargs
  .demand('f')
  .nargs('f', 1)
  .describe('f', 'JSON file to parse')
  .argv;
const file = argv.f;
readFile(file, (err, dataBuffer) => {
  const value = JSON.parse(dataBuffer.toString());
  console.log(JSON.stringify(value));
});
```

Requires –f to run

Tells yargs –f needs one argument after it

Using yargs is easier than manipulating the `process.argv` array, and it's better because rules can be enforced. Listing 11.1 uses `demand` to force an argument, and then declares that it requires a single parameter, which will be the JSON file to parse. To make the program easier to use, you can provide usage text with yargs as well. The convention here is to print the usage text when `-h` or `--help` is passed. You can add these with the help of yargs, as shown in this snippet:

```
yargs
  // ...
  .usage('parse-json [options]')
  .help('h')
  .alias('h', 'help')
  // ...
```

Now your JSON parser can accept a file argument and process the file. File handling isn't yet finished for this project, however, because it also needs to accept stdin. Read on to learn how to do that with a common UNIX convention.

Shell tips: history

Your shell stores a log of the commands you've typed previously. Type `history` to view the log; this is often aliased to `h`.

11.3.3 *Passing stdin as a file*

If a file parameter is given as a hyphen (`-f -`), it means grab the data from stdin. This is another common command-line convention. You can use the mississippi package to do this easily. You have to concatenate all the data piped to your application prior to calling `JSON.parse`, though, because it expects a full JSON string to parse. With the mississippi module, the example now looks like the following listing.

Listing 11.2   Reading a file from stdin

```
#!/usr/bin/env node
const concat = require('mississippi').concat;
const readFile = require('fs').readFile;
const yargs = require('yargs');
const argv = yargs
  .usage('parse-json [options]')
  .help('h')
  .alias('h', 'help')
  .demand('f') // require -f to run
  .nargs('f', 1) // tell yargs -f needs 1 argument after it
  .describe('f', 'JSON file to parse')
  .argv;
const file = argv.f;
function parse(str) {
  const value = JSON.parse(str);
  console.log(JSON.stringify(value));
}
```

```
if (file === '-') {
  process.stdin.pipe(concat(parse));
} else {
  readFile(file, (err, dataBuffer) => {
    if (err) {
      throw err;
    } else {
      parse(dataBuffer.toString());
    }
  });
}
```

This code loads mississippi and calls it concat. It then uses concat with the stdin stream. Because mississippi accepts a function that receives the final full set of data, the original parse function from listing 11.1 can still be used. This is done only when the filename is -.

11.4 *Sharing command-line tools with npm*

Any application that you want others to be able to use should be easily installed with npm. The simplest way to make npm see a command-line application is to use the bin field in package.json. This field makes npm install an executable available to any scripts in the current project. The bin field also tells npm to install the executable globally if you use npm install --global. This isn't useful only for Node developers, but also for anyone else who might want to use your scripts.

This snippet and the #!/usr/bin/env node line in listing 11.2 are all you need for the JSON parser example in this chapter:

```
...
    "name": "parse-json",
    "bin": {
      "parse-json": "index.js"
    },
...
```

If you install this package with npm install -global, it will make the parse-json command available systemwide. To try it, open a terminal (or command prompt in Windows) and type parse-json. Note that this works even in Windows, because npm will automatically install a wrapper enabling it to work in Windows transparently.

11.5 *Connecting scripts with pipes*

The parse-json program is simple—it accepts text and validates it. What if you have other command-line tools that you want to use it with? Imagine you have a program that can add syntax highlighting to JSON files. It would be great if the JSON could be parsed first and then highlighted. In this section, you'll learn about pipes, which can do all of this and more.

You'll be using parse-json and other programs to perform fancy workflows with pipes. Windows and Unix shells differ, but the important bits are (luckily) the same in both shells. A few differences arise during debugging, but they shouldn't affect you when you're writing command-line applications.

11.5.1 *Piping data into parse-json*

The main way to connect command-line applications is called *piping*. Piping is taking an application's stdout and attaching it to a different process's stdin stream. It's the central component of interprocess communication: enabling programs to talk to each other. You can access stdin in Node with `process.stdin` because it's a readable stream. Look at the following code to parse JSON coming in from stdin:

```
echo "[1,2,3]" | parse-json -f -
```

Notice the | character. This tells the shell that `echo '{}'` should send its output to parse-json's stdin.

Shell tips: keyboard shortcuts

Now that you've seen how pipes work, you can search the command history by combining `history` with `grep`:

```
history | grep node
```

An even better way to access previous commands is by using the up and down arrows on the keyboard. People do this all the time—but there's an even better way! Type Ctrl-R to recursively search through the command history. This lets you fish out lengthy commands based on a partial text match.

Here are more shortcuts: Ctrl-S does a forward search, and Ctrl-G aborts the search. You can also edit text more efficiently with these shortcuts: Ctrl-W deletes words, ALT-F/B moves forward or backward one word, and Ctrl-A/E moves to the start or end of the line.

11.5.2 *Working with errors and exit codes*

Right now the program doesn't output anything. But if you give it incorrect data, how do you know that it was able to complete successfully, even if you don't know the expected output of an executable? The answer is the exit code. You can see the exit code of the last command you ran, but note that the `echo` and `node` commands are treated as a single command unit because of piping.

On Windows, you can inspect the exit code with the following:

```
echo %errorlevel%
```

On UNIX, you can see the exit code by using this command:

```
echo $?
```

If a command is successful, it has an exit code of 0 (zero). So if you feed incorrect JSON to the script, it should exit with a nonzero value:

```
parse-json -f invalid.json
```

If you run this, the application will exit with a nonzero status and print a message indicating the reason. This is because when an error is thrown but not caught, Node automatically exits and prints the error message.

ERROR STREAMS

Although printing your output to the console can be useful, saving it to a file to read is even better, because you can keep it for debugging purposes. Luckily, you can do this with the shell by redirecting the stdout stream:

```
echo 'you can overwrite files!' > out.log
echo 'you can even append to files!' >> out.log
```

When you try this with invalid JSON, it would make sense for parse-json to save the error message:

```
parse-json -f invalid.json >out.log
```

But doing this won't log any errors. This is the expected behavior once you understand the difference between stderr and stdout:

- stdout is for other command-line applications to consume.
- stderr is for developers to consume.

Node logs to stderr when `console.error` is called or an error is thrown. This is different from echo, which logs to stdout, just like `console.log`. With that knowledge, you may want to redirect stderr to a file instead of to stdout. Luckily, that's a simple change.

The stdin, stdout, and stderr streams all have associated numbers, from 0 to 2, respectively. stderr has a stream number of 2. You can redirect it by using `2>` `out.log`, which tells the shell the stream number you want to redirect and the file in which to place the output:

```
parse-json -f invalid.json 2> out.log
```

Redirecting output is what piping does, but with processes instead of files. Take the following snippet:

```
node -e "console.log(null)" | parse-json
```

You're logging `null` and piping it to parse-json. `null` won't be logged to the console here because it's being piped to only the next command. Say you do something similar, but use `console.error`:

```
node -e "console.error(null)" | parse-json
```

You'll see an error because no text is being sent over to parse-json to consume. `null` was logged to stderr and will be printed to the console. The *data* should be piped to stdout and not stderr.

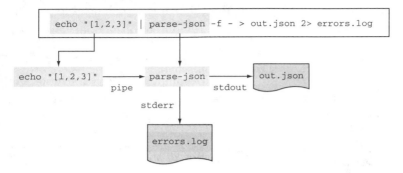

Figure 11.2 Combining pipes and output streams

Figure 11.2 shows how pipes and numbered output streams can be used to connect programs and then route the output into separate files.

Node also has an API for working with pipes. It's based on Node streams, so you can use it with anything that implements Node's stream classes. Read on to learn more about pipes in Node.

Shell tips: clearing a line

Some of these commands are pretty long; what do you do when you need to delete a long command and don't want to run it? One useful shortcut is Ctrl-U, which deletes the current line. If you type Ctrl-Y, you'll get the line back, so you can use these keyboard commands as you'd use copy and paste.

11.5.3 *Using pipes in Node*

You're now going to learn how pipes work by using Node's API. To do this, you'll write a short script that displays how long it takes a program to run, without interrupting piping.

A program can monitor a pipe without interrupting it by waiting for stdin to close and then piping the results to stdout. Because Node programs end when there's no more input to consume, you can print a message when the program is exiting. Here's an example, which you can save as time.js to try it out:

```
process.stdin.pipe(process.stdout);
const start = Date.now();
process.on('exit', () => {
  const timeTaken = Date.now() - start;
  console.error(`Time (s): ${timeTaken / 1000}`);
});
```

By piping to stdout again, you can put time.js in the middle of commands you pipe together and still have them work! In fact, both parse-json and time.js can easily be used together with pipes. For example, this shows how long it takes to parse JSON and send the data:

```
parse-json -f test.json | node time.js
```

Now that you have a basic idea of what to output and how to get input from other applications, you can start making applications that are much more complex. But first, we should talk about timing while processes are piping to each other.

> **Shell tips: completion**
>
> In addition to providing command history, most shells are capable of matching commands or files when the Tab key is pressed. Some even allow you to see the completions with Alt-?.

11.5.4 *Pipes and command execution order*

When you pipe commands, each command starts immediately. The commands don't wait for each other in any way. This means piping data won't wait for any command to exit, and you can consume only the data it gives you. Because the commands don't wait, you can't know how the previous command exited.

Imagine you want to log a message only when JSON is successfully parsed. To do this, you need new operators. The && and || operators act similarly in a shell to the way they do in JavaScript when used on numbers. Using && executes the next command if the previous exit code is zero, and || executes the next command if the exit code is a nonzero number.

Let's see how to make a little script that logs a message when a process is exiting over stderr. It's important to note that this is different from echo, because it's printing to stderr—it's meant for developers to use rather than other programs. All you need to do is listen for the process exit event, and then write the arguments to stderr:

```
process.stdin.pipe(process.stdout);
process.on('exit', () => {
  const args = process.argv.slice(2);
  console.error(args.join(' '));
});
```

Using &&, you can call exit-message.js if the JSON parsed successfully:

```
parse-json -f test.json && node exit-message.js "parsed JSON successfully"
```

But exit-message.js won't get the output of parse-json. The && operator must wait for parse-json.js to finish, to see whether it should execute the next command. While using &&, there's no automatic redirection as there is when piping.

REDIRECTING INPUT

You've already seen how to redirect output, but you can also redirect input in a similar fashion. This is a rare need, but can be a valuable asset if an executable doesn't accept

a filename as an argument. If you want a command to read a file into stdin, use
`<filename` to do so:

```
parse-json -f - <invalid.json
```

By combining both forms of redirection, you can use a temporary file to recover the
output of parse-json:

```
parse-json -f test.json >tmp.out &&
  node exit-message.js "parsed JSON successfully" <tmp.out
```

Now that you've learned how to handle streams, exit codes, and command order, you
should be able to write scripts with Node commands for your own packages. The next
section demonstrates how to use Browserify and UglifyJS together using pipes.

> **Shell tips: clearing the display**
> You may sometimes cat binary data to the terminal and basically break it. Like a
> scene from *The Matrix*, garbled characters will appear everywhere. In cases like this,
> you can either press Ctrl-L to refresh the display or type `reset` to reset the terminal.

11.6 *Interpreting real-world scripts*

You're ready to start writing your own `scripts` fields in package.json files. As an
example, let's look at how to combine the browserify and uglifyjs packages from npm.
Browserify (http://browserify.org/) is an application that takes Node modules and
bundles them up for use in the browser. UglifyJS (https://github.com/mishoo/
UglifyJS2) is an application that minifies a JavaScript file so that it takes up less bandwidth and time to send to a browser. Your script will take a file called main.js (found in
the book's listings under ch11-command-line/snippets/uglify-example), concatenate
it for use in a browser, and then minify the concatenated script:

```
{
  "devDependencies": {
    "browserify": "13.3.0",
    "uglify-js": "2.7.5"
  },
  "scripts": {
    "build": "browserify -e main.js > bundle.js && uglifyjs bundle.js >
    bundle.min.js"
  }
}
```

You can run the build script by typing `npm run build`. The build script in this example makes bundle.js. Then, if creating bundle.js is successful, the script creates bun-
dle.min.js. By using the `&&` operator, you can ensure that the second stage runs only if
the first stage succeeds.

Using the techniques demonstrated in this chapter, you can create and use
command-line applications. Remember, you can always use the command lines to

combine scripts from other languages together—if you have a useful Python, Ruby, or Haskell command-line program, you can easily use it with your Node programs.

11.7 Summary

- Command-line arguments can be read from process.argv.
- Modules such as yargs make it easier to parse and validate arguments.
- A handy way to add scripts to your Node projects is by defining npm scripts in the package.json file.
- Data is read and written to command-line programs by using standard I/O pipes.
- Standard input, output, and errors can be redirected to different processes and files.
- Programs emit exit codes that are used to determine whether they ran successfully.
- Command-line programs adhere to established conventions that other users will expect.

Conquering the desktop
with Electron

12

This chapter covers

- Building desktop apps with Electron
- Showing desktop menus
- Sending desktop notifications
- Creating cross-platform builds

In the preceding chapter, you learned about building command-line tools with Node. Node is starting to become prominent in another area, however: desktop software. Programmers are increasingly harnessing web technology to solve the problems of cross-platform development. In this chapter, you'll learn how to make a desktop web application based on native desktop features, Node, and client-side web technology. You can develop and run this application in Linux, macOS, and Windows. You'll also use Node modules in a model that isn't too far removed from client-server web application development.

12.1 Introducing Electron

Electron, originally known as Atom Shell, enables you to build desktop applications with web technology. The application and user interface are left up to you to create

279

with HTML, CSS, and JavaScript, but some of the "hard parts" of desktop software are provided for you. These include the following:

- Automatic updates
- Crash reporting
- Installers for Microsoft Windows
- Debugging
- Native menus and notifications

Some famous applications have been made with Electron. The first was Atom, GitHub's text editor, but more recent applications include Slack, the popular chat service, and Visual Studio Code by Microsoft, shown in figure 12.1.

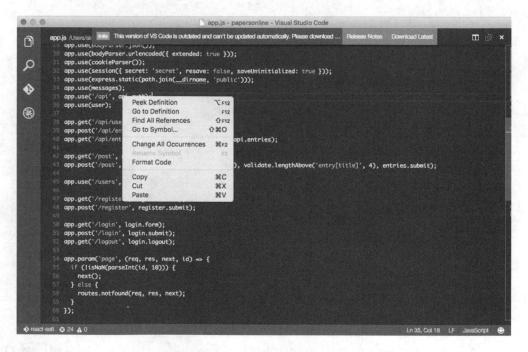

Figure 12.1   Visual Studio Code's application window and a native context menu

You should try out some of these applications to see the kinds of things that are possible with Electron. It's exciting to think that armed with Node and JavaScript skills, you can build compelling desktop software.

12.1.1   *Electron's stack*

Before getting started with Electron, you should familiarize yourself with the way Electron fits in with Node, HTML, and CSS. An Electron app has the following components:

- *The main process*—A Node script that boots the application and provides access to native Node modules
- *The render process*—A web page managed by Chromium

A real application, however, has several other dependencies. The previous list can be fleshed out as follows:

- Includes the main process
- Connects to a native database (for example, SQLite)
- Communicates with web APIs
- Reads and writes any local files (for example, configuration files)
- Provides access to native features (for example, context menus)
- Includes the render process
- Shows a modern rich web application using your preferred client-side technology (for example, React or Angular)
- Triggers native features (for example, context menus and notifications)
- Provides build scripts
- Generates the front-end JavaScript by using your preferred build system (Grunt, Gulp, npm scripts)
- Prepares releases for distribution

Figure 12.2 shows an overview of the three main parts of a typical Electron app. As you can see, Node is used to run the main process and to communicate with the operating system for services including opening files, reading and writing to a database, and communicating with web services. Although a large part of the focus is on the UI in the rendering process, Node is still used for a critical part of the application's architecture.

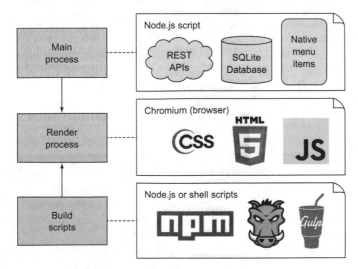

Figure 12.2 The main parts of a typical Electron application

12.1.2   *Interface design*

Now that you've seen the main components of an Electron app, let's look at how to design suitable interfaces. Electron applications are based on HTML, CSS, and Java-Script, so you can't pull in native widgets. Imagine that you want to make a native Mac-style interface. You can fake the macOS toolbar by using CSS gradients. Using native fonts provided by macOS and Windows is possible through CSS, and you can even tweak the antialiasing to look like a native application. You can also remove text selection for certain UI components, and make the UI work with drag-and-drop. Currently, most Electron apps use CSS that uses the same colors, border styles, icons, and gradients as macOS and Windows.

Some applications go the extra mile in terms of duplicating the native experience; one example is the N1 email application (https://github.com/nylas/N1). Other applications, such as Slack (https://slack.com/), have their own unique branding and identity that's clean enough to work well without too much modification on each platform.

When you build your own Electron apps, you'll have to decide which approach is right for your project. If you want to make an app that looks like it uses native desktop widgets, you have to create styles that suit each platform. That requires more time designing each target UI. Your customers may prefer it, but it may also result in more overhead when deploying new features.

In the next section, you'll use a skeleton Electron application to create a new one. This is the standard way to build new projects with Electron.

12.2   *Creating an Electron app*

The easiest way to get started with Electron is to use the electron-quick-start project, available on GitHub (https://github.com/atom/electron-quick-start). This small repository contains the dependencies necessary to run a basic Electron application.

To use it, check out the repository and install the dependencies with npm:

```
git clone https://github.com/atom/electron-quick-start
cd electron-quick-start
npm install
```

After everything has finished downloading, you can start the main process with npm start. It's safe to use this project as the basis for the rest of your Electron application; you shouldn't need to create your own project from scratch.

When the application starts, you should see a window with a web page and the Chromium Developer Tools. If you're a web developer who uses Chrome, this might not seem that exciting: the app looks like a web page with no CSS rendering in Chrome. But a lot more is going on under the hood to make this work. Figure 12.3 shows what this looks like in macOS.

This is a self-contained macOS application bundle: it includes a version of Node that's different from the one running on my system, and it has its own menu items and About window.

Figure 12.3 The electron-quick-start project running in macOS

At this point, you can start to build your web application in index.html by using HTML, JavaScript, and CSS. But as a Node programmer, you're probably eager to use Node for something, so let's see how to do that first.

Electron comes with a module called *remote* that uses interprocess communication (IPC) between the rendering process and the main Node process. The remote module can even provide access to Node modules. To try it, add a file called readfile.js to your Electron project, and add the code in the following listing.

Listing 12.1 A simple Node module

```
const fs = require('fs');

module.exports = (cb) => {
  fs.readFile('./main.js', { encoding: 'utf8' }, cb);
};
```

Now open index.html and change it to add an element with an ID of source, and a script that loads readfile.js, as shown in the next listing.

Listing 12.2 Loading Node modules from the rendering process

```
<!DOCTYPE html>
<html>
  <head>
    <meta charset="UTF-8">
    <title>Hello World!</title>
  </head>
  <body>
    <h1>Hello World!</h1>
    <pre id="source"></pre>
    <script>
var readfile = require('remote').require('./readfile');
readfile(function(err, text) {
  console.log('readfile:', err, text);
  document.getElementById('source').innerHTML = text;
```

```
});
    </script>
  </body>
</html>
```

Listing 12.2 uses the remote module to load readfile.js and then run it on the main process. The interaction between the two processes is seamless, so it doesn't seem that much different from using standard Node modules. The only real difference is the use of `require('remote').require(file)`.

12.3   *Building a full desktop application*

Now that you've seen how to create a basic Electron app and how to use Node modules, let's go a step further and see how to build a fully fledged desktop app with native features. The application you'll create is intended to be a developer tool for making and viewing HTTP requests. Think of it as a GUI for the request module (www.npmjs.com/package/request).

Although you can build Electron apps with pure HTML, JavaScript, CSS, and Node, for this example you'll use modern front-end development tools to make the app more maintainable and extensible. Here's a list of what you'll use:

- electron-quick-start as the basis for the project
- request module for making HTTP requests
- React for the user-interface code
- Babel for converting modern ES6 into browser-friendly ES5
- webpack for building the client-side app

Figure 12.4 shows what the finished application should look like.

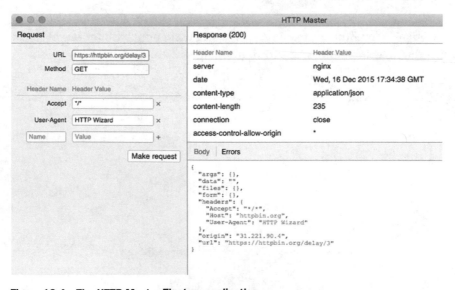

Figure 12.4   The HTTP Master Electron application

Next you'll learn how to set up a React-based project with webpack and Babel.

12.3.1 *Bootstrapping React and Babel*

The biggest challenge in building a new app with a sophisticated front end is setting up libraries such as React and Babel with a maintainable build system. You have many choices, including Grunt, Gulp, and webpack. And what makes things even more difficult is that these libraries change over time, so books and tutorials quickly become out-of-date.

To mitigate the fast-paced world of front-end development, we specify the exact versions of each dependency, so you should be able to follow the tutorial and obtain similar results. If you get lost, you can use tools such as Yeoman (http://yeoman.io/) to generate a skeleton app. Then you can modify it to work like the app outlined in this chapter.

12.3.2 *Installing the dependencies*

Create a new electron-quick-start project. To recap, you must clone the project from GitHub:

```
git clone https://github.com/atom/electron-quick-start
cd electron-quick-start
npm install
```

Now install react, react-dom, and babel-core:

```
npm install --save-dev react@0.14.3 react-dom@0.14.3 babel-core@6.3.17
```

Next, you need to install Babel plugins. The main one is babel-preset-es2015, which may be overkill for a project limited to Chromium, but including it makes it easier for you to experiment with ES2015 features that Chromium doesn't yet support. Use these commands for installation:

```
npm install --save-dev babel-preset-es2015@6.3.13
npm install --save-dev babel-plugin-transform-class-properties@6.3.13
```

This plugin adds JSX support to Babel:

```
npm install --save-dev babel-plugin-transform-react-jsx@6.3.13
```

Then install webpack:

```
npm install --save-dev webpack@1.12.9
```

You also need babel-loader for webpack to work with Babel:

```
npm install --save-dev babel-loader@6.2.0
```

Now that most of the dependencies are ready, add a .babelrc file to your project. It tells Babel to use the ES2015 and React plugins:

```
{
  "plugins": [
```

```
    "transform-react-jsx"
  ],
 "presets": ["es2015"]
}
```

Finally, open package.json and update the `scripts` property to include a webpack invocation:

```
"scripts": {
  "start": "electron main.js",
  "build": "node_modules/.bin/webpack --progress --colors"
},
```

This allows the application to be built with `npm run build`. Webpack plugins are available for React hot-loading, but we don't cover that here. If you want to automatically build your client-side code when files change, you could use something like fswatch or nodemon.

12.3.3 *Setting up webpack*

To use webpack, you need a webpack.config.js file. Add it to the root of your project. The basic format is JavaScript, using a Node-style CommonJS module:

```
const webpack = require('webpack');
module.exports = {
  setting: 'value'
};
```

Our project requires settings for finding React files (.jsx), loading the entry point (/app/index.jsx), and then placing the output in a place where the Electron UI can find it (js/app.js). The React files also have to be processed with Babel. Putting those requirements together produces the file in the following listing.

> **Listing 12.3   webpack.config.js**

```
const webpack = require('webpack');
module.exports = {
  module: {
    loaders: [
      { test: /\.jsx?$/, loaders: ['babel-loader'] }
    ]
  },
  entry: [
    './app/index.jsx'
  ],
  resolve: {
    extensions: ['', '.js', '.jsx']
  },
  output: {
    path: __dirname + '/js',
    filename: 'app.js'
  }
};
```

In this listing, webpack is told to transform .jsx (React) files with Babel through the `module.loaders` property. Babel has already been set up to handle React files with transform-react-jsx in .babelrc. Next, the `entry` property is used to define the main entry point for the React code. This works well because React components are based on HTML elements. Because HTML elements must have one parent node, a single entry point can encompass the entire application.

The `resolve.extensions` property tells webpack that .jsx files must be treated as modules. If you use a statement such as `import {Class} from 'class'`, it'll check class.js and class.jsx.

Finally, the `output` property tells webpack where to write the output file. Here I've used js/, but you could use any path that's accessible to the Electron UI.

This is a good time to start fleshing out the React app. Let's start by looking at the main entry point and how it'll pull in the request and response UI elements.

12.4 The React app

In figure 12.4, you saw a preview of what this app should look like. It has two main groups of UI components that can be divided into seven items:

- Request
- URL: String
- Method: String
- Headers: Object of string pairs
- Response
- HTTP status code
- Headers: Object of string pairs
- Body: String
- Errors: String

But in React, you can't render two things side by side: they need to be contained by a single parent. You need a top-level app object, which contains the UI elements for the request and response.

Given classes for `Request` and `Response`, which you'll implement later, the `App` class itself should look like the following listing.

Listing 12.4 The `App` class

```
import React from 'react';
import ReactDOM from 'react-dom';
import Request from './request';
import Response from './response';

class App extends React.Component {
  render() {
    return (
      <div className="container">
        <Request />
        <Response />
```

```
      </div>
    );
  }
}

ReactDOM.render(<App />, document.getElementById('app'));
```

Save this file as app/index.jsx. It first loads the `Request` and `Response` classes, and then renders them in a div. The last line uses ReactDOM to render the DOM nodes for the `App` class. React allows you to refer to the `App` class with `<App />`.

To make this work, you also need to define the `Request` and `Response` components.

12.4.1 *Defining the Request component*

The `Request` class takes input for the URL and HTTP method, and then generates a request that's posted with the Node request module. It renders the interface by using JSX, but unlike the previous example, it doesn't render the element directly with ReactDOM; this happens when it's included into the main app class in app/index.jsx.

The following listing (app/request.js) contains the code for the full class. We've removed the header-editing capability to reduce the length of the example; for an example with more features, including header editing, see our HTTP Wizard GitHub repository (https://github.com/alexyoung/http-wizard).

Listing 12.5 The `Request` class

```
import React from 'react';
import Events from './events';

const request = remote.require('request');

class Request extends React.Component {
  constructor(props) {
    super(props);
    this.state = { url: null, method: 'GET' };
  }

  handleChange = (e) => {
    const state = {};
    state[e.target.name] = e.target.value;
    this.setState(state);
  }

  makeRequest = () => {
    request(this.state, (err, res, body) => {
      const statusCode = res ? res.statusCode : 'No response';
      const result = {
        response: `(${statusCode})`,
        raw: body ? body : '',
        headers: res ? res.headers : [],
        error: err ? JSON.stringify(err, null, 2) : ''
      };

      Events.emit('result', result);
```

```
      new Notification(`HTTP response finished: ${statusCode}`)
    });
  }

  render() {
    return (
      <div className="request">
        <h1>Request</h1>
        <div className="request-options">
          <div className="form-row">
            <label>URL</label>
            <input
              name="url"
              type="url"
              value={this.state.url}
              onChange={this.handleChange} />
          </div>
          <div className="form-row">
            <label>Method</label>
            <input
              name="method"
              type="text"
              value={this.state.method}
              placeholder="GET, POST, PATCH, PUT, DELETE"
              onChange={this.handleChange} />
          </div>
          <div className="form-row">
            <a className="btn" onClick={this.makeRequest}>Make request</a>
          </div>
        </div>
      </div>
    );
  }
}

export default Request;
```

The bulk of the listing is taken up by the `render` method's HTML. Let's focus on the rest before going over how the UI is built up. First, we've used a descendent of Node's `EventEmitter` in app/events.jsx to communicate between this component and the response component. The following snippet is app/events.jsx:

```
import { EventEmitter } from 'events';
const Events = new EventEmitter();
export default Events;
```

Notice that `Request` is a `React.Component` descendant class. It defines a constructor that sets up a default state: the `state` property is special in React and can be set this way only in a constructor. Elsewhere, you must use `this.setState`.

The `handleChange` method sets state based on the HTML element's `name` attribute. To understand how this works, skip ahead to the URL `<input>` element in the render method:

```
<input
  name="url"
```

```
type="url"
value={this.state.url}
onChange={this.handleChange} />
```

The name specified here is used to set the URL when it's edited. Setting the state also causes `render` to run, and React will update the value attribute with the updated state. Let's move on to look at how the request module is used by this class.

This class is client-side code that runs in a web view, so you need a way of accessing the request module to make HTTP requests. Electron provides a way of loading remote modules without any unnecessary boilerplate. Near the top of the class, you use the global `remote` object to require the Node request module:

```
const request = remote.require('request');
```

Then later in `makeRequest`, the HTTP request can be made with a simple call to `request()`. The arguments for the request have been set in the class's state, so all you need to do is handle the callback that runs when the request is complete. Here that's very little imperative code: the class's state is set based on the outcome of the request, and then the result is emitted so the `Response` component can use it. A desktop notification is also displayed; if the request is slow, the user will be notified visually by using the operating system's notification pop-up:

```
new Notification(`HTTP response finished: ${statusCode}`)
```

Figure 12.5 shows a typical notification.

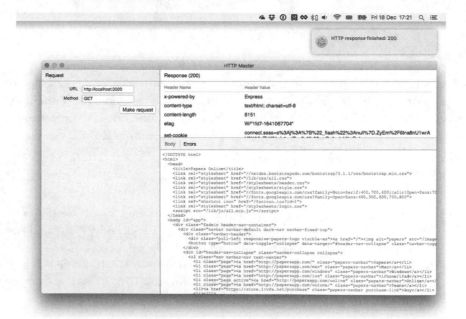

Figure 12.5   A desktop notification

Now let's look at how the Response component displays the HTTP response.

12.4.2 Defining the Response component

The Response component listens for result events and then sets its state to contain the results of the last request. It displays the results by using a table for headers, and divs for the request body and any errors.

The following listing has the whole Response component. This file is app/response.jsx.

Listing 12.6 The Response component

```
import React from 'react';
import Events from './events';
import Headers from './headers';

class Response extends React.Component {
  constructor(props) {
    super(props);
    this.state = { result: {}, tab: 'body' };
  }

  componentWillUnmount() {
    Events.removeListener('result', this.handleResult.bind(this));
  }

  componentDidMount() {
    Events.addListener('result', this.handleResult.bind(this));
  }

  handleResult(result) {
    this.setState({ result: result });
  }

  handleSelectTab = (e) => {
    const tab = e.target.dataset.tab;
    this.setState({ tab: tab });
  }

  render() {
    const result = this.state.result;
    const tabClasses = {
      body: this.state.tab === 'body' ? 'active' : null,
      errors: this.state.tab === 'errors' ? 'active' : null,
    };
    const rawStyle = this.state.tab === 'body'
      ? null
      : { display: 'none' }
    const errorsStyle = this.state.tab === 'errors'
      ? null
      : { display: 'none' };

    return (
```

```
        <div className="response">
          <h1>Response <span id="response">{result.response}</span></h1>
          <div className="content-container">
            <div className="content">
              <div id="headers">
                <table className="headers">
                  <thead>
                    <tr>
                      <th className="name">Header Name</th>
                      <th className="value">Header Value</th>
                    </tr>
                  </thead>
                  <Headers headers={result.headers} />
                </table>
              </div>
              <div className="results">
                <ul className="nav">
                  <li className={tabClasses.body}>
                    <a data-tab='body' onClick={this.handleSelectTab}>Body</a>
                  </li>
                  <li className={tabClasses.errors}>
                    <a data-tab='errors' href="#"
      onClick={this.handleSelectTab}>Errors</a>
                  </li>
                </ul>
                <div
                  className="raw"
                  id="raw"
                  style={rawStyle}>{result.raw}</div>
                <div
                  className="raw"
                  id="error"
                  style={errorsStyle}>{result.error}</div>
              </div>
            </div>
          </div>
        </div>
      );
    }
  }

  export default Response;
```

The `Response` component doesn't have any code specific to handling HTTP responses; it displays its state in various HTML elements. It's able to switch tabs by binding an `onclick` event to the `handleSelectTab` method that switches between the body and errors by using an attribute (`data-tab`).

The `Response` component uses another component, `Headers`, to render the HTTP response headers. Breaking components into ever smaller components is standard practice in React. The values of each header are passed to the subcomponent by using an attribute; in React, these are known as *props*, or *properties*:

```
<Headers headers={result.headers} />
```

The following listing shows the `Headers` component. This is in the app/headers.jsx file.

```
import React from 'react';

class Headers extends React.Component {
  render() {
    const headers = this.props.headers || {};
    const headerRows = Object.keys(headers).map((key, i) => {
      return (
        <tr key={i}>
          <td className="name">{key}</td>
          <td className="value">{headers[key]}</td>
        </tr>
      );
    });

    return (
      <tbody className="header-body">
        {headerRows}
      </tbody>
    );
  }
}

export default Headers;
```

Notice how the props are accessed near the top of the `render()` method, at `this.props.headers`.

12.4.3 Communicating between React components

The `Request` and `Response` classes are fairly well isolated; they're focused on solving their particular tasks without directly calling each other. React has other, more sophisticated state-management approaches, but they're beyond the scope of this chapter. This example application doesn't need a sophisticated communication mechanism, because it has only two main components, so instead it uses `EventEmitter` from Node to communicate.

To use `EventEmitter` this way, instantiate it inside its own file and then export the instance. This file is app/events.jsx in the example project for this chapter:

```
import { EventEmitter } from 'events';
const Events = new EventEmitter();
export default Events;
```

Now components can require `events` and either emit events or attach listeners to communicate. The `Request` component does this in the `makeRequest` method, with the result of the HTTP request:

```
Events.emit('result', result);
```

Then in the `Response` class, you can capture results by setting up a listener early in the component's life cycle:

```
componentWillUnmount() {
  Events.removeListener('result', this.handleResult.bind(this));
}
```

As an application grows, this pattern becomes harder to maintain. One particular problem is tracking the names of events. Because they're strings, it's easy to forget them or write them incorrectly. An extension of this pattern is to use a list of constants for event names. If you extend this pattern again to split the responsibility of dispatching events and storing data, you end up with something similar to Facebook's Redux state container (http://redux.js.org/), which is why many React programmers use it to design and build larger applications.

12.5 Builds and distribution

Now that you have a usable desktop application, you can bundle it for macOS, Linux, and Windows. App distribution with Electron has three stages:

1 Rebrand the Electron app with your application's name and icon
2 Package your app into a file
3 Create a binary for each platform

The electron-quick-start project is already almost suitable for distribution. You just need to copy your code into Electron's Contents/Resources/app folder in macOS, or electron/resources/app in Windows and Linux.

But manually copying files isn't the best way to build a redistributable binary. A more foolproof method is to use electron-packager (www.npmjs.com/package/electron-packager) by Max Ogden. This package provides a command-line tool for building executables for Windows, Linux, and macOS.

12.5.1 Building with Electron Packager

To install electron-packager, install it globally. This will allow you to build any project that you want to create platform-specific binaries for:

```
npm install electron-packager -g
```

After it's installed, you can run it from your application's directory. You must invoke it with the path to your application, the application name, platform, architecture (32- or 64-bit), and the Electron version:

```
electron-packager . HttpWizard --version=1.4.5
```

This downloads Electron version 1.4.5 and generates binaries for all supported platforms and architectures. This may take some time (Electron is about 40 MB), but when it's done, you'll have binaries that can be run on all major operating systems.

> ### Hiding the developer tools
>
> Before sharing builds, you should remove or change the line in main.js that opens the Chromium development tools:
>
> ```
> mainWindow.webContents.openDevTools();
> ```
>
> Alternatively, you could wrap this with a flag to hide it when working on the app:
>
> ```
> if (process.env.NODE_ENV === 'debug') {
>   mainWindow.webContents.openDevTools();
> }
> ```

12.5.2 Packaging

To further improve your application's performance, you can package the client-side and Node JavaScript file by using Atom Shell archives (https://github.com/atom/asar). These archives are known as *asar files,* and they work like the UNIX `tar` command. They hide your JavaScript but don't obscure it enough to stop people from decoding the packages, so you can't use it to truly obfuscate code. But they solve the issue of long filenames breaking in Windows, which you might run into if you have deeply nested dependencies.

In Electron, Chromium can read asar files as well as Node, so you don't have to do anything special to support it. Also, electron-packager can create asar packages for you with the `--asar` command-line option.

Figure 12.6 shows what an application packaged without asar looks like.

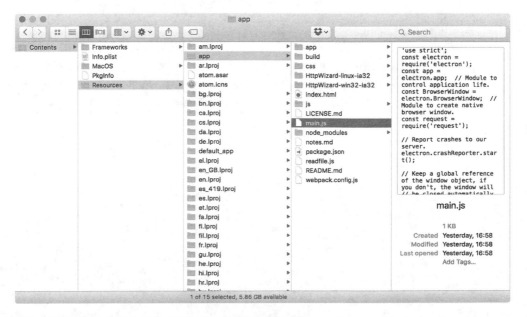

Figure 12.6 A typical Electron application bundle's contents

Notice that you can open the JavaScript files to view the source. The only binary files in an Electron application are resources such as images, or binary Node modules.

To generate a build with asar files, you can use electron-packager with the `--asar` flag:

```
electron-packager . HttpWizard --version=0.36.0 --asar=true
```

This is the easiest way to do it, because electron-packager runs all the necessary commands. To do it manually, you need to install asar, and then you need to invoke the command-line tool to create a package:

```
npm install -g asar
asar pack path-to-your-app/ app.asar
```

After you have the asar archive, download an Electron binary (https://github.com/atom/electron/releases) for the platform you want to support, and add the archive to the resources directory, as shown in figure 12.6. Running the application executable or bundle should cause your application to run.

Editing the vendor-supplied binaries is also how Electron applications are branded. You can change the application's name and icons this way. If you run an Electron binary with no modifications, it provides a window that allows you to run Electron apps made with the electron-quick-start repository.

12.6   *Summary*

- Using Electron, you can make desktop applications with Node, JavaScript, HTML, and CSS.
- You can generate native menus and notifications without using C++, C#, or Objective-C.
- If you have useful Node modules, you can use them from the client-side JavaScript within the Electron application's UI.
- Electron uses a fully fledged browser, so you can build UIs with the latest JavaScript technology, such as React or Angular.

appendix A
Installing Node

This appendix provides more details on installing Node.js. If you're fairly new to Node, we recommend installing it with a prebuilt package. We explain this for each major operating system.

Depending on your requirements, you can install Node in other ways instead. If you're more experienced with Node or have specific DevOps requirements, skip ahead to review other ways you can install Node.

A.1 Installing Node by using an installer

Node has two installers and several prebuilt binary packages. If you use macOS or Windows, you can use either binaries or installers. The binary packages contain executable files, but the installers have installation wizards that help you put Node on your system in a place that's easy to find when you're running commands such as node or npm in the terminal.

If you're new to Node, use an installer. All of the versions can be found on Node's website under Downloads (https://nodejs.org/en/download/).

A.1.1 The macOS installer

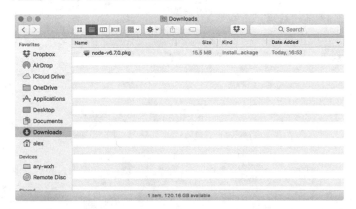

For macOS, download the 64-bit .pkg file from Node's website (https://nodejs.org/en/download/). You can use either the LTS or Current release. You should see a package file, as shown in figure A.1.

Figure A.1 The installer .pkg file

297

After you've downloaded the installer, double-click it to open the installation wizard (Figure A.2).

Click the Continue button and follow the instructions; the default options will install Node correctly. After the installation process has finished, you should be able to open a terminal and type node to run the Node REPL. Figure A.3 shows what this should look like.

The next section includes the same instructions for Windows users.

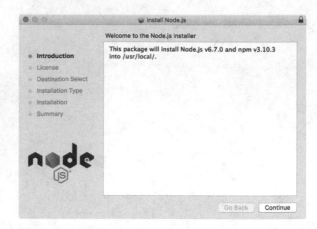

Figure A.2   The installation wizard

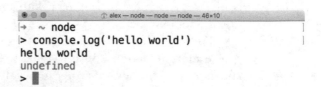

Figure A.3   Node's REPL

A.1.2   *The Windows installer*

On the Node Downloads page (https://nodejs.org/en/download/), click the Windows Installer icon, or click the Windows Installer .msi link. There are 32- and 64-bit options, but you probably want 64-bit. After the file has downloaded, double-click it to run the installation wizard, shown in figure A.4.

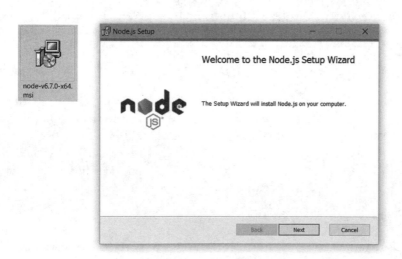

Figure A.4   The Windows .msi installer

Accept all of the default options, and then open cmd.exe to try out the Node REPL. Figure A.5 shows Node's REPL in Windows.

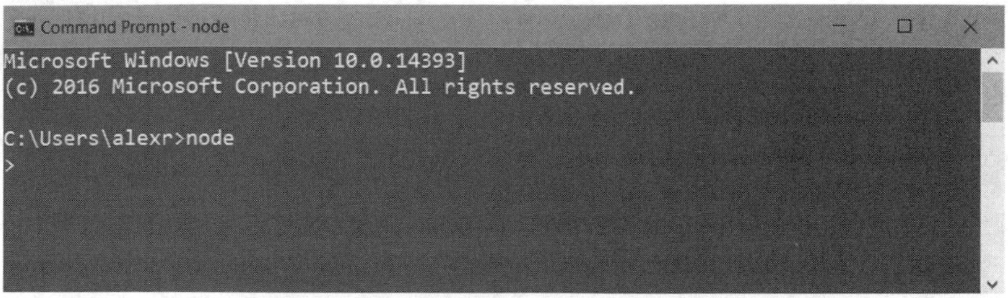

Figure A.5   Node's REPL in Windows

If you don't usually install software this way or don't want to install Node systemwide, continue reading to see how else Node can be installed.

A.2   *Using other ways to install Node*

You can install Node from source, through your operating system's package manager, or by using a Node version manager. If you install it from source, you'll need a working build system and Python installed.

A.2.1   *Installing Node from source*

You can download Node's source from the nodejs.org downloads page, but it's also available via Git on GitHub (https://github.com/nodejs/node). The full build guide is also on GitHub under node/Building.md (https://github.com/nodejs/node/blob/master/BUILDING.md). You'll need the following prerequisites to build Node:

- *Linux*—Python 2.6 or 2.7, gcc and g++ 4.8 or newer, or clang and clang++ 3.4 or newer. The easiest way to get this is with the build-essentials package in Debian-like distributions, or its equivalent for other distributions.
- *macOS*—Xcode and the command-line tools, which can be installed with Xcode.
- *Windows*—Python 2.6 or 2.7, Visual C++ Build Tools, Visual Studio 2015 Update 3.

When your build tools are ready, you can run `./configure` and `make` in UNIX-like operating systems. In Windows, you can run `.\vcbuild nosign`.

A.2.2   *Installing Node with a package manager*

If you use Linux or macOS, you may want to install Node with a package manager. This can make it easier to update Node. For example, if you're using a Linux web server, you might want to install Node so that it gets automatic security updates.

Node's website has a large list of installation instructions for operating systems that provide Node as a package (https://nodejs.org/en/download/package-manager/). In Debian and Ubuntu-based systems, for example, you can get Node from the Node-Source binary distribution repository. This has its own repository on GitHub with more details (https://github.com/nodesource/distributions).

In macOS, you can install Node with Homebrew (http://brew.sh/). If you have Homebrew installed, you just need to run `brew install node`.

Node is also available from Docker Hub. If you add `FROM node:argon` to your Dockerfile, you'll get the LTS version of Node installed into your image.

appendix B
Automating the web with scraping

This appendix covers

- Creating structured data from web pages
- Performing basic web scraping with cheerio
- Handling dynamic content with jsdom
- Parsing and outputting structured data

In the preceding chapter, you learned some general Node programming techniques, but now we're going to start focusing on web development. Scraping the web is an ideal way to do this, because it requires a combination of server and client-side programming skills. Scraping is all about using programming techniques to make sense of web pages and transform them into structured data. Imagine you're tasked with creating a new version of a book publisher's website that's currently just a set of old-fashioned, static HTML pages. You want to download the pages and analyze them to extract the titles, descriptions, authors, and prices for all the books. You don't want to do this by hand, so you write a Node program to do it. This is *web scraping*.

Node is great at scraping because it strikes a perfect balance between browser-based technology and the power of general-purpose scripting languages. In this

301

chapter, you'll learn how to use HTML parsing libraries to extract useful data based on CSS selectors, and even to run dynamic web pages in a Node process.

B.1   Understanding web scraping

Web scraping is the process of extracting useful information from websites. This usually involves downloading the required pages, parsing them, and then querying the raw HTML by using CSS or XPath selectors. The results of the queries are then exported as CSV files or saved to a database. Figure B.1 shows how scraping works from start to finish.

Web scraping may be against the terms of use of some websites, because of its cost or because of resource limitations. If thousands of scrapers hit a single site that runs on an old and slow server, the server could be knocked offline. Before you scrape any content, you should ensure that you have permission to access and duplicate the content. You can tech-

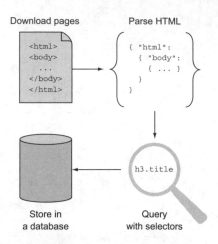

Download pages   Parse HTML

Store in a database   Query with selectors

Figure B.1   Steps for scraping and storing content

nically check the site's robots.txt (www.robotstxt.org) file for this information, but you should contact the site's owners first. In some cases, the site's owners may have invited you to index its information—perhaps as part of a larger web development contract.

In this section, you'll learn how people use scrapers for real sites, and then you'll look at the required tools that allow Node to become a web-scraping powerhouse.

B.1.1   Uses of web scraping

A great example of web scraping is the vertical search engine Octopart (https://octopart.com/). Octopart, shown in figure B.2, indexes electronics distributors and manufacturers to make it easier for people to find electronics. For example, you can search for resistors based on resistance, tolerance, power rating, and case type. A site like this uses web crawlers to download content, scrapers to make sense of the content and extract interesting values (for example, the tolerance of a resistor), and an internal database to store the processed information.

Figure B.2   Octopart allows users to search for electronic parts.

Web scraping isn't used for only search engines, however. It's also used in the growing fields of data science and data journalism. Data journalists use databases to produce stories, but because there's so much data that isn't stored in easily accessible formats, they may use tools such as web scraping to automate the collection and processing of data. This allows journalists to present information in new ways, through data-visualization techniques including infographics and interactive graphics.

B.1.2 Required tools

To get down to business, you need a couple of easily accessible tools: a web browser and Node. Browsers are one of the most useful scraping tools—if you can right-click and select Inspect Element, you're already partway to making sense of websites and converting them into raw data. The next step is to parse the pages with Node. In this chapter, you'll learn about two types of parser:

- Lightweight and forgiving: cheerio
- A web-standards-aware, Document Object Model (DOM) simulator: jsdom

Both of these libraries are installed with npm. You may need to parse loosely structured human-readable data formats such as dates as well. We'll briefly look at Java-Script's `Date.parse` and Moment.js.

The first example uses cheerio, which is a fast way to parse most static web pages.

B.2 Performing basic web scraping with cheerio

The cheerio library (www.npmjs.com/package/cheerio), by Felix Böhm, is perfect for scraping because it combines two key features: fast HTML parsing, and a jQuery-like API for querying and manipulating the HTML.

Imagine you need to extract information about books from a publisher's website. The publisher doesn't yet have an API that exposes book details, so you need to download pages from its website and turn them into usable JSON output that includes the author name and book title. Figure B.3 shows how scraping with cheerio works.

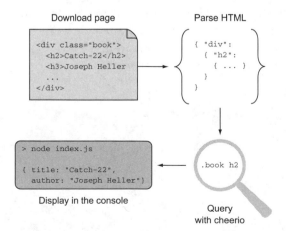

Figure B.3 Scraping with cheerio

The following listing contains a small scraper that uses cheerio. Sample HTML has been included, so you don't need to worry about how to download the page itself yet.

Listing B.1   Extracting a book's details

```
const html = `                          ◁──┐ Defines HTML
<html>                                        │ to parse
<body>
  <div class="book">
    <h2>Catch-22</h2>
    <h3>Joseph Heller</h3>
    <p>A satirical indictment of military madness.</p>
  </div>
</body>
</html>`;
const cheerio = require('cheerio');           ┐ Parses the entire
const $ = cheerio.load(html);             ◁──┘ document

const book = {
  title: $('.book h2').text(),           ◁──┐ Extracts the fields by
  author: $('.book h3').text(),              │ using CSS selectors
  description: $('.book p').text()
};

console.log(book);
```

Listing B.1 uses cheerio to parse a hardcoded HTML document by using the `cheerio`
`.load()` method and CSS selectors. In a simple example like this, the CSS selectors are simple and clear, but often real-world HTML is far messier. Unfortunately, poorly structured HTML is unavoidable, and your skill as a web scraper is defined by coming up with clever ways to pull out the values you need.

Making sense of bad HTML requires two steps. The first is to visualize the document, and the second is to define the selectors that target the elements you're interested in. You use cheerio's features to define the selector in just the right way.

Fortunately, modern browsers offer a point-and-click solution for finding selectors: if your browser has development tools, you can usually right-click and select Inspect Element. Not only will you see the underlying HTML, but the browser should also show a representation of the selector that targets the element.

Let's say you're trying to extract book information from a quirky site that uses tables without any handy CSS classes. The HTML might look like this:

```
<html>
  <body>
    <h1>Alex's Dated Book Website</h1>
    <table>
      <tr>
        <td><a href="/book1">Catch-22</a></td>
        <td>Joseph Heller</td>
      </tr>
    </table>
  </body>
</html>
```

Figure B.4   Viewing HTML in Chrome

If you open that in Chrome and right-click the title, you'll see something like figure B.4.

The white bar under the HTML shows "html body table tbody tr td a"—this is close to the selector that you need. But it's not quite right, because the real HTML doesn't have a tbody. Chrome has inserted this element. When you're using browsers to visualize documents, you should be prepared to adjust what you discover based on the true underlying HTML. This example shows that you need to search for a link inside a table cell to get the title, and the next table cell is the corresponding author.

Assuming the preceding HTML is in a file called messy_html_example.html, the following listing will extract the title, link, and author.

Listing B.2   Dealing with messy HTML

```
const fs = require('fs');
const html = fs.readFileSync('./messy_html_example.html', 'utf8');    ⟵ Loads the HTML from a file
const cheerio = require('cheerio');
const $ = cheerio.load(html);

const book = {                                          Uses cheerio's first() method
                                                        to get the specific link
  title: $('table tr td a').first().text(),    ⟵
href: $('table tr td a').first().attr('href'),    ⟵ Uses cheerio's attr()
                                                      method to get the URL
  author: $('table tr td').eq(1).text()    ⟵
};

                        Uses cheerio's eq() method to
                        skip to the second element
console.log(book);
```

You use the fs module to load the HTML; that's so you don't have to keep printing HTML in the example. In reality, your data source might be a live website, but the data could also be from a file or a database. After the document has been parsed, you use `first()` to get the first table cell with an anchor. To get the anchor's URL, you use cheerio's `attr()` method; it returns a specific attribute from an element, just like jQuery. The `eq()` method is also useful; in this listing, it's used to skip the first td, because the second contains the author's text.

> **Web-parsing dangers**
>
> Using a module such as cheerio is a quick and dirty way of interpreting web documents. But be careful of the type of content that you attempt to parse with it. It may throw an exception with binary data, for example, so using it in a web application could crash the Node process. This would be dangerous if your scraper is embedded in the same process that serves your web application.
>
> It's best to check the content type before passing it through a parser, and you may want to consider running your web scrapers in their own Node processes to reduce the impact of any serious crashes.

One of cheerio's limitations is that it allows you to work only with a static version of a document; it's used for working with pure HTML documents rather than dynamic pages that use client-side JavaScript. In the next section, you'll learn how to use jsdom to create a browser-like environment in your Node applications, so client-side JavaScript will be executed.

B.3 Handling dynamic content with jsdom

jsdom is the web scraper's dream tool: it downloads HTML, interprets it according to the DOM as found in a typical browser, and runs client-side JavaScript. You can specify the client-side JavaScript that you want to run, which typically means including jQuery. That means you can inject jQuery (or your own custom debugging scripts) into any pages. Figure B.5 shows how jsdom combines HTML and JavaScript to make otherwise unscrapeable content accessible.

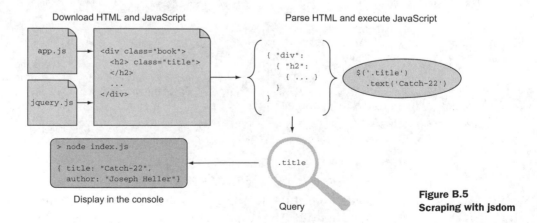

**Figure B.5
Scraping with jsdom**

jsdom does have a downside. It's not a perfect simulation of a browser, it's slower than cheerio, and the HTML parser is strict, so it may fail for pages with poorly written markup. Some sites don't make sense without client-side JavaScript support, however, so it's an indispensible tool for some scraping tasks.

The basic usage of jsdom is through the `jsdom.env` method. The following listing shows how jsdom can be used to scrape a page by injecting jQuery and pulling out useful values.

Listing B.3 Scraping with jsdom

```
const jsdom = require('jsdom');
const html = `                        ◄─┐  Includes a suitable
<div class="book">                        │  HTML fragment
  <h2>Catch-22</h2>
  <h3>Joseph Heller</h3>
  <p>A satirical indictment of military madness.</p>
</div>                                        Parses the document
`;                                            and loads jQuery

jsdom.env(html, ['./node_modules/jquery/dist/jquery.js'], scrape);  ◄─

function scrape(err, window) {                                  Aliases the jQuery
  var $ = window.$;                                             object for
  $('.book').each(function() {    ◄─  Iterates over the books   convenience
    var $el = $(this);                using jQuery's $.each method
    console.log({
      title: $el.find('h2').text(),   ◄─
      author: $el.find('h3').text(),     Uses jQuery's traversal
      description: $el.find('p').text()  methods to get the
    });                                  values of the book
  });
}
```

To run listing B.3, you need to save jQuery locally and install jsdom.[1] You can install both with npm. The modules are called jsdom (www.npmjs.com/package/jsdom) and jQuery (www.npmjs.com/package/jquery), respectively. After everything is set up, this code should print out the title, author, and description of the HTML fragment.

The `jsdom.env` method is used to parse the document and inject jQuery. jQuery is injected by downloading it from npm, but you could supply the URL to jQuery on a content delivery network (CDN) or your filesystem; jsdom will know what to do. The `jsdom.env` method is asynchronous and requires a callback to work. The callback receives error and window objects; the window object is how you access the document. Here the window's jQuery object has been aliased so it can be easily accessed with `$`.

A selector is used with jQuery's `.each` method to iterate over each book. This example has only one book, but it demonstrates that jQuery's traversal methods are indeed available. Each value from the book is accessed by using jQuery's traversal methods as well.

---

[1] jsdom 6.3.0 is the current version at the time of writing.

Listing B.3 is similar to the earlier cheerio example in listing B.1, but the main difference is that jQuery has been parsed and run by Node, within the current process. Listing B.1 used cheerio to provide similar functionality, but cheerio provides its own jQuery-like layer. Here you're running code intended for a browser as if it's really running in a browser.

The `jsdom.env` method is useful only for working with static pages. To parse pages that use client-side JavaScript, you need to use `jsdom.jsdom` instead. This synchronous method returns a window object that you can manipulate with other jsdom utilities. The following listing uses jsdom to parse a document with a `script` tag, and `jsdom.jQueryify` to make scraping it easier.

Listing B.4   Parsing dynamic HTML with jsdom

```
const jsdom = require('jsdom');
const jqueryPath = './node_modules/jquery/dist/jquery.js';    ◁──┐ Specifies the
const html = `                                                      jQuery path
<div class="book">
  <h2></h2>          ◁──┐ HTML with no
  <h3></h3>              static values
  <script>
document.querySelector('h2').innerHTML = 'Catch-22';         ◁── A script that
document.querySelector('h3').innerHTML = 'Joseph Heller';        dynamically
  </script>                                                       inserts
</div>                                                            the values
`;
                                              Creates an object that
const doc = jsdom.jsdom(html);        ◁──┘   represents the document
const window = doc.defaultView;

jsdom.jQueryify(window, jqueryPath, function() {   ◁──┐ Inserts jQuery into
  var $ = window.$;                                      the document
  $('.book').each(function() {
    var $el = $(this);
    console.log({
      title: $el.find('h2').text(),      ◁──┐ Extracts the
      author: $el.find('h3').text()          book values
    });
  });
});
```

Listing B.4 requires jQuery to be installed, so if you're creating this listing by hand, you need to set up a new project with `npm init` and `npm install --save jquery jsdom`. It uses a simple HTML document in which the useful values that you're looking for are dynamically inserted. They're inserted using client-side JavaScript found in a `script` tag.

This time, `jsdom.jsdom` is used instead of `jsdom.env`. It's synchronous because the document object is created in memory, but won't do much until you attempt to query or manipulate it. To do this, you use `jsdom.jQueryify` to insert your specific version of jQuery into the document. After jQuery has been loaded and run, the callback is run, which queries the document for the values you're interested in and prints them to the console. The output is shown here:

```
{ title: 'Catch-22', author: 'Joseph Heller' }
```

This proves that jsdom has invoked the necessary client-side JavaScript. Now imagine this is a real web page and you'll see why jsdom is so powerful: even websites made with very little static HTML and dynamic technologies such as Angular and React can be scraped.

B.4 Making sense of raw data

After you finally get useful data from a page, you need to process it so it's suitable for saving to a database or for an export format such as CSV. Your scraped data will either be unstructured plain text or encoded using microformats.

Microformats are lightweight, markup-based data formats that are used for things like addresses, calendars and events, and tags or keywords. You can find established microformats at microformats.org. Here's an example of a name represented as a microformat:

```
<a class="h-card" href="http://example.com">Joseph Heller</a>
```

Microformats are relatively easy to parse; with cheerio or jsdom, a simple expression such as `$('.h-card').text()` is sufficient to extract *Joseph Heller*. But plain text requires more work. In this section, you'll see how to parse dates and then convert them into more database-friendly formats.

Most web pages don't use microformats. One area where this is problematic but potentially manageable is date values. Dates can appear in many formats, but they're usually consistent on a given website. After you've identified the format, you can parse and then format the date.

JavaScript has a built-in date parser: if you run `new Date('2016 01 01')`, an instance of `Date` will be returned that corresponds to the first of January, 2016. The supported input formats are determined by `Date.parse`, which is based on RFC 2822 (http://tools.ietf.org/html/rfc2822#page-14) or ISO 8601 (www.w3.org/TR/NOTE-datetime). Other formats may work and are often worth trying out with your source data to see what happens.

The other approach is to match values in the source data with a regular expression, and then use `Date`'s constructor to make new `Date` objects. The signature for the constructor is as follows:

```
new Date(year, month[,day[,hour[,minutes[,seconds[,millis]]]]]);
```

Date parsing in JavaScript is usually good enough to handle many cases, but it falls down in reformatting dates. A great solution to this is Moment.js (http://momentjs.com), a date-parsing, validation, and formatting library. It has a fluent API, so calls can be chained like this:

```
moment().format("MMM Do YY"); // Sep 7th 15
```

This is convenient for turning scraped data into CSV files that work well with programs such as Microsoft Excel. Imagine you have a web page with books that include title and published date. You want to save the values to a database, but your database requires dates to be formatted as YYYY-MM-DD. The following listing shows how to use Moment with cheerio to do this.

Listing B.5   Parsing dates and generating CSV

```
'use strict';
const cheerio = require('cheerio');
const fs = require('fs');
const html = fs.readFileSync('./input.html');          ◁──┐ Loads the
const moment = require('moment');        ◁──                 input file
const $ = cheerio.load(html);
const books = $('.book')                                    Requires moment
  .map((i, el) => {                      ◁──  Maps each book into author,
    return {                                  title, and published date
      author: $(el).find('h2').text(),
      title: $(el).find('h3').text(),
      published: $(el).find('h4').text()
    };
  })
  .get();
                                                        ┌ The headers for
console.log('title, author, sourceDate, dbDate');  ◁──┘   the CSV file

books.forEach((book) => {
  let date = moment(new Date(book.published));   ◁──  Parses the date
  console.log(
    '%s, %s, %s, %s',
    book.author,
    book.title,
    book.published,
    date.format('YYYY-MM-DD')
  );
});
```

Listing B.5 requires that you install cheerio, Moment, and books. It takes as input HTML (from input.html) and then outputs CSV. The HTML should have dates in h4 elements, like this:

```
<div>
  <div class="book">
    <h2>Catch-22</h2>
    <h3>Joseph Heller</h3>
    <h4>11 November 1961</h4>
  </div>
  <div class="book">
    <h2>A Handful of Dust</h2>
    <h3>Evelyn Waugh</h3>
    <h4>1934</h4>
  </div>
</div>
```

After the scraper has loaded the input file, it loads up Moment, and then maps each book to a simple JavaScript object by using cheerio's `.map` and `.get` methods. The `.map` method iterates over each book, and the callback extracts each element that you're interested in by using the `.find` selector traversal method. To get the resulting text values as an array, `.get` is used.

Listing B.5 outputs CSV by using `console.log`. The header is printed, and then each row is logged in a loop that iterates over each book. The dates are converted to a format compatible with MySQL by using Moment; first the date is parsed using `new Date`, and then it's formatted using Moment.

After you've become used to parsing and formatting dates, you can apply similar techniques to other data formats. For example, currency and distance measurements can be captured with regular expressions, and then formatted by using a more generic number-formatting library such as Numeral (www.npmjs.com/package/numeral).

B.5 Summary

- Web scraping is the automated transformation of sometimes badly structured web pages into computer-friendly formats such as CSV or databases.
- Web scraping is used for vertical search engines but also for data journalism.
- If you're going to scrape a site, you should get permission first. You can do this by checking the site's robots.txt file and contacting the site's owner.
- The main tools are static HTML parsers (cheerio) and parsers capable of running JavaScript (jsdom), but also browser developer tools for finding the right CSS selector for the elements you're interested in.
- Sometimes the data itself is not well formatted, so you may need to parse things such as dates or currencies to make them work with databases.

appendix C
Connect's officially supported middleware

Connect is a minimal wrapper around Node's built-in HTTP client and server modules. The Connect authors and contributors have also produced officially supported middleware components that implement low-level features used by most web frameworks, including things like cookie handling, body parsing, sessions, basic auth, and cross-site request forgery (CSRF). This appendix demonstrates all of the officially supported modules so you can use them to build lightweight web applications without a larger framework.

C.1 Parsing cookies, request bodies, and query strings

Node's core doesn't provide modules for higher-level web application concepts such as parsing cookies, buffering request bodies, or parsing complex query strings, so Connect modules implement these features. This section covers four modules that parse request data:

- *cookie-parser*—Parses cookies from web browsers into `req.cookies`
- *qs*—Parses the request URL query string into req.query
- *body-parser*—Consumes and parses the request body into `req.body`

The first module we'll look at is cookie-parser. This makes it easy to retrieve data stored by a website visitor's browser so you can read things such as authorization status, website settings, and so on.

C.1.1 cookie-parser: parse HTTP cookies

The cookie-parser module supports regular cookies, signed cookies, and special JSON cookies (www.npmjs.com/package/cookie-parser). By default, regular unsigned cookies are used, populating the `req.cookies` object. If you want signed cookie support, which helps prevent cookies from being tampered with, you'll want to pass a secret string when creating the `cookie-parser` instance.

> **SETTING COOKIES ON THE SERVER SIDE** The `cookie-parser` module doesn't provide any helpers for setting outgoing cookies. For this, you should use the `res.setHeader()` function with `Set-Cookie` as the header name. Connect patches Node's default `res.setHeader()` function to special-case the `Set-Cookie` headers so that it just works, as you'd expect it to.

REGULAR COOKIES

To read cookies, you need to load the module, add it to the middleware stack, and then read the cookies in a request. The following listing illustrates each of these steps.

Listing C.1   Reading cookies sent in a request

```
const connect = require('connect');
const cookieParser = require('cookie-parser');          ←  ❶ Loads the cookie-
                                                              parser middleware
connect()                          ❷ Adds it to the middleware
  .use(cookieParser())      ←        for this application
  .use((req, res, next) => {
    res.end(JSON.stringify(req.cookies));     ←  ❸ Responds with a string
  })                                               version of the cookies
  .listen(3000);
```

This example loads the middleware component ❶. Remember that you need to install the middleware with `npm install cookie-parser` for this to work. Next it adds an instance of the cookie parser to the middleware stack for this application ❷. The final step is to send back the cookies to the browser as a string ❸, so you can see it working.

If you run this example, you'll need to set cookies with the request. If you go to http://localhost:3000 in a browser, you probably won't see much; it should return an empty object (`{}`). You can use cURL to set a cookie like this:

```
curl http://localhost:3000/ -H "Cookie: foo=bar, bar=baz"
```

SIGNED COOKIES

Signed cookies are better suited for sensitive data, as the integrity of the cookie data can be verified, helping to prevent man-in-the-middle attacks. Signed cookies are placed in the `req.signedCookies` object when valid. The reasoning behind having two separate objects is that it shows the developer's intention. If you were to place both signed and unsigned cookies in the same object, a regular cookie could be crafted to contain data to mimic a signed cookie.

A signed cookie looks something like `s:tobi.DDm3AcVxE9oneYnbmpqxoy[...]`,[1] where the content to the left of the period (`.`) is the cookie's value, and the content to

---

[1]   The signed values have been shortened.

the right is the secret hash generated on the server with SHA-256 HMAC (hash-based message authentication code). When Connect attempts to unsign the cookie, it will fail if either the value or HMAC has been altered.

Suppose, for example, you set a signed cookie with a key of `name` and a value of `luna`. `cookieParser` would encode the cookie to `s:luna.PQLM0wNvqOQEObZX[...]`. The hash portion is checked on each request, and when the cookie is sent intact, it will be available as `req.signedCookies.name`:

```
$ curl http://localhost:3000/ -H "Cookie:
➥ name=s:luna.PQLM0wNvqOQEObZXU[...]"
{}
{ name: 'luna' }
GET / 200 4ms
```

If the cookie's value were to change, as shown in the next `curl` command, the `name` cookie would be available as `req.cookies.name` because it wasn't valid. It might still be of use for debugging or application-specific purposes:

```
$ curl http://localhost:3000/ -H "Cookie:
➥ name=manny.PQLM0wNvqOQEOb[...]"
{ name: 'manny.PQLM0wNvqOQEOb[...]' }
{}
GET / 200 1ms
```

The first argument to `cookieParser` is the secret to be used for signing cookies. In the following listing, the secret is *tobi is a cool ferret*.

Listing C.2   Parsing signed cookies

```
const connect = require('connect');
const cookieParser = require('cookie-parser');
const secret = 'tobi is a cool ferret';

connect()
  .use(cookieParser(secret))                           ❶  The signed cookies are automatically
  .use((req, res) => {                                     added to the request object
    console.log('Cookies:', req.cookies);
    console.log('Signed cookies:', req.signedCookies);  ❷  Access the signed cookies
    res.end('hello\n');                                     from the request object
  }).listen(3000);
```

In this example, the signed cookies are parsed automatically because the `secret` argument was passed to the `cookieParser` middleware component ❶. The values can be accessed on the `request` object ❷. The cookie-parser module also makes the cookie parsing functionality available through the `signedCookie` and `signedCookies` methods.

Before moving on, let's look at how to use this example. As with listing C.1, you can use `curl` with the `-H` option to send a cookie. But for it to be considered a signed cookie, it needs to be encoded in a certain way.

Node's crypto module is used to unsign cookies in the `signedCookie` method. If you want to sign a cookie to test listing C.2, you need to install `cookie-signature` and then sign a string with the same secret:

```
const signature = require('cookie-signature');
const message = 'luna';
const secret = 'tobi is a cool ferret';
console.log(signature.sign(message, secret));
```

Now if the signature or message were modified, the server would be able to tell. In addition to signed cookies, this module supports JSON-encoded cookies. The next section shows how these work.

JSON COOKIES

The special JSON cookie is prefixed with `j:`, which informs Connect that it's intended to be serialized JSON. JSON cookies can be either signed or unsigned.

Frameworks such as Express can use this functionality to provide developers with a more intuitive cookie interface, instead of requiring them to manually serialize and parse JSON cookie values. Here's an example of how Connect parses JSON cookies:

```
$ curl http://localhost:3000/ -H 'Cookie: foo=bar,
bar=j:{"foo":"bar"}'
{ foo: 'bar', bar: { foo: 'bar' } }
{}
GET / 200 1ms
```

As mentioned, JSON cookies can also be signed, as illustrated in the following request:

```
$ curl http://localhost:3000/ -H "Cookie:
 cart=j:{\"items\":[1]}.sD5p6xFFBO/4ketA1OP43bcjS3Y"
{}
{ cart: { items: [ 1 ] } }
GET / 200 1ms
```

SETTING OUTGOING COOKIES

As noted earlier, the cookie-parser module doesn't provide any functionality for writing outgoing headers to the HTTP client via the `Set-Cookie` header. Connect, however, provides explicit support for multiple `Set-Cookie` headers via the `res.setHeader()` function.

Say you want to set a cookie named `foo` with the string value `bar`. Connect enables you to do this in one line of code by calling `res.setHeader()`. You can also set the various options of a cookie, such as its expiration date, as shown in the second `setHeader()` call here:

```
var connect = require('connect');

connect()
  .use((req, res) => {
    res.setHeader('Set-Cookie', 'foo=bar');
    res.setHeader('Set-Cookie',
```

```
        'tobi=ferret; Expires=Tue, 08 Jun 2021 10:18:14 GMT'
    );
  res.end();
})
.listen(3000);
```

If you check out the headers that this server sends back to the HTTP request by using the `--head` flag of `curl`, you can see the `Set-Cookie` headers set as you would expect:

```
$ curl http://localhost:3000/ --head
HTTP/1.1 200 OK
Set-Cookie: foo=bar
Set-Cookie: tobi=ferret; Expires=Tue, 08 Jun 2021 10:18:14 GMT
Connection: keep-alive
```

That's all there is to sending cookies with your HTTP response. You can store any kind of text data in cookies, but it has become usual to store a single session cookie on the client side so that you can have full user state on the server. This session technique is encapsulated in the express-session module, which you'll learn about later in this appendix.

Now that you can handle cookies, you're probably eager to handle the other usual methods for accepting user input. The next two sections cover parsing query strings and request bodies, and you'll discover that even though Connect is relatively low-level, you can still get the same features as more complicated web frameworks without writing lots of code.

C.1.2 Parsing query strings

One method for accepting input is to use GET parameters. You place a question mark after a URL, with a list of arguments separated by ampersands:

```
http://localhost:3000/page?name=tobi&species=ferret
```

This type of URL can be presented to your application by a form that's set to use the GET method, or by anchor elements within your application's templates. You've probably seen this used for pagination.

The request object that's passed to each middleware component in Connect applications includes a `url` property, but what you want is the last part of the URL: just the portion after the question mark. Node comes with a URL-parsing module, so you could technically use `url.parse` to get the query string. But Connect also has to parse the URL, so it sets an internal property with a parsed version.

The recommended module for parsing query strings is qs (www.npmjs.com/package/qs). This module isn't officially supported by Connect, and alternatives are available through npm. To use qs and similar modules, you need to call its `.parse()` method from your own middleware component.

The following listing uses the `qs.parse` method to create an object that's stored on the `req.query` property for subsequent middleware components to use.

> **Listing C.3　Parsing query strings**

```
const connect = require('connect');
const qs = require('qs');
connect()
  .use((req, res, next) => {
    console.log(req._parsedUrl.query);              ❶ Uses qs to parse
    req.query = qs.parse(req._parsedUrl.query);        the query string
    next();
  })
  .use((req, res) => {
    console.log('query string:', req.query);        Displays the parsed
    res.end('\n');                                  query string
  })
  .listen(3000);
```

This example uses a custom middleware component to obtain the parsed URL, parse it using `qs.parse` ❶, and then display it in a subsequent component.

Suppose you're designing a music library app. You could offer a search engine and use the query string to build up the search parameters, like this:

`/songSearch?artist=Bob%20Marley&track=Jammin.`

This example query produces a `res.query` object like this:

`{ artist: 'Bob Marley', track: 'Jammin' }`

The `qs.parse` method supports nested arrays, so complex query strings such as `?images[]=foo.png&images[]=bar.png` produce objects like this one:

`{ images: [ 'foo.png', 'bar.png' ] }`

When no query-string parameters are given in the HTTP request, such as `/song-Search`, `req.query` will default to an empty object:

`{}`

Higher-level frameworks such as Express tend to have query-string parsing built in, because it's such a common requirement for web development. Another common feature of web frameworks is parsing request bodies, so you can accept data posted in forms. The next section explains how to parse request bodies, handle forms and file uploads, and validate these requests to ensure they're safe.

C.1.3　*body-parser: parse request bodies*

Most web applications have to accept and process user input. This can be from forms or even other programs in the case of RESTful APIs. HTTP requests and responses are collectively known as *HTTP messages*. The format of a message consists of a list of headers and then a message body. In Node web applications, the body is usually a stream, and it can be encoded in various ways: a POST from a form will usually be `application/x-www-form-urlencoded`, and a RESTful JSON request could be `application/json`.

That means your Connect applications need middleware that's capable of decoding streams of form-encoded data, JSON, or even compressed data using gzip or deflate. In this section, we'll show how to do the following:

- Handle input from forms
- Parse JSON requests
- Validate bodies based on content and size
- Accept file uploads

FORMS

Suppose you want to accept registration information for your application though a form. All you have to do is add the body-parser component (www.npmjs.com/ package/body-parser) before any other middleware that will access the `req.body` object. Figure C.1 shows how this works.

The following listing shows how to use the body-parser module with HTTP POSTs from forms.

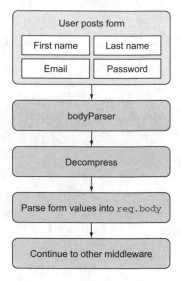

Figure C.1   How a form is processed by body-parser

Listing C.4   Parsing form requests

```
const connect = require('connect');
const bodyParser = require('body-parser');

connect()
  .use(bodyParser.urlencoded({ extended: false }))      ①
  .use((req, res, next) => {
    res.setHeader('Content-Type', 'text/plain');
    res.end('You sent: ' + JSON.stringify(req.body) + '\n');   ②
  })
  .listen(3000);
```

① Adds the body parser to the middleware stack

② Returns the request body as a string

To use this example, you need to install the body-parser module,[2] and then you need a way to make a simple HTTP request with a URL-encoded body. The easiest way is to use `curl` with the `-d` option:

```
curl -d name=tobi http://localhost:3000
```

---

[2]   We used version 1.11.0.

This should cause the server to display `You sent: {"name":"tobi"}`. To make this work, the body parser is added to the middleware stack ❶, and then the parsed body in `req.body` is converted to a string ❷ so it can be displayed more easily. The `urlencoded` body parser accepts a UTF-8 encoded string, and it'll automatically decompress request bodies encoded with gzip or deflate.

In this example, the options passed to the body parser are `extended: false`. When set to `true`, this option causes the body parser to use another library to parse the query-string format. This allows you to use more complex, nested, JSON-like objects in forms. The other options are presented in the next section, where you'll look at validating requests.

VALIDATING REQUESTS

Each parser that comes with the body-parser module supports two options for validating requests: `limit` and `verify`. The `limit` option allows you to block requests over a certain size: the default is 100 KB, so you can increase it if you want to accept larger forms. If you're making something like a content management system or blog, where people can potentially enter valid but lengthy fields, this would be useful.

The `verify` option allows you to use a function to validate requests. It's useful if you want to get the raw request body and check that it's in the correct format. For example, you could use this to ensure that API methods that accept XML always start with the correct XML header. The following listing shows how to use both of these options.

Listing C.5 Validating form requests

```
const connect = require('connect');
const bodyParser = require('body-parser');

function verifyRequest(req, res, buf, encoding) {
  if (!buf.toString().match(/^name=/)) {
    throw new Error('Bad format');          ⟵──┐  ❶ Throws an error when
  }                                              the format is incorrect
}

connect()
  .use(bodyParser.urlencoded({
    extended: false,
    limit: 10,                    ❷ Sets the request limit
    verify: verifyRequest         ⟵──
  }))                                    ⟵──┐ ❸ Adds a verify
  .use(function(req, res, next) {              function
    res.setHeader('Content-Type', 'text/plain');
    res.end('You sent: ' + JSON.stringify(req.body) + '\n');
  })
  .listen(3000);
```

Notice that an `Error` object should be thrown by using the `throw` keyword ❶. The body-parser module is set up to catch these before parsing the request, so it'll pass the error back to Connect. After a request validation function has been created, you need to pass it to the body-parser middleware component by using the `verify` option ❸.

The body size limit is in bytes; here it's quite small, at 10 bytes ❷. You can easily see what happens when the request is too large by using the previous `curl` command with a larger name value. Also, if you want to see what happens when the validation error is thrown, use `curl` to send another value instead of `name`.

WHY IS LIMIT NEEDED?

Let's take a look at how a malicious user can render a vulnerable server useless. First, create the following small Connect application named server.js, which does nothing other than parse request bodies by using the `bodyParser()` middleware component:

```
const connect = require('connect');
const bodyParser = require('body-parser');

connect()
  .use(bodyParser.json({ limit: 99999999, extended: false }))
  .use((req, res, next) => {
    res.end('OK\n');
  })
  .listen(3000);
```

Now create a file named dos.js, as shown in the following listing. You can see how a malicious user could use Node's HTTP client to attack the preceding Connect application, simply by writing several megabytes of JSON data:

```
const http = require('http');
let req = http.request({
  method: 'POST',
  port: 3000,
  headers: {
    'Content-Type': 'application/json'      ◁——  Notifies server that you're
  }                                                sending JSON data
});
req.write('[');                   ◁——  Begins sending a large
let n = 300000;                          array object
while (n--) {
  req.write('"foo",');            ◁——  Array contains 300,000
}                                        "foo" string entries
req.write('"bar"]');
req.end();
```

Fire up the server and run the attack script:

```
$ node server.js &
$ node dos.js
```

If you watch the `node` process in `top(1)`, you should see that it starts to use more CPU and RAM as dos.js runs. This is bad, but thankfully it's exactly why all the body parsing middleware components accept a `limit` option.

PARSING JSON DATA

If you're making web applications with Node, you're going to be dealing with a lot of JSON. The body-parser module's JSON parser has a few handy options that you've seen in the previous examples. The following listing shows how parsing JSON and using the resulting values works.

> **Listing C.6   Validating form requests**

```
const connect = require('connect');
const bodyParser = require('body-parser');

connect()                                              ❶ Adds the JSON
  .use(bodyParser.json())                                  body parser
  .use((req, res, next) => {
    res.setHeader('Content-Type', 'application/json');  ❷ Gets a value from
    res.end(`Name: ${req.body.name}\n`);                    the body object
  })
  .listen(3000);
```

After the JSON parser has been loaded ❶, your request handlers can treat the `req.body` value as a JavaScript object rather than a string. This example assumes that a JSON object with a `name` property has been sent, and it'll send the value back in the response ❷. That means your request has to have a `Content-Type` of `application/json`, and you need to send valid JSON. By default, the `json` middleware component uses strict parsing, but you can relax encoding requirements by setting this to `false`.

> ### Setting the JSON Content-Type option
>
> One option that you need to be aware of is `type`. This allows you to change the `Content-Type` that'll be parsed as JSON. In the following example, we use the default, which is `application/json`. But in some cases your application might have to interact with HTTP clients that don't send this header, so be warned.

The following `curl` request could be used to submit data to your application, and will send a JSON object with the `username` property set to `tobi`:

```
curl -d '{"name":"tobi"}' -H "Content-Type: application/json"
➥ http://localhost:3000
Name: tobi
```

PARSING MULTIPART <FORM> DATA

The body-parser module doesn't handle multipart request bodies. You need to handle multipart messages to support file uploads, so anything such as uploading a user's avatar needs multipart support.

There's no officially supported multipart parser for Connect, but some popular ones are well maintained. Two examples are busboy (www.npmjs.com/package/busboy) and multiparty (www.npmjs.com/package/multiparty). Both of these modules have associated connect modules: connect-busboy and connect-multiparty. The reason for this is that the multipart parsers themselves are dependent on Node's lower-level HTTP modules, so a wide range of frameworks can use them. They're not specifically tied into Connect.

The following listing is based on multiparty, and will print out the details of an uploaded file in the console.

Listing C.7   Handling uploaded files

```
const connect = require('connect');
const multipart = require('connect-multiparty');

connect()
  .use(multipart())                          ──◄── ❶ Adds the multipart
  .use((req, res, next) => {                             middleware component
    console.log(req.files);                  ──◄── ┐
    res.end('Upload received\n');                  │ Logs the files
  })                                           ❷ that were sent
  .listen(3000);
```

This short example adds the multiparty middleware component ❶ and then logs the received files ❷. The files will be uploaded to a temporary location, so you have to use the fs module to delete the files when your application is finished with them.

To use this example, make sure you've installed connect-multiparty.[3] Then start the server and send it a file with `curl`'s `-F` option:

```
curl -F file=@index.js http://localhost:3000
```

The filename is placed after the @ symbol, and it's prefixed with a field name. The field name will be available in the `req.files` object, so you can distinguish between separate uploaded files.

If you take a look at the output of the application, you'll see something similar to the following example output. As you can see, `req.files.file.path` would be available to your application, and you could rename the file on disk, transfer the data to a worker for processing, upload to a content delivery network, or do anything else your app requires:

```
{ fieldName: 'file',
  originalFilename: 'index.js',
  path: '/var/folders/d0/_jqj3lf96g37s5wrf79v_g4c0000gn/T/60201-p4pohc.js',
  headers:
   { 'content-disposition': 'form-data; name="file"; filename="index.js"',
     'content-type': 'application/octet-stream' },
```

Although body-parser copes with compression, you may be wondering about compressing outgoing responses. Read on to learn about the compression middleware component that can reduce your bandwidth bills and make your web applications feel faster.

---

[3]   We used version 1.2.5 to test this example.

C.1.4 *compression: compressing outgoing responses*

In the preceding section, you may have noticed that the body parsers are capable of decompressing requests that used gzip or deflate. Node comes with a core module for handling compression called zlib, and this is used to implement both compression and decompression methods. The compression middleware component (www.npmjs .com/package/compression) can be used to compress outgoing responses, which means the data your server sends can be compressed.

Google's PageSpeed Insights tool recommends enabling gzip compression,[4] and if you look at requests made by your browser in the developer tools, you should see that many sites send gzipped responses. Compression adds CPU overhead, but because formats such as plain text and HTML compress well, it can improve your site's performance and reduce bandwidth usage.

Deflate or gzip?

Having two compression options can be confusing. You're probably wondering which is best, and why two exist at all. Well, according to the standards (RFC 1950 and RFC 2616), both use the same compression algorithm, but they differ in the way the header and checksum are handled.

Unfortunately, some browsers don't correctly handle deflate, so the general advice is to use gzip. In the case of body parsing, it's best to be able to support both, but if you're compressing your server's output, use gzip to be on the safe side.

The compression module detects the accepted encodings from the `Accept-Encoding` header field. If this field isn't present, the identity encoding is used, meaning the response is untouched. Otherwise, if the field contains `gzip`, `deflate`, or both, the response will be compressed.

BASIC USAGE

You should generally add compression high in the Connect stack, because it wraps the `res.write()` and `res.end()` methods.

In the following example, the content will be compressed:

```
const connect = require('connect');
const compression = require('compression');
connect()
  .use(compression({ threshold: 0 }))
  .use((req, res) => {
    res.setHeader('Content-Type', 'text/plain');
    res.end('This response is compressed!\n');
  })
  .listen(3000);
```

---

[4] See https://developers.google.com/speed/docs/insights/EnableCompression for more information.

To run this example, you need to install the compression module from npm. Then, start the server and try making a request with `curl` that sets `Accept-Encoding` to `gzip`:

```
$ curl http://localhost:3000 -i -H "Accept-Encoding: gzip"
```

The `-i` argument makes cURL show you the headers, so you should see the `Content-Encoding` set to `gzip`. The output should be garbled, because the compressed data won't be standard characters. Try piping it through `gunzip` without the `-i` option to see the output:

```
$ curl http://localhost:3000 -H "Accept-Encoding: gzip" | gunzip
```

This is powerful and relatively simple to set up, but you won't always want to compress everything your server sends. To skip compression, you can use custom filter functions.

USING A CUSTOM FILTER FUNCTION

By default, `compression` includes the MIME types `text/*`, `*/json`, and `*/javascript` in the default `filter` function to avoid compressing these data types:

```
exports.filter = function(req, res){
  const type = res.getHeader('Content-Type') || '';
  return type.match(/json|text|javascript/);
};
```

To alter this behavior, you can pass a `filter` in the options object, as shown in the following snippet, which will compress only plain text:

```
function filter(req) {
  const type = req.getHeader('Content-Type') || '';
  return 0 === type.indexOf('text/plain');
}
connect()
  .use(compression({ filter: filter }));
```

SPECIFYING COMPRESSION AND MEMORY LEVELS

Node's zlib bindings provide options for tweaking performance and compression characteristics, and they can also be passed to the `compression` function.

In the following example, the compression `level` is set to 3 for less but faster compression, and `memLevel` is set to 8 for faster compression by using more memory. These values depend entirely on your application and the resources available to it. Consult Node's zlib documentation for details:

```
connect()
  .use(compression({ level: 3, memLevel: 8 }));
```

That's all there is to it. Next we'll look at middleware that covers core web application needs, such as logging and sessions.

C.2 Implementing core web application functions

Connect aims to implement and provide built-in middleware for the most common web application needs so that they don't need to be reimplemented over and over by every developer. Core web application functions such as logging, sessions, and virtual hosting are all provided by Connect out of the box.

In this section, you'll learn about five useful middleware components that you'll likely use in your applications:

- *morgan*—Provides flexible request logging
- *serve-favicon*—Takes care of the /favicon.ico request without you having to think about it
- *method-override*—Enables incapable clients to transparently overwrite `req.method`
- *vhost*—Sets up multiple websites on a single server (virtual hosting)
- *express-session*—Manages session data

Up until now, you've created your own custom logging middleware, but the Connect maintainers provide a flexible solution named morgan, so let's explore that first.

C.2.1 morgan: log requests

The morgan module (www.npmjs.com/package/morgan) is a flexible request-logging middleware component with customizable log formats. It also has options for buffering log output to decrease disk writes, and for specifying a log stream if you want to log to something other than the console, such as a file or socket.

BASIC USAGE

To use morgan in your own application, invoke it as a function to return a middleware function, as shown in the following listing.

> **Listing C.8 Using the morgan module for logging**

```
const connect = require('connect');
const morgan = require('morgan');

connect()
  .use(morgan('combined'))                                    ❶ The "combined" logging
  .use((req, res) => {                                          option is used for each request
    res.setHeader('Content-Type', 'application/json');
    res.end('Logging\n');                                     ❷ Responds to the
  })                                                            request with a message
  .listen(3000);
```

To use this example, you need to install the morgan module from npm.[5] It adds the module at the top of the middleware stack ❶ and then outputs a simple text response

---

[5] We used version 1.5.1.

❷. By using the `combined` logging format argument ❶, this Connect application will output the Apache log format. This is a flexible format that many command-line utilities can parse, so you can run your logs through log-processing applications that can generate useful statistics. If you try making requests from different clients, such as `curl`, `wget`, and a browser, you should see the user agent string in the logs.

The `combined` logging format is defined like this:

```
:remote-addr - :remote-user [:date[clf]] ":method :url
➥ HTTP/:http-version" :status :res[content-length] ":referrer" ":user-agent"
```

Each of the `:something` pieces are *tokens*, and in a log entry they'd contain real values from the HTTP request that's being logged. For example, a simple `curl(1)` request would generate a log line similar to the following:

```
127.0.0.1 - - [Thu, 05 Feb 2015 04:27:07 GMT]
                    ➥ "GET / HTTP/1.1" 200 - "-"
                    ➥ "curl/7.37.1"
```

CUSTOMIZING LOG FORMATS

You can also create your own log formats. To do this, pass a custom string of tokens. For example, the following format would output something like `GET /users 15 ms`:

```
connect()
  .use(morgan(':method :url :response-time ms'))
  .use(hello)
  .listen(3000);
```

By default, the following tokens are available for use (note that the header names aren't case-sensitive):

- `:req[header]` example: `:req[Accept]`
- `:res[header]` example: `:res[Content-Length]`
- `:http-version`
- `:response-time`
- `:remote-addr`
- `:date`
- `:method`
- `:url`
- `:referrer`
- `:user-agent`
- `:status`

You can even define custom tokens. All you have to do is provide a token name and callback function to the `connect.logger.token` function. For example, say you want to log each request's query string. You might define it like this:

```
var url = require('url');
morgan.token('query-string', function(req, res){
  return url.parse(req.url).query;
});
```

The morgan module comes with predefined formats other than the default one, such as `short` and `tiny`. Another predefined format is `dev`, which produces concise output for development, for situations when you're usually the only user on the site and you don't care about the details of the HTTP requests. This format also color-codes the response status codes by type: responses with a status code in the 200s are green, 300s are blue, 400s are yellow, and 500s are red. This color scheme makes it great for development.

To use a predefined format, you provide the name to `logger()`:

```
connect()
  .use(morgan('dev'))
  .use(hello);
  .listen(3000);
```

Now that you know how to format the logger's output, let's look at the options you can provide to it.

LOGGER OPTIONS: STREAM, IMMEDIATE, AND BUFFER

As mentioned previously, you can use options to tweak how morgan behaves.

One such option is `stream`, which allows you to pass a Node `Stream` instance that the logger will write to instead of stdout. This allows you to direct the logger output to its own log file, independent of your server's own output, by using a `Stream` instance created from `fs.createWriteStream`.

When you use these options, it's generally recommended to also include the `format` property. The following example uses a custom format and logs to /var/log/myapp.log with the `append` flag, so that the file isn't truncated when the application boots:

```
const fs = require('fs');
const morgan = require('morgan');
const log = fs.createWriteStream('/var/log/myapp.log', { flags: 'a' })
connect()
  .use(morgan({ format: ':method :url', stream: log }))
  .use('/error', error)
  .use(hello)
  .listen(3000);
```

Another useful option is `immediate`, which writes the log line when the request is first received, rather than waiting for the response. You might use this option if you're writing a server that keeps its requests open for a long time, and you want to know when the connection begins. Or you might use it for debugging a critical section of your app. Tokens such as `:status` and `:response-time` can't be used, because they're related to the response. To enable immediate mode, pass `true` for the `immediate` value, as shown here:

```
const app = connect()
  .use(connect.logger({ immediate: true }))
  .use('/error', error)
  .use(hello);
```

That's it for logging! Next we'll look at the favicon-serving middleware component.

C.2.2 *serve-favicon: address bar and bookmark icons*

A *favicon* is that tiny website icon your browser displays in the address bar and bookmarks. To get this icon, the browser makes a request for a file at /favicon.ico. It's usually best to serve favicon files as soon as possible, so the rest of your application can simply ignore them. The serve-favicon module (www.npmjs.com/package/serve-favicon)   causes

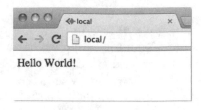

Figure C.2   A favicon

Connect's icon to be displayed by default. This can be configured by passing arguments for other icons. This favicon is shown in figure C.2.

BASIC USAGE

The serve-favicon middleware component can be placed at the top of the stack, which causes favicon requests to be ignored by any subsequent logging components. The icon is cached in memory for fast responses.

The following example shows serve-favicon sending an .ico file by passing the file path as the only argument:

```
const connect = require('connect');
const favicon = require('serve-favicon');
connect()
  .use(favicon(__dirname + '/favicon.ico'))
  .use((req, res) => {
    res.end('Hello World!\n');
  });
```

Note that you need a file called favicon.ico to test this out. Optionally, you can pass in a maxAge argument to specify how long browsers should cache the favicon in memory.

Next we have another small but helpful middleware component: method-override. It provides the means to fake the HTTP request method when client capabilities are limited.

C.2.3 *method-override: fake HTTP methods*

Sometimes it's useful to use HTTP verbs beyond the common GET and POST methods. Imagine that you're building a blog, and you want to allow people to create, update, and delete articles. It feels more natural to say DELETE /article rather than GET or POST. Unfortunately, not every browser understands the DELETE method.

A common workaround is to allow the server to get a hint about which HTTP method to use from the query parameters, form values, and sometimes even the HTTP headers. One way this is done is by adding <input type=hidden> with the value set to the method name you want to use. The server can then check the value and pretend it's the request method.

Most web frameworks support this technique, and the method-override module (www.npmjs.com/package/method-override) is the recommended way to do it with Connect.

BASIC USAGE

By default, the HTML input name is _method, but you can pass a custom value to methodOverride, as shown in the following snippet:

```
connect()
const connect = require('connect');
const methodOverride = require('method-override');
connect()
  .use(methodOverride('__method__'))
  .listen(3000)
```

To demonstrate how methodOverride() is implemented, let's see how to create a tiny application to update user information. The application consists of a single form that will respond with a simple success message when the form is submitted by the browser and processed by the server, as illustrated in figure C.3.

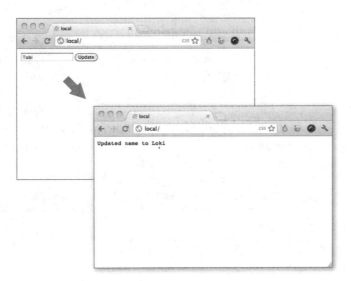

Figure C.3 Using method-override to simulate a PUT request to update a form in the browser

The application updates the user data through the use of two separate middleware components. In the update function, next() is called when the request method isn't PUT. As mentioned previously, most browsers don't respect the form attribute method="put", so the application in the following listing won't function properly.

Listing C.9 A broken user-update application

```
const connect = require('connect');
const morgan = require('morgan');
const bodyParser = require('body-parser');

function edit(req, res, next) {
  if ('GET' != req.method) return next();
```

```
  res.setHeader('Content-Type', 'text/html');
  res.write('<form method="put">');
  res.write('<input type="text" name="user[name]" value="Tobi" />');
  res.write('<input type="submit" value="Update" />');
  res.write('</form>');
  res.end();
}
```

A form that sends
a PUT instead of
a GET or POST ❶

```
function update(req, res, next) {
  if ('PUT' != req.method) return next();
  res.end('Updated name to ' + req.body.user.name);
}
```

Ensures the request
❷ has been sent with a PUT

```
connect()
  .use(morgan('combined'))
  .use(bodyParser.urlencoded({ extended: false }))
  .use(edit)
  .use(update)
    .listen(3000);
```

In this example, a form has been set up that sends a PUT to the server ❶. The form should send data to the update function, but only if it's sent with a PUT ❷. You can try this with different browsers and HTTP clients; you can send a PUT with curl by using the -X option.

To improve browser support, you'll add the method-override module. Here an additional input with the name _method has been added to the form, and method-Override() has been added below the bodyParser() method because it references req.body to access the form data.

Listing C.10 Using method-override to support HTTP PUT

```
const connect = require('connect');
const morgan = require('morgan');
const bodyParser = require('body-parser');
const methodOverride = require('method-override');

function edit(req, res, next) {
  if ('GET' != req.method) return next();
  res.setHeader('Content-Type', 'text/html');
  res.write('<form method="post">');
  res.write('<input type="hidden" name="_method" value="put" />');
  res.write('<input type="text" name="user[name]" value="Tobi" />');
  res.write('<input type="submit" value="Update" />');
  res.write('</form>');
  res.end();
}

function update(req, res, next) {
  if ('PUT' != req.method) return next();
  res.end('Updated name to ${req.body.user.name}');;
}
```

Sends a hint for the HTTP
method by including the
_method form variable

```
connect()
  .use(morgan('dev'))
  .use(bodyParser.urlencoded({ extended: false }))
  .use(methodOverride('_method'))
  .use(edit)
  .use(update)
  .listen(3000);
```

◁──── **Uses the methodOverride middleware component to watch for the form variable**

If you run this example, you should see that you can now send PUT requests from almost any browser.

ACCESSING THE ORIGINAL REQ.METHOD

`methodOverride()` alters the original `req.method` property, but Connect copies over the original method, which you can always access with `req.originalMethod`. The previous form would output values like these:

```
console.log(req.method);
  // "PUT"
console.log(req.originalMethod);
  // "POST"
```

To avoid including extra form variables, HTTP headers are supported as well. Different vendors use different headers, so you can create servers that support several header field names. This will help if you want to support client tools and libraries that assume a specific header. In the following example, the three header field names are supported:

```
app.use(methodOverride('X-HTTP-Method'))            ◁──────── Microsoft
app.use(methodOverride('X-HTTP-Method-Override'))   ◁──────── Google/GData
app.use(methodOverride('X-Method-Override'))        ◁──────── IBM
```

Routing based on headers is a common task. One good example of this is supporting virtual hosts. You may have seen Apache servers that do this when you want to host multiple websites on a smaller number of IP addresses. Apache and Nginx can determine which website should be served based on the `Host` header.

Connect can do this too, and it's easier than you might think. Read on to learn about virtual hosts and the vhost module.

C.2.4 *vhost: virtual hosting*

The vhost (virtual host) module (www.npmjs.com/package/vhost) is a simple, lightweight middleware component that routes requests via the `Host` request header. This task is commonly performed by a reverse proxy, which then forwards the request to a web server running locally on a different port. The vhost component does this in the same Node process by passing control to a Node HTTP server associated with the vhost instance.

BASIC USAGE

Like most middleware, a single line is all it takes to get up and running with the vhost component. It takes two arguments: The first is the hostname string that this vhost instance will match against. The second is the http.Server instance that'll be used when an HTTP request with a matching hostname is made (all Connect apps are subclasses of http.Server, so an application instance will work as well):

```
const connect = require('connect');
const server = connect();
const vhost = require('vhost');
const app = require('./sites/expressjs.dev');
server.use(vhost('expressjs.dev', app));
server.listen(3000);
```

In order to use the preceding ./sites/expressjs.dev module, it should assign the HTTP server to module.exports, as in the following example:

```
const http = require('http')
module.exports = http.createServer((req, res) => {
  res.end('hello from expressjs.com\n');
});
```

USING MULTIPLE VHOST INSTANCES

As with any other middleware, you can use vhost more than once in an application to map several hosts to their associated applications:

```
const app = require('./sites/expressjs.dev');
server.use(vhost('expressjs.dev', app));
const app = require('./sites/learnboost.dev');
server.use(vhost('learnboost.dev', app));
```

Rather than setting up the vhost middleware manually like this, you could generate a list of hosts from the filesystem. That's shown in the following example, with the fs.readdirSync() method returning an array of directory entries:

```
const connect = require('connect')
const fs = require('fs');
cons app = connect()
const sites = fs.readdirSync('source/sites');
sites.forEach((site) => {
  console.log('  ... %s', site);
  app.use(vhost(site, require('./sites/' + site)));
});
app.listen(3000);
```

The benefit of using vhost instead of a reverse proxy is simplicity. It allows you to manage all your applications as a single unit. This is ideal for serving several smaller sites, or for serving sites that are largely composed of static content, but it also has the downside that if one site causes a crash, all your sites will be taken down (because they all run in the same process).

Next we'll take a look at one of the most fundamental middleware components that Connect provides: the session management component, appropriately named express-session.

C.2.5 *express-session: session management*

The way web applications handle sessions is dependent on varying requirements. For example, one important choice is the storage back end: some applications benefit from high-performance databases such as Redis; others require simplicity and use the same database as the main application. The express-session module (www.npmjs.com /package/express-session) provides an API that can be extended to suit different databases. It's robust and easy to extend, so it has many community-supported extensions. In this section, you'll learn how to use the memory-backed version and Redis.

First, let's see how to set up the middleware and explore the options available.

BASIC USAGE

Listing C.11 implements a small application that counts the number of times a given user has accessed the page. The data is stored in the user's session. By default, the cookie name is connect.sid, and it's set to be `httpOnly`, meaning client-side scripts can't access its value. The data in the session itself is stored in-memory on the server. The listing shows the basic usage for express-session in Connect.[6]

Listing C.11   Using sessions in Connect

```
const connect = require('connect');
const session = require('express-session');

connect()
  .use(session({
    secret: 'example secret',        ❶ These are the basic options
    resave: false,                     required to use sessions
      saveUninitialized: true
  }))
  .use((req, res) => {
    req.session.views = req.session.views || 0;      Sets up a "views" session
    req.session.views++;                             variable and increments it
    res.end('Views:' + req.session.views);      Sends the value back
  })                                              to the browser
  .listen(3000);
```

This short example sets up sessions and then manipulates a single session variable called `views`. First, the session middleware component is initialized with the required options: `secret`, `resave`, and `saveUninitialized` ❶. The `secret` option is required and determines whether the cookie used to identify the session is signed. The `resave` option is used to force the session to be saved on each request, even if it

---

[6]   This was tested with express-session 1.10.2.

hasn't changed. Some session storage back ends require this, so you need to check before enabling it. The last option, `saveUninitialized`, causes a session to be created even if no values were saved. You can turn this off if you want to comply with laws that require consent before saving cookies.

SETTING THE SESSION EXPIRATION DATE

Suppose you want sessions to expire in 24 hours, to send the session cookie only when HTTPS is used, and to configure the cookie name. You can control how long the session lasts by setting the `expires` or `maxAge` properties on the expression object:

```
const hour = 3600000
req.session.cookie.expires = new Date(Date.now() + hour * 24);
req.session.cookie.maxAge = hour * 24;
```

When using Connect, you'll often set `maxAge`, specifying a number of milliseconds from that point in time. This method of expressing future dates is often written more intuitively, expanding to `new Date(Date.now() + maxAge)`.

Now that sessions are set up, let's look at the methods and properties available when working with session data.

WORKING WITH SESSION DATA

The express-session data management API is simple. The basic principle is that any properties assigned to the `req.session` object are saved when the request is complete; then they're loaded on subsequent requests from the same user (browser). For example, saving shopping cart information is as simple as assigning an object to the `cart` property, as shown here:

```
req.session.cart = { items: [1,2,3] };
```

When you access `req.session.cart` on subsequent requests, the `.items` array will be available. Because this is a regular JavaScript object, you can call methods on the nested objects in subsequent requests, as in the following example, and they'll be saved as you expect:

```
req.session.cart.items.push(4);
```

One important thing to keep in mind is that this session object gets serialized as JSON between requests, so the `req.session` object has the same restrictions as JSON: cyclic properties aren't allowed, `function` objects can't be used, `Date` objects can't be serialized correctly, and so on. Keep those restrictions in mind when using the session object.

Connect will save session data for you automatically, but internally it's calling the `Session#save([callback])` method, which is also available as a public API. Two additional helpful methods are `Session#destroy()` and `Session#regenerate()`, which are often used when authenticating a user to prevent session fixation attacks. When you build applications with Express, you'll use these methods for authentication.

Now let's move on to manipulating session cookies.

MANIPULATING SESSION COOKIES

Connect allows you to provide global cookie settings for sessions, but it's also possible to manipulate a specific cookie via the `Session#cookie` object, which defaults to the global settings.

Before you start tweaking properties, let's see how to extend the previous session application to inspect the session cookie properties by writing each property into individual `<p>` tags in the response HTML, as shown here:

```
...
res.write('<p>views: ' + sess.views + '</p>');
res.write('<p>expires in: ' + (sess.cookie.maxAge / 1000) + 's</p>');
res.write('<p>httpOnly: ' + sess.cookie.httpOnly + '</p>');
res.write('<p>path: ' + sess.cookie.path + '</p>');
res.write('<p>domain: ' + sess.cookie.domain + '</p>');
res.write('<p>secure: ' + sess.cookie.secure + '</p>');
...
```

Express-session allows all the cookie properties (such as `expires`, `httpOnly`, `secure`, `path`, and `domain`) to be altered programmatically on a per-session basis. For example, you could expire an active session in 5 seconds like this:

```
req.session.cookie.expires = new Date(Date.now() + 5000);
```

An alternative, more intuitive API for expiry is the `.maxAge` accessor, which allows you to get and set the value in milliseconds relative to the current time. The following also expires the session in 5 seconds:

```
req.session.cookie.maxAge = 5000;
```

The remaining properties, `domain`, `path`, and `secure`, limit the cookie *scope*, restricting it by domain, path, or to secure connections, whereas `httpOnly` prevents client-side scripts from accessing the cookie data. These properties can be manipulated in the same manner:

```
req.session.cookie.path = '/admin';
req.session.cookie.httpOnly = false;
```

So far you've been using the default memory store to store session data, so let's take a look at how to plug in alternative data stores.

SESSION STORES

In the previous examples, we've been using the built-in `MemoryStore` session storage. It's a simple, in-memory data store, which is ideal for running application tests because no other dependencies are necessary. But during development and in production, it's best to have a persistent, scalable database backing your session data; otherwise, you'll keep losing your session when you restart the server.

Just about any database can act as a session store, but low-latency key/value stores work best for such volatile data. The Connect community has created several session stores for databases, including CouchDB, MongoDB, Redis, Memcached, PostgreSQL, and others.

Here you'll use Redis with the connect-redis module (https://www.npmjs.com/package/connect-redis). Redis is a good backing store because it supports key expiration, provides great performance, and is easy to install.

Invoke `redis-server` to make sure you've got Redis installed:

```
$ redis-server
[11790] 16 Oct 16:11:54 * Server started, Redis version 2.0.4
[11790] 16 Oct 16:11:54 * DB loaded from disk: 0 seconds
[11790] 16 Oct 16:11:54 * The server is now ready to accept
➥ connections on port 6379
[11790] 16 Oct 16:11:55 - DB 0: 522 keys (0 volatile) in 1536 slots HT.
```

Next, you need to install connect-redis by adding it to your package.json file and running `npm install`, or by executing `npm install --save connect-redis` directly.[7] The connect-redis module exports a function that should be passed connect, as shown in the following listing.

Listing C.12 Using Redis as a session store

```
const connect = require('connect');
const session = require('express-session');
const RedisStore = require('connect-redis')(session);   ←── Passes the instance
const favicon = require('serve-favicon');                    of express-session
const options = {                                            to RedisStore
  host: 'localhost'
};

connect()
  .use(favicon(__dirname + '/favicon.ico'))
  .use(session({
    store: new RedisStore(options),        ←── Configures the session with the
    secret: 'keyboard cat',                    recommended defaults and RedisStore
    resave: false,
    saveUninitialized: true
  }))
  .use((req, res) => {
    req.session.views = req.session.views || 0;   ←── Changes session values
    req.session.views++;                              the usual way
    res.end('Views: ' + req.session.views);
  })
  .listen(3000);
```

This example sets up a session store that uses Redis. Passing the `connect` reference to `connect-redis` allows it to inherit from `connect.session.Store.prototype`. This is important because in Node a single process may use multiple versions of a

---

[7] We used version 2.2.0 when writing this book.

module simultaneously; by passing your specific version of Connect, you can be sure that connect-redis uses the proper copy.

The instance of `RedisStore` is passed to `session()` as the `store` value, and any options you want to use, such as a key prefix for your sessions, can be passed to the `RedisStore` constructor. After both of these steps are done, you can access session variables the same way as with `MemoryStore`. One small detail about this example is that we included the favicon middleware component to prevent the session variable from being incremented twice; otherwise, the `views` value will appear to be increased by 2 on each request as the browser fetches the page and /favicon.ico.

Whew! `session` was a lot to cover, but that finishes up all the core concept middleware. Next we'll go over the built-in middleware that handles web application security. This is an important subject for applications that need to secure their data.

C.3 Handling web application security

As we've stated many times, Node's core API is intentionally low-level. This means it provides no built-in security or best practices when it comes to building web applications. Fortunately, Connect middleware components implement these security practices.

This section will teach you about three security-related modules that you can install from npm:

- *basic-auth*—Provides HTTP Basic authentication for protecting data
- *csurf*—Implements protection against cross-site request forgery (CSRF) attacks
- *errorhandler*—Helps you debug during development

First, let's see how to set up an application that uses basic-auth to provide HTTP Basic authentication.

C.3.1 basic-auth: HTTP Basic authentication

In chapter 4, you created a crude Basic authentication middleware component. Well, it turns out that several Connect modules can do this for you. As previously mentioned, Basic authentication is a simple HTTP authentication mechanism, and it should be used with caution because user credentials can be trivial for an attacker to intercept unless Basic authentication is served over HTTPS. That being said, it can be useful for adding quick and dirty authentication to a small or personal application.

When your application has the basic-auth module in use, web browsers will prompt for credentials the first time the user attempts to connect to your application, as shown in figure C.4.

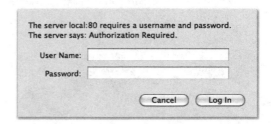

Figure C.4 Basic authentication prompt

BASIC USAGE

The basic-auth module (www.npmjs.com/package/basic-auth) allows you to get the credentials from the HTTP Authorization header field. The following listing shows how to use it with your own password verification function.

Listing C.13   Using the basic-auth module

```
const auth = require('basic-auth');
const connect = require('connect');

function passwordValid(credentials) {              ◁──  Checks the password is valid
  return credentials                                    using a hardcoded username
    && credentials.name === 'tj'
    && credentials.pass === 'tobi';           ◁──  Gets the parsed
}                                                   credentials

connect()
  .use((req, res, next) => {
    const credentials = auth(req);

    if (passwordValid(credentials)) {
      next();
    } else {
      res.writeHead(401, {
        'WWW-Authenticate': 'Basic realm="example"'
      });                                                ◁──  Sends back the WWW-
      res.end();                                              Authenticate header when
    }                                                         the password is incorrect
  })
  .use((req, res) => {
    res.end('This is the secret area\n');      ◁──  Otherwise, next() will cause
  })                                                 execution to continue to
  .listen(3000);                                     the "secret area"
```

The basic-auth module provides only the Authorization header field parsing part of the authentication process. You have to check the password yourself by calling it in a middleware component and then the basic-auth module sends back the right headers when authentication fails. This example calls next() when authentication has succeeded so execution will continue to the protected parts of the application.

AN EXAMPLE WITH CURL

Now try issuing an HTTP request to the server with curl, and you'll see that you're unauthorized:

```
$ curl http://localhost:3000 -i
HTTP/1.1 401 Unauthorized
WWW-Authenticate: Basic realm="Authorization Required"
Connection: keep-alive
Transfer-Encoding: chunked
Unauthorized
```

Issuing the same request with HTTP Basic authorization credentials (notice the beginning of the URL) will provide access:

```
$ curl --user tj:tobi http://localhost:3000 -i
HTTP/1.1 200 OK
Date: Sun, 16 Oct 2011 22:42:06 GMT
Cache-Control: public, max-age=0
Last-Modified: Sun, 16 Oct 2011 22:41:02 GMT
ETag: "13-1318804862000"
Content-Type: text/plain; charset=UTF-8
Accept-Ranges: bytes
Content-Length: 13
Connection: keep-alive
I'm a secret
```

Continuing on with the security theme of this section, let's look at the csurf module, which is designed to help protect against cross-site request forgery attacks.

C.3.2 *csurf: cross-site request forgery protection*

Cross-site request forgery (CSRF) is a form of attack that exploits the trust that a web browser has in a site. The attack works by having an authenticated user on your application visit a different site that an attacker has either created or compromised, and then making requests on the user's behalf without them knowing about it.

It's easier to understand this process with an example. Suppose that in your application the request `DELETE /account` will trigger a user's account to be destroyed (though only while the user is logged in). Now suppose that user visits a forum that happens to be vulnerable to CSRF. An attacker could post a script that issues the `DELETE / account` request, thus destroying the user's account. This is a bad situation for your application to be in, and the csurf module can help protect against such an attack.

The csurf module (https://www.npmjs.com/package/csurf) works by generating a 24-character unique ID, the *authenticity token*, and assigning it to the user's session as `req.session._csrf`. This token can then be included as a hidden form input named `_csrf`, and the CSRF component can validate the token on submission. This process is repeated for each interaction.

BASIC USAGE

To ensure that csurf can access `req.body._csrf` (the hidden input value) and `req.session._csrf`, you need to make sure that you add the module's middleware function below body-parser and express-session, as shown in the following listing.[8]

> **Listing C.14 CSRF protection**

```
const bodyParser = require('body-parser');
const connect = require('connect');
const csurf = require('csurf');
```

---

[8] We tested this example with csurf 1.6.6.

```
const session = require('express-session');
const sesionOptions = {
  resave: false,
  saveUninitialized: false,
  secret: '1234'
};

connect()
  .use(bodyParser.urlencoded({ extended: false }))
  .use(session(sesionOptions))
  .use(csurf())
  .use((req, res, next) => {
    if ('/' != req.url) return next();

    const token = req.csrfToken();
    const html = `
      <form method="post" action="/save">
        <input type="text" name="_csrf" value="${token}">
        <button type="submit">Submit</button>
      </form>`;

    res.setHeader('Content-Type', 'text/html');
    res.end(html);
  })
  .use((req, res) => {
    const html = `
      <p>Body: ${req.body._csrf}</p>
      <p>Session secret: ${req.session.csrfSecret}</p>
    `;
    res.end(html);
  })
  .use((err, req, res, next) => {
    console.error(err);
    res.end('Did you get the csrf token wrong?');
  })
  .listen(3000);
```

Annotations:
- **Loads the csurf middleware component after the body parser and session handler**
- **Shows a form for the / route**
- **Gets the current CSRF token by using this method added by csurf**
- **This function will run after a POST with the right token**
- **This is an error handler for when the token is incorrect**

To use csurf, you have to first load the body-parser and session middleware components. This example then shows a form, which includes a text field with the current CSRF token. This token will cause all requests of certain method types to be checked based on the secret in the session. You can get the current token with `req.csrf-Token`, which is a method added by csurf. Posts with invalid tokens will automatically be flagged by csurf, so we've included a "token successful" handler and an error handler. This example uses a text field so you can see what happens if you change it.

This example shows that csurf automatically kicks in for certain kinds of requests. This is defined by the `ignoreMethods` option that you can pass to csurf. By default, HTTP GET, HEAD, and OPTIONS are ignored, but you could add others if required.

Another aspect of web development is ensuring that verbose logs and detailed error reporting are available both in production and development environments. Let's look at the errorhandler module, which is designed to do exactly that.

C.3.3 errorhandler: displaying errors during development

The errorhandler module (www.npmjs.com/package/errorhandler) is ideal for development, providing verbose HTML, JSON, and plain-text error responses based on the `Accept` header field. It's meant for use during development and shouldn't be part of the production configuration.

BASIC USAGE

Typically, this component should be the last used so it can catch all errors:

```
connect()
  .use((req, res, next) => {
    setTimeout(function () {
      next(new Error('something broke!'));
    }, 500);
  })
  .use(errorhandler());
```

RECEIVING AN HTML ERROR RESPONSE

If you view any page in your browser with the setup shown here, you'll see a Connect error page like the one shown in figure C.5, displaying the error message, the response status, and the entire stack trace.

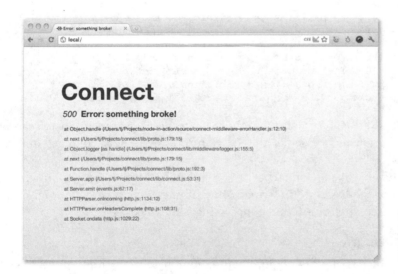

Figure C.5
The default errorhandler HTML as displayed in a web browser

RECEIVING A PLAIN-TEXT ERROR RESPONSE

Now suppose you're testing an API built with Connect. It's far from ideal to respond with a large chunk of HTML, so by default `errorHandler()` will respond with `text/plain`, which is ideal for command-line HTTP clients such as `curl(1)`. This is illustrated in the following stdout:

```
$ curl localhost:3000 -H "Accept: text/plain"
Error: something broke!
```

```
   at Object.handle (/Users/tj/Projects/node-in-action/source
⇨ /connect-middleware-errorHandler.js:12:10)
   at next (/Users/tj/Projects/connect/lib/proto.js:179:15)
   at Object.logger [as handle] (/Users/tj/Projects/connect
⇨ /lib/middleware/logger.js:155:5)
   at next (/Users/tj/Projects/connect/lib/proto.js:179:15)
   at Function.handle (/Users/tj/Projects/connect/lib/proto.js:192:3)
   at Server.app (/Users/tj/Projects/connect/lib/connect.js:53:31)
   at Server.emit (events.js:67:17)
   at HTTPParser.onIncoming (http.js:1134:12)
   at HTTPParser.onHeadersComplete (http.js:108:31)
   at Socket.ondata (http.js:1029:22)
```

RECEIVING A JSON ERROR RESPONSE

If you send an HTTP request that has the `Accept: application/json` HTTP header, you'll get the following JSON response:

```
$ curl http://localhost:3000 -H "Accept: application/json"
{"error":{"stack":"Error: something broke!\n
⇨   at Object.handle (/Users/tj/Projects/node-in-action
⇨ /source/connect-middleware-errorHandler.js:12:10)\n
⇨   at next (/Users/tj/Projects/connect/lib/proto.js:179:15)\n
⇨   at Object.logger [as handle] (/Users/tj/Projects
⇨ /connect/lib/middleware/logger.js:155:5)\n
⇨   at next (/Users/tj/Projects/connect/lib/proto.js:179:15)\n
⇨   at Function.handle (/Users/tj/Projects/connect/lib/
proto.js:192:3)\n
⇨   at Server.app (/Users/tj/Projects/connect/lib/connect.js:53:31)\n
⇨   at Server.emit (events.js:67:17)\n
⇨   at HTTPParser.onIncoming (http.js:1134:12)\n
⇨   at HTTPParser.onHeadersComplete (http.js:108:31)\n
⇨   at Socket.ondata (http.js:1029:22)","message":"something broke!"}}
```

We've added additional formatting to the JSON response, so it's easier to read on the page, but when Connect sends the JSON response, it gets compacted nicely by `JSON.stringify()`.

Are you feeling like a Connect security guru now? Maybe not yet, but you should have enough of the basics down to make your applications secure. Now let's move on to a common web application function: serving static files.

C.4   *Serving static files*

Serving static files is another requirement common to many web applications that's not provided by Node's core. Fortunately, with some simple modules, Connect has you covered here as well.

In this section, you'll learn about two more of Connect's officially supported modules—this time focusing on serving files from the filesystem. These types of features are provided by HTTP servers such as Apache and Nginx, but with a little bit of configuration you can add them to your Connect projects:

- *serve-static*—Serves files from the filesystem from a given root directory
- *serve-index*—Serves pretty directory listings when a directory is requested

First we'll show you how to serve static files with a single line of code by using the server-static module.

C.4.1 *serve-static: automatically serving files to the browser*

The serve-static module (www.npmjs.com/package/serve-static) implements a high-performance, flexible, feature-rich static file server supporting HTTP cache mechanisms, `Range` requests, and more. It also includes security checks for malicious paths, disallows access to hidden files (beginning with a period) by default, and rejects poison `null` bytes. In essence, serve-static is a secure and compliant static file-serving middleware component, ensuring compatibility with the various HTTP clients out there.

BASIC USAGE

Suppose your application follows the typical scenario of serving static assets from a directory named ./public. This can be achieved with a single line of code:

```
app.use(serveStatic('public'));
```

With this configuration, serve-static will check for regular files that exist in ./public/ based on the request URL. If a file exists, the response's `Content-Type` field value will be defaulted based on the file's extension, and the data will be transferred. If the requested path doesn't represent a file, the `next()` callback will be invoked, allowing subsequent middleware (if any) to handle the request.

To test it out, create a file named ./public/foo.js with `console.log('tobi')`, and issue a request to the server by using `curl(1)` with the `-i` flag, telling it to print the HTTP headers. You'll see that the HTTP cache-related header fields are set appropriately, the `Content-Type` reflects the .js extension, and the content is transferred:

```
$ curl http://localhost/foo.js -i
HTTP/1.1 200 OK
Date: Thu, 06 Oct 2011 03:06:33 GMT
Cache-Control: public, max-age=0
Last-Modified: Thu, 06 Oct 2011 03:05:51 GMT
ETag: "21-1317870351000"
Content-Type: application/javascript
Accept-Ranges: bytes
Content-Length: 21
Connection: keep-alive
console.log('tobi');
```

Because the request path is used as is, files nested within directories are served as you'd expect. For example, you might have a `GET /javascripts/jquery.js` request and a `GET /stylesheets/app.css` request on your server, which would serve the files ./public/javascripts/jquery.js and ./public/stylesheets/app.css, respectively.

USING SERVE-STATIC WITH MOUNTING

Sometimes applications prefix pathnames with /public, /assets, /static, and so on. With the mounting concept that Connect implements, serving static files from multiple directories is simple. Just mount the app at the location you want. As mentioned in chapter 5, the middleware itself has no knowledge that it's mounted, because the prefix is removed.

For example, a request to `GET /app/files/js/jquery.js` with serve-static mounted at /app/files will appear to the middleware as `GET /js/jquery`. This works out well for the prefixing functionality because /app/files won't be part of the file resolution:

```
app.use('/app/files', connect.static('public'));
```

The original request of `GET /foo.js` won't work anymore, because the middleware isn't invoked unless the mount point is present, but the prefixed version `GET /app/files/foo.js` will transfer the file:

```
$ curl http://localhost/foo.js
Cannot get /foo.js
$ curl http://localhost/app/files/foo.js
console.log('tobi');
```

ABSOLUTE VS. RELATIVE DIRECTORY PATHS

Keep in mind that the path passed to serve-static is relative to the current working directory. Passing in `"public"` as your path will essentially resolve to `process.cwd() + "public"`.

Sometimes, though, you may want to use absolute paths when specifying the base directory, and the `__dirname` variable helps with that:

```
app.use('/app/files', connect.static(__dirname + '/public'));
```

SERVING INDEX.HTML WHEN A DIRECTORY IS REQUESTED

Another useful feature of serve-static is its ability to serve index.html files. When a request for a directory is made and an index.html file lives in that directory, it will be served.

Serving static files is useful for web application assets, such as CSS, JavaScript, and images. But what if you want to allow people to download a list of arbitrary files from a list of directories? That's where serve-index comes in.

C.4.2   *serve-index: generating directory listings*

The serve-index module (www.npmjs.com/package/serve-index) is a small directory-listing component that provides a way for users to browse remote files. Figure C.6 illustrates the interface provided by this component, complete with a search input field, file icons, and clickable breadcrumbs.

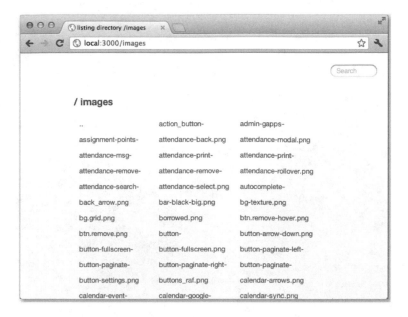

Figure C.6 Serving directory listings with Connect's `directory()` **middleware component**

BASIC USAGE

This component is designed to work with serve-static, which will perform the file serving; serve-index simply serves the listings. The setup can be as simple as the following snippet, where the request GET / serves the ./public directory:

```
const connect = require('connect');
const serveStatic = require('serve-static');
const serveIndex = require('serve-index');

connect()
  .use(serveIndex('public'))
  .use(serveStatic('public'))
  .listen(3000);
```

USING DIRECTORY() WITH MOUNTING

Through the use of middleware mounting, you can prefix both the server-static and serve-index modules to any path you like, such as GET /files in the following example. Here the icons option is used to enable icons, and hidden is enabled for both components to allow the viewing and serving of hidden files:

```
connect()
  .use('/files', serveIndex('public', { icons: true, hidden: true }))
  .use('/files', serveStatic('public', { hidden: true }))
  .listen(3000);
```

It's now possible to navigate through files and directories with ease.

Glossary

Chapter 1

abstract interface A programmatic description of an API that doesn't include an implementation. In Node.js, a good example is the Streams API.

arrow function A function written in a shorthand syntax. Instead of writing `function ()
{}`, write `() => {}` when passing functions as arguments to other functions. If the function accepts only one argument, the parentheses can be omitted.

asynchronous Describes code that doesn't necessarily run in the order in which it appears. In Node.js, this term is used to distinguish APIs that accept callbacks that will be run at a point in the future. For example, `fs.readFile` accepts a callback that receives the file's contents after it has been read.

core modules The libraries that are built into Node.

destructuring ECMAScript 2015 introduced destructuring, which allows objects and arrays to be broken into variables and constants. For example, `const { name } = { name:
'Alex' }` creates a constant called `name` with the value `alex`.

ECMAScript standard ECMAScript is a scripting language specification standardized by Ecma International. There are several ECMAScript standards; this book focuses on ECMAScript 2015 (ECMAScript 6th Edition). JavaScript implementers use the ECMAScript standard to make sure their interpreter is compatible with JavaScript written for other implementations.

event A string that causes a function to be called. The function is known as an object listener. An emitter sends the named event. The basic class for creating emitters in Node is `EventEmitter`.

event loop Node's event loop waits for external events and converts them into callback invocations. Other systems use similar things—message dispatchers and run loops—to quickly route events to the corresponding event handler.

JSON (JavaScript Object Notation) JSON is a lightweight data-interchange format, intended to be easy to read and write, and based on a subset of JavaScript.

libuv A multiplatform library for asynchronous I/O. It's used in Node, but also other libraries and languages such as Julia.

nonblocking I/O   Blocking operations halt execution until the operation completes. Node uses nonblocking I/O, which means reads from a network or file resource won't block execution.

npm   Node's package manager. It allows you to install Node packages from a large central repository and to manage dependencies in Node projects.

Promise   The `Promise` object is a standardized ECMAScript 2015 API for representing values that may be available now, in the future, or never.

REPL (read-eval-print loop)   A command-line interface enabling you to evaluate code and see the results.

rest parameters   The rest parameter syntax in ECMAScript 2015 allows an unknown number of arguments in a function to be represented as an array. To name two arguments but put the rest in an array, use `function (a, b, ...rest)`. It can also be used with destructuring to copy objects: `const newObject = { ...oldObject }`.

semantic versioning   A convention for specifying library compatibility using three numbers: major, minor, and patch, written as 1.0.2 (major: 1, minor: 0, patch: 2). An application that depends on version 1.0.2 should be compatible with 1.1.1, but not 2.0.0.

Chapter 2

callback   A function that has been passed to a function and may run later.

closure   JavaScript functions capture the variables defined in their enclosing scope. If you define function B inside function A, B will have access to all of A's values.

CommonJS module specification   A module format for defining which values should be exported from the current JavaScript file. See *module*.

content management system (CMS)   Web application used to edit text and images that will be displayed on a public-facing website.

flow control (or control flow)   The order in which statements will be executed. Because Node is asynchronous, control flow is of interest, as JavaScript offers many ways of dealing with control flow, including callbacks, promises, generators, basic looping primitives, and iterators. In Node, *flow control* refers to the way we group sequences of asynchronous tasks.

global scope   *Scope* means the parts of the program that can access a value, so *global scope* means a value is accessible everywhere within a program.

module   Node modules are single files that contain JavaScript. Values (typically, functions and constants) can be exported so they can be used in other files.

nested callback   A callback within a callback; when a callback has been passed to a function, it's sometimes necessary to define another callback inside the first callback.

package.json   A file that defines a Node project's name, author, license, and dependencies. Every Node program and library you create should have a package.json file.

property   JavaScript objects are collections of keys and values, and keys and values are known as the object's properties.

stack trace   A list of program instructions that had executed up to the point when an error occurred.

state   The value of all the variables in a program at a given time.

Chapter 3

boilerplate   Code that's frequently duplicated and that could be automated.

client-side bundle   Preprocessed JavaScript code from several source files that's usually minified and compressed, and then served to clients.

cURL   A command-line tool and programmer library for making HTTP requests. It's often used as a debugging tool for quickly checking how web servers respond to requests.

database model   A programmer-friendly data model that makes it easier to interact with database tables or documents than using the database's native language.

form encoding   When an HTTP POST is made to a web server, including a simple form POST, the form's contents are encoded into the request body. The most common format, `application/x-www-form-urlencoded`, is similar to URL encoding, which replaces unsafe ASCII characters with percent signs.

MIME (Multipurpose Internet Mail Extensions)   An internet standard for adding nontextual data to emails and multipart message bodies. This allows email clients to show HTML, images, and text in non-ASCII character sets.

object-relational mapping (ORM)   A library that maps between programmer-friendly data structures (for example, JavaScript objects) and database data structures (for example, tables and foreign keys).

REST (Representational State Transfer), RESTful API   Stateless web API using a set of predefined operations in HTTP. The operations are based on HTTP verbs; the most common are GET, POST, PUT, and DELETE.

route   The URL fragment and HTTP verb that a given route handler should process.

route handler   A user-defined callback that runs when an HTTP request is made to a web application. The route handler usually generates content, perhaps from a database, or modifies a database, and then generates the response by using a template or format such as JSON.

static asset   A file that's served by a web server without any additional processing. Typically, images, CSS files, and client-side JavaScript files are static assets.

template   Plain-text format that can include embedded data or JavaScript code and be used to generate HTML to streamline HTML's syntax.

Chapter 4

build system   A set of tools and configuration files for generating JavaScript that will run efficiently in a browser.

linter   A program that checks the correctness of a source file's format. Linters can be used to enforce a given programming style on a project by checking against a set of linting rules.

method chain   Running a method on the return value of a previously called method.

pipe   Connecting a data output to an input. In UNIX, processes are pipelined by using the vertical bar character (|); in Node, streams are connected by using method chaining.

source map   A file that allows browser debuggers to map from a line in a transpiled source file to the original code.

stream   An efficient data input and/or output channel that may be text or binary data. Node supports readable, writable, and other stream types, and these streams can be linked together by using pipes.

test runner   A program that runs and collates the results of unit tests found in one or more files.

transpile   Also known as source-to-source compilers, JavaScript transpilers convert one type of ECMAScript to another. The most common use is to convert modern ES2015 to backward-compatible ECMAScript 5, which can run in more browsers. Another example is TypeScript, which is a superset of JavaScript that gets transpiled into ES5 or ES2015.

webpack loader   Transforms or transpiles source code.

webpack plugin   Changes the behavior of the build process itself, rather than the output files.

Chapter 5

database adapter   Some database libraries are written in a generic fashion and can be extended with specific adapters that implement functionality for the desired database.

decoupled   If a function, class, or module can easily be changed in a project, or reused in another project, then it is loosely coupled.

full-stack framework   A framework that includes features for working with both client-side and server-side code. That usually means it has libraries for dealing with HTTP requests, request routing, database modeling, and communication with code running in a browser.

GET parameters   URL parameters that appear after a question mark and are separated by ampersands.

HTTP verb   The HTTP method (GET, POST, PUT, PATCH, DELETE) representing the action that should be performed on a remote resource.

isomorphic   JavaScript applications that run both client-side and server-side by sharing the same code.

middleware   Functions that can be called in sequence to modify an HTTP request and response.

Model-View-Controller (MVC)   Design pattern for separating software into components; the model manages data and logic, the view transforms the data into a user interface, and the controller converts interactions into operations for the model or view.

relational database   A database structure based around relations between the stored entities.

single-page web app   An application that's served to the browser once and doesn't require a full-page reload. If the application needs to change the URL in the browser for any reason, the HTML5 History API is used to give the impression that the URL has changed and the browser has loaded a new page from the server.

web framework   A set of libraries for developing a web application with support for extensibility through plugins or middleware.

Chapter 6

bcrypt   A password-hashing function. This function maps arbitrary amounts of data to a string of fixed size that can be stored safely in a database, so the user's plain-text password isn't stored.

content negotiation   Part of the HTTP standard that deals with serving different versions of a document at the same URI. User agents (browsers) can request a different data format if the server supports it.

CSS preprocessor   Programs that convert supersets of CSS to CSS that a browser can interpret. The Sass and LESS stylesheet languages both include CSS preprocessors, and these languages add features such as variables, nesting, and mixins.

password salt   Random data used in addition to the input of a hash function, making dictionary attacks harder.

Redis database   An in-memory database that's also used as a cache and message broker. It's useful for storing user sessions and dealing with push messages in web applications.

Redis hash   A map from a string field and a value, used to represent objects in a Redis database.

response object   An object that determines how your server will respond to a given HTTP request. It includes the response body, which is usually a web page, and the headers.

single-threaded   A running program (process) can be made up of threads that execute concurrently. JavaScript's model is to use a single thread, but allow the thread to switch context and run different code when events happen. The events in a browser are interactions such as the user clicking a button; in Node, they're typically I/O events, such as network operations or data being read from a disk.

template language   Lightweight markup languages that are converted to HTML and add features that make it easier to inject values from code, and iterate over arrays or objects.

third-party middleware   Middleware components that aren't distributed by the authors of the original web library or framework.

Chapter 7

lexical scope   The visibility of a variable is determined by its scope. In JavaScript, adding a function adds a new level of scope. Any variables defined in that function are visible by any functions defined within that function.

mixin   This usually means a class that contains methods for use in other classes. In Sass, mixins are groups of CSS declarations that can be reused in multiple places; in Pug, mixins are used to define reusable template fragments.

partial   Small, reusable template.

section lambda   A *lambda* is an anonymous function, so a *section lambda* in Hogan is a way of associating a function with a tag in a template.

significant whitespace   In JavaScript, curly brackets, semicolons, and newlines are used to separate statements. If a new lexical block is required, a function or control statement is used. In languages with significant whitespace, such as Pug, lines of code are grouped together by the number of spaces used to indent each line.

XSS (cross-site scripting) attack   If a web application accepts user input from forms or URL parameters, and those values are redisplayed in templates, then it may be possible to inject malicious code. Values must be escaped first to be safe from this type of attack.

Chapter 8

ACID (atomicity, consistency, isolation, durability)   For a database to be ACID-compliant, it must support operations that are atomic (the operation succeeds, or the operation fails and the database is left unchanged), consistent (the data changes only in the allowed ways), isolated (ensuring concurrent execution), and durable (after a change has been made, it will remain, even if the system crashes or is rebooted).

BSON   A binary format used by MongoDB for representing objects. Objects consist of an ordered set of elements; the elements are made up of a field name, a type, and a value. The types supported by BSON include string, integer, date, and JavaScript code.

daemon   A program that runs in the background, usually starting automatically when the system boots.

database schema   A formal definition of the data and relationships between items in a database. It's the design of the database.

database transaction   One or more database operations that are grouped together and run according to the ACID properties.

distributed database   A database stored on multiple computers, potentially but not necessarily in different geographical locations.

leaky abstraction   An attempt to hide complexity that exposes too many details and issues of the underlying implementation.

document-oriented database   A database that stores semistructured data without a predefined schema, sometimes in JSON or XML. Examples include MongoDB and CouchDB.

memoize   An optimization technique that stores the result of a function so it doesn't have to be called again.

NoSQL   A database that doesn't use tabular relations as found in relational databases.

primary key   A column in a database table that's used to uniquely identify each row.

publish-subscribe   A pattern in which messages can be sent to multiple receivers.

query builder   An API that's more convenient for programmers than writing SQL queries by hand.

relational algebra   Used as the theoretical basis for relational databases to model the stored data and queries that can be performed on it.

replica set   A group of MongoDB processes that maintain the same dataset.

web worker   A way of allowing JavaScript to run on background threads in browsers.

Chapter 9

assert, assertion   Ensure that an expression matches an expectation. This can be a simple Boolean statement, equality, or practically anything else. In Node, assertions throw exceptions when they fail. A test runner can catch and collate these exceptions to produce test reports.

BDD (behavior-driven development)   An extension of TDD that uses a different API style to encourage a focus on where in the process the test occurs, what to test and what not to test, and how much to test in one go. It also tries to improve understanding of test failures, and the naming of test units.

functional testing   Testing a slice of functionality through the whole system. In web development, that means full-stack testing: the browser and server are tested at the same time.

mocks   Objects or values that behave like real counterparts, but are usually a simple veneer that provides just enough behavior to allow a test to run. Rather than accessing real files or networks in tests, which could be slow or dangerous if destructive operations occur, mocks can be used to safely simulate their behavior.

test-driven development (TDD)   Writing tests before the code under test.

test runner   A program that manages loading tests, running them, and then collecting the results so they can be displayed. Mocha is a test runner.

typeof   A JavaScript operator that returns a string for a given object or value.

unit testing   Small parts of a module, such as functions or methods of a class, are tested in isolation against assertions in small test cases (units).

Chapter 10

Amazon EC2 (Amazon Elastic Compute Cloud)   Amazon's virtual computer service.

container   A type of virtualization, containers are isolated user-space instances of an operating system, running on top of a host operating system. Containers offer additional control over resource usage and security benefits, and they can be quickly started up and destroyed.

Content delivery network (CDN)   Distributed servers that deliver static content.

Docker image   An image of the filesystem that Docker will use to create a container.

dyno   Heroku's term for a container; this is used to run both servers and arbitrary commands in an isolated environment on Heroku's servers.

Elastic Beanstalk   An orchestration service run by Amazon for scripting deployments to Amazon's other services, such as EC2.

log rotation   A command that runs periodically and renames log files based on the date, and then optionally compresses them to use less storage space.

SSH (Secure Shell)   Provides an encrypted command-line (or X11) interface to a remote computer for running commands. It can form the workflow of a web developer when initially configuring a new server, or connecting to servers to run maintenance or debugging commands.

sudo   A program for running programs with other user privileges. It's usually used to run commands that need special privileges, such as editing system configuration files.

Chapter 11

arguments   Program arguments are the flags provided on the command line that enable or disable certain features.

exit status   Value returned by a program when it completes. Nonzero values indicate an error.

interprocess communication   The methods an operating system provides to allow running programs to communicate. An example is pipes, which use the output of one program as the input of another, but even files can be considered a form of interprocess communication.

Open Group   A consortium that publishes the Single UNIX Specification, a family of standards that qualifies producers of operating systems to use the UNIX trademark.

shell   Command-line user interface enabling commands to be entered and the results viewed. It's called a *shell* because it's a layer around the operating system.

redirection   Capturing the output from a program and sending it as input to another program or file.

stderr   The error stream for outputting error messages from a running program.

stdin   The input stream for a running program.

stdout   The output stream for messages printed by a program.

Chapter 12

Chromium   An open source browser from which Google's Chrome browser derives its code.

Electron main process   A Node process that manages the Electron app and access to files and the network.

Electron render process   The Chromium web view.

JSX   React applications use a mix of HTML fragments alongside JavaScript. This is preprocessed into pure JavaScript before it runs in a browser. This language is called JSX.

native   A program or library that's written using the operating system's built-in APIs.

React   A library by Facebook for building data-driven web and mobile user interfaces.

Appendix A

constructor   A function that creates and initializes a JavaScript object.

CSV (comma-separated values)   A text format for tabular data that's typically used with databases or spreadsheet programs. The values are split into columns by using commas, and rows by using new lines.

DOM (Document Object Model)   The standards that define the API for JavaScript working with HTML. The DOM is a language-independent interface working with HTML.

microformats   A way of including structured data in HTML that's readable by both humans and software. Because HTML doesn't always represent structured data clearly, microformats can be used to embed data such as addresses, geographical locations, and calendar entries in HTML without any special tags.

regular expression   An expression that matches patterns in a string.

robots.txt   A standard used by websites to tell web crawlers and scrapers what content can be scanned or excluded from scraping.

vertical search engine   Search engine that focuses on a niche.

web scraping   Converting HTML into structured data that can be stored in files or a database.

XPath   A query language for selecting nodes from an XML document.

index

RELATED MANNING TITLES

Node.js in Practice
by Alex Young and Marc Harter

ISBN: 9781617290930
424 pages, $49.99
December 2014

Secrets of the JavaScript Ninja, Second Edition
by John Resig, Bear Bibeault, and Josip Maras

ISBN: 9781617292859
464 pages, $44.99
August 2016

Getting MEAN with Mongo, Express, Angular, and Node, Second Edition
by Simon D. Holmes

ISBN: 9781617294754
450 pages, $44.99
April 2018

The Tao of Microservices
by Richard Rodger

ISBN: 9781617293146
275 pages, $49.99
September 2017

For ordering information go to www.manning.com